Dear Pat

With best wishes

Martin Dee
9/15/02

THE SECURITIES HANDBOOK

A
Comprehensive
Reference Guide
for
The Securities Industry

Martin Torosian

MTA Financial Services Corporation

Library of Congress Cataloging in Publication Data

Torosian, Martin
    The Securities Handbook
    Includes Index
        I. Securities Trading — United States
    1. Title
ISBN 0-9603592-2-2

TOROSIAN, MARTIN
The Securities Handbook
MTA Financial Services Corporation

This publication is designed to provide accurate and authoritative information in regard to the subject matter covered. It is sold with the understanding that the publisher is not engaged in rendering legal, accounting, or other professional service. If legal advice or other expert assistance is required, the services of a competent professional person should be sought.

> *–From a Declaration of Principles jointly adopted by a Committee of the American Bar Association and a Committee of Publishers and Associations.*

Other Books By Martin Torosian
  Legal Transfer Guide
  Securities Transfer — Principles and Procedures
  Modern Stock Market Handbook
  The Margin Book
  Options — A Comprehensive Guide to Options

Printed in the United States of America
    10 9 8 7 6 5 4 3 2 1

MTA Financial Services Corporation
1010 Hunter Court
Deerfield, Illinois 60015
(312)945-3649, (312)945-3735

For Amy and our three sons — Craig, Brian, and Jeffrey

CONTENTS

CHAPTER THREE
DISTRIBUTIONS OF SECURITIES TO THE PUBLIC, 56

CHAPTER FOUR
EQUITY SECURITIES, 96

CHAPTER FIVE
INVESTMENT COMPANIES, 103

CHAPTER SIX
TRANSACTIONS ON THE NEW YORK STOCK EXCHANGE, 132

CHAPTER SEVEN

THE SPECIALIST SYSTEM OF THE NEW YORK STOCK EXCHANGE, 149

CHAPTER EIGHT

TRANSACTIONS ON THE OVER-THE-COUNTER MARKET, 162

CHAPTER NINE

STOCK MARKET TICKER TAPE AND FINANCIAL TABLES, 187

CHAPTER TEN

THE SECURITY ORGANIZATIONS, 202

PREFACE

This is a study of securities — what they are and how they are created, purchased, and sold in today's securities markets.

Within the past several years, members of the financial community have been forced to develop cost-saving methods to stay competitive and profitable. New products and ideas have changed the economics of the business. What was standard operating procedure a few years ago has been replaced by new techniques of securities trading and processing. In a highly competitive industry such as this, a thorough understanding of the investment principles and practices is of utmost importance to the individual entering the field and to personnel already engaged in stock market activities.

This book presents an up-to-date description of the securities operation with emphasis on the latest information on the mechanism of the markets, over-the-counter trading, the functions of the clearing corporations and depositories, and distribution of securities to the public. It is written for the individual who wishes to obtain a broad knowledge of all facets of the securities industry and to understand how various segments of the securities operation fit together. It is also written for the professional who wants to have a deeper understanding of the procedures of securities ownership and processing.

Please note: In referring to the professional (broker) and the customer (investor), the pronoun *he* is used for continuity and to increase the readability of the text. It is not meant as a gender preference.

Martin Torosian

CHAPTER ONE

HISTORICAL OVERVIEW OF THE SECURITIES BUSINESS

The earliest public interest in the securities business was made during the American Revolution. Under the direction of its first Secretary of the Treasury, Alexander Hamilton, the federal government financed the Revolution through the issuance of war bonds. Earlier, Congress had assumed the outstanding debts of the thirteen colonies and was given authorization to issue "bills of credit" to finance its obligations.

As the country achieved political stability, corporate and industrial development followed. By 1800, there were approximately 300 publicly owned corporations, 29 banks, and 15 insurance companies.

The first attempt of securities operation was made in Philadelphia in 1791. In New York where the auction market was flourishing, stock brokers gradually moved away from general merchants and started to conduct securities transactions under a buttonwood tree at 68 Wall Street. Eventually the brokers organized themselves into a group, and in March of 1792, in a meeting held at Corre's Hotel, they drew up an agreement. The agreement established rules of negotiations for the purchase and sale of public stock.

This is known in history as the Buttonwood Tree Agreement. It was the first document of what was later to be the cornerstone of the New York Stock Exchange and opened the stage for New York to assume its role as the nation's financial center.

In 1793 with the construction of the Tontine Coffee House on Wall Street, the newly formed organization of stock brokers moved indoors. This formal organization and centralized trading were not enough, however, to attract the public to deal in securities.

THE START OF THE NEW YORK STOCK EXCHANGE

It was not until 1815 that the newspapers started publishing quotations of securities transactions. The economy of the country was improving and new corporations were being formed. In 1817, the New York group drew up a constitution, elected officers, and established rules. They also adopted the name "New York Stock and Exchange Board."

The period between 1812 and the Civil War is one of the most important periods in the nation's economic life. In the 1830s, a new speculative fever swung the country toward speculation in real estate. Banks started to lend large sums of money for land purchases. Farmers were more interested in selling their acres than raising crops. In the mid 1830s, the securities listed on the Exchange Board doubled in price. Shares of railroads and canals tripled. There was speculation in every facet of commercial activity — bond, securities, and commodities. As in the case of every speculative fever, this was short-lived. A bad crop in 1836 brought on an economic collapse, first in land prices, then in securities and commodities. The stock market crashed. Many banks failed, corporations went bankrupt, and states refused to honor their obligations. This occurred in 1837. Two years earlier, a fire had destroyed the headquarters of the Exchange Board.

The panic of 1837 was the first economic depression in the United States. It lasted five years until 1842 when gold was discovered in the West and money started to pour in from California. Networks of railroads were established all around the country. The public started to buy shares in railroads, utilities, and government securities.

THE PERIOD OF THE CIVIL WAR

The Civil War brought a new dimension to the securities business. Because of the war related expenditures, Washington relied heavily on the advice of investment bankers. The brokers were able to underwrite securities and sell them to the public. The result was a well-run financial operation that made a major contribution to Union victory.

The trading of securities became so hectic that it was necessary for New York brokers to organize new stock exchanges. An "outdoor" exchange, which later became the American Stock Exchange, was formed to handle the after-hour trading of the New York Exchange's listed securities. Another exchange was organized in the room next to the Exchange Board and still another in the basement of the same building. In 1863, the New York Stock and Exchange Board changed its name to New York Stock Exchange (NYSE).

The period immediately following the Civil War gave birth to the era of financial giants in the securities business. Daniel Drew, Commodore Vanderbilt, Leonard W. Jerome, Addison Jerome, W. R. Travers, Jay Cooke, Anthony Morse, Russell Sage, James R. Keene were some of the most colorful and shrewd manipulators in history. At a time when there were no laws or governmental controls in the securities markets, these men created their own laws and their own ethics as they played the securities business game.

It was during this period that the New York Stock Exchange started to expand. Industrial development was apparent in new railroad construction, new manufacturing companies, and new scientific inventions. The West was opening up, and the telegraph provided communications between East and West. Other inventions were instrumental in the development of the NYSE. Electric stock tickers started to transmit quotations, and the telephone provided an important link between the exchange floor and the brokerage offices. Because of its popularity and rapid expansion, the New York Stock Exchange had by now become the leading financial center. It had long surpassed the Philadelphia Stock Exchange as the nation's central marketplace. With expansion came consolidation of other exchange groups. In 1869 two important groups joined the New York Stock Exchange: the Open Board of Brokers and Government Bond Department.

Consolidation and the increase in membership forced the New York Stock Exchange to change its administrative format and adopt a new constitution. It stiffened the membership requirements to reduce financial manipulation and helped maintain the integrity of the marketplace. To safeguard against over-issuance of corporate shares, the Exchange required that listed corporations maintain two separate agencies as record keepers for their books — the transfer agent and the registrar. The transfer agent was assigned to register the shares, and the registrar to authenticate the issuance of securities.

As new companies came into existence, trading continued to be heavy. Securities of industrial corporations became attractive vehicles for investment and speculation. The country was in the midst of a post-Civil War reconstruction. Rockefeller's Standard Oil Company started its operation and J. P. Morgan became a dominant figure in American finance.

The activity came to an abrupt halt, however, as the financial community witnessed yet another panic. The year was 1873. It erupted when Jay Cooke and Company went bankrupt. The panic caused 57 other exchange members and several banks to go under. The financial community was shaken — trading stopped and the New York Stock Exchange closed its doors for several days.

THE START OF CLEARING SECURITIES TRANSACTIONS

In 1892, exactly 100 years after its organization, the New York Stock Exchange created a clearing entity to process settlement of securities transactions. This was an important development in the history of the stock market. Before the installation of this system, securities transactions were handled on a cash basis. Each firm settled its own transaction by delivering or receiving certificates sold or purchased against payment. There was no netting process. A selling broker had to deliver the certificates and receive payment, and the buying broker had to receive certificates against payment. As the volume increased, settlement of individual cash transactions became difficult.

The experiment of clearing started in May 1892. The concept of clearing originated in Europe. The stock exchange in Frankfurt, Germany, had a clearing organization dating back to 1867.

On the first day's clearing in 1892, the system eliminated individual cash transactions valued at $7 million. The operation was a success. (Formal organization of clearing and settlement did not start, however, until 1920 — 28 years later.)

Trading in speculative issues was heavy during the last

decade of the nineteenth century. New men and industrialists were on the scene this time with more capital, imagination, and prestige than the earlier generation. J. P. Morgan, Harriman, Hill, Rockefeller, Flagler, Schiff, Carnegie, and Schwab were the financial leaders of the day, replacing the old manipulators of Wall Street. These financial leaders were in oil, steel, banking, railroad, and industrial companies.

The speculative fever lasted until 1893 when the country witnessed another panic. A severe economic crisis created havoc not only for the financial community but also for railroads and industrial corporations. Most of the railroads went bankrupt, and the stock brokers were hit very hard. By the turn of the century, however, the stock market had bounced back.

AT THE TURN OF THE TWENTIETH CENTURY

The stock market flourished during the first seven years of the twentieth century. Corporate profits were up, new companies were being organized, and the stock prices started to rise. This inflationary trend, mixed with speculative activity, soon led the market to a serious financial crisis. In March of 1907, the stock market crashed and a panic broke out. Brokerage houses and financial institutions were severely shaken. Many banks were forced to close their doors.

The crash of 1907 triggered a congressional investigation of the securities industry. The investigation brought to light highly questionable practices, such as financial manipulations, fictitious accounts, and bucket shops.

But corporate America continued to grow. American Telephone & Telegraph Company and United States Steel were the leading industrial companies of the day. In 1910, a company called General Motors was organized out of 24 small and worthless corporations. The master and chief promoter was William C. Durant, one of the greatest bull market operators of his time. Though Durant made vast fortunes in the stock market, he twice suffered bankruptcy and died a comparatively poor man.

Then came World War I. The advent of the War affected the stock market. In the summer of 1914, the NYSE decided to close its door to prevent the flow of selling orders from Europe. This was the third time the Exchange ceased its operations. The first was in 1835 when a fire forced the Exchange to close down temporarily; the second was in 1873 caused by the failure of Jay Cooke and Company. And in 1914, it took several months before the market resumed trading. By mid 1915, operation was back to normal.

On the whole, World War I had a positive impact on the stock market. Up to that point, the Exchange was an exclusive club for its members — the marketplace was only for the professionals, promoters, operators, and speculators. In general, the public was not interested. There were only 200,000 stockholders throughout the country, and several panics and financial crises had given the market an unfavorable reputation. The war brought a new consciousness, however. When Liberty Bonds were being sold to aid the government's war efforts, public interest was stimulated. The war ended, the nation emerged as a world power, and Wall Street assumed the role as the principal money center of the world. For the first time in history, America was extending loans to foreign powers and exporting goods, commodities, and war supplies to its allies. In return, gold was being shipped to the United States in huge quantities, as London had suspended payment in gold at the outbreak of the War.

THE NINETEEN TWENTIES

By 1920 the Treasury Department had become the custodian of an enormous supply of the world's monetary gold. This was a time for transition not only for Wall Street, but for the nation as a whole. America had a sound economic system and a growing productive system in every field — automobiles, foods, chemicals, motion pictures, public utilities, banking, oil, aviation, and radio. As a result, the nation had become a creditor on the international scene and Wall Street played a prominent role to that effect. There were financial giants on Wall Street who were at times more powerful than the politicians in Washington. The impact of such individual bankers as J. P. Morgan, Schiff, and Otto Kahn was enormous. They wielded financial power as few people did at any time, before or since. But the center of activity was always the New York Stock Exchange. By now, the Exchange had become one of the most influential financial institutions in the world. Controlled by none but governed by its own rules and regulations, it was still the most important arena for shrewd manipulators and operators. The year 1920 was the start of a new era. Prosperity was everywhere, and the world was at peace. The public was involved in the stock market as never before, and new security issues were being distributed at a rapid pace. Common stock had achieved tremendous popularity, and speculative fever was about to start.

THE ROLE OF THE FEDERAL RESERVE

The establishment of the Federal Reserve System in the United States was an important milestone for banking and finance — and for the national economy. Created by the Federal Reserve Act in 1913, it eventually developed into one of the strongest banking systems in the world. As in the case of the securities clearance and settlement, the concept originated in Europe. European countries had successfully developed central banking systems for their own economic and monetary needs.

One of the functions of the Federal Reserve System was to implement credit and monetary policy and then to accommodate business with bank credit in accordance with that policy. One of the tools to accomplish this was the discount window. Banks made adjustments in their reserve positions by borrowing at the discount window of the Federal Reserve Bank.

During the 1920s, banks made extensive use of the discount window to adjust their reserve positions. Throughout the decade, average daily borrowings exceeded $500 million and at times amounted to more than $1 billion.

Starting in the fall of 1921, the speculative craze acquired dangerous proportions. It has been said that the Federal Reserve Bank was a major contributor to this speculative mania. By progressively lowering its discount rate, it created uncontrolled economic expansion and skyrocketed stock market speculation to unmanageable heights. People borrowed money from banks to buy stocks, and banks borrowed from the Fed's discount window to lend to the people. Margin requirements were only 10 percent or 20 percent. One would need a mere $1,000 to own $10,000 worth of stock. This heavy demand for credit was fueled by continued stock market expansion, persistent inflation, and higher stock prices. This was an unusual situation and a heyday for bankers. They would borrow from the Fed at 5 percent and lend it in the call money-market at 10 percent or 12 percent. There were no risks or legal impediments. The Federal Reserve Board had issued several warnings against this practice but found itself powerless to do anything about it.

THE CRASH OF 1929

In the summer of 1929, all stock averages were at their highs and still going higher. People everywhere were speculating. Even foreigners were lured into Wall Street by soaring stock market prices. Every morning the brokerage offices were jammed with people watching the quotation board.

On Thursday, October 24, 1929, an enormous crowd was gathered on Wall Street when the market opened. The prices of stocks went down so rapidly and precipitously on that day, that news from the White House and a syndicate of bankers could not stop the avalanche of sell orders. This was the day America crashed, bringing a dramatic end to the prosperity and affluence that had started a decade earlier. Four days later, on Tuesday, October 29 came the day of the financial disaster. This day will go down in history as the worst day in stock market history, with echoes heard throughout the world. This was unlike any other crash, panic, or depression. The crash was so complete that Tuesday will be remembered as the start of America's National Depression.

The crash of 1929 was the tenth disaster in the history of American finance. The first was the panic of 1792, with the signing of the Buttonwood Tree Agreement, followed by the crash of 1837, the disaster of 1857, the manipulative period between 1865 and 1869, the crisis of 1873, the panic of 1884, the period between 1893 and 1895, the crisis of 1901, and the panic of 1907. With the crash of 1929 came the end of an era of crises and panics and the beginning of regulation.

THE FRAMING OF SECURITIES LAWS AND
THE START OF THE SEC

The crash of 1929 was the end of one period in America and the beginning of another. This was the end of the raucous, "Roaring Twenties" and the beginning of a period of tremendous social change.

From the Buttonwood Tree Agreement in 1792 until 1933, the world of Wall Street and finance was not regulated. There were no federal laws governing the stock market. The issuance, the underwriting, sale and transfer of corporate securities were done at the discretion of the corporate officer and the stock brokers. There were congressional concerns at various periods of America's financial disasters, but those concerns did not result in any sort of legislation. Congress and the Executive Branch viewed the affairs of Wall Street as those of the private sector. It took a major disaster to shake the conscience of the country's legislators to regulate this business. And that major disaster — the Crash of 1929 — forced the President and Congress to enact laws to regulate the banking and the securities industry.

President Roosevelt's New Deal brought a series of legislation under the jurisdiction of a federal commission. The creation of the Securities and Exchange Commission in 1934 ushered in a new period for Wall Street. This was followed by the Glass-Steagall Act, which separated the investment banking and stock brokerage business from commercial banking activities.

With SEC as regulator, Congress enacted these seven different but interrelated securities laws to protect the American public from fraud and manipulative activities:

- The Securities Act of 1933
- The Securities Exchange Act of 1934
- The Public Utility Holding Company Act of 1935
- The Trust Indenture Act of 1939
- The Investment Company Act of 1940
- The Investment Advisers Act of 1940
- The Securities Act of 1975

Since October of 1929, it is safe to assume that because of these laws, America has been spared financial disasters, panics, and crashes.

THE NINETEEN SIXTIES

The 1960s brought one of the most active bull markets the world had ever known. After a dormant period following World War

II, Americans started to be actively interested again in the stock market. In order to stimulate this activity, the New York Stock Exchange adopted the slogan "Own Your Share in American Business" in an advertising campaign, not unlike that promoted by Madison Avenue.

Wall Street was coming back to life. This was a different era — more complex, more sophisticated, and more fascinating. The American Stock Exchange, the nation's second largest exchange, had completed a massive reorganization program by throwing out the old guard and bringing in a new management team and a new constitution. In the securities trading, there were high flyers not only on the over-the-counter market, but also on organized stock exchanges, conglomerates, computer leasers, franchisers, and electronics companies that led the market to the point of paralleling the decade of the Roaring Twenties. John Kennedy's election to the Presidency pushed the Dow Jones Industrial Average to 616, and the financial analysts coined this period as the "Roaring Sixties."

There were strong bullish expectations in every facet of economic activity. People saw the end of financial stagnation that marked the Eisenhower years and the beginning of the nation's technological advances that guaranteed economic progress. The post war period had brought new investment ventures, such as mutual funds and pension funds, and cash started to flow again into Wall Street. Unlike the 1920s, however, there was stability along with a growing economy. There were also the SEC, the Federal Reserve, and the stock exchanges ready to curb the activities of the speculators and prevent manipulation. The period initiated a boom in the new issues market. The little guy and the middle class rushed to buy new issues in a way reminiscent to the fever of 1929. Trading volume soared, setting new highs.

The Back-Office Problems of Nineteen Sixties

It was during this period of tremendous volume that Wall Street experienced a paperwork crunch of unusual dimension.

The so-called back-office problem was officially inaugurated on April 1, 1968, the day following President Johnson's dramatic withdrawal as candidate for reelection. On that day, the stock exchange volume shattered the 1929 record. This was the beginning of one of the most active periods in the history of the securities industry. It was also the beginning of one of the most tragic, sad, and embarrassing periods in the American financial system. Wall Street lost control. The brokerage houses simply could not handle the enormous volume of transactions.

Wall Street did not have the technology nor the manpower to run its back offices. This paperwork convulsion almost paralyzed the financial mechanism to the point that the stock exchanges decided to close shop on Wednesdays.

Firms spent millions of dollars to modernize their operations, automate procedures, and train operational personnel. The paperwork crisis lasted until the recession of 1972. It came perilously close to destroying the mechanism of the American economy. Twenty thousand people in the securities industry lost their jobs, 200 member organizations of the New York Stock Exchange went bankrupt, hundreds of brokerage offices around the world closed their doors, capital fled from the brokerage industry in search of safer grounds.

THE SECURITIES MARKET TODAY

There have been significant changes in the securities business since 1968. Some of the examples of the changes in this evolutionary period are: unprecedented operational stress, elimination of fixed commission rates, explosive trading volume, institutional participation, option trading, the emergence of discount brokerage houses. The most important changes, however, were legislative as well as operational. To ensure the continued fairness of the nation's capital markets and to increase their operational efficiency, Congress enacted legislation called the Securities Acts Amendments of 1975, giving the Securities and Exchange Commission a mandate to implement a national market system with the following objectives:

1. Efficient execution of securities transactions
2. Fair competition between and among securities markets and market participants
3. The collection and dissemination of information with respect to securities transactions and quotations
4. The execution of customers' orders in the best market available

5. The execution, to the extent practicable, of customers' orders without the participation of a dealer

6. Facilitation of the establishment of a national system for clearance and settlement of securities transactions

Since 1975, some progress has been made to achieve these congressional mandates, but not much.

From the operational standpoint, the decade of the 1970s brought new technology for the securities markets. Automation and the use of sophisticated computers have dramatically changed the mechanism and the operation of the marketplace. These new developments include:

1. *Consolidated Transaction Reporting System.* Information with respect to all securities transactions is now made available to brokers, dealers, and investors. The system gives the last sale information of listed securities traded at major and regional stock exchanges and the over-the-counter market.

2. *The development of a high speed data transmission system.* Vendors are now able to supply information with respect to securities trading on a timely basis.

3. *Market linkage for securities transaction.* A system called Intermarket Trading System (ITS) has been developed by several stock exchanges to facilitate the flow of orders from one exchange to the Specialists of another exchange.

4. *National Securities Trading System.* This is a fully automated trading system to execute retail orders.

5. *Automated Order Executions at several exchanges.*

6. *Designated Order Turnaround (DOT).* This is an internal order handling system developed by the New York Stock Exchange and designed to transmit smaller market and day limit orders from brokerage firms directly to the Specialist on the floor of the stock exchange.

7. *Institutional Network System (INSTINET).* INSTINET is a computerized network through which institutional accounts may buy and sell securities without a broker–dealer acting as an intermediary.

8. *National Association of Securities Dealers Automated Quotation System* (NASDAQ). This is an interdealer quotation system developed by the NASD.

With these changes, it is still difficult to predict the structure of the National Market System (NMS) in the foreseeable future.

This is an ongoing evolutionary process. Full implementation of the NMS will be for the best interest of the public investor.

The congressional mandate, however, was a turning point for the New York Stock Exchange. There was a general consensus in 1975 that the establishment of a national market system would be detrimental to the New York Stock Exchange. In its battle for survival, the New York Stock Exchange installed a program of unprecedented automation of trading and operation. Some day in the future, this massive program may even begin to keep the doors of the stock exchange open for 24 hours of trading.

The American capital market — as it represents the stock, bond, and the money market — is the most efficient market in the world today. It provides versatility, and its ability to raise money for the free enterprise system is unique in the world. It plays a dominant role in America's economic viability.

CHAPTER TWO

FUNDAMENTALS OF CORPORATE FINANCE

In planning an enterprise, a person usually selects a form of organization which is best suited to his needs and is advantageous to the nature of his particular business.

Primary consideration in any undertaking is given to the profit, its potential yield, and the manner in which it will be shared. This is an important economic factor, outweighing all other considerations in starting a venture. The manner in which a person decides to form the business is, therefore, dependent on this fundamental investment principle.

TYPES OF BUSINESS ORGANIZATIONS

There are basically three forms of business organizations:

- Sole-proprietorship
- Partnership
- Corporation

SOLE-PROPRIETORSHIP

In a sole-proprietorship the control of the business is in the hands of the individual owner. The owner is responsible for the conduct of his business and he shares the risks and the profits with no one.

This form of business organization is generally applicable for small businesses where expansion of the business is not a necessity. It has its advantages and its disadvantages.

Advantages:

1. The owner controls the activities of the business.
2. All profits of the business belong to the owner.
3. It is easy to organize. There are no legal requirements or restrictions to organize a sole-proprietorship. If the owner has the license to conduct the business, he may organize it immediately.
4. The owner has complete freedom to do whatever he wishes. He may enlarge or discontinue his operation at will.

Disadvantages:

1. The sole-owner of the business has unlimited liabilities. All his assets, whether business or personal, are subject to liquidation to satisfy the claims of creditors.
2. It is difficult to expand the business.
3. It is difficult to raise money for the business.
4. The business may require an amount of money beyond the owner's means. The capital is limited to the personal resources of the individual owner.
5. The business may not have continuity. The death or the incapacitation of the owner may terminate the business.

PARTNERSHIP

In a partnership type of organization, the business is owned jointly by all the people involved. The partners sign an agreement and organize the business. The agreement will specify the terms of the partnership, control of management, division of profits, and the proportional liabilities of each partner.

Advantages:

1. The capital contributed by each partner may be utilized to finance the business.

2. It is easy to organize the partnership. The management of the organization is divided among the partners.

3. The success of the organization depends on each partner's contribution to the firm.

4. The combined judgment of the partners governs the organization.

5. The amount of capital is not limited to the resources of one individual. Capital may be increased by bringing in additional partners.

Disadvantages:

1. The partners have unlimited liability for the debts of the firm.

2. It is difficult to expand the business.

3. The partnership may lack continuity. It may be subject to dissolution if a partner dies or withdraws from the business.

Types of Partnership

1. *General partnership.* In a general partnership, each general partner has unlimited liabilities for the debts of the organization.

2. *Limited partnership.* In a limited partnership, the limited partner has limited liabilities without any active role in the affairs of the organization. A general partnership may choose to have limited partners along with general partners.

3. *Joint ventures.* This type of partnership is organized for a particular purpose. One of the partners will have the authority to run the organization and the others will assume limited liabilities without any responsibility for the debts of the firm beyond the amount of their investment.

SUBCHAPTER S CORPORATION

The Subchapter S Corporation is a hybrid type of organization. It is similar to a corporation, but the profits and losses are allocated to individual owners. The business losses are passed through to the owners to offset income from other sources. The law permits the maximum number of shareholders to be 35. A Subchapter S organization is primarily used for personal, financial, estate planning, and new venture activities.

CORPORATION

Corporations are distinct legal entities. The word "corporation" comes from the Latin word "corpus," meaning body. Corporations are generally organized under state laws.

Advantages:

1. The stockholders are protected from the liabilities of the corporation. The stockholder is under no obligation to pay the debts of the corporation.
2. The stockholder will have a proportionate interest in the corporation. He will buy shares, and the extent of his loss will be the cost of the purchase of the shares in the event of liquidation.
3. It is easy to expand the business. It is easy to raise capital for the expansion or the operation of the business. The managers of the corporation do not have to rely on personal resources to raise money.
4. It is easy to transfer interest in the corporation. If it is a public corporation, one may buy or sell shares at any time.
5. The interests and assets of the corporation are divided into shares, and each stockholder, as a member of this corporate family, is eligible to receive dividends.

Disadvantages:

1. Paperwork and record-keeping requirements
2. Higher taxes
3. Governmental supervision over corporate affairs

The Organization of a Corporation

The corporate form of business organization consists of the following:

- The stockholders
- The board of directors

- The president
- The treasurer and/or secretary

The stockholders are the owners of the corporation. They have the power to elect the board of directors. The board of directors will elect the chairman of the board, the president, and other officers. The board is responsible for the general direction of the corporation. The board members are responsible for formulating company policies and establishing objectives and guidelines for management. The president is the officer directly responsible for the operation of the company. He must fulfill the objectives of the board and keep the board informed of the activities of the business. The president may be assisted by other officers, such as the vice president, the treasurer, the secretary, and so on.

HOW TO RAISE MONEY FOR YOUR BUSINESS

Let us assume you wish to start a business venture and you do not have adequate personal resources. You know now that there are three forms of business organizations, and you may choose any one that suits your purpose. What are the mechanics for raising money for your business? The discussion that follows will give you an idea of the requirements and steps that one must take to raise money for his business venture.

Whether you go to a bank, a relative, or a financial institution to borrow money, you will have to make a presentation of your company and the purpose of the loan. Raising cash is like selling a product. The conduct, the operation, and the future growth of your business may well depend on the way you will make the presentation to the person who will agree to lend you money. If you have adequate financial resources, the problem is easily solved. This is the simplest way of financing the business. But if you already have an operating business and you would like to raise money to meet the growing demands of your company, your individual resources might not be sufficient.

What is this growing demand of your company? It is possible that your company has an economic stimulus, such as a scientific invention, and its implementation with limited funds will be difficult. Or, your business might have increased its productivity and it will be necessary for you to devise new and more expensive methods of production. The increase of output requires increase of capital.

There is always a flow of funds from one hand to another. A businessman needs money to manufacture his goods. He sells his goods and buys more raw materials to manufacture more goods. The operation of the business will be successful if the demand and supply of money are simultaneous. The businessman needs tools and equipment to produce goods. He needs his manufactured goods to be stockpiled to meet delivery schedules to the market-place. He may also want to stockpile raw materials necessary to produce his goods.

There is, therefore, a demand for capital on a continuing basis. The businessman is always confronted with the problem of raising funds to meet the constantly changing economic and business requirements.

SOURCES OF CAPITAL. WHERE DOES ONE GO TO RAISE MONEY?

Individual Savings

The most obvious source of capital is the accumulation of funds through the process of saving. The prosperity of the country depends, in large measure, on the existence and the availability of funds. This act of saving is an important first step. The accumulation of money, however, has little value if the funds are not invested wisely. If you are in a business for yourself, you may use your own savings to operate the business, or you may entrust your savings to another businessman. You may even wish to participate in a public offering. You may buy a company's stock and turn over your money to a corporation. You may deposit your money at a bank and the bank officers will utilize your funds in your behalf. *No matter what method you select, you must always remember that the utilization of capital must be done in a manner capable of yielding profits.* This is the science of investment. Monies are placed in the hands of those who have convinced the owner of the money that they have sufficient ability to utilize the funds wisely and generate profits for the owner. The most obvious source of capital is private investors. But nobody will lend you money until he is thoroughly convinced that his money will be safe with you and he can expect a reasonable return. If you have a good plan that can be developed into a profitable enterprise, you can convince people to participate for their own immediate or long-range benefit.

You may find people in your immediate circle who will be willing to participate in your undertaking. There are several important factors that the lender will consider before making a commitment.

A. Does he trust you?

B. Is his money safe with you?

C. What will be the return on his investment. What is the long-term potential of his investment in your business?

D. Will there be additional liabilities on the part of the lender? This will depend on your type of organization and the nature of his participation.

E. What are the tax consequences of his investment?

Banks

The bank is an obvious source to raise cash. You go to a bank to borrow money. The lending officer must be convinced that the loan is for a worthy cause. You must be prepared to make a detailed presentation of the reasons and the purpose of the loan. The presentation must include:

- The nature of your business
- The products that you are manufacturing
- The services that you are providing
- The industry of your business
- Your financial and managerial background
- Short-term and long-range projections of your business venture

You must be able to convince the loan officer that you are a good businessman, capable of running the business. He must be convinced that you will use the borrowed funds properly and that you will honor the terms of the loan agreement. The most effective way of making a presentation is through the use of a *financial statement* of yourself or your business. The financial statement is a report listing all your assets, your liabilities, the operating expenses of your business, the anticipated revenues, the net earnings, etc.

THE FINANCIAL STATEMENT

It is relatively easy to prepare a financial statement. Your financial background or the condition of your business is best expressed through this medium. The financial statement comes in two different forms: the Balance Sheet and the Income Statement.

• *The Balance Sheet.* The Balance Sheet lists all the assets and liabilities of your business. On the asset side there are cash, securities, real estate, automobiles, equipment, inventory, etc. If this is a personal balance sheet, the list on the asset side will include everything that you own, whether you own it in full or a portion of it. If the current market price of your house is $50,000, put down $50,000 even though you may have a mortgage on it. If you have assets that you think are worthless, investigate, see if they have any value. If they have, mark it down on the asset side of the Balance Sheet. Put down the value of your car, your insurance, and everything else that you consider to be your own. By checking each aspect of your property, you'll be able to evaluate what you own to see if you can raise some cash against those assets. Real estate, for instance, gives the owner an opportunity to refinance to raise additional cash. If the value of the real estate has appreciated considerably since the time you purchased it, you may borrow against the present equity through a refinancing procedure or through an application for a second mortgage. You may do the same for your other assets. The securities that you own may be converted into cash without losing ownership. You may borrow against the market value of the securities.

The other part of the Balance Sheet will have all the liabilities. These are your loans, your monthly bills, your mortgage on the house, personal debt, credit charges, etc. After putting down all your liabilities, total up all of your assets and liabilities. Subtract the liabilities from the assets. The difference is your net worth or the equity. If your liabilities exceed your assets, the excess portion will be the degree of your indebtedness.

A personal Balance Sheet will look like this:

Assets		Liabilities and Net Worth	
1. Cash on hand	$ 300.00	1. Bank loan	$ 2,000.00
2. Bank accounts	$10,000.00	2. Loan from a relative	$ 500.00
3. Car	$ 3,000.00	3. Mortgage on house	$25,000.00
4. House	$50,000.00	4. Property taxes payable	$ 2,500.00
5. Furniture	$ 2,000.00	Total Liabilities	$30,000.00
		Net Worth	$35,300.00
Total	$65,300.00	Total	$65,300.00

A personal Balance Sheet tells you what financial resources you have and the funds you will need to meet your obligations. The equity will be determined by the following formula:

$$\text{Assets} - \text{Liabilities} = \text{Equity}$$

• *The Income Statement.* After preparing a personal balance sheet, you will be ready to prepare a statement of revenue and expense. The revenue will include the salary, wages, dividends, and interests on investments. The revenue is the inflow of assets for goods sold or services performed. The expenses will include the household bills or other liabilities. The expenses are the outflow of assets, or the use of assets. The expense portion of the statement also will show the depreciation of your properties. If you own a car, you will show a portion of its original cost for that year. If the life of the car is 5 years you must show ⅕ of its cost as an annual depreciation expense. By doing this, you are allocating the cost of an asset to expense over its useful life.

The following is an example of a personal statement of Revenue and Expense:

STATEMENT OF REVENUE AND EXPENSE
(As of December 31, 1986)

1. Cash on hand and in bank as of Dec. 31, 1985		$10,000.00
2. Add receipts:		
Salary	$25,000.00	
Dividends	$ 300.00	
Interest	$ 500.00	
	$25,800.00	$25,800.00
		$35,800.00

3. Subtract expenses:

Medical bills	$ 400.00	
Utility expense	$ 3,000.00	
Income Tax	$ 2,500.00	
Property Tax	$ 1,500.00	
Others	$ 500.00	
	$ 7,900.00	$ 7,900.00

4. Cash on hand and in bank as of
   December 31, 1986 $27,900.00

For your business, the statement of Revenue and Expense will be the statement of the previous year and the projected profit and loss. This will give a comparative picture of your last year's versus the coming year's business activity. A bank loan officer or institution interested in extending credit to you would like to see this together with your financial statement. This will only be a projection of what type of business activity you think you anticipate to have in the coming year. It is merely an intelligent exercise that will give you a guideline of what to expect. It will also give the moneylender an idea about the strengths or weaknesses of your business.

The form starts with total sales. Put down your estimate of the gross monthly sales of the products that you are manufacturing or services you are providing. Next is the cost of sales. This will be the cost of the raw materials you need to manufacture, the product and the cost of direct labor; no other expenses. If you are not the manufacturer of the product but merely the seller or the distributor of someone else's product, just put down the amount that it is costing you to buy the product from the manufacturer. After determining the total sales and the total cost of sales, you will calculate the gross profit. This will also give you the percentage of gross margin. If the cost of the product is 50 cents a unit and you are selling it for a dollar, that means your gross margin is 50 percent. You can reduce or increase this percentage if the market can bear or if your other expenses are controllable enough to make a profit.

Next comes the column for controllable expenses. You can control these expenses through effective management. These are the salaries, payroll taxes, advertising, dues, subscriptions, supplies, telephone, utilities, etc. — all expenses that are controllable or *variable* in nature. Total all your variable expenses.

Then come the expenses that are *fixed* in nature. These are the expenses that you have no control, such as depreciation of your equipment, insurance, rent, taxes, licenses, cost of interest on loan. Total the fixed expenses. Make a total of both your variable and fixed expenses. Subtract this total from your gross profit. The difference is your net profit or loss before taxes.

This entire exercise will give you an idea of your financial and operating condition for the coming year. If you can effectively manage the controllable side of your expenses and increase your gross sales, you can minimize the impact of your fixed expenses provided that your percentage of gross margin is reasonable.

INTEREST AND COST OF MONEY

The interest rate must be reasonable enough for you to borrow money. What is interest? Interest is the price one pays for the use of someone else's money. The rate of interest that one pays is governed by the same principle that governs other activities of commerce, that of supply and demand. Often times the government or federal agencies dictate interest-rate policies. Their decisions are based on economic, monetary, or the business conditions of the country or world at large. The rates will go up if the demand for capital is high; the rates will decline if the demand is low and the supply of credit is high.

When you borrow money from a bank or from a financial institution, the rate of interest that you will be charged is generally determined on the basis of pure interest plus an amount that will measure the risk of the transaction. If you are a prime customer of the bank, you will be charged on the basis of prime rate. For other borrowers, the lender will consider the element of risk. It is this measure of risk that the lender will add to the prime rate when lending money to non-prime customers.

Cash Utilization

Money brings money. If you cut your expenses down, you save money. If you make money, you accumulate and save money. If you store your savings at a place that brings you interest, the interest will bring you more interest. The interest will be compounded. You will be amazed how an insignificant amount of money kept in a savings account with interest compounded will grow into a large amount in a period of time.

Let us say you save $1 each year for 5, 10, 15 years. What will be the sum of money at the end of the 5th, 10th, and the 15th year at the following interest rates compounded?

Interest Rates	5 Years Later	10 Years Later	15 Years Later
6%	$5.64	$13.18	$23.28
8%	$5.87	$14.49	$27.15
10%	$6.11	$15.94	$31.77
12%	$6.35	$17.55	$37.28
14%	$6.61	$19.54	$43.84
16%	$6.88	$21.32	$51.66
18%	$7.15	$23.52	$60.97
20%	$7.44	$25.96	$72.04
22%	$7.74	$28.66	$85.19
24%	$8.05	$31.64	$100.82

You can use this table to calculate compound interest. Let us say you wish to save $500 a year for 10 years. You will multiply the figure in Column 2 by $500. $500 saved each year for 10 years at 8% interest compounded will amount to $7,245.00 (500 × 14.49). $500 saved each year at 12% interest compounded will amount to $8,775.00 (500 × 17.55). $1,000 saved each year for 10 years at 10% compound interest will amount to $15,940.00 (1,000 × 15.94).

We may use another table that will show the value of a single investment over a period of years, with interest compounded. Let us say you keep only $1,000 in an account as opposed to adding $1,000 in fresh money each year. What will be the value of that $1,000 over a period of years at different rates of interest:

Interest Rates	6 Years Later	12 Years Later	23 Years Later
6%	$1,420	$2,010	$4,050
8%	$1,590	$2,520	$6,340
10%	$1,770	$3,140	$9,850
12%	$1,974	$3,896	$15,179

At what point do you double your original investment? This is an important question that is of interest to all investors. Just remember 72. If you divide 72 by the interest rate that the investor receives on his investment, the result will be the number of years that will be required to double the original investment, regardless of the amount involved. Examples:

A. An investment of funds earning 10% each year will double in 7.2 years.

$$\frac{72}{10} = 7.2$$

B. An investment earning 8% interest every year will double in 9 years.

$$\frac{72}{8} = 9$$

HOW TO INCORPORATE YOUR BUSINESS

Now that we know how to raise money, the sources of capital, the importance of interest rates, and the cost of money, let us study the mechanics of incorporating a business organization and the fundamentals of corporate finance.

1. You must choose a state where you wish to incorporate your company. The requirements vary from state to state, but there are certain standard procedures.
2. One of the organizers of the corporation must be a U.S. citizen, not necessarily a resident of the state where the corporation is being organized.
3. You must file a Certificate of Incorporation with that state's Secretary of State. The Certificate of Incorporation will include the following:
   A. *The name of the corporation.* The name must be unique in that state. You may not use a corporate name that has already been used.
   B. *The names of the incorporators and their addresses.* The number of incorporators vary from state to state. Some states require only one, some three, etc.
   C. *The location of the corporation.* The place of business for the corporation does not have to be the state of incor-

poration. You may conduct your business in any other state, but you must maintain an office address in the state of incorporation.

D. *The purpose of incorporation.* The corporation will be required to restrict its business activities to that purpose.

E. *Capital stock.* You must indicate the number of shares to represent the capital of your corporation. You will petition the Secretary of State to authorize the issuance of a number of shares for your corporation.

When the Certificate of Incorporation is filed with the Secretary of State, you must wait until you receive the approval. Let us say the Secretary will approve the issuance of 500,000 shares representing the capital of your corporation. These shares will be called authorized shares. When approval is obtained, you will have a meeting with the board of directors. The board will decide to sell some of these shares to the public or to the employees of the corporation. The board will not sell the entire amount of shares authorized. It will leave some shares for future purposes. Those future purposes may be:

- to sell additional shares to raise more cash
- to issue shares as stock dividends to the stockholders
- to give bonuses to the employees in the form of shares
- to use the shares to acquire another company

The shares will have par value or no par value. This is an arbitrary determination of the value of the shares by the corporation and has nothing whatever to do with the market value of the stock. A corporation may have fractional par value — 37½ cents, for instance.

After selling some of the shares of the 500,000 authorized stock, the corporation will start its operation. Sometime later the corporation may decide to repurchase some of the shares back from the stockholders. These repurchased shares are called Treasury shares and will be kept by the corporation.

To summarize:

1. Authorized shares   500,000
   (These are the total shares authorized by the Secretary of State.)

2. Issued and outstanding   400,000
   (This is the number of shares sold to the
   public.)
3. Treasury stock   50,000
   (This is the number of shares previously sold to
   the public but repurchased by the corporation.)
4. Authorized but unissued.   50,000

The Treasury stock has no voting and dividend privileges. It can
be used to finance corporate activity. It also may be sold back to
the public. The difference in money between the purchase and
sale will be a profit or loss to the corporation. The Treasury stock
will appear in the corporate balance sheet in the section of stockholders' equity, with a bracket around the funds invested to purchase the shares. It will be a reduction of the stockholders' equity.
It will be listed in the Balance Sheet at the average purchase price
of the shares and not on the basis of par value. The average purchase price is determined by taking the average of the cost of purchasing the security by the corporation.

The corporation may select different types and classes of
securities, common, preferred, etc. It also may issue bonds or
money market instruments to finance the operation.

THE BALANCE SHEET OF A CORPORATION

As in the case of a personal financial statement, a corporation also
will prepare a financial statement or a Balance Sheet to demonstrate the net worth of the corporation. The Balance Sheets will
have the total assets and the total liabilities. The difference
between the two will be the stockholders' equity. It is called a
"Balance" Sheet because both sides of the equation are balanced.
Using the formula discussed above:

$$ASSETS - LIABILITIES = NET\ WORTH$$

The net worth in this case is the stockholders' equity in the corporation. It is the amount of money invested by the stockholders
in the corporation. Placing the formula in a different way:

$$ASSETS = LIABILITIES + STOCKHOLDERS'\ EQUITY$$

Public corporations, particularly those listed on the stock exchanges, are required to publish their financial statements annually. The confidence that one places in the financial statements is based on the integrity of the independent auditor or the accountant preparing the statements. Outside auditors are approved by the stockholders and cannot arbitrarily be dismissed by the management of the company.

The financial statements, however, do not provide all the answers to analyze a corporation's financial health. The missing elements in the statements are the quality of the management and its ability to run the company profitably and efficiently. The statements on the Balance Sheet do not provide clues as to the company's financial policies, the management's ability to promote and sell the products, or the company's competitive posture with regards to other companies in the same industry. The assets on the Balance Sheet represent the value of the properties of the corporation, whether they are real estate, securities, equipment, or inventory. The stockholders' equity will be the amount of money that the stockholders will receive if all the assets on the Balance Sheet are liquidated and the liabilities are paid off.

STOCKHOLDERS' EQUITY = ASSETS − LIABILITIES

The Preparation of a Corporate Balance Sheet

ASSETS

Current Assets. The current assets on the Balance Sheet will include those assets of the corporation that can be converted into cash within a year or less. These are:

- Cash
- Marketable securities. The Balance Sheet will indicate the value of the securities at their lowest cost, or their current market value.
- Accounts Receivable. This represents the amount of money due the corporation. It must not include the bad debts. The bad debts must be subtracted from the amount in the Accounts Receivable. The difference will be the amount that the corporation is expected to collect.

- Inventory. This figure will include the raw materials, the finished products, and the work in progress. As in the case of securities, the inventory is carried on the Balance Sheet at its lowest cost or the current market value. Cost accounting for inventory is based on two methods:
  - First-in-first-out (FIFO). This method assumes that items placed in inventory most recently stay in inventory. The first items placed in inventory are sold first.
  - Last-in-first-out (LIFO). This method assumes that the last items placed in inventory are sold first. Therefore, goods placed in inventory earlier tend to remain in inventory.

The corporation may choose either one. The FIFO method will provide a lower deduction for cost of goods sold. This will result in higher profit and higher taxes.

Placing these four figures together will have the following picture as the *Current Assets of Bee Corporation.*

1. Cash	$ 120,000
2. Marketable securities at cost (current market value $176,000)	$ 170,000
3. Accounts Receivable (250,000 minus 30,000 for bad debts)	$ 220,000
4. Inventory	$ 630,000
Total Current Assets	$1,140,000

By looking at this Balance Sheet of current assets, one may also determine the portion that is considered as Quick Assets. The Quick Assets represent those current assets that can be converted into cash readily by the corporation within 30 days. They will include:

- Cash
- Marketable securities
- Accounts Receivable

The only figure excluded in the Quick Assets is the inventory. The inventory cannot be converted into cash readily. The Quick Assets are determined, therefore, by subtracting the inventory from the total current assets.

QUICK ASSETS = TOTAL CURRENT ASSETS

− INVENTORY

In our example above, the Quick Assets of this corporation will be:

Quick Assets = $1,140,000 - $630,000 = $510,000

Fixed Assets. The fixed assets in the Balance Sheet include real estate, properties, furniture, machinery, etc. They are generally categorized on the Balance Sheet as property, plant and capital equipment valued at cost minus accumulated depreciation. Depreciation means a decrease in value of the property as the property gets older. When a corporation buys a property, it does not charge that property as a business expense in the year of the purchase. Because the property will last for a number of years, the corporation charges it as an expense over a number of years. The corporation spreads out the expense. If the cost of the property is $10,000 and the usable life of the property is five years, the corporation will spread out the expense of $10,000 for a period of five years. This is called Annual Depreciation.

Under the Economic Recovery Tax Act (ERTA) of 1981, the depreciation of properties is much simplified. The law provides a schedule of useful lives that are basically 3, 5, 10, and 19 years. These lives must be used for all purchases made after January 1, 1981. The schedule of depreciation under ERTA is as follows:

1. Transportation equipment (cars, trucks, etc.), research and development, equipment, and other short-term tangible property: 3-year life.
2. Everything else except items in the 10-year and 15-year category: 5-year life.
3. Railroad tank cars, public utility and moving equipment, manufactured home: 10-year life.
4. Real estate buildings: 19-year life.

It must be noted that only buildings will depreciate and not the raw land. The land may be depleted, such as for oil and gas exploration, and so on.

There are three different methods in determining depreciation: Straight Line, Sums-of-Years Digits, and Double Declining Balance.

1. *Straight-line.* Through this method the annual depreciation is determined by dividing the net cost of the property by the

number of years of usable life of the property. The net cost of the property is the actual cost minus the salvage value. The annual depreciation formula under the Straight-Line method will be:

$$\text{Annual Depreciation} = \frac{\text{Net Cost (actual cost-salvage value)}}{\text{Number of years of usable life}}$$

EXAMPLE

The corporation purchases equipment for $10,000. This is the actual cost. The salvage value of the equipment is $2,000. Therefore, the net cost will be $8,000. If the usable life of the property is 5 years, the annual depreciation will be: 8,000/5 = $1,600.

As mentioned above, the fixed assets are carried on the Balance Sheet at cost minus accumulated depreciation. The cost in our example above is $10,000; the annual depreciation is $1,600. The fixed asset on the Balance Sheet for the first year will be:

First year:

$$\$10,000 - \$1,600 = \$8,400.$$

This annual depreciation of $1,600 will accumulate every year. At the end of the second year, the fixed asset on the Balance Sheet will be:

Second year:

$$\$10,000 - \$3,200 = \$6,800$$

(3,200 is determined by multiplying $2 \times 1,600$).

Third year:

$$\$10,000 - \$4,800 = \$5,200$$

(4,800 is determined by multiplying $3 \times 1,600$).

Fourth year:

$$\$10,000 - \$6,400 = \$3,600$$

(6,400 is determined by multiplying $4 \times 1,600$).

Fifth year:

$$\$10,000 - \$8,000 = \$2,000$$

(8,000 is determined by multiplying $5 \times 1,600$).

At the end of the fifth year, which is the last year of the property's usable life, the fixed asset on the Balance Sheet will be $2,000, which is exactly the salvage value of the property as discussed above.

2. *Sums-of-Years Digits depreciation.* To determine the annual depreciation of the property, the number of years of the property's usable life is added together. In our example above, the life of the property is 5. Add the number of years counting down to 1.

$$5 + 4 + 3 + 2 + 1 = 15$$

The annual depreciation is determined by the following formula:

$$\text{Annual Depreciation} = \frac{\text{Usable Life} \times \text{Net Cost}}{\text{Sum-of-Years' Digit}}$$

Using the example above:

$$\frac{5}{15} \times 8,000 = \$2,666.66$$

For subsequent years, the annual depreciation is determined by taking the next lower number in the sequence.

Second year:

$$\frac{4}{15} \times 8,000 = \$2,133.34$$

The depreciation will accumulate each year. At the end of the second year, the accumulated depreciation will be:

$$\$2,666.66 + \$ 2,133.34 = \$4.800$$

Third year:

$$\frac{3}{15} \times 8,000 = \$1,600$$

Accumulated depreciation:

$$\$1,600 + \$4,800 = \$6,400$$

Fourth year:

$$\frac{2}{15} \times 8,000 = \$1,066.67$$

Accumulated depreciation:

$$\$6,400 + \$1,066.67 = \$7,466.67$$

Fifth year:

$$\frac{1}{15} \times 8,000 = \$533.33$$

Accumulated depreciation:

$$\$7,466.67 + \$533.33 = \$8,000$$

As in the straight-line determination, the fixed assets on the Balance Sheet are calculated at actual cost minus accumulated depreciation. For each year the fixed assets will be shown as:

First year:	$10,000 − $2,666.66	= $7,333.34
Second year:	$10,000 − $4,800	= $5,200
Third year:	$10,000 − $6,400	= $3,600
Fourth year:	$10,000 − $7,466.67	= $2,533.33
Fifth year:	$10,000 − $8,000	= $2,000

Under the Sums-of-Years Digit method, more depreciation is charged off in the early years of the property's life.

3. *Double Declining Balance depreciation.* This method does

not consider the salvage value of the property. In determining depreciation, the actual cost is considered and not the net cost. The property is written down from its actual cost to the expected salvage value. In the example above, that will be from $10,000 to $2,000. To determine each year's write-off under this method, the accountant will double what it would be under the straight-line method. This again provides an accelerated depreciation in the early years. Therefore, it will produce a higher expense and a lower tax.

This type of accelerated depreciation is known as ACRS (Accelerated Cost Recovery System). Under this method, the assets are undervalued in the early years.

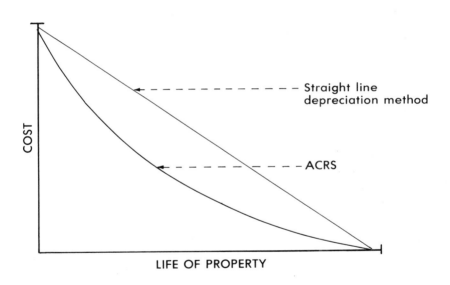

Sundry Assets. The sundry assets are miscellaneous assets on the Balance Sheet. They include such things as unimproved land, deferred charges, and prepaid expenses. Prepaid expenses are payments for materials in advance of their receipts, rent payments, insurance premiums, etc. Deferred charges are charges incurred in the organization of a new division or the manufacturing of a new product.

Intangible Assets. The intangible assets of a company are the patents, goodwill, and franchises.

These are the four major areas of the asset side of the Balance Sheet. Let us now construct the asset portion by using the previous example of the Current Assets of Bee Corporation.

ASSETS

1. Cash	$ 120,000
2. Marketable securities at cost	$ 170,000
(current market value $176,000)	
3. Accounts Receivable	$ 220,000
($250,000 minus $30,000 for bad debts)	
4. Inventory	$ 630,000
Total Current Assets	$1,140,000
5. Fixed Assets (property, plant, and equipment)	$ 750,000
6. Sundry Assets	$ 57,500
(unimproved land, deferred charges, prepaid expenses)	
7. Intangible Assets (patents, franchises, goodwill)	$ 50,000
Total Assets	$1,997,500

LIABILITIES

Now we turn to the liabilities side of the Balance Sheet.

Current Liabilities. The Current Liabilities will include all obligations that the company must make within a year's time. These are the debts of the corporation scheduled to be paid within a year. They include:

- Accounts Payable. This is the amount owed to creditors.
- Accrued Expenses. These are the interest on debt and salaries to employees.
- Accrued Taxes. These are taxes owed to federal, local and state governments, the FICA withholding deductions.
- Notes Payable. This is the amount owed to banks, money lenders, and bondholders scheduled to be paid within a year's time.

Placing all these items together on the liability side of the Balance Sheet, we will have the following picture for Bee Corporation:

CURRENT LIABILITIES

1.	Accounts Payable	$100,000
2.	Accrued Expenses	$ 75,000
3.	Accrued Taxes	$ 35,000
4.	Notes Payable	$ 21,000
	Total Current Liabilities	$231,000

RATIO OF CURRENT ASSETS TO CURRENT LIABILITIES

At this point, it is important to determine the company's ability to honor these current obligations. The source that the company will tap to make these current obligations is the current assets itemized on the left side of the Balance Sheet. We must, therefore, relate the current liabilities to current assets. The corporation must also make sure that the current assets are more than the current liabilities so that after all the current debts are paid, the management will have enough working capital to run the company. The rule of thumb for this ratio is 2 to 1, or better.

The excess portion of the current assets over current liabilities is the *working capital*.

WORKING CAPITAL = CURRENT ASSETS

– CURRENT LIABILITIES

An increase in net income, sale of securities, sale of non-current assets, and cash flow generated from depreciation and depletion will increase the working capital of the corporation.

In our example of Bee Corporation's Balance Sheet, the *Working Capital* is:

$1,140,000 − $231,000 = $909,000

After determining the working capital, the accountant will determine the ratio between the current assets and current liabilities. This is called the *Current Ratio*, which is computed by simply dividing the current assets by current liabilities.

$$\text{Current Ratio} = \frac{\text{Current Assets}}{\text{Current Liabilities}}$$

In our example above, the *Current Ratio* will be:

$$\frac{1,140,000}{231,000} = 4.9$$

This means Bee Corporation has $4.9 in current assets for every $1 it owes in current liabilities. Even though we have a healthy ratio of 4.9, it is important for us to realize that not all the current assets can be converted into cash readily to meet the current liabilities. As discussed previously, the only items in the current assets that are readily convertible into cash are the *Quick Assets*. The Quick Assets are all the current assets minus the inventory. They are the cash, the marketable securities, and the Accounts Receivable — all liquid assets available to cover the current liabilities. In our example of Bee Corporation, the Quick Assets amount is $510,000. Quick Assets are items that may be converted into cash within 30 days:

$$\$1,140,000 - \$630,000 = \$510,000$$

Taking the Quick Assets into consideration, the accountant will compute the ratio between the Quick Assets and the Current Liabilities. This ratio is called the Quick Asset Ratio, the Liquidity Ratio, or the Acid Test Ratio. It is a measuring device to test a corporation's liquidity.

$$\text{Quick Asset Ratio} = \frac{\text{Quick Assets}}{\text{Current Liabilities}}$$

For Bee Corporation the Quick Asset Ratio is:

$$\frac{510,000}{231,000} = 2.2$$

Higher figure indicates good performance. This means there is $2.2 in Quick Assets for every $1 needed to cover the short-term current liabilities.

Cash Assets represent cash and money market instruments, such as CDs, Treasury Bills, and money market funds.

The *Cash Asset Ratio* is computed by:

$$\frac{\text{Cash Assets}}{\text{Current Liabilities}}$$

Fixed Liabilities

The fixed liabilities are the company's long-term obligations. They include bonds maturing in 5 years or more, long-term bank loans, mortgages, or notes. This is the company's funded debt. Let us assume the fixed liabilities for Bee Corporation are:

Bee Corporation Bonds 7% due in 2002: $300,000

The bonds are carried on the Balance Sheet at their face value. It is the face value or the par value of the bonds that the corporation is obligated to pay the bondholders, regardless whether the market value is higher or lower than the par value.

Current Debt to Tangible Net Worth

This ratio indicates the relationship between short-term credit and the owner's investment in the business. It is determined by:

$$\frac{\text{Current Debt}}{\text{Tangible Net Worth}}$$

(Lower percentage indicates better performance.)

Total Debt to Tangible Net Worth

This ratio indicates whether the management is relying heavily on debt to finance the business. It is determined by:

$$\frac{\text{Total Debt}}{\text{Tangible Net Worth}}$$

(Lower percentage indicates better performance.)

Placing all these items on the liability side of the Balance Sheet, we will have the following picture for Bee Corporation:

LIABILITIES

1. Accounts Payable	$100,000
2. Accrued Expenses	$ 75,000
3. Accrued Taxes	$ 35,000
4. Notes Payable	$ 21,000
Current Liabilities	$231,000
4. Fixed Liabilities	
Bonds — 7% due in 2002	$300,000
Total Liabilities	$531,000

STOCKHOLDERS' EQUITY

The difference between the total assets and the total liabilities is the net worth of the company. The net worth of the company is the stockholders' equity. This is the amount of money that the stockholders have in the company.

In our example, the stockholders' equity is $1,997,500 − $531,000 = $1,466,500.

The stockholders' equity means that at the time of the dissolution of the company, the stockholders would receive this amount if all the assets on the Balance Sheet are sold at the values stated and all the liabilities are paid off.

The Common Stockholders' Equity is determined by excluding the Preferred Stock from the Stockholders' Equity.

The stockholders' equity is categorized in the following manner:

1. Preferred stock.
2. Common stock.
3. Capital surplus.
4. Retained earnings.

A. Preferred Stock

The preferred stock, which is similar to common stock, is carried on the Balance Sheet as to its par value — the amount of money that the company received when it sold the original issue to stockholders. The market value of the preferred stock is not considered.

Let us assume that Bee Corporation has a total of 1,000

shares of 8 percent preferred stock issued and outstanding with a par value of $100 a share. This means that the stockholders are holding a total of 1,000 shares and are entitled to receive 8 percent dividends annually — 8 percent of the par value or 8 percent of $100, $8 a share.

$$1,000 \text{ shares} \times \$100 \text{ Par} = \$100,000 \text{ (total par value)}$$

B. Common Stock

The Balance Sheet will state the par value of all the common shares issued and outstanding. These are the shares sold to the public and the par value generally represents the total money that the corporation received at the original sale of the security to the public. Most corporations assign par value to their common stock at prices well below the original issue price.

For Bee Corporation, the Balance Sheet will indicate:

50,000 shares of common stock issued and outstanding

$10 par value

$$50,000 \times 10 = \$500,000$$

C. Capital Surplus

This represents the amount of money that the company received from the sale of the common stock to the public in excess of the par value. Let us assume Bee Corporation originally sold to the public 40,000 shares of common stock at a par value of $10, which brought to the company $400,000. At a later date, the company issued another 10,000 shares and sold to the public at $15 a share. This extra $5 a share over the par value is the capital surplus and must be stated as such on the Balance Sheet.

Common Stock	$500,000
($10 par value × 50,000 shares)	
Capital Surplus	$ 50,000
[10,000 out of 50,000 sold at a later date.	
Amount in excess of original sale is $50,000.]	
(10,000 × 5)	
	$550,000

The total of the two — $550,000 — will indicate the amount that Bee Corporation received as a result of the sale of its common stock.

D. Retained Earnings

The retained earnings represent the amount of the profits that have not yet been distributed to the common stockholders in the form of dividends. They may not be in the form of liquid cash that the company has at its disposal ready to distribute to stockholders. They may be amounts reinvested in additional inventory or spread out among various assets. If the company decides to distribute dividends to the stockholders, it will use the amount in the Retained Earnings. Dividends distributed to the stockholders, therefore, reduce the Retained Earnings.

Let us assume the Retained Earnings for Bee Corporation are: $816,500.

We are now ready to construct the entire Balance Sheet of Bee Corporation (see Balance Sheet on p. 43).

The sheet is balanced.

ASSETS = LIABILITIES + STOCKHOLDERS' EQUITY.

ANALYSIS OF THE BALANCE SHEET

Now that we have constructed the Balance Sheet, let us analyze the condition of the corporation: what kind of capitalization does it have, what is the Book Value, and what is the financial picture?

Capitalization. The capitalization of the company is the total of bonds, preferred stock, common stock, capital surplus, and retained earnings. Each component of capitalization is measured separately in relationship to the total capitalization. These are measured in ratios: ratios for bonds, preferred stock, common stock, the bond ratio in relationship to the total capitalization, the common stock ratio in relationship to the total capitalization and the preferred stock ratio in relationship to the total capitalization.

BALANCE SHEET

BEE CORPORATION, January 6, 1986

ASSETS

Cash	$ 120,000
Marketable Securities	$ 170,000
Accounts Receivable	$ 220,000
Inventory	$ 630,000
Total Current Assets	$1,140,000
Fixed Assets — capital equipment	$ 750,000
Sundry Assets	$ 57,500
Intangible Assets	$ 50,000
Total Assets	$1,997,500

LIABILITIES

Accounts Payable	$ 100,000
Accrued Expenses	$ 75,000
Accrued Taxes	$ 35,000
Notes Payable	$ 21,000
Total Current Liabilities	$ 231,000
Bonds — 7% due 2002	$ 300,000
Total Liabilities	$ 531,000

STOCKHOLDERS' EQUITY

Preferred Stock — 8% $100 par (1000 shares)	$ 100,000
Common Stock — $10 par (50,000 shares)	$ 500,000
Capital Surplus (AKA Paid-in Capital or Capital excess)	$ 50,000
Retained Earnings	$ 816,500
Total Stockholders' Equity	$1,466,500
Total Liabilities + Stockholders' Equity	$1,997,500

If the corporation is highly capitalized with debt instruments, it is said to be speculatively capitalized. The chances for bankruptcy will increase if it is highly leveraged. If it is capitalized with equity securities, it is known to have conservative capitalization. The stockholders' equity is increased when convertible bonds are converted into common shares. This conversion does not provide dilution of per share equity and per share earnings of the corporation.

Taking our example of Bee Corporation, let us determine the total capitalization and the ratios.

$$\text{Capitalization} = \begin{cases} \text{Bonds} & \$\ 300{,}000 \\ \text{Preferred stock} & \$\ 100{,}000 \\ \text{Common stock} & \$\ 500{,}000 \\ \text{Capital surplus} & \$\ 50{,}000 \\ \text{Retained earnings} & \underline{\$\ 816{,}500} \\ & \overline{\$1{,}766{,}000} \end{cases}$$

A. The Bond Ratio $= \dfrac{\text{Bonds}}{\text{Total capitalization}}$

$$\frac{300{,}000}{1{,}766{,}000} = 0.169 \text{ or } 16\%$$

B. The Preferred Stock Ratio $= \dfrac{\text{Preferred stock}}{\text{Total capitalization}}$

$$\frac{100{,}000}{1{,}766{,}000} = 0.056 \text{ or } 5.6\%$$

C. The Common Stock Ratio $= \dfrac{\text{Common} + \left(\begin{array}{c}\text{Capital}\\\text{surplus}\end{array}\right) + \left(\begin{array}{c}\text{Retained}\\\text{earnings}\end{array}\right)}{\text{Total capitalization}}$

$$\frac{500{,}000 + 50{,}000 + 816{,}500}{1{,}766{,}000} = 0.773 \text{ or } 77.3\%$$

All three combined will add up to 100 percent.

Book Value. The Book Value of a common share is the amount of cash that the stockholder will receive for each share of common stock if all the tangible assets are sold at prices stated on the Balance Sheet and all the liabilities, the bondholders, and the preferred stockholders are paid off. It is determined by the following formula:

Book Value per share

$$= \frac{\left[\left(\begin{array}{c}\text{Common}\\\text{stock}\end{array}\right) + \left(\begin{array}{c}\text{Capital}\\\text{surplus}\end{array}\right) + \left(\begin{array}{c}\text{Retained}\\\text{earnings}\end{array}\right)\right] - \left(\begin{array}{c}\text{Intangible}\\\text{assets}\end{array}\right)}{\text{Number of shares of common}}$$

$$= \frac{(500{,}000 + 50{,}000 + 816{,}500) - 50{,}000}{50{,}000} = \$27.33 \text{ per share}$$

The Book Value of Bee Corporation as stated on the Balance Sheet is $27.33 per share.

The Book Value for preferred stock is determined by:

$$\frac{\text{Total assets} - (\text{Intangible assets} + \text{Total liabilities})}{\text{Number of preferred shares}}$$

The Book Value for a $1,000 face value of a bond is determined by:

$$\frac{\text{Total assets} - (\text{Intangible assets} + \text{Current liabilities})}{\text{Number of \$1,000 bonds}}$$

The total assets of Bee Corporation are $1,997,500, the intangible assets are $50,000, and the current liabilities are $231,000. Bee Corporation has only $300,000 face value of outstanding bonds. That will mean 300 bonds for $1,000 each. Placing these items in the formula:

$$\frac{1,997,500 - (50,000 + 231,000)}{300} = 5,721.66$$

The Book Value of each $1,000 bond is $5,721.66.

THE PREPARATION OF INCOME STATEMENT

The Income Statement is the profit and loss statement of the corporation over a one-year period. It will contain the net sales, the cost of goods sold, expenses, depreciation, operating and other income, interest on bonds, taxes, net income, dividends on preferred stocks, and net earnings.

Let us study each item and construct an Income Statement for Bee Corporation:

1. Net sales or operating revenues. This is the total revenue that the company took in.

2. Cost of goods sold.

3. Selling, general, and administrative expenses. This is the cost of running the sales office — payroll, commissions, advertising, etc.

4. Depreciation. This is the annual depreciation of fixed assets.

5. Operating Income. This figure represents net sales minus the operating expense.

6. Other Income. Related or unrelated income derived from various sources — dividends or interest on securities, rental income, etc.

7. Total income. This is also known as "EBIT" — earnings before interest and taxes.

8. Interest on Bonds of the corporation. This is the interest cost on the bonds.

9. Taxes. These are federal and state income taxes.

10. Net income. This is the net profit. All income minus all expenses.

11. Dividends on Preferred Stock. The interest on bonds in item number 8 is a tax-deductible item. It is figured before the tax liability is determined. The dividend on preferred stock is not a tax-deductible item.

12. Net earnings. This is the net earning per each share of common stock. The management may decide to reinvest this in the company or pay out as cash dividends to stockholders of common stock. The amount not paid out as dividends will be considered as Retained Earnings.

In preparing the Income Statement, we must also determine the number of days sales are outstanding. This is known as DSO (Days Sales Outstanding). This shows the effect of the flow of cash into the organization.

The collection period is determined by:

$$\frac{\text{Accounts Receivable}}{\text{Annual Net Credit Sales}} \times 365$$

(Lower figure indicates better performance.)

EXAMPLE

Net Credit Sales:	$500,000
Accounts Receivable	$ 50,000

Collection Period: $\dfrac{50,000}{500,000} \times 365 = 36.5$ days

Higher figure may be caused by poor collection program, delinquent accounts, increased sales volume, and general economic conditions.

STATEMENT OF INCOME

BEE CORPORATION, Jan. 1–Dec. 31, 1986

Net sales	$ 4,000,000
Cost of goods sold	$-2,100,000
Selling, general, and administrative expenses	$ -220,000
Depreciation	$ -35,000
Operating income	$ 1,645,000
Other income	$ 25,000
Total income (EBIT)	$ 1,670,000
Interest on bonds (7% interest on 300M Bonds)	$ -21,000
Taxes (50%)	$ -824,500
Net income	$ 824,500
Dividends on preferred stock (8% on 1000 shares)	$ -8,000
Net earnings (available to common stockholders)	$ 816,500

Analysis of Income Statement

Now that we have constructed the Income Statement of Bee Corporation, let us analyze each item to determine the company's financial posture.

1. The Operating or the Expense Ratio. The Expense Ratio is measured by the following formula:

$$\text{Expense Ratio} = \frac{\left(\begin{array}{c}\text{Cost of}\\\text{goods sold}\end{array}\right) + \left(\begin{array}{c}\text{Selling, general}\\\text{administrative}\\\text{expenses}\end{array}\right) + \text{Depreciation}}{\text{Net Sales}}$$

This is, in fact, the operating cost divided by net sales. In the case of Bee Corporation it is:

$$\frac{2,100,000 + 220,000 + 35,000}{4,000,000} = 0.588 \text{ or } 58.8\%$$

2. Margin of Profit Ratio. This is determined by dividing the operating income by net sales.

$$\frac{1,645,000}{4,000,000} = 0.411 \text{ or } 41.12\%$$

The Expense Ratio plus the margin of Profit Ratio is equal to 100%.

$$(58.8\% + 41.12\%)$$

Significance: It measures the profitability of the sales force.

Higher percentage indicates larger profits. Lower percentage may be the result of reduced sales price, high cost of inventory, high cost of labor, and high cost of material.

Another measuring device will be the ratio of net profit on net sales. This is determined by:

$$\frac{\text{After tax profit}}{\text{Net sales}}$$

This will indicate profits earned per dollar of sales. Higher figure reflects operational efficiency.

Ratio Net Sales to Tangible Net Worth

This will indicate the turnover on investment. It is determined by:

$$\frac{\text{Annual net sales}}{\text{Tangible net worth}}$$

Lower figure indicates good performance.

3. Cash Flow. The cash flow is the actual cash the company has before it pays out dividends on preferred and common stock. It is measured by the following formula:

$$\text{Cash flow} = \text{Net income} + \text{Annual depreciation}$$
$$\$824,500 + \$35,000 = \$859,500$$

4. Interest Coverage. This determines the company's ability to pay interest to the bondholders on its outstanding bonds.

$$\text{Interest coverage} = \frac{\text{Total income (EBIT)}}{\text{Interest on bonds}}$$

$$= \frac{1,670,000}{21,000} = 79.52 \text{ times}$$

The company's income covers the interest on bonds 79.52 times.

5. Preferred Dividend Coverage. This measures the company's ability to pay dividends on preferred stock.

$$\text{Preferred Dividend Coverage} = \frac{\text{Net income}}{\text{Preferred dividends}}$$

$$= \frac{824,500}{8,000} = 103.06 \text{ times}$$

This means that the company's earnings cover the dividends on preferred stock 103.06 times.

6. Earning Per Share. This is a very important measuring device of the corporate financial picture. It is determined by the following formula:

$$\text{Earnings per share} = \frac{\text{Net earnings}}{\text{Number of common shares outstanding}}$$

$$= \frac{816,500}{50,000} = 16.33$$

If the intent is to measure the earnings per share on a fully diluted basis, the accountant will use the same formula but the number of common shares must also include all potential common shares after a type of security of the corporation is converted into common stock. This corporation might have a convertible security or a warrant that will give the holder the privilege to convert them into a corresponding number of shares of common stock. Let us assume that if all the convertible securities are converted into common stock, the number of common shares will be increased by 10,000 shares. In order to measure the fully diluted earnings per share, the net earnings will be divided by the total number of shares of common after the conversion.

7. Pay-Out Ratio. This is determined by dividing the total dividends paid on common stock by the total net earnings. The net earnings of Bee Corporation as stated in the Income Statement is $816,500. The corporation elects to distribute $1 a share cash dividend to stockholders of common stock. There are 50,000 shares of common outstanding, which means the corporation will distribute $50,000 to the stockholders. This distribution will be done out of the net earnings of $816,500. (Remember: The net earnings are determined after the dividends on the preferred stock have been distributed.)

$$\text{The pay-out ratio will be} = \frac{\text{Common stock dividends}}{\text{Net earnings}}$$

$$= \frac{50,000}{816,500} = 0.061$$

Cash dividends also may be paid out of retained earnings, but not from stockholders' equity.

Stocks with a high pay-out ratio are known as *Income Stocks*. A *defensive stock* is one that continues to earn income during periods of economic downturn.

8. Inventory Turnover Ratio. This will determine the turnover of the company's inventory. The accountant will simply divide the net sales by the year-end inventory. For Bee Corporation, the net sales as stated in the Income Statement is $4,000,000, and the inventory at the end of the year as stated on the Balance Sheet is $630,000. The Inventory Turnover is 6.34 times, as determined by the following formula:

$$\text{Inventory Turnover Ratio} = \frac{4,000,000}{630,000} = 6.34$$

A higher figure indicates good performance. The lower figure may be caused by low sales volume, excessive purchases for inventory, or obsolete items in inventory.

9. Current Yield on Common Stock. This is determined by dividing the stock's annual dividends by its current market price.

$$\text{Current Yield} = \frac{\text{Annual dividend rate}}{\text{Market price}}$$

If the market price is $24 a share and the annual dividend per share is $2, the current yield is $2.00/24 = 0.083 or 8.3%.

10. Price Earning Ratio (PE). This is determined by dividing the current market price of the common stock by the common stock earnings per share.

$$PE \ Ratio = \frac{Current \ market \ price \ of \ common}{Common \ stock \ earnings \ per \ share}$$

The current price is $24 a share and the earnings per share is $16.33. The PE ratio is 24/16.33 = 1.46. This means each share of common is selling at 1.46 times earnings per share. A *growth* company usually has a high price earning ratio. A growth company is a company that is growing faster than other companies in the same industry. Their pay-out ratio is usually 25 percent or less. A company with a reputation of earnings, stability, and marketability is known as a *Blue Chip* company.

11. Return on Equity. This is determined by dividing the net income by stockholders' equity. The net income of Bee Corporation as stated in the Income Statement is $824,500 and the Stockholders' Equity is $1,466,500 as stated in the Balance Sheet. The sum of preferred stock, common stock, capital surplus and retained earnings is $1,260,000. The return on equity of this corporation will be:

$$\frac{824,500}{1,466,500} = 0.562 \ or \ 56.22\%$$

The formula used is:

$$Return \ on \ Equity = \frac{Net \ income}{Stockholders' \ Equity}$$

12. Return on Invested Capital. To determine the return on Invested Capital, the accountant will use the following formula:

$$Return \ on \ Invested \ Capital = \frac{Net \ income + Interest \ on \ debt}{Total \ capitalization}$$

The capitalization is the capital invested by the company. The net income for Bee Corporation is $824,500, the interest on bonds is

$21,000, and the total capitalization of Bee Corporation is $1,766,000. This is the sum of bonds, preferred stock, common stock, capital surplus, and retained earnings. The return on invested capital of Bee Corporation will be:

$$\frac{824,500 + 21,000}{1,766,000} = 0.478 \text{ or } 47.87\%$$

RULE OF THUMB STANDARDS

The following is the "rule of thumb" standards of a well-run company:

1. Gross margin ratio:	40–50%
2. Net margin ratio:	5–15%
3. Current ratio:	3 to 1
4. Quick ratio:	2 to 1
5. Collection period (DSO):	2 times credit terms
6. Ratio of current debt to tangible net worth:	50–75%
7. Ratio of total debt to tangible net worth:	100% or less
8. Ratio of net sales to tangible net worth:	4–6 times
9. Ratio of net profit to tangible net worth:	5–8%
10. Inventory turnover:	6 times a year; 60 days of inventory

These standards vary — different industries may have different standards.

STOCK SPLITS AND DISTRIBUTIONS

What happens to the financial picture of Bee Corporation if the board of directors elects to take the following actions?

- Stock split, reverse split
- Stock dividends
- Cash dividends
- Retiring the bond

Let us consider each one and analyze the impact on the Balance Sheet and the Income Statement.

1. *Stock split.* Let us assume that the board decides to have a stock split of 2 to 1 for its common stock. This means for every old share, the stockholder will receive two new shares. In a stock split, the number of common shares will increase and the par value will decrease. Bee Corporation currently has 50,000 shares of common stock at $10 a share par value, and the Balance Sheet states the following:

Common Stock – $10 par	$ 500,000
Capital Surplus	$ 50,000
Retained Earnings	$ 816,500
Total of Common Stockholders' Equity	$1,366,500

After a 2 to 1 split, the Balance Sheet will indicate 50,000 shares, outstanding will be 100,000, and the par value will be reduced from $10 to $5 a share but the total money figures will be the same:

100,000 shares at $5 par	$ 500,000
Capital Surplus	$ 50,000
Retained Earnings	$ 816,500
Total of Common Stockholders' Equity	$1,366,500

The market price of the share will also be reduced — in this case it will be half of the original price. If the market price was $50 a share after a 2 to 1 split, the price will be $25 a share. Stock splits resulting in distribution of shares of 25 percent or less of the total outstanding shares of the corporation are treated as stock dividends. The stock splits will make the stock more marketable.

In a reverse split, the price of the security will increase but the number of shares will decrease. In a 1 for 2 reverse split, the 50,000 shares become 25,000 shares, and the par value becomes $20. The total money figure will remain the same.

2. *Stock dividend.* If the board of directors declares a stock dividend, it issues additional shares and delivers them to the stockholders of record. In a stock split, the par value of the stock is changed. Stock dividends do not alter the par value of the stock. The common stock account increases, and the retained earnings are reduced. The accounting treatment will be different if the stock dividend is less than 25 percent. The corporation may offer the dividend in cash to be invested in more shares. The stock-

holder will have the choice to participate in a dividend reinvestment program. This is known as Constructive Receipt and it is taxable upon receipt.

3. *Cash dividend.* If the board declares to distribute cash dividends to stockholders of record, it must change the Balance Sheet when the dividends are actually paid out. Between the declaration date and the payable date, therefore, the Balance Sheet must indicate a liability, obligating the corporation to pay out the dividend. An item called "dividend payable" will be added to the Current Liability on the Balance Sheet. Let us assume Bee Corporation declares to distribute 50 cents a share dividend. The total number of shares issued is 50,000, therefore, $25,000 will be added to the Current Liability as "dividends payable." The $25,000 will come from retained earnings. The accountant will reduce the retained earnings by $25,000 and increase the Current Liability by $25,000. By doing this, however, several different ratios, as discussed earlier, will be affected. After the payable date of the dividend, the "dividend payable" item in the Current Liability will disappear and the cash will be reduced.

In summary

Between the declaration date and the payable date, create a dividend payable on the Balance Sheet by:

- Increasing current liability and decreasing the retained earnings by the amount of cash dividend
- Reducing the working capital, or the difference between the Current Assets and Current Liabilities
- Reducing capitalization or the net worth and the long-term debt.

After the payable date, the Current Liability item of the dividend will disappear and cash is reduced.

4. *Calling the bonds.* The corporation may elect to call the bond if the market price of the bond is favorable. It will purchase the bonds, thus reducing its liability. For Bee Corporation the Balance Sheet indicates $300,000, the face value or the par value of the outstanding bonds. Let us assume the corporation redeems $100,000 face value of the bonds paying a discount price of $85,000 to the bondholders. This purchase will reduce the bond figure on the Balance Sheet by $100,000 leaving a balance of

$200,000. But since the corporation used only $85,000 to redeem the bonds, there will be a $15,000 cash generated on the Balance Sheet. This $15,000 will increase the stockholders' equity. If, on the other hand, the company calls the bonds at a price higher than the face value of the bonds, it will use cash from retained earnings. For example, let us assume Bee Corporation calls 100,000 bonds and pays out $110,000. The bond figure on the Balance Sheet will be reduced by $100,000; and to compensate for that extra $10,000, the retained earnings will also be reduced by $10,000.

CHAPTER THREE

DISTRIBUTION OF SECURITIES TO THE PUBLIC

The underwriting and distribution of securities to the public are governed by various laws, rules, and regulations. There are federal laws, the rules of the Securities and Exchange Commission, the NASD, the stock exchanges, and the requirements of each individual state. This chapter will discuss the practices and the requirements of underwriting and distributing securities to the public.

THE FEDERAL LAWS AND THE REQUIREMENTS OF THE SEC

After the 1929 stock market crash, Congress enacted a series of laws to protect the public from fraudulent activities in the securities business. One of the first congressional acts was the Securities Act of 1933, which governs the issuance and distribution of corporate securities to the public. The Act states that a corporation when issuing and distributing its securities to the public must make full disclosure pertaining to all aspects of its financial and operational conditions.

The Securities Act of 1933 defines a "security" as any one of the following:

- Note
- Stock
- Bond

- Evidence of debt
- Interest in a participation in a profit sharing agreement
- Investment contract
- Voting trust certificates
- Fractional interest in oil, gas, and other mineral rights
- Warrants granting the holder the privilege to subscribe to or purchase any one of the above.

The following securities are exempt from the Securities Act of 1933.

1. Securities issued and guaranteed by the United States government
2. Securities issued and guaranteed by state and municipal entities
3. Securities issued by domestic banks (securities issued by bank holding companies are not exempted)
4. Commercial papers and Banker's Acceptances maturing within 270 days
5. Securities issued by savings and loan associations
6. Securities issued by farmers' cooperative groups
7. Securities issued by common carriers (rails, airlines, etc.)
8. Securities issued as receivers' or trustees' certificates under a court order
9. Securities issued by SBIC (Small Business Investment Companies)
10. Securities issued and sold exclusively within a state
11. Securities issued by religious, educational, charitable, or nonprofit organizations
12. Insurance policies and fixed annuity contracts (variable annuity contracts are not exempted)

All other securities must be registered with the Securities and Exchange Commission before they are distributed to the public. In registering a security, the issuer is required to prepare a Registration Statement, which will include the following information:

1. The name of the issuer

2. The name of the state in which the issuer is organized

3. The location of the issuer's principal place

4. The names and addresses of the directors and other senior officials

5. The names and addresses of the underwriters (if any)

6. The names and addresses of persons owning 10 percent or more of any class of stock of the issuer

7. The amount of securities owned by directors, senior officials, underwriters, and 10 percent holders

8. The general character of the issuer's business

9. A statement of the issuer's capitalization

10. A statement of securities reserved for options outstanding, with names and addresses of persons allotted 10 percent or more of these options

11. The amount of capital stock of each class included in this offer

12. The issuer's funded debt

13. The purposes to which the proceeds of this offering will be applied

14. Remuneration payable to the issuers directly, naming them specifically when annual payments exceed $25,000

15. The estimated net proceeds to be derived from the offering

16. The price at which the public offering will be attempted

17. Commissions, fees, and service charge to be paid to the underwriters

18. Itemized detail of expenses incurred by the issuer in connection with this offering

19. The net proceeds derived from any securities sold by the issuer in the preceding two years and the pertinent details of that sale

20. Any payments made to a promoter in the preceding two years

21. The names and addresses of any vendor of property or goodwill to be acquired with the proceeds of this offering

22. Full particulars of any dealings between the issuer and its officers, directors, and holders of 10 percent or more of its stock that were transferred in the preceding two years

23. The names and addresses of counsel passing upon the legality of the issue

24. The dates and details of material contracts created outside the issuer's ordinary course of business within the preceding two years

25. A certified and detailed Balance Sheet of the issuer drawn within the preceding 90 days

26. A certified profit-and-loss statement of the issuer for the latest fiscal year and the preceding two years

27. Certified financial statements of any issuer or businesses to be acquired with proceeds of this offering

28. A copy of the underwriting contract or agreement

29. A copy of all material contracts referred to in item number 24

30. A copy of the issuer's charter, by-laws, trust agreements or the partnership agreement, as the case may be

A section of the Registration Statement will be used to prepare the prospectus.

Registering securities with the SEC is cumbersome, time consuming, and costly. There are certain transactions under the Act that exempt the corporation to register the security with the SEC.

Exempt Transactions

The following transactions are exempt from registration requirements:

A. If the transaction is done by anyone other than the issuer, a dealer, or an underwriter, that transaction does not have to be registered with the SEC.

B. Transactions by brokers executed in behalf of a customer on an unsolicited basis.

C. Transactions by the issuer in a private placement. In this case, the securities will be sold privately and not through a public offering. The purchaser must submit a letter to the issuer stating that he has no immediate intention to sell or transfer the security.

These letters are known as Investment Letters. The purchaser may sell or transfer the security to another person, again through a private placement, but he must receive another Investment Letter from the second purchaser. The second transaction is called a secondary private placement. Here again, the transaction will be exempt from the SEC's registration requirements.

The securities offered through a private placement may either be stocks or bonds. They are generally known as Letter Stocks and Letter Bonds.

Rule 506 of Regulation D:

Private placements offered to a limited number of investors are generally done through the SEC Rule 506 of Regulation D. The provisions of Rule 506 are:

1. The corporation may offer the security to accredited investors — such as financial institutions and wealthy individuals — without any limitation as to the number of sales, number of investors, or the amount of money to be raised. A wealthy individual is defined as a person with a net worth of at least $1 million and a minimum of $200,000 annual income.

2. The issuer may offer the security in a private placement to no more than 35 nonaccredited investors.

3. The offering of the security must be on a negotiated basis between the buyer and the issuer, or between the buyer's representative and the issuer.

4. The issuer must receive an Investment Letter from each purchaser and must place a "stop" on the certificate with the transfer agent, preventing the stockholder to sell or transfer the security within a specified period of time.

5. The issuer may not advertise the private offering through a promotional medium. No group solicitations, mailings, or general advertisements are allowed.

6. The individual purchasing the security must be suitable for this type of investment. He must sign a form entitled "Prospective Purchaser–Investor Suitability Statement."

7. The individual purchasing the security must have such knowledge and experience in financial and business matters that he is capable of evaluating the merits and the risks of prospective investments.

PROSPECTIVE PURCHASER–INVESTOR SUITABILITY STATEMENT

1. Customer's Name _____
2. Name of Spouse _____
3. Customer's Age _____
4. Number of Dependent Children _____
   Ages of Children _____
5. Residence Address _____
   _____
6. Number of Years at the Address _____
7. Telephone _____
8. Business Address _____
9. Employer _____
10. Position _____
11. Nature of Employer's Business _____
12. Years with the Firm _____
13. Educational Background _____
14. Estimate of Present Net Worth
    (excluding home furnishings, automobiles) _____
15. Estimate of Present Liquid Net Worth (cash or assets readily convertible into
    cash) _____
16. Estimated Annual Income for the Year Ending _____
    A. Earned Income _____
    B. Long-Term Capital Gains _____
17. Face value of life insurance (including group protection) _____
18. Investment Objectives _____
    _____
    _____
19. Investment Experience Including the Following:

| Estimate of Amount of | Number of Years of Investment |
| Investment $_____ | Experience in Securities |

A.	Stocks	H.	Oil & Gas Drilling Programs
B.	Corporate Bonds	I.	Real Estate Syndications & Partnership
C.	Municipal Bonds	J.	Direct Ownership of Real Estate
D.	U.S. Gov't Sec.	K.	Cattle Feeding and Breeding Programs
E.	Mutual Funds	L.	Agricultural Programs
F.	Options	M.	Leasing Programs
G.	Commodities	N.	Other

20. Considering the foregoing and all other factors in my financial and personal circumstances, I am able to bear the economic risk of an investment in such a private placement including a loss of my entire investment in such a private placement.
21. If I decide to purchase an interest in such a private placement, I will do so for investment purposes only and with no present intention, agreement or arrangement for the distribution, transfer, assignment, resale, subdivision or hypothecation thereof, and I understand that in any event, such interest will in all likelihood be subject to restrictions against transferability thereof.
22. Additional Comments _____
    _____
    _____
23. All of the foregoing answers that I have provided to the questions above are true, correct, and complete to the best of my knowledge.

_____
Signature of Customer

_____
Date

_____
Branch Office

The execution of this document does not indicate an intent to purchase any private placement interest that may be offered.

8. In the event the purchaser is not financially sophisticated, he may obtain the services of an agent to evaluate the security for him. The agent must use the Prudent Man's Law for the interest of the purchaser. If an account executive of a brokerage firm is selected for evaluating the issue for the purchaser, that selection must be made by the purchaser and not by the issuing corporation. The agent cannot be related to the customer.

9. The purchaser must receive information about the issue.

10. The purchaser must be informed in writing that the security may not be sold without a Registration Statement or the use of an available exemption. The purchaser must sign an agreement to that effect.

11. The issuer must file Form D with the SEC within 15 days after the first sale.

Rule 504 of Regulation D:

Under Rule 504 of Regulation D a corporation may offer securities valued up to $500,000 to an unlimited number of investors during a 12-month period.

Rule 505 of Regulation D:

Rule 505 of Regulation D allows a corporation to offer securities valued up to $5 million to 35 investors during a 12-month period.

SEC Rule 144:

An investor who had purchased a restricted security in a private placement is allowed to sell the security in modest amounts under the SEC Rule 144 without the necessity of filing a Registration Statement. The provisions of Rule 144 are as follows:

1. If the intended sale exceeds 500 shares or $10,000 in aggregate value, Form X-144 must be filed with the SEC and with the stock exchanges where the security is traded. The filing remains effective for 90 days. A new form must be filed if the security is not sold within the 90-day period.

2. The offering of the security cannot be advertised or solicited.

3. The security to be sold under Rule 144 must be fully paid for and held by the owner for at least two years.

   The period of time in which the previous owner held the securities may be tacked on to the holding period of the seller in the following manner:
   A. The period of time a pledgor held the restricted securities may be tacked on to the time the pledgee held the securities, provided the pledgee acquires the securities after a default by the pledgor.
   B. Gifts — The period of time a donor held the securities may be tacked on to the time the donee held the securities.
   C. Trusts — The period of time the seller of a trust held the securities may be tacked on to the period of time held by the trust or its beneficiaries, provided that the seller donates rather than sells the security to the trust.
   D. Estates — The period of time that the securities were held by the deceased may be tacked on to the time held by the estate or its beneficiaries that are non-affiliates and are not subject to holding period or volume limitations. If the person dies prior to the two-year period, the holding period will be deemed to be satisfied.

4. Restricted securities held more than three years by a non-affiliated customer are relieved from all conditions, provided the issuer is current in the reporting requirements pursuant to Section 13 and 15 (d) of the Securities Exchange Act of 1934 for at least 90 days prior to any sales under Rule 144.

   If the issuer is not subject to these reporting requirements, he must make the following information available to the public:
   A. Name of issue
   B. Address of the principal office
   C. State of incorporation
   D. Title and class of security, number of shares outstanding and the stated par value
   E. Name and address of the transfer agent
   F. Description of the issuer's business, products, services, and facilities
   G. Name of the Chief Executive Officer and the members of the Board of Directors

H. The most recent Balance Sheet, profit and loss, and retained earning statements

I. A statement whether the broker–dealer or any associated person is affiliated directly with the issuer

A customer acting alone or in concert with others may not sell more than 1 percent of the total outstanding shares in an over-the-counter trade within a three-month period. If the security is traded on the stock exchange, the investor is not allowed to sell the greater of:

- 1% of the outstanding shares, or
- the average weekly volume of the security traded in all stock exchanges within the last four consecutive weeks

If the transaction is done on an exchange, the security will be cleared from all restrictions and the new buyers will receive unrestricted certificates. If the transaction is being done on the over-the-counter market, the market maker must be advised that the trade is being done under Rule 144. The market maker may be considered as a statutory underwriter if he acts as a principal in the transaction.

Insiders, such as officers, directors, and major stockholders, are allowed to sell unrestricted securities without a Registration Statement; the two year holding period does not apply. For restricted securities, the insider must consider the two-year holding period before he is allowed to sell. In both cases, the number of shares to be sold have the same volume limitations as discussed above.

Insider Rules:

The Insider Rules of the Securities Exchange Act of 1934 prohibit insiders — such as officers, directors, major stockholders holding 10 percent or more of the outstanding shares and members of their immediate families — to sell the company security short or short against the box, and to accept capital gains in the security transaction if the security is sold within six months of purchase. Any gain in this type of short-term trade must be given to the corporation.

Bee Securities Company
300 Wall St.
New York, N.Y. 10005

Gentlemen:

In connection with my order placed with you to sell for my account _____ shares of the stock of _____ in the manner permitted by Rule 144 of the Securities and Exchange Commission, I represent to you as follows:

1. I have not made, and will not make, any payment in connection with the execution of the above order to any person other than the usual and customary broker's commissions payable to you for the performance of your usual and customary broker's function, if you act as broker in the execution of this order.

2. I have not solicited or arranged for the solicitation of, and will not solicit or arrange for the solicitation of, orders to buy in anticipation of or in connection with my order to you.

3. I herewith deliver to you a signed copy of the Form 144 that has been placed in the mail to the Securities and Exchange Commission in Washington, D.C. The Form 144 states that I do not have any material adverse information about the issuer, or such securities that has not been publicly disclosed. If prior to the completion of the execution of this order I obtain any such information, I will notify you forthwith so that you may terminate sales until after it has been publicly disclosed.

4. Except as indicated below, no sale or orders for shares of such security will be placed with any other broker, pending execution or cancellation of this order and no other dispositions of any kind of shares of such security are intended,

    a) by me or any person related to me or by any person, firm, corporation, trust, or estate acting in my behalf, jointly or in concert with me or over which I have control

    b) by any pledgor, donor, or trust from which I may have acquired shares of such security

    c) by any pledgee, donor, or trust to which I may have given shares of such security

5. Except as indicated below, no sales of shares of such security have been made in the last three months by the persons enumerated in Paragraph 4.

6. I am not aware of any facts or circumstances indicating that I am or might be deemed an underwriter within the meaning of the Securities Act of 1933 with respect to such securities. I am not individually or together with others engaged in making a distribution.

I am familiar with Rule 144 of the Securities and Exchange Commission and agree that you may rely upon the above statements in executing the order that I have given you.

I understand that you will not pay me the net proceeds of any sales made pursuant to this order nor will I receive interest credit on such proceeds until the certificates have been transferred by the issuer or its transfer agent at the issuer's instruction to the purchasers or to you, or your correspondent broker's street name for delivery to the purchaser, and until you have been paid in full by the buying brokers. I also understand that if for any reason the shares being sold cannot be transferred, you will be required to purchase shares in the open market to cover my sale.

I hereby accept responsibility for any such buy-in and any deficit resulting therefrom.

Very truly yours,

Dated:

The rules also have strict provisions for insiders who buy or sell the security based on information not available to the public.

Regulation A of the SEC:

Under the SEC Regulation A, a corporation is permitted to use an abbreviated statement when registering securities with the SEC. The abbreviated statement is filed with the SEC's regional office rather than the main office in Washington, D.C. This will save the corporation considerable time and expense. The corporation is required, however, to publish an Offering Circular that will contain most of the information in the Registration Statement. It is this circular that will be sent to prospective customers and not the full prospectus. The corporation will be allowed to use Regulation A if the value of the security to be distributed to the public during a 12-month period does not exceed $1.5 million. Offerings by affiliated persons must not exceed $100,000 under Regulation A. An affiliated person is one who may influence management decisions in the corporation. Affiliated persons may be officers, directors, principal stockholders, or members of their immediate families.

Under Regulation A, the "cooling off" period is reduced to 10 days, and there is no need for an audited financial statement.

The Offering Circular is effective for up to nine months. For offerings valued less than $100,000, an Offering Circular is not needed. Any sales literature must be filed with the SEC at least five business days prior to its use. Regulation A offerings are not allowed for oil and gas programs and investment companies.

SEC Rule 147: Intrastate Offering

The securities sold to the residents of a state by a corporation registered in the same state are exempt from the SEC's registration requirements. This type of offering is called "Intra State" or "Safe Harbor." The corporation will register the security with the securities commissioner of the state under the state's Blue Sky requirements.

To qualify for this exemption, the corporation must receive at least 80 percent of its gross revenue within that state and must maintain its principal office in that state. At least 80 percent of the proceeds of the offering must be used within the state.

Broker–dealers interested in underwriting the issue must have an office (a main office or branch office) in that state. The broker must obtain a written statement from the prospective customer that the customer is a legal resident of the state. The purchasers may not sell the security to anybody outside the state for at least nine months.

SEC Rule 237:

The SEC Rule 237 allows certain nonaffiliated persons to sell restricted securities without an effective Registration Statement filed with the SEC. The issuer must be a domestic corporation, and the seller of the security cannot be the issuer or a broker–dealer.

Schedule E: Self-Underwriting

A broker–dealer may distribute its own securities or that of an affiliate through a self-underwriting procedure known as Schedule E. The offering price for this distribution must be recommended by two qualified independent underwriters. The qualified underwriters must be members of the NASD and must have been engaged in the securities business for at least five years and have been profitable for at least three years.

An NASD member may also offer the securities owned by an associated person. The person must have owned the security for at least a year. A Schedule E security cannot be purchased in a discretionary account without prior written approval of the customer.

The broker–dealer may sell its own securities under Schedule E to any employee without any limitation. But these securities will be restricted for a period of one year if there is no available market at the time of the offering, and for a period of 90 days if an open market exists at the time of the offering.

SEC Rule 415:

The SEC Rule 415, also known as Shelf Registration Rule, allows an issuer to file only one Registration Statement detailing its long-term plans for sale of certain securities. When the issuer feels that the market conditions are favorable, it will arrange to sell the securities covered by shelf registration without having to reregister them with the SEC.

STATE LAWS REGARDING DISTRIBUTION OF SECURITIES

In addition to SEC and federal requirements for distribution of securities, most states have their own securities laws. The issuer must also comply with those laws before the securities are sold to the residents of that state. The filing with the securities commissioner of the state is usually done by the underwriters on behalf of the issuer. This procedure is known as the "Blue Sky" requirements. (The term "Blue Sky" originated in a ruling made by a judge referring to certain securities schemes as "so many feet of blue sky.")

The Blue Sky law contains three elements: Coordination, Qualification, and Notification. *Coordination* refers to the timing and the effectiveness of the Registration Statement. The state's Registration Statement becomes effective after the SEC Registration Statement has become effective. *Notification* relates to the registration of certain securities to be sold within the state. *Qualification* refers to the registration within the state separate from the SEC registration requirement.

REGISTRATION OF SECURITIES UNDER
BLUE SKY REQUIREMENTS

The following are the provisions of the Uniform Securities Act for registration of securities under state Blue Sky requirements:

1. *Registration requirement.* It is unlawful for any person to offer or sell any security in this state unless:
   a. It is registered under this Act.
   b. The security or the transaction is exempt.

2. *Types of securities registrations.*
   a. Registration by notification. Registration by notification is generally available for securities of companies that have achieved a specified level of earnings for the

past three years. This type of registration is rare. Consent to Service of Process Form must be submitted to the securities commissioner.

b. Registration by coordination. An application to register securities by coordination may be filed for any security that is currently under pending application to register with the SEC under the Securities Act of 1933. Registration by coordination is effected by filing the following documents with the Securities Commissioner:

- The Registration Statement
- Three copies of the prospectus
- The articles of incorporation
- The underwriting agreement
- The sample of the security
- Other documents filed with the SEC
- Amount of securities to be offered to the public
- Consent to Service of Process Form

This registration becomes effective upon clearance by the SEC.

c. Registration by qualification. Any security may be registered by qualification by filing with the Securities Administrator a Registration Statement containing specified information about the issuer including a balance sheet and a copy of the proposed circular.

The Registration Statement must include:

1. The name, the address of the business, and the state of incorporation
2. Directors' names and addresses and their occupations for the last 5 years
3. The promoter's compensation for the last 3 years
4. Purpose of the funds raised by the offering
5. Any stock option created by the issuing corporation
6. The accountant's and the legal opinion
7. Consent to Service of Process Form
8. Amount of securities to be offered

The securities administrator may require a quarterly report during the effective period of the Registration Statement. The Registration Statement remains effective for one year after the effective date. It becomes effective after the approval of the administrator is received.

As in the case of the SEC registration, the broker is required to send a prospectus to the customer purchasing the security.

The securities administrator has the power to deny, revoke, or suspend the effectiveness of any registration by issuing a "stop order." The "stop order" will be issued if the registration has been revoked by the SEC; if the business is engaged in fraudulent activities; if the company does not maintain adequate record keeping; and if a partner, a director, or an officer has been found guilty of any violation. In the latter case the entire firm will be found guilty.

The securities administrator may also deny, revoke, or suspend the registration of any broker–dealer or their agents under the following circumstances:

- The individual has violated the law.
- The individual has filed a misleading application.
- The individual has been convicted during the past ten years.
- He has been found guilty of a dishonest activity.
- His license has been suspended or revoked in the last five years.
- The individual is subject to an injunction.
- He is insolvent.

The penalty for criminal violation of the Act is $5,000 and/or three years in jail. Criminal liabilities cease at the time of death of the individual or five years from the date of the activity, whichever comes first. The individual may also be sued for any civil violations of the Act. The statute of limitation is two years. The person seeking remedies for civil cases must sue the broker–dealer or his agent within two years after the sale of the security. Civil liabilities continue after the death of the broker–dealer or his agent.

3. Exempt Securities. The following securities are exempt from state registration requirements:

   a. Governmental securities

   b. Securities of banks, savings and loan associations, and credit unions authorized to do business in the state

   c. Securities of public utility companies, mortgages, and securities of cooperatives

   d. Securities listed on stock exchanges

   e. Securities of railroads and common carriers authorized to do business in the state

   f. Securities of nonprofit organizations

   g. Securities of insurance companies authorized to do business in the state except variable annuities

   h. Commercial papers with maturities of 270 days or less

   i. Foreign securities

4. Exempt transactions. The following transactions are exempt from registration requirements:

   a. Isolated "non-issuer" transaction

   b. Unsolicited transactions — any nonissuer transactions effected by a broker–dealer, pursuant to an unsolicited order

   c. Fiduciary transactions — transactions by executors, administrators, guardians, conservators, receivers, or trustees in bankruptcy

   d. Transactions with financial institutions

   e. Private placement transactions — any transaction in a private placement offered to not more than 10 persons in this state during a period of 12 consecutive months, provided that the purchase is made for investment purposes only and the broker–dealer is not paid a commission for the transaction.

   f. Transactions by a pledgee to liquidate a loan

   g. Sales and distribution of securities to stockholders where no commissions are charged, such as rights and warrants

   h. Transactions between issuing corporations and underwriters

i. Nonissuer transactions in outstanding securities when the security is listed in a securities manual — such as Moody's, Fitch, Standard & Poor's, Best's Life, Best's Fire and Casualty. These manuals must indicate the names of the officers and directors, current balance sheet, a current profit and loss statement, and a statement that there has been no default on any interest or dividend for at least three years.

j. Sale of securities to a professional investor who is a person with a net worth of $1 million or more

k. Transactions involving mortgages and chattel mortgages.

The following exemptions may be revoked by the securities commissioner:

- Security exemptions in a pension contract
- Security exemptions of a charitable organization

If other securities of the issuer are being sold through an exempt transaction, then the issuer does not have to register the security with the securities commissioner.

Selling Group Members and Blue Sky Laws

1. Selling group members who participate in offerings will be required to submit a statement indicating that all payments to the escrow agent were made by using the free credit balances of the respective customers, and that no firm funds have been used as payment for customer purchases as referred under Section 11 (d) (1) of the Securities Exchange Act of 1934.

2. The offering must be registered in the states where the security is intended to be sold under the state's Blue Sky requirements. Some states review the qualification of an issue on a "merit" basis.

Blue Sky Requirements for Registration of Broker–Dealers

1. Broker–dealers and agents must register in states where they intend to conduct securities business. For Blue Sky require-

ments, the account executive, the broker–dealer, and the security must be registered with the state.

2. The account executive's license becomes ineffective if the broker–dealer becomes insolvent.

3. The account executive's license may be transferred to another broker–dealer. The securities administrator of the state must be notified.

4. To register, the account executive must file an application and post a security bond of $10,000.

5. Registration becomes effective on the 30th day after filing the application.

6. The account executive must pass the licensing examination.

Investment advisers also are required to register with the state securities commissioner as investment advisers, and they must pass the licensing examination.

The securities administrator has the power to deny, suspend, cancel, or revoke the registration of account executives and investment advisers if the applicant has furnished misleading information, has engaged in unethical practices, has been suspended by the SEC during the past five years, is not qualified to act as agent for the broker–dealer, has been convicted of a felony in the last 10 years, has failed to pass the licensing examination twice, is subject to injunction, or if his registration has been suspended or revoked within the last five years.

The license must be renewed a year or two years later. Renewal schedule varies from state to state.

Any document is deemed to be filed after it has been received by the securities commissioner.

PROHIBITED ACTIVITIES

The following practices are prohibited:

- Employing fraudulent devices or making fraudulent statements about a price quotation.
- Making incorrect statements about the company's earnings and about commissions and markups to be charged.
- Making a statement that the security will be listed at a stock exchange without having knowledge to that effect.

- Making a statement that the SEC or state registration means the approval of the security.

- Churning security activities to generate commissions.

- Recommending securities beyond the customer's means or failure to understand customer's objectives.

- Using customer's funds or securities without the approval of the customer.

- Guaranteeing profits or protection against losses.

- Conducting wash sales and matched orders.

- Accepting orders from a third party for a customer account without the approval of the customer.

- Not complying with customer's instructions.

- Using insider information for securities transactions.

- Soliciting orders for unregistered securities; securities that are nonexempt under the Securities Act of 1933.

THE UNDERWRITING PROCESS

The underwriting process starts when the corporation approaches an investment banking firm and offers to sell the security wholesale. The underwriter buys the security from the issuer and sells it to his customers hopefully at a higher price; the difference in money will be his profit or the underwriting spread. A voluntary underwriter is one that purchases the security from the issuer and offers it for sale to the customers after the SEC Registration Statement has become effective. An involuntary or statutory underwriter is one that purchases an unregistered security and sells it in a public distribution to his customers.

In underwriting a security, the investment banker acts as an intermediary between the issuer and the public investor. The underwriter assumes the risk of taking a position in a security and selling it to the public.

The investment banker acting as an underwriter or a financial adviser provides a wide range of financial services to the issuer.

In deciding to underwrite the security, the investment banker will consider the following factors:

- The corporation's financial needs and the amount of money needed
- The charter and the by-laws of the corporation
- The type of business and the industry
- The quality of management and the purpose for issuing the security

After analyzing these factors, the investment banker will decide the type of security to be issued — stocks or bonds, common or preferred.

The Procedure to Underwrite a Security

1. After the agreement is made to underwrite the issue, the underwriter, with the help of the corporation, will file a Registration Statement with the Securities and Exchange Commission.

2. The SEC staff will examine the Registration Statement for at least 20 days. This 20-day period is called the "cooling-off" period. It starts at 5:30 p.m. on the day of filing the Registration Statement.

3. During the "cooling off" period, a Purchase Agreement is signed between the issuer and the underwriter.

4. If the SEC staff finds any omissions or misrepresentations in the statement, it will send a Deficiency Letter to the issuer. The effective date of the registration will be postponed until all deficiencies are corrected. The SEC may issue a "stop order" to stop the registration process indefinitely.

5. If there are no deficiencies, the effective date will be the 20th calendar day after the Registration Statement has been filed.

6. The SEC may delay the effective date beyond the 20th calendar day if it has not completed the examination of the statement. The SEC will notify the corporation, and the underwriter must wait before selling the security to the public.

7. The SEC in examining the Registration Statement does not guarantee the adequacy or the accuracy of the Registration Statement or pass judgment on the quality of the security being offered. If there are any misrepresentations or inaccuracies in the Registration Statement, the purchasers have the right to sue the officers, the underwriters, the directors, and the potential insiders of the corporation for reimbursement of financial losses. The

prospectus, which is a section of the Registration Statement, must have an SEC Disclaimer Statement.

8. During the 20-day "cooling off" period, the underwriter may solicit indications of interest from his customers. The indication of interest may be used to establish the public offering price of the security. The security may not be sold and the customer is not allowed to make any commitments to purchase the security. These are only indications that the customer *may be* interested to purchase the security. The indication of interest is often called "circle."

9. During the "cooling off" period, it may be necessary for the underwriter to issue a preliminary prospectus to solicit indications of interest. The preliminary prospectus is called a "Red Herring" because of the red lettering on the border of the front page, stating that it is a preliminary prospectus and the sale of the security may not be consummated before the effective date of the Registration Statement. The "Red Herring" will not have the public offering price, the effective date, commissions, dealer discounts, and the net proceeds to the company. It may have a price range but not the actual offering price. It will contain, however, all other pertinent information. A "Red Herring" may not be used to solicit purchase orders.

10. The underwriter will file the offering documents with the Committee of Corporate Financing of the NASD. The committee will review the underwriting spread and the compensation to underwriters.

11. The underwriter may form a syndicate. He will be the managing underwriter, and the members of the syndicate will be the co-underwriters.

12. Before the effective day, the managing underwriter will arrange a meeting between the officials of the corporation and the members of the syndicate. This meeting is known as the "due diligence" meeting. It is generally held on the day before the effective date. It is mandatory for all underwriters to attend this meeting. At this meeting the underwriters will prepare the final prospectus, discuss the underwriting agreement, check the accuracy of the Registration Statement, the payment price to the corporation, and the public offering price of the security.

13. If some of the conditions discussed at the "due diligence" meeting are not satisfactory to an underwriter, he will have the right to withdraw without any loss or liability.

14. On the effective date the security will be offered to the public. A final prospectus must be presented to all customers purchasing the security with the confirmations of the trade. If the customer has not received the final prospectus, he will have the right to cancel the order. The customer may not purchase the security on margin. No margin transactions are allowed in a primary distribution until up to 30 days after the distribution of the security is completed.

15. The effective period of the Registration Statement is 90 days after the effective date for original primary issues and 40 days for additional distributions of registered securities. During this period, the broker is required to send a copy of the final prospectus to customers purchasing the security. This 90-day or 40-day period is called the "Quiet Period."

16. The managing underwriter may advertise the security in a newspaper or a periodical. This advertisement is called the "tombstone." The "tombstone" is not a solicitation to sell nor an offer to buy the security.

17. On a given day the managing underwriter will hold a meeting with the officials of the corporation. This is called the "closing" date. The underwriter will present a check to the corporation in exchange of securities. The difference between the public offering price (POP) and the proceeds to the corporation will be the *underwriting spread*. This spread will be divided among the members of the syndicate in the following manner:

- The manager will receive between 10 percent and 15 percent of the spread.

- The manager will allot between 25 percent and 35 percent to cover the underwriting expenses.

- Between 40 percent and 60 percent will be given to the members of the selling group as dealers' concessions. The manager may decide to reduce his fee to increase the dealers' concession. It is important for the underwriter to have selling group brokers to help sell the security, particularly if the underwriter does not have a retail customer base.

18. During the first few days after the effective date, the underwriter must make sure that the price of the security in the secondary market is stabilized. The secondary market is the "after

market," the market immediately following the effective date. The managing underwriter's responsibility, as part of the Underwriting Agreement, is to maintain a bid price of the security in the after market at or even below the public offering price of the security. Through this stabilization process, the underwriter will enhance the ability of other underwriters or the selling group members to continue to sell the security at the public offering price. This stabilization activity, if conducted under the SEC guidelines, is not considered fraudulent.

The SEC guidelines for stabilization are as follows:

a. The underwriter may not purchase more than 15 percent of the average daily volume of the security being traded.

b. A stabilizing bid may not be placed at a price higher than the public offering price.

c. The SEC must be notified within three days after the start of the stabilization period and three days after the conclusion of the stabilization.

d. The prospectus must include a statement to the effect that "the underwriters may over-allot or effect transactions to stabilize or maintain the market price of the security at a level above that which might otherwise prevail in the open market. Such stabilizing, if commenced, may be discontinued at anytime."

e. If the underwriter starts stabilizing the security prior to the effective date of the Registration Statement, the amount of the securities purchased and the price must be disclosed in the prospectus.

Forming a Syndicate

In order to reduce his risk in underwriting an issue, an investment banker may form a syndicate with other investment bankers. The first underwriter is the managing underwriter and the others are the co-underwriters. The selection of the co-underwriters is made on the basis of traditional ties within the financial community. Each co-underwriter is allocated a number of shares by the managing underwriters. This allocation is based on the distribution capabilities of the securities firm. If the co-underwriter has a good track record of distributing shares to the public, he will be classified as a major-bracket underwriter. Others in the group will follow as sub-major bracket, middle-bracket, and minor-bracket underwriters.

If a member of the syndicate is a market maker of the security, he must stop purchasing the security as a dealer–principal 10 days prior to the effective date and stop selling the security as a dealer–principal five days prior to the effective date. He is allowed to publish quotations on the NQB list or Nasdaq starting 10 days prior to the effective date.

If an underwriter had recommended the security as a "buy" to his customer prior to the filing of the Registration Statement, this recommendation may be continued throughout the offering.

After the formation of the syndicate, an agreement is prepared among the underwriters sharing the duties and the responsibilities of the managing underwriter. The agreement may have a "market-out" provision that allows the underwriter to cancel the agreement in the event that condition becomes adverse and the underwriter would be unable to sell the issue. The agreement is signed on the effective date of the Registration Statement.

The managing underwriter's responsibilities are as follows:

a. Choose the co-underwriters.
b. Select the selling group members.
c. Stabilize the market price of the security.
d. Conduct sales meetings to ensure success of distributing the security.
e. Oversee the "Penalty Syndicate Bid." This bid denies the concession to the selling group member whose customers' shares are repurchased on the managing underwriter's bid.

After choosing the selling group members, the underwriter will prepare the "Selected Dealer Agreement" that will disclose the amount of the dealer's concession and the agreement to comply with the terms of the underwriting and warranty of NASD membership.

The selling group members are not at risk with regard to the underwriting. They cannot, however, compete with the underwriters. They must sell the security at the public offering price until the syndicate is broken.

If the security is a "hot issue," the distribution must be in accordance with the prescribed rules and regulations. A "hot issue" is one that is expected to trade in the after market at a higher price than the public offering price immediately following the effective date. The rules prohibit the sale of hot issues to the following individuals:

1. Underwriters for their inventory positions.

2. Other broker–dealers for their inventory positions.

3. Any employee, agent, or director of the broker–dealer, or to any member of his immediate family.

4. Senior officers of banks, insurance companies, or other financial institutions, and their immediate families. If the bank is purchasing the security for an undisclosed customer, the banker must make sure that the undisclosed customer is not a prohibited person. The order ticket must indicate such findings and must be initialed by a principal of the broker–dealer.

5. Any person whose activities are related to the function of buying or selling securities for a financial institution and his immediate family.

6. Any accounts in which the person specified above have beneficial interests.

7. A person who has made the habit of buying only "hot issues" without any investment history with the brokerage firm.

Sales in insubstantial amounts to nonbroker–dealers may be acceptable to the NASD. These insubstantial amounts may be 100 shares, but not blocks of 5,000 or 10,000 shares.

The rules define *immediate family* as: parents, parents-in-law, husband, wife, brother, sister, brother-in-law, sister-in-law, children, ex-wives, ex-husbands (if any support payments are made), or any relative to whose support the person contributes directly or indirectly.

The Underwriting Agreement

On the effective date of the Registration Statement, the Underwriting Agreement is signed by the underwriters, stating the final terms and the public offering price of the security. The agreement must be filed with the SEC as part of the Registration Statement. The agreement must state the type of account on which the syndicate is formed. There are two types of underwriting accounts: Eastern account or United account, Western account or Divided account. If the syndicate is formed in an Eastern account, the underwriters will be responsible to sell not only their allocated portion but also the unsold portion of the other underwriters. In a Western account, each party will be responsible for his own portion of the commitment. An underwriter is not held responsible if another underwriter is unable to distribute his allocated amount. In the Eastern account when the syndicate is broken, the unsold portion is divided among the underwriters.

Types of Underwriting

There are three types of offerings when the security is being distributed to the public. When the proceeds of the sale go to the issuer, that is called a *Primary Offering;* when the proceeds go to a person other than the issuer, it is called a *Secondary Offering;* and when the proceeds are divided between the issuer and another person, it is called a *Split Offering.*

The following are different types of procedures to underwrite a security:

Firm Commitment:

Firm commitment underwriting is a type of underwriting in which the investment banker commits to purchase the entire issue at a set price from the issuer.

Best Efforts:

In a "best efforts" offering, the underwriter agrees to act as agent for the issuing entity. There is no commitment on the part of the underwriter to sell the entire issue, however. He will do his best to sell the shares to the public, but the unsold portion will be returned to the issuer.

All or Nothing:

In an "all or nothing" underwriting, the corporation advises the underwriter to cancel the issue if all the shares are not sold to the public. The customers' funds are held in escrow until the underwriting is completed.

Mini–Maxi Underwriting:

Through this method, the corporation establishes a minimum and a maximum amount of shares to be sold to the public. When the minimum amount is sold, the offering will continue until the maximum amount is reached. If the underwriter fails to sell the minimum, the offering will be cancelled and the proceeds returned to the investors. The customers' funds are held in escrow until the minimum is reached.

Statutory Underwriting:

A statutory underwriter is a broker–dealer who will purchase an unregistered security and sell it to the public without the necessity of registering it with the SEC.

Competitive Underwriting:

The competitive underwriting is usually done for municipal securities. The issuer accepts competitive bids from various underwriters. After receiving all the bids, the issuer chooses the one which will have the most favorable price.

The procedure is as follows:

    a. The issuer announces the creation of the security and invites investment bankers to send their bids by a specific time and to a specific place.

    b. All bids are sent in sealed envelopes and the envelopes are opened at a designated time with all interested parties in attendance. No consideration is given to the bid that is presented after the designated time.

    c. For a bond issue, a bid may cover the price of the issue and the interest rate.

    d. The issuing entity will decide the winning bid, and the investment bankers will then proceed to accept the security and offer it to the public hopefully at a price higher than the bid price.

Negotiated Underwriting:

In a negotiated underwriting, the terms of the offering are negotiated between the issuer and the investment banker.

Standby Underwriting:

The standby underwriting is done when a corporation issues rights to stockholders giving them the privilege to subscribe for additional shares. If the stockholder does not exercise the rights, the standby underwriter will purchase the shares of all unexercised rights and sell them. The underwriter may either receive a flat commission or a flat commission plus a percentage of the market price of the sold issue. A standby agreement will be signed which will state that the investment banker must stabilize the market of the shares during the 30- or 60-day life of the rights. He will stabilize the open market price of the security in such a way that the old stock trades above the subscription price of the new stock. The procedure for stabilization is as follows:

a. The underwriter will purchase the stock through stabilization. The stock will be "laid-off" to the underwriters. They will then re-offer the stock to their customers at a set market price.

b. The underwriter will purchase the rights in an open market below the market level. If a stockholder is not interested to exercise his rights, he may dispose of them at a price lower than the mathematical value of the right. After purchasing the right, the underwriter will subscribe to new shares. The underwriter's profit will be the difference between the discounted price of the security and the subscription price. In addition, the underwriter will receive a fee from the corporation.

c. The underwriter will take any abandoned or neglected rights and subscribe to purchase additional shares. The underwriter will acquire the abandoned right generally at no cost.

Summary of the Underwriting Process:

A public offering of a security evolves around the following periods of time:

1. *Pre-filing period.* Prior to the filing of the Registration Statement with the SEC, no offers, written or oral, may be made. The broker may not discuss the public offering with anybody. This is called "gun jumping."

2. *After the Registration Statement has been filed but before it becomes effective:* Oral offers may be made, but they must be limited to the information set forth in the "Red Herring." During this period, indications of interest may be received and orders may be noted, but sales may not be made or confirmed. Indications of interest should not be accepted from a customer unless the firm expects the security to be qualified in the state in which the customer resides.

Ten days prior to the effective date, the underwriter will stop purchasing the security as principal and stop publishing quotes if he has been acting as a market maker of the security being offered.

Five days prior to the effective date, the underwriter will stop selling the security as principal if he has been acting as a market maker of the security being offered.

The underwriting statement must be filed with the Corporate Finance Committee of the NASD. The NASD will only check the underwriting spread and will not be concerned with the disclosure statement.

The following activities take place during the "cooling off" period:

   a. Form of a syndicate
   b. Blue Sky registration
   c. Selection of selling group members
   d. Filing with the NASD
   e. Due Diligence meeting

3. *Effective and post-effective date.* The security may be offered and sales may be confirmed. The broker must make sure that the customer receives a prospectus within 48 hours after the trade is confirmed. Offers to sell or solicitation of orders to buy the securities being distributed should be made by means of the final prospectus as required by the SEC Rule 10b-6.

No written communication other than the final prospectus may be sent to the customer during the applicable 40 or 90 days of the post-effective period. This is known as the "Quiet Period." During this period, research recommendations and other literature on the security may not be distributed to the customers.

The prospectus delivery requirement continues in effect for the longest of the following periods:

a. Until the firm's allotment is sold

b. For a period of 90 days after the effective date of the Registration Statement if the securities of the issuer have not been previously sold

c. For a period of 40 days after the effective date of the Registration Statement if the securities of the issuer have previously been sold

This does not apply in cases where the firm is acting as a broker–agent pursuant to a customer's *unsolicited* order.

What is the meaning of *unsolicited* order? It is instructions given to a broker without solicitation. Solicitation would be involved if an employee of the firm has attempted to interest a customer in an issue. The order will be regarded as *solicited* unless the customer voluntarily, without any prior mention about the issue on the part of any employee of the firm, instructs the broker to purchase the security for his account.

When the firm is participating in an underwriting, no *solicited* orders may be accepted from a customer on an agency basis prior to the termination of the trading restrictions. If an order from a customer to whom a prospectus has been sent can only be partially filled, the balance of the order may not be filled on any agency basis prior to the termination of the trading restrictions.

If the underwriters have overallocated the shares or oversold the security, the issuer may agree to issue more shares. This is called "Green Shoe"; or the managing underwriter will sell short to satisfy the demand of the buying customers. The short sale may be a loss to the manager. In that case, the loss will be divided among the underwriters.

TRUST INDENTURE ACT OF 1939

The Trust Indenture Act of 1939 provides protection to the holders of public and private debt securities.

Under the Act, a corporation issuing a debt security in excess of $2 million in principal amount, must appoint a trustee to assume the terms of the bond indenture and to safeguard the interests of the bond-holders. The trustee, usually a bank, must file an annual report with the SEC indicating its continued qualification to serve as trustee.

For corporate issues, an "Indenture Qualification Statement" is filed with the SEC if the corporate issue is exempted from the registration requirement of the Securities Act of 1933.

RULES OF THE NASD FOR DISTRIBUTION OF SECURITIES TO THE PUBLIC

The rules of the NASD state that members who participate in the distribution of securities, whether as an underwriter or a member of a selling group, must act in accordance with high standards of commercial honor and just and equitable principles of trade. The managing underwriter is charged with the responsibility of ensuring that the conditions of the underwriting are fair and reasonable.

All documents for underwriting a security are filed with the Committee on Corporate Financing of the NASD. The Committee will review all filings and make recommendations as to the terms and conditions of the underwriting arrangements. In the event the Committee determines that the underwriting terms are not reasonable, it will notify the managing underwriter to modify the terms. Violations are referred to the District Business Conduct Committee.

The Committee on Corporate Finance in reviewing the documents is not charged with the responsibility to evaluate the merits of any issue being underwritten.

A. Filing Requirements.

All filings for corporate finance must be submitted to the Director, Corporate Financing Department of the NASD.

1. Filing for Interstate Offerings.

- The full Registration Statement that the corporation files with the SEC must be presented together with copies of preliminary prospectus, and the Underwriting Agreement. These offerings must be filed at the same time the Registration Statement is being filed with the SEC.
- For Regulation A offerings, the underwriter must file the initial offering circular and the Underwriting Agreement. These must be filed within 10 business days from the offering.

- The final prospectus or definitive offering circular with the list of the members of the underwriting syndicate must be presented at the time of the offering.

  No filing with the NASD is necessary for the public offering of the following securities:
  a. Securities exempt under Section 3(a) of the Securities Exchange Act of 1934
  b. Securities of investment companies (except issues of closed-end mutual funds)
  c. Variable contracts
  d. Straight bond issues rated "B" or better by a rating service

2. Filing for Intrastate Offerings.

- Copy of the Registration Statement filed with the securities commissioner of the state must be filed with the NASD at the same time of the filing with the state securities commissioner, but at least 15 business days prior to the offering date.
- Copy of the preliminary prospectus together with the Underwriting Agreement.
- Copy of the final prospectus and the offering circular. In addition to these documents, the underwriter is also required to notify the NASD as to the following:

  1. Maximum and minimum public offering price per share.
  2. The underwriting discount or commission.
  3. The reimbursement for underwriter's expenses, counsel's fees, counsulting fees, finder's fees, etc.
  4. The purchase price and date of any warrant or option acquired by the underwriter.
  5. The list of individuals who may have purchased the security in a private placement within 18 months prior to the filing of the security.
  6. Securities that the underwriter had purchased from the issuer or affiliated persons within 12 months prior to the filing. Purchases within six months will be considered as part of the offering; the underwriter's compen-

sation will be the difference between the original cost
and the offering price.

B. Certain NASD Restrictions.

Stocks acquired directly by an underwriter and related persons whether acquired prior to, at the time, or after the public
offering shall not be more than 10 percent of the total number of
shares being offered to the public. The maximum limitation in the
case of "best efforts" underwriting is one share for every 10 actually sold to the public. There are certain exceptions to this 10 percent rule for warrants, options, and convertible securities. A
warrant of a security expiring in five years may not be exercised
in the first year of the offering.

C. Venture Capital and Other Investments by NASD
   Members Prior to Public Offerings.

1. All NASD members making such investments prior to the
public offering must hold their securities for a period of at least
18 months from the date of purchase.
2. Upon the termination of the 18-month holding period, if
a member selects to sell a portion of that security in a public offering, he must hold the balance for an additional period of three
months beyond the effective date of the public offering. When
selling this security in a public offering, the member cannot act
as an underwriter.
The NASD may allow shorter holding periods in certain
cases.

D. Free Riding and Withholding Rules.

An NASD member has an obligation to make a bona fide
public distribution at the public offering price of securities that
are considered "hot issues." As previously described, security is
considered a hot issue, when the underwriter expects the security
to trade at a price higher than the offering price immediately after
the public offering date. The "Free Riding and Withholding"
Rules prohibit the underwriter:

1. To purchase these securities for his own account.

2. To sell these securities to any officer, employee, director, or agent of the broker–dealer, or to a member of his immediate family.

3. To sell these securities to a person who is a finder in respect to the public offering, including attorneys, consultants, accountants, and members of his immediate family.

4. To sell these securities to a senior officer of a bank, savings and loan association, insurance company, investment companies, or any other institutional type accounts.

5. To sell these securities to customers who do not have an investment history with the member firm.

E. Private Securities Transactions.

Private securities transactions are transactions that involve a limited number of purchases and sales other than transactions in public offerings. No employee of a member organization may be involved in any way in a private securities transaction outside the regular course or scope of his employment without prior notice to the member organization.

F. Maintaining the Public Offering Price.

The NASD members must maintain the public offering price of the security not only to customers as required by law, but also to nonmember broker–dealers.

G. Solicitation of Purchases on an Exchange to Facilitate a Distribution of Securities.

An NASD member participating in the primary or secondary distribution of any security must not offer any compensation to any person for soliciting another to purchase the security on a stock exchange. This rule does not apply to any person who receives a salary as a regularly employed person of the NASD member organization.

H. Disclosure of Control.

An NASD member controlled by or controlling an issuer of a security must disclose to his customer the existence of such a control.

I. Participating in Underwriting or Selling Groups.

A member of the NASD may not enter into a joint account, underwriting or selling group, or join a syndicate or group with any nonmember broker–dealer or with a member of a stock exchange, who is not also a member of the NASD, for the purposes of acquiring and distributing securities. The same rule also applies to bankers and trust companies. A broker–dealer, who is a member of the NASD, participating in an underwriting whether as an underwriter or a member of the selling group, may not allow any selling concessions, discounts, or other allowances in connection with the sale of such securities to any bank or trust company.

An NASD member may not join an underwriting or a selling group with a dealer who has been suspended or expelled from NASD membership. If the member has been suspended from NASD membership after the underwriting group has been organized, the suspended member may continue his association in the underwriting. He must buy or sell the security at the public offering price. The rule also applies to a suspended member who has joined a selling group before his suspension from the NASD.

J. Direct Participation Programs.

A Direct Participation Program is a program that provides for flow-through tax considerations. Direct Participation Programs include oil and gas programs, real estate programs, agricultural programs, cattle programs, condominium securities, Subchapter S corporate offerings, etc. A program may be composed of one or more legal entities or plans. This definition of Direct Participation Program does not include real estate investment trusts, tax qualified pension and profit sharing programs, or individual retirement plans.

An NASD member shall not underwrite or sponsor for the purposes of distributing to the public units of Direct Participation

Programs if the programs are inconsistent with the rules and regulations of the NASD. The NASD provides safeguards against unreasonable profits, unreasonable commission rates and charges. The NASD member before sponsoring or selling such programs must check the terms and conditions concerning the operation, structure, and management of programs. He must make sure that the programs are suitable investments for his customers. He must file the necessary reports with the NASD in connection with the distribution and advertising of the programs.

RULES OF THE NEW YORK STOCK EXCHANGE REGARDING SPECIAL OFFERINGS AND DISTRIBUTIONS.

The New York Stock Exchange has adopted special procedures to facilitate the distribution of blocks of listed securities that cannot be absorbed in the regular auction market within a reasonable time and at a reasonable price.

The following are rules and regulations governing these special procedures:

Rule 391: Special Offerings and Special Bids

The Exchange may permit a "Special Offering" or a "Special Bid" to be made through the facilities of the Exchange, if a determination has been made that the regular auction market cannot absorb the block of a security. To make such a determination the following factors must be considered:

1. The price range and the volume of the transaction in the security on the floor of the Exchange during the preceding month

2. Attempts that have been made to dispose of the security on the floor of the Exchange

3. The existing condition of the specialist's book and the floor quotation of the security

4. The public's interest in the security in the regular auction market

5. The number of shares or bonds and the current market value of the block of the security proposed to be sold or purchased through this special procedure

A Special Offering or a Special Bid will not be permitted unless it involves at least 1000 shares with an aggregate market value of $25,000 or at least $15,000 face amount of a bond with an aggregate market value of $10,000.

A Special Offering is an offering by a member for sale of a block of a listed security at a price not in excess of the last sale or the current offer of such security in the regular market on the Exchange floor, whichever is the lower price. This offering price cannot be lower than the current bid for the security.

A "Special Bid" is a bid designated as a fixed price bid by a member for the purchase of a block of a listed security. This bid cannot be lower than the last sale of the security on the floor or the current bid, whichever is the higher price. This bid cannot be higher than the current offer of the security on the floor.

Conditions for Special Offering or Special Bid

No Special Offering or Special Bid shall be made unless all of the following conditions are complied with:

1. The person for whose account the Special Offering is to be made shall be the owner of the entire block of the security to be offered.

2. The person for whose account the Special Bid is to be made shall be the bidder for the entire block of the security to be purchased.

3. The person for whose account such offerings are to be made shall include in this offering or bid all of the security that he intends to offer or bid within a reasonable time. A written statement must be submitted to the Exchange to that effect.

4. Unless exempted by the Exchange, every Special Offering and Special Bid shall remain open for a minimum period of 15 minutes. The Offer or the Bid shall not be withdrawn before completion without the approval of the Exchange.

5. The Special Offering or the Special Bid shall be automatically suspended as long as an offering or a bid exists "regular way" at a price that would permit a purchase at a lower net cost than the Special Offering or that would permit a sale at higher net proceeds than the Special Bid.

6. The person for whose account such Special Offering or the Special Bid is made, shall not, during the period of the trans-

action, offer or bid for, in the regular market on the floor the same security without the approval of the Exchange.

7. The member organization, directly or indirectly involved in a Special Offer or Bid transaction cannot charge any commission in the trade. A member may accept commission, however, if the securities are being purchased or sold as principal for the purpose of distribution or acquisition from others even though the member broker has been unable to distribute or acquire the securities.

8. A Special Offering or Bid shall not be made unless it can be accepted in a lesser amount than the total of the securities offered or bid. If the transaction is being made in odd-lot, no odd-lot differential must be charged.

9. The Offerer or the Bidder, may, at the time of the announcement of the offer or the bid, allot on a firm basis to a broker not more than 50 percent of the securities being offered or bid.

Announcement of the Special Offer or Bid

1. The terms of the Special Offer or Bid must be printed on the tape before it becomes effective. The transaction, after completed, must be printed on the tape as with commissions, if there are:

SP OFF (BID) 100 BEE Corp. Comm. ½. If the transaction is for the purpose of stabilization, the tape must include this information.

2. The broker in the transaction, if the trade is being done for a customer, must confirm the transaction, to the customer and cannot charge any commission in the transaction to the customer. The confirmation must include:

  a. The purchase or sale price
  b. A statement that no commissions are charged to the customer
  c. A statement that the seller or the buyer, as the case may be, is to pay a commission to the broker if such be the fact
  d. The amount of such commissions
  e. The return of the broker's interest in the transaction other than the interest to collect commission. Any stabilizing activity, if any, must be stated in the confirmation ticket.

Type of Information Required

Rule 391 is intended primarily to provide for Special Offerings and Special Bids on an agency basis by members in behalf of their customers. The rule does not prohibit a member to act for his own account. There are certain limitations on the size of the offering or bid. Piecemeal or successive offerings or bids of the same security by the same offerer or bidder, or offerings or bids on an "All or None" basis are not permitted.

The broker must submit a report to the Exchange at the close of business after the day of the transaction.

Rule 392: Exchange Distributions and Acquisitions

A member may make an "Exchange Distribution" or "Acquisition" of a block of a listed security with any other member under which the member with whom the arrangement is made solicits others to purchase the security in the case of a Distribution or solicits others to sell the security in the case of an Acquisition. The selling or the buying member pays a commission to the broker with whom the arrangement is made. The commission must be totally agreeable.

Exchange Distribution or Acquisition may be made only with the prior approval of the Exchange. Before giving its approval, the Exchange must determine that the regular market on the floor cannot, within a reasonable time and price, handle the block transaction.

Conditions for Exchange Distribution or Acquisition

No Distribution or Acquisition shall be made unless all of the following conditions are complied with:

1. The person for whose account the transaction is to be made shall be the owner of the entire block of the security to be distributed or the bidder of the entire block of the security to be acquired.

2. A written statement must be submitted to the Exchange before the transaction.

3. The person for whose account the transaction is to be made shall agree that during the Distribution he will not bid for or purchase the security, or if it is an Acquisition, he will not offer

or sell the security through the regular market. The broker is also prohibited to do so.

4. If the broker is soliciting the order, he must advise the person solicited as to the capacity in which he is acting, whether he is acting as agent or principal and the type of commission he intends to charge.

5. No "Short Sale" may be made in connection with an Exchange Distribution.

6. The member broker shall report to the Exchange all transactions effected by him. After the transaction is completed, the tape will report as ACQ or DIST.

Rule 393: Secondary Distributions

With the prior approval of the Exchange, a member may participate in an over-the-counter or "off board" Secondary Distribution of a listed security. The Exchange's Market Surveillance Division will make the determination that the regular auction market cannot, with a reasonable time and price, absorb the particular block of securities and that a Special Offering or Exchange Distribution is not feasible.

A Secondary Distribution is an offering by a member or a nonmember, acting as agent or principal of a block of a listed security off the floor, at a price not exceeding the last sale price of the security on the floor. The terms of the Secondary Distribution must be reported on the ticker tape.

When a Secondary Distribution is in effect during market hours, the distributor must make the security available on the floor of the Exchange in sufficient quantity to permit the maintenance of an orderly market.

Confirmations and comparisons used by underwriters or selling group members in connection with Secondary Distributions must clearly describe the capacity in which the broker is acting — agent or principal.

The distributor shall make daily reports to the Exchange regarding his activities in the secondary distributions. The Exchange may withdraw its approval at any time.

CHAPTER FOUR

EQUITY SECURITIES

There are basically four classifications of securities in America today: stocks, bonds, U.S. government securities, and money market instruments.

STOCKS

Stocks are generally categorized as capital stocks issued by a corporation upon approval of the Secretary of State of the state of incorporation. Capital stocks may be issued in two different types — common and preferred. It is a requirement for a corporation to have a common stock, but the issuance of a preferred security is not mandatory.

COMMON STOCK

Common stock may have a par value or may be issued with no par. The par value has nothing to do with the market value of the security. The par value is determined by the accountant of the corporation representing the capital of the company. The Secretary of State of the state of incorporation assesses the corporation on the basis of the par value. If the stock is issued with no par, the assessment will be made on a nominal basis.

Characteristics of Common Stock

The common stockholder has voting privileges. He may attend meetings and vote on company matters, such as election of directors, auditors, reorganization of the company, etc. He may attend a meeting personally or appoint another person to represent him, in which case, the stockholder will be given a proxy form, and he will use this form to indicate his voting preferences.

Voting procedures are either statutory or cumulative.

I. Statutory Voting

In this procedure, the stockholder will have one vote for each share he holds. If he is the owner of 50 shares, he will have 50 votes. He will use these votes for each of the proposals at the meeting. Let us say, there are three different proposals or three nominees for the board of directors, he will cast his 50 votes for each proposal or for each nominee. The votes will be counted, and the majority of the votes will win.

II. Cumulative Voting

In this procedure, the stockholder has again one vote for each share he holds, but, unlike the statutory procedure, his votes are multiplied by the number of proposals or nominees for directorship. Instead of casting his 50 votes, as in the above example, for each proposal or nominee, he will cast 150 votes for the proposal or the nominee of his choice. Cumulative procedure is more popular than the statutory method. Through the cumulative method, minority stockholders may gain control of the board. This method is used to make the security more attractive to the public.

STATUTORY METHOD			CUMULATIVE METHOD		
Nominee 1	*Nominee 2*	*Nominee 3*	*Nominee 1*	*Nominee 2*	*Nominee 3*
50 votes	50 votes	0 votes	0 votes	150 votes	0 votes

The New York Stock Exchange requires that common stocks listed at the Exchange offer voting privileges to stockholders.

The common stockholder has the right to examine the books of the corporation. These rights of the stockholder are known as Shareholders' Derivative Rights.

Voting Trust Certificates

Sometimes a group of stockholders in a corporation give their voting privileges to a bank that will act in the capacity of a trustee. The stockholders will deposit their shares at the bank, and the bank will issue a security called Voting Trust Certificate based on the deposited shares. In exchange for his shares, the stockholder will receive a Voting Trust Certificate from the bank. The bank will vote on behalf of the stockholder. Until the dissolution of this trust, the company shares will be traded as VTC (Voting Trust Certificate). There may be two different markets, therefore, for the security — one for the regular shares and one for the VTC.

Dividend Distribution

The common stockholder may receive dividends when they are declared by the board of directors. The board may choose the dividends to be paid in cash or in shares. When it decides to issue shares as dividends, it does so by using the shares that are authorized but unissued. But there is no contractual obligation on the part of the corporation to pay dividends to common stockholders.

The common stockholder is last in priority to receive dividends or his proportionate interest of the company assets in the event of liquidation.

Rights Offering

The common stockholder may purchase additional shares of the company through the subscription of rights.

The corporation will issue rights and distribute them to stockholders. The stockholder will purchase shares based on the subscription formula specified by the company. This may be two rights to purchase one new share, three rights to purchase one new share, etc.

The rights are traded in the stock market as interim securities. Their market value is determined by the following formula:

$$\text{Value of 1 Right} = \frac{\left(\begin{array}{c}\text{Market price}\\\text{of stock}\\\text{with rights}\\\text{attached}\end{array}\right) - \left(\begin{array}{c}\text{Subscription price to}\\\text{purchase new stock}\\\text{through subscription}\\\text{of rights}\end{array}\right)}{\text{Number of rights to buy 1 share} + 1}$$

Let us say the market price of the stock is $37 a share, the subscription price to purchase one new share is $28 a share, and the stockholder needs two rights to purchase one new share at $28. The above formula will give the stockholder the following value for one right:

$$\text{Value of 1 Right} = \frac{37 - 28}{2 + 1} = \$3$$

The subscription price usually will be less than the market price of the security.

These subscription rights are temporary instruments. They usually have a life between 30 and 60 days after issuance. The stockholder must act during that period, otherwise the rights will expire worthless.

"Cum-Rights" and "Ex-Rights"

In offering subscription rights to stockholders, the corporation determines a record date for the rights. On the basis of this record date, the stock exchange will establish a date called Ex-Right date, similar to the Ex-Dividend date. The Ex-Right date is usually four business days before the record date. When the security trades on the basis of "Cum-Rights," it means the customer purchasing the security on that day will receive the subscription rights; otherwise, he will not be entitled to receive them. This may be explained by the following illustration:

Declaration Date	Record Date
March 16	April 6
Monday	*Friday*
The corporation announces rights offering to stockholders of record.	

Four business days before the record date is Monday, April 2. On this day, the security will trade on the basis of Ex-Rights. An investor purchasing the security on that day will not receive the rights, because his trade will settle on a business day following the record date. The business day before the Ex-Rights day (April 2) is Friday, March 30; this will be the last day to purchase the shares Cum Rights (with rights). The trades of March 30 will settle on Friday, April 6, which is the record date entitling the stockholder to receive the rights.

In order not to penalize the buyer of the security on the Ex-Right day, the stock exchange will adjust the price of the security in the same way that cash dividends are adjusted on the Ex-Dividend date.

Exercise of Warrants

The stockholder may purchase additional shares through the exercise of warrants. A warrant is similar to a subscription right but it has a longer term to maturity. The exercise price established by the corporation will generally be higher than the prevailing market price of the common stock at the issuance of the warrant. A company will issue warrants in a public offering of a security to make the security more attractive to the public.

Warrants pay no dividends. They may be listed on the stock exchange if the underlying security is also listed.

PREFERRED STOCK

The preferred stockholder generally has no voting privileges. Instead, he will receive a set percentage of dividends from the corporation. The market value of preferred stock is inverse to interest rates. When interest rates rise, the value of preferred stock goes down—except for convertible preferred. If the preferred stock has a par value, the dividends will be distributed as a percentage of that par value. A stockholder of 6 percent preferred will receive $6 a share cash dividend each year if the par value of the security is $100 a share. Six percent will be the maximum that the corporation will pay in this case. It may pay a dividend, lower than 6 percent. The dividends generally are paid on a quarterly basis.

There are six different types of preferred stocks:

1. *Cumulative Preferred.* The stockholder of a cumulative preferred stock does not lose his right to receive dividends. The corporation accumulates the dividends in a corporate account and will distribute them at some future date, before dividends on common stock are distributed.

2. *Non-Cumulative Preferred.* This preferred stock does not have any cumulative feature. The undistributed dividends are lost forever.

3. *Convertible Preferred.* This preferred stock may be con-

verted into common shares. The conversion becomes irrevocable. The stockholder will receive a set number of shares of common stock based on the conversion ratio. The conversion privilege may have an expiration date. If the stockholder does not convert his security by that date, it becomes a straight preferred with no conversion privilege.

The conversion ratio may vary during the life of the preferred stock. For instance, a preferred stock may be converted into three shares of common during the first 15 years and then into two shares for the next five years, etc.

The conversion value of the preferred stock is the current price of the common stock multiplied by the conversion ratio. If the conversion ratio is three (that means the stockholder will get three shares of common for every one share of preferred) and the market price of the common is $15 a share, the conversion value is $45 a share (3 × 15). If the market price of the convertible preferred is $55 a share, that means there is a conversion premium of $10 a share (55–45).

Some convertible preferred stocks may be called by the company. These are classified as callable convertible preferred.

4. *Participating Preferred.* The stockholder of a participating preferred may receive additional dividends. When a corporation has extra dividends left over after distributing the annual dividends, it will distribute the extra cash to the holders of participating preferred. A 5 percent participating preferred, for instance, may receive 8 percent dividend. There may be a ceiling established by the corporation.

5. *Callable Preferred.* The callable preferred stock may be called, or redeemed, by the corporation. The corporation will simply take the stock and give the stockholder cash based on a specified value of the shares. The corporation may offer a higher price to the stockholder than the prevailing price of the security. The recall may be partial or total.

6. *Prior Preferred or Preference Preferred.* The stockholder of a prior preferred stock has seniority over any other preferred.

In the event of liquidation or distribution of dividends, the prior preferred stockholder will have priority over any other preferred.

Taking all of these securities into consideration, the following is the priority order through which stockholders and creditors are satisfied in the event of a corporate liquidation:

1. Employees
2. Internal Revenue Service
3. Trade creditors
4. Holders of debentures
5. Holders of subordinated debentures
6. Prior preferred stockholder
7. Preferred stockholder
8. Common stockholder

AMERICAN DEPOSITARY RECEIPTS (ADR)

The American Depositary Receipts are created by a U.S. bank to accommodate U.S. investors interested in owning foreign securities.

A U.S. bank with a foreign branch will create an ADR that will represent the actual shares of the underlying foreign security physically located at the foreign branch of the U.S. bank. The bank will have the power to transfer ownership of the ADR in its books and maintain the company's stockholder records. The underlying foreign security will be registered in the name of the bank's nominee even though the ADR's are registered in the name of the U.S. investor.

The ADR's are subject to SEC registration requirements and as such the holders are entitled to receive full protection under U.S. laws as accorded to investors of domestic securities.

The ADR stockholder will have voting power by means of proxy. He is also entitled to receive dividends if they are declared by the foreign corporation.

If the foreign corporation elects to issue subscription rights, the U.S. bank will send the rights to ADR holders. But if the foreign corporation decides not to register the rights with the SEC, those rights may not be distributed. In that case, the U.S. bank will sell the rights and distribute the cash to the holders of record.

CHAPTER FIVE

INVESTMENT COMPANIES

An investment company is a holding company that invests funds in groups of securities for the interest of investors. Investment companies offer diversification in security ownership. Instead of investing funds in individual corporations, the investor can invest in a portfolio of securities managed by the investment company in accordance with its policies.

There are certain regulatory requirements. Those requirements include:

1. The company must have a minimum net worth of $100,000 and at least 100 stockholders.

2. Forty percent of its board of directors must be composed of individuals outside the company.

3. The investment company is required to send audited financial statements to outstanding stockholders once a year and unaudited statements every six months.

4. The company may borrow money to operate its business; but the borrowed funds may not exceed one-third of the company's net asset value. Its asset to debt ratio, therefore, should be at least 3 to 1.

There are basically three types of investment companies:

- Face amount certificate company
- Unit investment trust
- Management company

The management companies are further classified into the following:

— Subclass I
  • Closed-end investment companies
  • Open-end investment companies
— Subclass II
  • Diversified investment companies
  • Non-diversified investment companies

FACE AMOUNT CERTIFICATE COMPANY

A face amount certificate company will accept the investor's deposits on a lump sum or installment basis and issue a bond instrument with a face amount in excess of the amount deposited. The company will promise to pay the face amount of the bond at the time of maturity. The difference between the amount deposited and the face value is considered as compound interest that is predetermined by the company at the time of issuance on a yield-to-maturity basis.

The investor may redeem the bond at any time before maturity. The redemption value will be the amount of money deposited up to that point plus the compound interest and minus commissions and administrative fees. This redemption value is known as the *cash surrender value* of the certificate. The investor may discontinue his installment payments anytime before maturity.

Regulations require that the company invests the customers' funds in safe instruments, such as U.S. government obligations, municipal securities, real estate mortgages, and blue chip instruments. Because of changes in the federal tax codes, these certificates are no longer popular.

UNIT INVESTMENT TRUST

The unit investment trust is organized under a trust agreement. The company will issue redeemable shares of beneficial interests known as SBIs. The SBIs represent a participation in a unit of specified securities in the portfolio administered by a board of trustees.

There are two types of unit investment trusts—fixed and participating.

Fixed Trust

The shares in a fixed trust represent units of tax-exempt government obligations. The maturity dates of the securities will determine the maturity date of the trust. The size and the value of the trust fund will diminish as the securities in the portfolio approach their maturity dates. At maturity, the board of trustees will liquidate the trust and distribute the assets to the shareholders.

Participating Trust

A participating trust invests its funds in other investment companies. Its shares of beneficial interest will represent ownership in the investment companies in the portfolio.

MANAGEMENT COMPANY

The majority of investment companies are management companies. They are divided into two large subclassifications—closed-end and open-end, diversified and non-diversified.

Closed-End Management Company

A closed-end management company has a fixed capitalization. It issues its shares and sells them to the public at a predetermined price through an underwriting process. After the initial offering, the shares will be traded on the stock exchange or in the over-the-counter market where forces of supply and demand will dictate the price of the security. If the shareholder wishes to dispose of the shares, he will sell them in the open market at the prevailing price. If the investment company wishes to repurchase its shares in the open stock market, it must give the stockholder a six-month notice and an opportunity to present the shares to the corporation for redemption.

Open-End Management Company

Open-end management companies are also known as *mutual funds*. They issue shares and continuously issue more shares to meet the demand of the investing public. Unlike the closed-end management company, their capitalization is not fixed. The price per share is not determined in the marketplace but rather by the Net Asset Value (NAV) of the management company.

The Net Asset Value per share of an open-end management company is determined by adding the market values of the securities in the portfolio, subtracting the liabilities from the sum, and dividing the difference by the number of shares outstanding.

$$\text{Net Asset Value per share} = \frac{\left[\left(\begin{array}{c}\text{Market Value}\\ \text{of the}\\ \text{securities}\end{array}\right) + \left(\begin{array}{c}\text{All}\\ \text{other}\\ \text{assets}\end{array}\right)\right] - \begin{array}{c}\text{Total}\\ \text{liabilities}\end{array}}{\text{Number of outstanding shares}}$$

Regulations require that mutual funds calculate their NAV per share on a daily basis. Some companies determine the value twice daily, once at 1:00 p.m. New York time and the other at the end of the trading session of the New York Stock Exchange. After calculating the NAV, the company will determine the bid and the offering price of the shares. The Net Asset Value will be the bid price and the offering price will be determined by adding a sales charge to the NAV.

EXAMPLE

BID PRICE		SALES CHARGE		OFFERING PRICE
$18.00	+	$1.50	=	$19.50

The sales charge of $1.50 may be expressed as a percentage of the offering price. This percentage will be determined by:

$$\frac{\text{Sales Charge}}{\text{Offering Price}} \times 100$$

$$\frac{1.50}{19.50} \times 100 = 7.6\%$$

The sales charge is 7.6 percent of the offering price which is $19.50.

If the percentage of the sales charge is known, one may determine the offering price by:

$$\frac{\text{Net Asset Value}}{1.00 - \text{Sales Charge (in decimal)}}$$

By using the above example, the formula will give us $19.50 as the offering price:

$$\frac{18.00}{1.00 - 0.076} = 19.50$$

The percentage of the sales charge is determined by the management company. The percentage of the sales charge is not the same for all purchases. For large dollar purchases, the company will offer a schedule of reduced sales charge. When the amount of deposit or purchase approaches a predetermined "breakpoint" level, the company will charge a reduced sales charge. For example, a person investing $25,000 in a mutual fund will be charged a sales charge equal to 8.10 percent of the public offering price, and a person investing $50,000 will be charged 6.75 percent. The investor does not have to deposit or invest these funds in a lump sum to qualify for the reduced sales charge. If his intention is to invest the funds during a period of time in the future, he will submit a *letter of intent* to the company stating his objective of investing a sum of money during a scheduled period. On the basis of this letter, the company will offer the investor a reduced sales charge. The letter of intent is not a binding contract. If the investor fails to deposit the stated sum of money during the scheduled period, his sales charge will be based on the amount of funds deposited up to that point. The letter of intent may be postdated for a period of 13 months.

The management company may even allow the investor to predate the letter of intent to take advantage of a large deposit he had made earlier. The letter of intent may be backdated for a period of 90 days. The use of the letter of intent is restricted to trustees of pension plans and fiduciaries who act on behalf of other individuals.

The sales charge will also be reduced based on the *right of accumulation* of shares by the investor. Through this program, the management offers a reduced sales charge if the investor's total value of shares already accumulated in the program reaches a "breakpoint" level. From that point on, all new purchases will be done on the basis of a reduced sales charge, regardless of the amount of purchase.

The mutual fund company is obligated to redeem the shares anytime the stockholder wishes to dispose of them. The redemption price will generally be the prevailing Net Asset Value per share. Mutual funds are allowed to issue only one class of stock and may not issue bonds or debt instruments.

Public Distribution of Mutual Fund Shares

The distribution of mutual fund shares to the public is done through one or the combination of the following methods:

1. *Direct sales method.* Through this method the company sells the shares directly to the public without any sales force and, therefore, without any sales charge. These funds are known as *no-load* mutual funds. The bid and the offering price of no-load mutual funds will be the same. The company will offer and redeem these shares at the Net Asset Value.

2. *Selling through an underwriter.* Through this method a broker–dealer acting as an underwriter will purchase the shares from the mutual fund company at the Net Asset Value and offer them to the public at the offering price. The difference between the NAV and the public offering price will be the underwriter's spread.

The underwriter, often referred to as the sponsor, the distributor, or the wholesaler, will maintain an exclusive relationship with the mutual fund company to distribute the shares to the public. He is not allowed, however, to act as the market maker for the shares. He may purchase the shares from the fund only *after* he has received the customer's purchase order. He may not hold shares in his inventory in *anticipation* of receiving customers' orders. The underwriter may, however, purchase the mutual fund shares for the firm's investment account.

3. *Selling through a selling group member.* The underwriter may seek the services of other broker–dealers who will act as members of the selling group to help sell the mutual fund shares to the public. He will compensate the selling group member by

giving him a portion of the underwriting spread. This is known as the *dealers' concession*. The selling group member is not allowed to sell the shares at prices different from the public offering price as set forth in the prospectus. He must also agree to return the dealers' concession to the underwriter if the customer redeems the mutual fund shares within seven business days after purchase.

4. *Selling through a plan*. An underwriter offering the shares to the public through a periodic payment plan will often utilize a *plan company* to facilitate the sale of the program. The plan company, acting as a sales manager, receives the periodic payments from investors and purchases mutual fund shares from the underwriter. The plan company will thus accumulate the shares in the planholder's account. The plan company usually utilizes its own sales force.

How to Purchase Shares in a Mutual Fund

There are three ways to purchase shares in a mutual fund:

1. *Single plan*. This is the simplest way. The customer will contact his broker, the underwriter, or the mutual fund company itself and place an order to purchase the shares. The purchase price will be the prevailing Net Asset Value plus the sales charge.

Mutual fund shares may be purchased only in a cash account. A customer may not purchase mutual fund shares on margin. Regulation T of the Federal Reserve does not allow brokers to extend credit to their customers on shares of mutual fund.

If the customer is purchasing the shares from a selling group member, the broker is required to make full payment to the underwriter no later than 10 business days after the trade date. If payment is not received on time, the underwriter will have the right to liquidate the customer's position. After the payment is made, the customer may request a certificate to be registered in his name and shipped to him.

2. *Voluntary accumulation plan*. The customer may purchase mutual fund shares through a voluntary accumulation program. The purchase plan may be based on set limits and payment schedule established by the company or the underwriter. The initial payment may be as low as $250 and the payment schedule may be arranged on a monthly, quarterly, or yearly basis. The record-keeping activities are performed by a commercial bank

that acts as the administrator of the plan. The investor will send the payment to the bank, which, after deducting a service fee, will use the money to purchase mutual fund shares from the underwriter. The shares are held by the bank for the account of the customer.

Distribution of dividends and capital gains are used to purchase more mutual fund shares in the program. This does not relieve the customer from declaring these distributions as taxable income for income tax calculation purposes. Dividends and capital gains are considered as income in the year the dividends or the capital gains are distributed.

The investor may redeem the shares at any time by submitting a written request to the custodian bank. The redemption price will be the prevailing Net Asset Value of the fund, and the check must be mailed to the customer within seven calendar days. The customer may also convert his accumulated shares into another type of mutual fund managed by the same company. This *swap* is accomplished at the Net Asset Value. The customer will save the redemption fee on the old share and the sales charge on the new fund. The company may also repurchase shares from the stockholder. A service fee may be associated with this transaction. The stockholder may make arrangements to have an automatic withdrawal of funds from his account. Some mutual funds have a reinstatement provision that allows the investor to withdraw the money from his account in case of emergency and redeposit without incurring a second sale charge. He must redeposit the money, however, within 30 days of withdrawal.

3. *Contractual payment plan.* Under a contractual payment plan, the investor agrees to deposit a fixed amount of money at specified intervals over a period of several years. The custodian bank must send a notification to the customer within 60 days of the purchase stating the terms of the transaction. The investor has the right to withdraw from the plan within 45 days of the mailing of the notice. If he decides to withdraw, he will receive the Net Asset Value and all charges in the transaction. This "45-day letter" is also known as "Free Look," which means the customer will have the opportunity to study the sales charges and other pertinent facts about the plan.

Most plans charge 20 percent sales charge on the first 12 monthly deposits, and 16 percent on deposits for the first 48 monthly deposits. The total sales charge of the plan over a

12½-year period may not exceed 9 percent of all the planned deposits.

If the plan is "front-loaded," it means that when 50 percent of the first 12 monthly deposits are applied to the sales charge, the customer will have *surrender rights*. He will have 18 months to rescind the balance of the contract and receive the Net Asset Value and all charges in excess of 15 percent of all the deposits that he had made up to that point. If the customer is three months late in payment, the custodian bank is required to send him a notice advising him of his *surrender right* and the amount of money that will be returned if the customer decided to rescind.

The *surrender right* applies only to front-end contractual plans.

DIVERSIFIED MANAGEMENT COMPANY

A diversified management company is an investment company that invests 75 percent of its assets in cash, government securities, and securities of other investment companies. The remaining 25 percent may be invested at the discretion of the management. The management must make sure that no more than 5 percent of its total assets are invested in any one company and the fund does not own more than 10 percent of the voting shares of a corporation.

NON-DIVERSIFIED MANAGEMENT COMPANY

The non-diversified management company is a venture capital company with no limitations or constraints. The company is registered as such with the SEC and the management is free to invest the assets in any way it chooses.

OTHER TYPES OF INVESTMENT COMPANIES

Diversified Common Stock Company

A diversified common stock company invests all its assets in a variety of securities, but will be flexible enough to shift security positions at any time. The value per share will be based on the market value of the securities in the portfolio.

Balanced Company

A balanced company holds inventory positions in different percentages of securities. For instance, it will maintain 60 percent of its assets in common stocks, 30 percent in bonds, 10 percent in preferred stocks, and so on.

Income Company

The management of the income company selects only those securities that pay high dividends and interests. Capital appreciation of securities in the portfolio will not be part of the company's objectives.

Specialized Company

A specialized company will select a group of securities only in one industry or in one geographic location for its portfolio. For instance, the management will select bank securities, utility corporations, foreign stocks, high-tech securities, and so on.

Bond and Preferred Stock Company

A bond and preferred stock company will select bonds or preferred securities for its portfolio.

Money Market Fund

A money market fund will select money market instruments, such as U.S. Treasury obligations, certificates of deposit, commercial papers, bankers' acceptances, and short-term municipal notes for its portfolio. The portfolio may not contain stocks. The funds are generally sold with "no-load."

Municipal Bond Fund

A municipal bond fund selects only municipal bonds for its portfolio.

Corporate Bond Fund

A corporate bond fund selects only corporate bonds for its portfolio.

Dual Purpose Company

A dual purpose company is an investment company that issues two classes of securities, each for a specific objective. One is the *Income Share* and the other the *Capital Share*. The income share will distribute dividends and interest that the company receives from the securities in the portfolio, and the capital share will distribute the capital gains from the transaction of the securities in the portfolio. The investment company will establish a maturity date at which time the company will redeem the income share, leaving the capital share as the only existing class. With one class in existence, the investment company becomes an open-end entity and starts issuing redeemable shares to investors.

Real Estate Investment Trusts – REIT

A real estate investment trust is an investment company that invests its funds in real estate and real estate related ventures. The REIT is organized under a trust indenture supervised by a board of trustees. It issues Certificates of Beneficial Interest (CBI) to investors subscribing to the plan. There are basically two types of REIT – *Mortgage Reit* and *Equity Reit*. The mortgage REIT finances the construction of commercial and residential properties; while equity REIT owns the properties outright.

As a regulated company under Subchapter M of the Internal Revenue Code, the REIT is required to distribute at least 95 percent of the net investment income annually to the beneficial owners.

ANNUITY CONTRACTS

Annuity contracts are offered by life insurance companies and are regulated by the insurance department of the state in which the insurance company conducts its business. They are also regulated by the Securities and Exchange Commission. The agent selling annuities, therefore, must be registered as an insurance agent and also pass the qualifying examination required by the SEC. If the insurance company is a member of the NASD, the agent must also comply with rules and regulations of that organization.

Annuities are programs through which the insurance company agrees to make periodic payments to a subscriber. The amount of payment is based on the following factors:

- Females receive smaller payments than males. This is because of longer-life expectancy of females.
- Age. The young will receive smaller payments than the old.
- Amount of money in the plan. The more money in the plan the larger the payment will be.
- Number of options attached to the plan. The more options the plan has, the smaller the payment will be.

Annuities are suitable investment vehicles for profit sharing and retirement accounts — pension, IRA, and Keogh accounts. Under these programs, all tax liabilities are deferred until payment or withdrawals begin. Payments to holders of annuity contracts are taxable as ordinary income.

The annuity program has two time periods — "pay-in" and "pay-out." These also are known as "accumulation" period and the "annuity" period.

The insurance company may offer the annuity programs with an option called "period certain," which means the customer may select a "period certain" during which he would like to receive the annuity payments. Let us say, the customer elects a "period certain" of five years; the annuity payments, therefore, will be for five years or until death, whichever is longer. If the customer dies two years later, the beneficiary will receive the payment for the remaining three years.

The following are different types of annuity contracts:

Fixed Annuity or Guaranteed Dollar Annuity

Under a fixed annuity contract the insurance company guarantees to pay a set amount of money to the subscriber periodically. The customer's funds will be invested in bonds and real estate mortgages. A major disadvantage of this program is inflation. The annuity payments are fixed; therefore, inflation will erode the purchasing power of the dollar.

Variable Annuity

Under this contract, the life insurance company guarantees to make periodic payments to the annuity holder. The amount of payment will be based on the investment performance of the securities in the portfolio. Payments are made through an account called "Separate Account."

The funds in the Separate Account will be invested in securities similar to mutual funds and, as such, they are considered as "securities" and, therefore, governed by the Securities Act of 1933 and the Investment Company Act of 1940.

The Separate Account of the variable annuity will have an Investment Adviser and a board of directors. As securities, they must offer voting privileges to the program holders and a right to a proxy. The laws require a delivery of the prospectus.

The value of the variable annuity contract is based on two time periods — the *accumulation period* and the *annuity period*. During the accumulation period when the customer is depositing money in the account, the contracts are known as "Accumulation Units." When he starts receiving payments, the units will be known as "Annuity Units." Like a mutual fund the Accumulation Units are valued at the end of the trading session at the New York Stock Exchange. This will be done by adding the total value of the portfolio, the total investment income for the day, the realized capital gains or losses, and unrealized capital gains or losses. From this total, the company will subtract management service charges, the mortality risk cost, tax liability, unrealized capital gain, and insurance tax premium for certain states. The result will be divided by the total accumulation units outstanding. This will be the current value per unit.

The value of the Annuity Unit is rather complicated. Since this is a variable annuity contract, the company establishes an assumed rate of return for the investment. This is known as Assumed Interest Rate (AIR). The company will assume that the investment will earn a certain percentage in a year, which will be "factored-out" based on the actuarial considerations. The monthly benefit check will be determined by:

(Size of the account) × [Actual Rate of Return Realized (ROR)]

× (Actuarial Factor) × (AIR factor-out)

If the ROR (Actual Rate of Return) is greater than AIR (Assumed Interest Rate), the customer will receive more money. But the company does not guaranty the AIR.

If the customer dies before the annuity payments start, the beneficiary will receive the greater of:

- total payments made by the customer, or
- the accumulated value of the contract at the time of death.

The customer may terminate the program at any time before the payments begin. There is no forfeiture of previous investment if the customer fails to make a deposit. The customer may borrow money during the accumulation period and may convert the plan into a fixed account or a combination of fixed and variable.

Procedure of Purchasing Variable Annuities

The customer may choose any one of the following three methods to purchase variable annuities:

1. Immediate Annuity Contract. Here the customer will make a lump sum payment and purchase Annuity Units.
2. Single Payment Deferred Contract. The customer will make a lump sum payment and purchase Accumulation Units.
3. Periodic Payment Deferred Contract. The customer will make systematic payments and purchase Accumulation Units.

Sales Charges and Option to Withdraw

For periodic payment deferred annuity plans, the maximum sales charge is 9 percent over the life of the program. There are "Breakpoints" as in mutual funds.

The customer has the option to withdraw from the plan within 45 days. He will receive the value of the plan plus all sales charges. For front-end plans, the company will refund any charges over 15 percent of total payment during the first 18 months of the plan.

Any proceeds from the annuity plan is taxed to the customer at the time of payment as ordinary income. If the customer makes a "random" withdrawal from the plan without annuitizing it, he will use LIFO method to pay his income tax plus 5 percent penalty on the amount withdrawn, if he is under 59½ years old.

After annuitization, when the customer receives periodic payments from the plan, the amount of tax will be determined by dividing the customer's investment by his life expectancy.

Hybrid Annuity

Hybrid annuities are part guaranteed dollar contracts and part variable contracts. The individual annuity holder will determine the percentages of each component. The programs also offer different methods of payment to the subscriber. The payment may be lump sum or the life annuity method.

Life Annuity with Specified Payment

These are monthly or periodic payments to the contract holder during his lifetime. If the holder dies before a specified number of payments are made, the insurance company will continue the payments to the decedent's beneficiary.

Unit Refund Annuity

These are monthly or periodic payments to the contract holder during his lifetime. If the holder dies before receiving payments equal to the contract's original purchase cost, the difference between the payments and the amount invested will be distributed to the decedent's beneficiary in a lump sum.

Joint and Survivor Annuity

These are monthly or periodic payments during the lifetime of two people. The payments will continue until both die.

DISTRIBUTIONS

Investment companies make distributions to stockholders generally on a quarterly basis. The statement accompanying the check
must indicate the distribution schedule as to the following:

- Net income
- Undistributed profits
- Paid-in surplus

Long-term capital gains are distributed no more than once
a year. The stockholder may elect to participate in a dividend
reinvestment program. The reinvestments are made at the Net
Asset Value of the shares.

Dollar Cost Averaging

Dollar Cost Averaging is an investment concept through
which the investor deposits a specific sum of money to be invested
in a number of shares of mutual funds on a regularly assigned
basis — monthly, quarterly, etc.

PROSPECTUS

All public offering of investment company shares must be done
through a prospectus, as required by the Securities Act of 1933.
     The prospectus must have the following information to aid
the customer in assessing the advantages and the disadvantages of
the fund:

1. The structure of the investment company — whether it is
   closed-end or open-end, diversified or non-diversified, corporation, trust or a divided partnership
2. The investment objectives of the company
3. Method of calculation of the net asset value and the offering price
4. Data on breakpoints, letters of intent, etc.
5. Explanation as to the method of redeeming shares

6. Description of sales charges; management and advisory fees paid by the company

7. Names and addresses of people owning more than 5 percent of the investment company shares

8. Description of systematic investment or withdrawal plans if provided

9. The Balance Sheet, income statement, list of current investments, and audit reported

The prospectus must be updated every 13 months.

INCOME TAX CONSIDERATIONS FOR INVESTMENT COMPANIES

If a corporate account receives dividends from a domestic corporation, its income tax liability will be calculated only on the basis of 15 percent of the dividends received. The Internal Revenue Code allows the corporate account to exclude 85 percent of the dividend for its corporate income tax purposes. If the dividend paying corporation is a foreign corporation, the entire amount of the dividend will be taxable.

This is true for all corporate accounts, but the investment companies have another provision. If an investment company or a unit investment trust is qualified under Subchapter M of the Internal Revenue Code, it may avoid income tax liability altogether, provided it distributes its Net Investment Income (NII) to the stockholders. The Net Investment Income is the dividends and interests that the investment company receives from securities in its portfolio. This is known as the Conduit or the Pipeline Theory, which means the dividends and interests will flow from the investment company to the stockholders. The investment company will be exempt from payment of income tax on the dividend and interest it receives. For the stockholder, this dividend and interest distribution will be considered as ordinary income. To be qualified, the investment company must meet the following requirements:

1. It must be a domestic and regulated investment company, registered with the Securities and Exchange Commission under the Investment Company Act of 1940.

2. It must have a diversified portfolio of securities.
3. At least 90 percent of its gross income must come from dividends, interest, and gains from the sale of securities.
4. It must distribute at least 90 percent of its net investment income to stockholders.

The stockholder will treat the distribution of capital gains as long term or short term, based on the holding period of the security in the investment company's portfolio. This tax treatment has nothing to do with the holding period of the investment company shares that the stockholder is holding. If the capital gain on the sale of the security by the investment company is short term and when that gain is distributed to the stockholder of the investment company, the stockholder also will treat the gain as short term for his income tax purposes, regardless when he had purchased his investment company shares.

The Conduit Theory applies to all investment trusts including the Real Estate Investment Trust (REIT).

The Investment Adviser

The investment adviser is a company or a person that advises the type of securities to be purchased or sold by the investment company. The investment advisers are often referred to as the Management Group. They are a group of professional people who advise the fund on what to buy and when to buy securities for the plan. The investment company will enter into a contractual agreement with the investment adviser. In most cases the officials of the investment advisory group are also the officials running the investment company; but each entity will be organized under a different charter. The advisers will be paid a fee in accordance with the contractual agreement. The fee is usually ½ percent of the average annual net asset, payable to the advisers on a monthly basis. Some advisory groups charge their fees according to their performance as compared with the Dow Jones Averages or the Standard & Poor's Index. The fee structure also may include a penalty clause for underperformance.

The Sponsor

The sponsor is the distributor or the principal underwriter of the fund shares.

The Custodian Bank

The Investment Company Act of 1940 requires the appointment of a commercial bank to act as the custodian for monies and securities of the mutual fund. The Custodian Bank will be responsible for the record-keeping and bookkeeping activities of the fund and will act as the transfer agent for the shares, as well as disbursing agent for dividends and capital gains.

FEDERAL REGULATIONS FOR INVESTMENT COMPANIES

The Securities Act of 1933 requires that the investment company files a Registration Statement with the SEC prior to the public distribution of the shares. No offering is allowed until the effective date of the Registration Statement. The offering must be done through a prospectus. Since the open-end mutual funds do not have a specified number of shares, the fund will file a Registration Statement specifying a certain number of shares; and when those shares are sold to the public, the fund is required to file a new statement with the SEC.

The Investment Company Act of 1940 and the Amendments of 1970 protect the investor against unfair and improper practices and activities by the investment company.

The SEC rules prohibit investment companies to purchase securities on margin, sell securities short, and acquire more than 3 percent of the voting shares of another investing company.

The Investment Company Act of 1940 also requires the investment company to keep the shareholders informed about the activities of the company. Every six months, the company must submit the following to its stockholders:

1. A Balance Sheet indicating the value of the investments in the portfolio
2. A list of securities in the portfolio as of the date of the Balance Sheet
3. A statement of income and expenses
4. A statement of all compensations made to the officers and directors of the company

5. A statement indicating the aggregate dollar amount of purchases and sales of securities by the company during the period covered by the report.

The Act requires the investment company to select an outside independent accounting firm to conduct an annual audit of its records. An audited statement certified by the public accounting firm must be submitted to the stockholders immediately after the conclusion of the audit.

Prohibitive Practices and Requirements

1. The sale of investment company shares in a primary offering must be done through a prospectus.
2. The salesperson will violate the securities laws if he advises the potential investor that the registration of the investment company shares with the SEC constitutes the approval of the issue by the SEC.
3. The salesperson may not imply to the investor that the investment company shares are safe investments.
4. The salesperson may not imply to the investor that the custodian bank assigned by the company to hold the customers' funds and securities will provide protection against possible depreciation of the mutual fund's assets.
5. The salesperson may not make exaggerated and flamboyant statements about the management of the investment company and that the investor will be protected against losses in value.
6. The salesperson is prohibited to use inaccurate charts and tables to illustrate the investment company's past performances.
7. The salesperson may not encourage the investor to switch investment companies if the switch is not for the interest of the customer. He must advise the customer that mutual funds are long-term investment vehicles.
8. The salesperson must clearly state the amount and rate of the sales commission.
9. Any representation as to the percentage return on investment in a mutual fund must be factual. To illustrate the rate of return on a historic basis, the salesperson must use the following formula:

$$\text{Historic Rate of Return} = \frac{\text{Net investment income paid in a year (per share)}}{\text{Average monthly offering price during the year (per share)}}$$

To illustrate the return of investment on a current basis, he will use the following formula:

$$\text{Current Rate of Return} = \frac{\text{Net investment income paid during the last 12 months (per share)}}{\text{Current offering price + Capital gains distributed during the past 12 months (per share)}}$$

If the fund had made a $.62 per share distribution as net investment to shareholders during the last 12 months and a $.98 per share capital gains distribution during the same 12 month period, and if the current offering price per share of the fund is $7.50, the current percentage of the rate of return based on the above formula will be:

$$\frac{.62}{(7.50 + .98)} = 7.31\%$$

The salesperson may not make any representations that the same rate of return will continue in the future.

10. It is improper for an underwriter or a salesperson to receive any gifts in addition to the discounts or concessions as set forth in the prospectus in connection with the sale or distribution of the investment company shares.

11. It is improper for a salesperson to solicit purchase orders for mutual fund shares solely on the basis of an impending dividend distribution to be made by the mutual fund.

12. The salesperson must exercise care in advising customers of the breakpoint level of the mutual fund. The customer will pay a reduced rate of sales charge if his total investment is above the fund's breakpoint level. It is improper for a salesperson to solicit new fund orders in dollar amounts just below the fund's breakpoint level.

13. A broker–dealer must not charge an unreasonable or excessive sales commission to the customer. For periodic contrac-

tual plans the maximum sales charge is 9 percent of the public offering price as set forth by the Investment Company Act of 1940. The Act does not specify sales charges for single payments or voluntary accumulation plans. Under the NASD's Rules of Fair Practice, however, the maximum sales charge on any single payment, voluntary accumulation, or contractual plans is 8½ percent of the offering price. The NASD will not allow a broker–dealer to charge this maximum sales charge unless the mutual fund offers the following benefits to the stockholders:

1. Dividend reinvestment privileges at Net Asset Value
2. Quantity sales charge discounts at breakpoint levels
3. Accumulation plan

If the mutual fund does not offer these benefits, the sales charge must be scaled down from 8½ percent to as low as 6¼ percent.

PROVISIONS OF THE INVESTMENT COMPANY AMENDMENTS ACT OF 1970

1. The maximum sales charge for contractual payment plans may not exceed 9 percent of the total investment.

2. The custodian bank must send the planholder a notice of the initiation of the plan and a schedule of charges. The notice must be sent within 60 days of the initiation of the plan.

3. The investor may cancel the plan within 45 days from the date of the bank's notification. If cancelled within the 45-day period, the investor will receive a full refund of all sales charges, custodian fees, and insurance premiums. He will also receive the current value of all the shares outstanding in his account.

4. Computations of sales charge under the 1970 Act: The Act provides two methods of levying sales charges for contractual periodical payment plans. The mutual fund company is free to choose either one of these two methods:

Method 1. Under Method 1, the company may deduct as much as 50 percent of the first 12 monthly payments in equal portions and apply these deductions toward the total sales charge of the plan. The remaining 50 percent of the sales charge will be deducted in equal amounts from the balance of payments over the remaining life of the plan.

If the investor's monthly payment is $100 for a 10-year plan, 50 percent of the first year's payments will be deducted as sales charge.

1. Total plan: $12,000
2. Annual Payment: $1,200
3. Monthly payment: $100
4. Sales charge for the total investment: 9 percent of $12,000 = $1,080.
5. First year's total payment = $1,200
6. Fifty percent of the first year's payment will be deducted and applied toward the total sales charge of $1,080: 50 percent of 1,200 = $600.
7. The remaining sales charge (1,080 − 600 = 480) will be deducted during the remaining nine years of the plan.
8. 480 ÷ 9 = $53.33 a year.

This is known as "Front-Load" application of sales charge.

Method 2. Under Method 2, the company may deduct as much as 20 percent from annual payments to cover the sales charge. This deduction may not be more than 16 percent from each annual deposit, based on the first four years of operation of the plan. Through this method, which is also known as *Spread-Load* application, concentration of sales charge deductions from any single payment is avoided; and relatively equal amount of deposits will be invested in the early years of the program.

Using the above example, this method may be illustrated as follows:

1. Total plan: $12,000
2. Annual payments: $1,200
3. Monthly payment: $100
4. Nine percent sales charge for the total program: $1,080 (9% of 12,000).
5. Maximum deduction of sales charges during the first 4 years
   4 × 1,200 = $4,800.
   16% of 4,800 = $768.

6. $768 is also equal to 64 percent of the annual payment of $1,200.

7. $768 can be deducted in equal or unequal annual increments in such a way that each monthly deduction is equal to: 200, 200, 200, 168.

8. The first year's payment is $1,200 from which the fund will deduct $200 as sales charge.

9. Amount of money invested in the plan in the first year is $1,000.

10. Remaining sales charge for the next three years: 768 − 200 = $568.

11. During the first four years, therefore, the company would have deducted $768 out of $1,080 of the total sales charge.

12. The remaining sales charge of $312 (1080 − 768) will be deducted during the remaining six years on a monthly basis:

$$6 \times 12 \text{ months} = 72 \text{ months}$$

$$312 \div 72 = \$4.33 \text{ per month}$$

In both these methods if the investor cancels the plan during the first 45 days after the initiation of the program, he will receive the full refund of all charges and his accumulated shares will be valued on the basis of the Net Asset Value prevailing at the time of the cancellation.

Through a contractual plan, the investor may redeem as much as 90 percent of the value of his holdings and then redeposit the money before the expiration date of the plan. This redeposited amount will be done on the basis of the Net Asset Value prevailing at the time. The investor does not pay a sales charge on the reinvestment portion of the withdrawn funds.

The contractual plan also provides a decreasing term insurance policy to guarantee the full payment of the plan should the investor die before the completion of the plan. The beneficiary of the insurance policy will be the custodian bank, which will then distribute the completed plan to the beneficiary of the decedent. It will be part of the decedent's estate.

RULES OF THE NATIONAL ASSOCIATION OF SECURITIES DEALERS REGARDING INVESTMENT COMPANIES

Discussed in simplified terms, the following are the rules of the NASD pertaining to practices and procedures of investment companies.

Sales Literature Filing Requirement

All members must file all sales literature with the Advertising Department of the NASD within 10 business days after first use or publication.

Contractual Plan Withdrawal and Reinstatement Privileges

It shall be considered inconsistent with just and equitable principles of trade and in violation of Section 1 of Article III of the Rules of Fair Practice for a member of the NASD to engage in the following practices:

1. Encourage an investor in an investment company program to make repeated or excessive use of the withdrawal and reinstatement privilege. Making use of the withdrawal privilege more than once a year is considered excessive.

2. Encourage an investor to reinstate the investment within 90 days after withdrawing.

3. Encourage the investor to use the withdrawal privilege to provide funds for temporary investment in other securities.

4. Encourage the investor to use the withdrawal privilege for the purpose of taking advantage of the fluctuations in the Net Asset Value per share of the investment company.

5. A member of the NASD shall not make arrangements whereby a custodian bank will accept telephone or telegraphic requests for the withdrawal or the reinstatement of shares or cash from the plan account.

6. A member of the NASD shall not make arrangements whereby a custodian bank will withdraw shares or cash from a plan account, or reinstate shares previously withdrawn upon a power of attorney executed by a planholder appointing the broker as the agent of the plan.

7. In presenting investment programs to customers, the broker cannot insure a profit or protect the customer against any loss.

Special Deals

It shall be deemed conduct in violation of Section 1 of Article III of the Rules of Fair Practice for a principal underwriter in connection with the sale or distribution of investment company shares to give to another broker–dealer or accept from another broker-dealer anything of material value in addition to discounts or concessions set forth in the prospectus.

Things of material value may include the following:

1. Gifts amounting in value to more than $50 per person per year
2. Gifts of securities or company stock
3. Special loans
4. Discounts from the offering price in excess of those set forth in the prospectus
5. Wholesale commissions not described in the prospectus
6. Payment or reimbursement of travel expenses, unless such payment is in connection of a business meeting
7. An occasional dinner or a ticket to a sporting event is allowable.

Selling Dividends

An investor who buys investment company shares must understand the difference between dividends paid from net investment income and distribution of capital gains paid from realized profits in securities transactions.

There is no advantage to the buyer if the buyer buys the investment company shares in anticipation of a dividend distribution. The amount of the dividend will be included in the price of the shares he is purchasing. The price per share will be reduced on the ex-distribution date by the amount of the dividend.

Consequently, a broker–dealer shall not induce the sale of investment company shares by implying to the customer a rate of return that is based upon distributions of capital gains or impending dividends.

Prompt Payment by Members for Shares of Investment Companies

Failure by broker–dealers to pay underwriters promptly for investment company shares sold to customers is contrary to the accepted standards of the business.

Broker–dealers are required to transmit payment to underwriters or custodians promptly after the date of the transaction. They must maintain records showing date of transaction, the date of the receipt of payment from the customer, and the date of payment to the underwriter.

In the event the underwriter does not receive payment from a broker–dealer within 10 business days after the date of the transaction, the underwriter must immediately notify the district office of the NASD.

Breakpoint Sales

The sale of investment company shares in dollar amounts just below the point at which the sales charge is reduced on quantity transactions so as to share in the higher sales charge is contrary to the just and equitable principles of trade. Breakpoint or reduced sales charges may be given to a fiduciary account or to a family with children under 21. Groups of individuals purchasing the fund shares are not eligible for breakpoints.

Broker–dealers are prohibited under Section 11(d)(1) of the Securities Exchange Act of 1934 from extending credit to a customer with respect to any transaction in a new issue in which the broker–dealer has participated as an underwriter or a member of the selling group.

Regulation T of the Federal Reserve System does not permit the extension of credit on open-end investment company shares by broker–dealers.

Policy with Respect to Continuing Commissions

The payment of continuing commissions in connection with the sale of securities is proper so long as the person receiving the commission remains a registered representative associated with the

NASD. A broker–dealer may make payment of compensation to a terminated registered representative or to his beneficiaries, however, if there is a bonafide contract between the broker–dealer and the registered representative. The NASD will consider improper any payment of continuing commissions to a registered representative who has been suspended or expelled from the NASD.

Maintaining the Public-Offering Price

Section 25(a) of Article III of the Rules of Fair Practice states that no member shall deal with any nonmember broker–dealer except at the same prices, for the same commission and fees, and on the same terms as are accorded to the general public.

Section 22(d) of the Investment Company Act of 1940 states that no principal underwriter of open-end investment company shall sell to any customer shares of mutual funds at prices other than those indicated in the prospectus.

The following transactions made at prices *less* than the public offering price as set forth in the prospectus may illustrate the above rules:

1. One member sells to another member. This is proper.

2. One member sells through a nonmember to another member. This is proper.

3. A member sells to customer. This is a violation of Section 22(d) of the Investment Company Act of 1940.

4. A member sells to a nonmember. This is a proper transaction under Section 22(d) of the Investment Company Act of 1940 but a violation of Section 25 of Article III of the Rules of Fair Practice of the NASD.

5. One member sells to another member who acts as agent for a nonmember. This is a proper transaction under Section 22(d) of the Investment Company Act of 1940 but a violation of Section 25 of Article III of the Rules of Fair Practice.

6. One member sells through another member (his agent) to a nonmember. This is a proper transaction under Section 22(d) of the Investment Company Act of 1940 but a violation of Section 25 of Article III of the Rules of Fair Practice.

7. One member sells to another member who acts as agent for a customer. This is a violation of Section 22(d) of the Investment Company Act of 1940.

8. One member sells through another member (his agent) to a customer. This is a violation of Section 22(d) of the Investment Company Act of 1940.

9. A customer sells to another customer through a member who acts as agent for either or both customers. This is a proper transaction.

Reciprocal Brokerage Rule

The NASD rules permit members who sell shares of an investment company to execute portfolio transactions for the investment company so long as they seek to obtain such orders for execution on the basis of the quality of their brokerage services, and not on the basis of their sales of investment company shares. This means that the selection of the broker–dealer to execute portfolio transactions must be based on the broker–dealer's professional capability.

Anti-Reciprocal Rule

Sections 1 and 26(k) of the Rules of Fair Practice prohibit broker–dealers to engage in any of the following activities:

1. To provide to sales personnel any incentive of additional compensation for the sales of shares of investment companies based on the amount of brokerage commission received.

2. To grant a salesperson any participation in brokerage commissions received by the broker–dealer from portfolio transactions of an investment company.

3. To use sales of shares of an investment company as a factor in negotiating the price of, or the amount of, the brokerage commissions to be paid on a portfolio transaction of an investment company.

4. These rules will not prevent a member from compensating its sales persons based on total sales of investment company shares attributable to such salesperson, whether by use of overrides, accounting credit, or other compensation methods, provided that such compensation is not designed to favor or disfavor sales of shares of a particular investment company.

5. A member, acting as an underwriter of an investment company, shall not sponsor any incentive campaign or special sales effort of another member based on the amount of the brokerage commissions that the member will receive from him.

CHAPTER SIX

TRANSACTIONS ON THE NEW YORK STOCK EXCHANGE

The New York Stock Exchange, popularly known as the Big Board, is the cornerstone of domestic and international finance. Its influence is felt in every segment of economics, finance, banking, securities, and even politics. It has played a dominant role in our nation's history for almost 200 years.

The New York Stock Exchange provides a central auction market for a selected group of securities where transactions in these securities are executed by Exchange members or personnel of member organizations. It is a nonprofit organization owned by 1,366 members. Memberships or seats may be transferred or sold to any individual who complies with the requirements of the Exchange.

FUNCTIONS

- The New York Stock Exchange provides the liquidity in listed securities.
- It provides market and trade publicity of listed securities.
- It provides a continuous market in listed securities.
- It provides opportunity for people or corporations to raise capital for business ventures.
- It provides the facility for determination of equitable prices for both the buyer and the seller of these securities.

- It supervises the trading activities to prevent unfair and fraudulent manipulation of security prices for the interest of investors, members, and corporations.

ADMINISTRATION

The board of directors is the governing body of the NYSE composed of 21 directors: 10 from the Exchange membership, 10 from the public, and a chairman. The chairman may appoint other officers to help him run the organization. The board has the full power to adopt, repeal, amend, and implement rules; to impose penalties; and to order the dismissal of any member.

MEMBERSHIP

A person applying for membership must purchase a seat and satisfy the Exchange's membership requirements. He must disclose all essential facts about his background, have letters of recommendation from three people, and be sponsored by at least two members of the Exchange.

The applicant will appear in front of a committee of the board of directors. If accepted, his membership application will be presented to the board for approval. He must receive at least two-thirds of the majority of directors to be accepted for membership.

When the membership is approved the person is obligated to pay for his seat and the initiation fee and sign the constitution of the NYSE, pledging to abide by all its provisions and rules. He also must pass a qualification examination.

The following are different methods for financing the cost of purchasing the seat:

1. Personal resources.

2. Gift. The donor's name and a release signed by the donor must be presented to the Exchange.

3. Subordinated loan. If the funds to buy the seat are financed through a subordinated agreement, the agreement must first be approved by the Exchange and the lender of the fund must agree not to lay claims to the seat in the event of default. The term of the subordinated agreement must be longer than one year.

4. ABC Agreement. The brokerage firm may advance the funds to its employee to purchase a seat at the Exchange. This will be done through a special contract called the ABC Agreement. The Agreement will specify the member's percentage of interest in the brokerage organization and the disposition of the seat in the event of death.

Besides individual memberships, there are three forms of business organizations allowed to become members. These are sole-proprietorships, partnerships, and corporations.

Individual members and sole-proprietorships are not allowed to carry customer accounts. Partnerships and corporations must have at least one person as a member of the Stock Exchange. When the member dies, the organization will transfer the deceased person's membership to another person to allow the firm to continue its business.

DEPARTMENTS

The following are some of the departments of the New York Stock Exchange:

Corporate Services — Listing Requirements

The Corporate Services Department determines the qualification and eligibility of corporations to have their shares listed at the Exchange. A corporation must meet the following requirements to have its security listed for trading:

1. Earning. At the time of listing, the corporation must show a pretax earning of a minimum of $2.5 million a year and at least $2 million for the preceding two years. For continued listing, the corporation must show an after tax earning of $600,000 a year for the preceding three years.

2. Net tangible assets. At the time of listing, the corporation's tangible net assets must be at least $16 million, and then a minimum of $8 million for continued listing.

3. Total market value of shares. The total market value of shares issued and outstanding must be at least $8 million at the time of listing and $2 million on a continuous basis.

4. Number of shares. At the time of listing, the number of shares publicly held must be at least 1 million, with 600,000 on a continuous basis.

5. Number of shareowners. At the time of listing, the corporation must have a minimum of 2,000 shareholders, with 1,200 on a continuous basis.

Proxies

The Corporate Services Department also is responsible for making sure that corporate proxy materials are mailed to stockholders within a scheduled period of time. A brokerage house holding securities in Street name is required to mail the proxy materials to customers and receive customers' voting instructions. If the brokerage firm does not receive the customers' voting instructions by the tenth day prior to the meeting date, the broker is allowed to vote according to his discretion on routine matters placed on the agenda. These routine matters may not include proxy contests or measures to authorize capital expenditures.

A dissident group may instruct a brokerage house to mail the proxy materials to customers of record. The brokerage house will mail the material after receiving proper compensation for administrative and mailing expenses.

The dissident group is required to file with the SEC a schedule 14B before it is allowed to represent the stockholders in a proxy contest.

Market Operations

The Market Operations Department is responsible for the ticker tape and quotation services, telephone, teletype, wire services, and the floor operation.

Member Firm Surveillance

The Member Firm Surveillance Department oversees the conduct of members and member organizations in the area of capital requirements, registration procedures for members, allied members, registered representatives, branch office managers, and other supervisory personnel. This Department's main concern is to protect the public customer from abuses and wrongdoings by broker–dealers.

Member organizations carrying customer accounts must have a Fidelity Bond Insurance and Broker's Blanket Bond to protect them from losses resulting from fraudulent practices. The required insurance coverage is based on the firm's net capital and the type of business.

Member organizations carrying customer accounts must have a minimum net capital of $\frac{1}{15}$th of their aggregate indebtedness pursuant to the SEC Rule 15c3-1. If the firm's net capital is less than $\frac{1}{10}$th of its aggregate indebtedness, the firm may not expand its business. If it is less than $\frac{1}{12}$th of its aggregate indebtedness, the firm must take steps to reduce its business.

The Member Firm Surveillance Department is responsible for screening applicants who wish to be registered as securities managers, supervisors, and salespersons. The Exchange requires the following criteria for registered representatives:

1. The applicant must agree to devote his full time to the securities business.

2. The applicant must be of legal age.

3. The applicant must have at least four months of on-the-job training in the securities business.

4. The applicant must pass a qualification examination.

The application for registration will include an agreement to be signed by the applicant whereby the prospective registered representative agrees to abide by the rules, by-laws, and the constitution of the exchange at all times. This agreement will include the following:

1. The registered representative may not guarantee a customer against any losses in securities transactions.

2. The registered representative may not share in the profit or loss of a customer's account.

3. The registered representative may not pay the debt of the customer to the firm.

4. The registered representative may not open a securities account with another firm without the consent of his employer.

5. The registered representative may not rebate part of his compensation to a customer.

6. The registered representative must respond to any inquiry made by the Exchange.

7. The registered representative may not accept any com-

pensation in connection with securities transactions other than from his employer.

8. The registered representative must notify his employer and the Exchange when he becomes subject of any arrest, fine, litigation, regulatory investigation, injunctions, civil judgment, contempt proceedings, etc.

9. The registered representative must agree to submit to arbitration by the Exchange of any dispute between him and his employer or other members of the Exchange community.

10. The registered representative must agree to cooperate with any Exchange inquiry and investigation even after his employment has been terminated.

The Member Firm Surveillance Department also regulates the firm's practices of communicating with the public. Market letters, research reports, and sales literature must be approved by a responsible employee before they are distributed to the public. All advertising materials must be approved, in advance, by a responsible employee of the firm. Once a year member organizations are required to send to the Member Firm Surveillance Department samples of their advertising materials that they have used during the course of the year.

Surveillance Coordination Department

The Surveillance Coordination Department is responsible to ensure that member organizations submit audit reports and financial statements to the Exchange. In accordance with SEC Rule 17a-13, every member organization carrying customer accounts must verify its security positions and resolve the differences. Once a year they are required to employ an outside accounting firm to conduct a comprehensive audit of the firm's records. The result of the audit must be submitted to the Exchange and the Securities and Exchange Commission.

The SEC Rule 17a-5 requires that member firms submit a monthly and a quarterly report called FOCUS (Financial and Operational Combined Uniform Single), to the Exchange and the SEC. This report will indicate the firm's capital structure, the aggregate indebtedness, the operational activities, and its profitability. The Surveillance Coordination Department will review the FOCUS Report and will monitor trends within each firm and request appropriate action if the report reflects any deterioration in the firm's operating and financial condition.

The SEC Rule 17a-5 also requires that firms send a certified statement of financial condition to customers once a year and an unaudited statement every six months.

ARBITRATION

The New York Stock Exchange provides facilities to resolve disputes among employees and customers, members, or member organizations. Disputes must be presented to arbitration in accordance with the Exchange's rules and regulations. A customer who is having a dispute with a broker may compel the broker to go into arbitration. The customer must sign an agreement in which he states that he will accept the arbitration decision as binding and will not resort to public court.

The Board of Arbitration is appointed by the Chairman of the Board of the Exchange. Disputes and controversies in amounts of less than $100,000 are resolved by a panel of three arbitrators, and disputes for amounts over $100,000 are resolved by a panel of five arbitrators.

The decision of the majority of the Board of Arbitration is final and binding. The parties in question do not have the right to appeal the decision to public courts or to the Exchange's Board of Directors.

PRINCIPLES OF THE AUCTION MARKET

The securities auction market has four principles. They are known as the 4 P's — Priority, Parity, Precedence, and Preference.

1. *Priority* refers to the timing of the entry of the order. The order that has entered the trading crowd first will have priority for execution.

2. *Parity* refers to equality. The orders of two brokers have entered the trading crowd at the same time. The brokers will toss a coin to execute the trade.

3. *Precedence* indicates size. If there is no priority or parity, the order with the largest number of shares will have priority for execution.

4. *Preference.* Here a broker claims that he entered the crowd earlier than other brokers. In that event, his order will be executed first.

TRANSACTIONS ON THE EXCHANGE FLOOR

All orders to buy or sell securities listed at the Exchange are transmitted to the floor by telephone, teletype, and through CRT equipment authorized by the Exchange. All transactions in NYSE listed securities must be executed on the Exchange floor with the following exceptions:

1. If the security is also listed at another exchange, the broker is allowed to have the order executed on the floor of that exchange.

2. For certain inactive securities, the Exchange may allow the broker to execute the trade elsewhere.

3. For certain block orders, the Exchange may allow the broker to execute the order in the over-the-counter market.

All orders submitted to the Exchange floor must be completely filled out with proper instructions as to the type of order, number of shares to be executed, and the account number of the customer.

After the order has entered the trading floor, the customer's account number may not be changed. The order ticket also must indicate the time of entry of the order and the time of execution of the trade.

The trading unit is a round lot. Round lots are 100 shares or multiples of 100 shares, and for inactive preferred securities, 10 shares and multiples of 10 shares. The unit of trading for bonds is either $1,000 or $5,000 face value of the bond. Odd lots are shares between 1 and 99 and 1 to 9 for preferred securities. Bonds with a face value of under $1,000 are called Baby Bonds and they are usually non-marketable securities.

The Exchange rules require that brokers keep the floor tickets for at least 12 months with time of entry and execution properly marked. Trade cancellations also must be kept for 12 months. If the customer has received an erroneous execution report and subsequently has received the corrected report, he must accept the corrected version with no right to cancel the order.

TYPES OF ORDERS

1. Market Orders. The order will be executed as soon as possible at the best available price.

2. Limit Orders. In a limit order, the customer instructs the broker to purchase or sell the security at a set price. The broker will try to execute the order at that requested price or better.

3. Stop Orders. There are two types of stop orders—buy stop order and sell stop order.

A. Buy Stop Order. The customer will place a buy stop order usually above the market level. This generally is done to reduce a loss on an existing short sale. Let us assume that the customer has sold short 100 Bee Corp. at 27. He expects the price to fall down. He may incur a loss, however, if the stock rises in value. To protect himself, he will place a buy stop order at a price usually higher than the prevailing price. In this case, he will place a buy stop order at 30. If the price rises to 30, his buy stop order becomes a market order, and he will purchase the security at that price and cover his short sale.

B. Sell Stop Order. The customer will place a sell stop order below the present market level to reduce a loss on his security holding. Let us assume that he purchases a security at 27, expecting the price to rise. To protect himself against a declining market, he will place a sell stop order at 25. When the security's price falls down to 25, his sell stop order will automatically become a market order and he will sell the security at that price.

Stop orders are memorandum orders, and there is no assurance that the execution price will be exactly the same as the stop order price. When the market reaches the stop order level, the order is activated and becomes a market order. It will then be executed at the best available price.

4. Stop Limit Order. This is a memorandum stop order that becomes a limit order instead of a market order when activated.

Each of these orders may be entered for a specific period of time in the following schedule:

A. Day Orders. A day order is valid only for that particular day.

B. GTC (Good-'Til-Cancellation). This order will be valid until executed or cancelled. It is also called an open order. The broker is required to reconfirm all open GTC orders to the customer periodically.

5. Not Held (NH). With this instruction, the customer allows the broker to use his judgment in deciding when to execute the order. The order is called "not held" because the customer will not hold the broker financially responsible.

6. Participate But Do Not Initiate (PNI). With this order, the customer instructs the broker to purchase or sell the security without creating a new price level or influencing the volatility of the security.

7. All or None (AON). With this order the customer instructs the broker to purchase or sell the entire amount on the order ticket. The broker must wait until the entire amount is available to buy or sell. The customer will not accept partial execution.

8. Fill or KILL (FOK). This is a variation of All or None. In this case, the customer will not wait until the shares are available for execution.

9. Immediate or Cancel (IOC). This order is a combination of both All or None and Fill or Kill. The customer instructs the broker to execute the order and agrees to accept any executed portion of the order, with the broker cancelling the unexecuted portion immediately.

10. Fractional Discretion. The customer, in entering a limit order, gives an ⅛ or ¼ of a point discretion to the broker to facilitate the execution of the trade.

11. Scale Orders. For volatile securities, the customer may enter a series of limit orders at prices scaled down or up. The customer will place an order to purchase 500 shares of Bee Corp. at $37 scaled down 1 point. This means that 100 shares are to be purchased at $37, another 100 at $36, another 100 at $35, another 100 at $34 and another 100 at $33. In a scaled up order, the customer will enter an order to sell 300 shares of Bee Corp. at $33 scaled up ½ point. This means that 100 shares are to be sold at $33, 100 shares at $33½, and another 100 shares at $34.

Executed orders may not be cancelled without the approval

of the floor official. Both parties in the trade must agree to the cancellation.

12. At the Close Order. The customer instructs his broker to enter the order at the end of the trading session, specifically during the last 30 seconds of the trading day. The broker is not responsible if he cannot accomplish the execution of the trade during that specific period.

13. At the Opening Order. The customer instructs the broker to enter the order at the opening of the trading session.

14. Alternative Order (Either/Or) The customer instructs the broker to enter the order as a limit order and a stop order at the same time for the same security at different prices. If the limit order is executed, the stop order will be cancelled automatically and vice versa.

15. Sell Plus. The customer instructs the broker to sell the security at a price higher than the previous differently priced transaction for that stock.

16. Buy Minus. The customer instructs the broker to purchase the security at a price lower than the previous differently priced transaction for that stock.

17. Switch Order (Contingent Order or Swap Order). The customer instructs the broker to enter a limit order to sell a stock and, when executed, enter a limit order to buy another stock, or vice versa.

TYPES OF MEMBERS

1. *Floor Brokers.* The floor brokers represent their own brokerage firms.

2. *Two-Dollar Brokers.* These are independent members who will execute orders in behalf of another member organization. In the early days they used to charge $2 for every 100 shares executed; thus the name Two-Dollar Brokers. They now charge a floor commission for services rendered.

3. *Specialists.* These are members of the Exchange who maintain a market of a group of securities assigned by the administration of the Exchange. The specialists are not allowed to deal with public customers.

4. *Traders.* These are members who trade only for their own accounts.

5. *Bond Brokers.* These are members who execute bond orders in the Bond Room of the Exchange.

PROCESSING OF ORDERS

1. After receiving the order on the floor of the Exchange, the telephone clerk will locate a floor broker to execute the trade. Only members are allowed to execute orders. If the telephone clerk cannot locate the firm's own floor broker, he will give the order to a Two-Dollar Broker to execute. The telephone clerk will use various electronic paging devices to locate a Two-Dollar Broker. Tickets for DOT (Designated Order Turnaround) orders are sent directly to the trading post for execution.

2. The floor broker or the Two-Dollar broker will then go to the trading post where this particular security is listed for trading.

3. Without revealing the size or the nature of his order, he inquires about the current price of the security.

4. His inquiry will be answered with a quotation indicating the highest bid price and the lowest offering price of the security at that point in time, with the number of shares available in the market. For instance, "35½ to 35¾ by 200 by 400." This means someone wants to purchase 200 shares at 35½ and someone wishes to sell 400 shares at 35¾ or, "35½ to 35¾ 2 up." This means someone wishes to purchase 200 shares at 35½ and someone else wishes to sell 200 shares at 35¾.

5. After receiving the quotation, the broker may propose his own price. But this proposal must be equal to, or better than, the existing quotation. Therefore, if the bid price to purchase is 35½, he will propose a bid price 35½ or higher. On the sell side, the broker's proposal should be equal to or lower than the prevailing offering price.

6. The broker may request the range of the security's prices. The price range will indicate:

Open   *High*   *Low*   *Last*

The price range is usually furnished by the specialist at the trading post. Electronic equipment located on the floor will also indicate the price range and the volume of the security.

7. If the floor broker finds the quotation agreeable, he will announce his acceptance by simply saying "Take 200." This means he agrees to purchase 200 shares for his customer at the offering price, which in our example is 35¾. Someone is offering to sell at 35¾, and this broker is agreeing to purchase.

8. If the floor broker has instructions to sell the security after receiving the bid and the offering prices, he will simply say, "Sold 200." He will sell 200 shares at the bid price because someone was bidding to purchase at that price.

9. This announcement "take" or "sold" will consummate the transaction.

10. The two brokers will then approach each other and identify the firm they each represent. If they are Two-Dollar brokers, they will give up the names of the brokerage firms they represent. Disputes between brokers are submitted to a floor official for resolution.

11. The specialist plays a very important role here. He is the market maker responsible for maintaining a fair and equitable price for securities. The specialist may guarantee a price on a customer order, while the broker continues to look for a better price without fear of missing the market. This is known as "Stopping the Stock." Let us assume that floor broker A, wishing to purchase 100 Bee Corp., is informed that the quotation for the security is 34 to 34¼. The broker is obligated to purchase the stock at 34¼. If he does not purchase it at that point in time, another broker may purchase it, and he will miss the market for the customer. To avoid this problem, floor broker A will ask the specialist to "stop" 100 Bee Corp. at 34¼. This means the broker will be assured a price no lower than 34¼. If the specialist agrees, the stock will be "stopped." If another broker purchases the stock at 34¼, floor broker A will be "stopped out"; that means he will be forced to pay the guaranteed price of 34¼ for his purchase.

For his services to "stop" the stock, the specialist will charge a floor brokerage fee to the broker. (The practice of "Stopping the Stock" must not be confused with stop orders discussed earlier.)

12. If the broker has two separate customers on opposite sides of the trade in the same security — one wishes to purchase and another wishes to sell 100 Bee Corp. — the broker will pair off the buy with the sell. This is known as "crossing" the trade. The crossing must be done at the trading post with at least ¼ of a point spread between the two trades.

OTHER PROCEDURES OF SECURITIES TRADING

Designated Order Turnaround (DOT)

This is a computerized procedure developed by the New York Stock Exchange in the mid-1970s to facilitate the trading of small round lot orders up to a specified number of shares. A switching system will connect the brokerage firm's order transmission system to the trading post of the particular security, bypassing the floor brokers. The trade will then be executed at the post by the specialist. The specialist does not charge a floor brokerage fee and executes the trade within the framework of the security's quotation — buy orders will be done at the offering price and sell orders at the bidding price. Obviously, only market orders are entered through this system.

Exchange Distribution

The floor department of the Exchange may allow a broker to effect a block transaction through a procedure referred to as Exchange Distribution. A customer who wishes to sell a block of securities must give a certification to the Exchange that he is the beneficial owner of the security (short sales are not allowed through this method).

After receiving the approval from the floor department, the selling customer's broker will solicit other brokers to buy the shares. The selling broker agrees to pay the buying brokers a special commission for the transaction.

A block trade is usually a trade of 10,000 shares or more. The seller of the block pays both commissions on the buy and on the sell. In making the block trade, the broker will find customers who will be willing to buy the shares. The buying customer pays no commission.

The same is true for a customer requesting to buy a block. The broker finds customers interested in selling the shares. Here again, the selling customer pays no commission. The block buyer pays commissions on both sides.

After the buy and the sell orders are paired off, the trades are crossed at the current market price within the framework of the security's price range. The crossing will be done at the trading post. The ticker tape will report this transaction as DIST.

Exchange Acquisition

The broker may decide to buy a block of securities from the customer as a principal to be sold to other customers at a later date. This transaction is called Exchange Acquisition, and it will be reported on the ticker tape as ACQ.

Special Offerings

A special offering is a trading procedure to allow a member firm to dispose of a large block of securities at a fixed price. This price may not be above the last sale or the current offering price in the market. After the execution, the ticker tape will report this as SP.

As in Exchange Distribution, short sales are not allowed and the selling customer must certify that he is the beneficial owner of the security and that this is the only amount to be sold within a reasonable period of time. The selling broker is required to indicate the terms of the transaction on the customer's confirmation ticket.

Special Bid

The procedure of Special Bid is used by customers who wish to purchase a block of shares at a fixed price. Again, approval is required before the transaction is effected. The order must be executed at a price of the last sale or the current bid price, whichever is higher. After execution, the ticker tape will report this as SP.

Secondary Distribution

A secondary distribution is done when the order is too large and cannot be accomodated through the procedures of Special Offering or Special Distribution. This transaction will be done "off-board," in the over-the-counter market.

There are two types of Secondary Distributions — Registered and Spot. A Registered Secondary Distribution requires the registration of the security with the Securities and Exchange Commission. Spot Secondary Distributions are sales by holders not connected with the issuing corporation. These sales are executed on the spot without any delay.

Because of the fact that this transaction is done off-board, it requires the approval of both the floor department and the Market Surveillance Division of the Exchange. The approval is granted after the Exchange considers the following factors:

1. The volume and the price range of the security during the last 30 days
2. The condition of the Specialist's records
3. The liquidity of the security in the marketplace

After the approval, the ticker tape will report the terms of the transaction. The fixed price of the Secondary Distribution cannot be higher than the last transaction on the floor at the time the offering starts.

THE AFFECT OF DIVIDENDS ON THE MARKET PRICE OF THE SECURITY

Cash Dividends

On the Ex-Dividend date the market price of the security will be reduced to reflect the amount of cash dividend. Let us assume that the day before the Ex-Dividend date the stock closed at $24 a share. If this corporation has declared to pay 50 cents a share cash dividend, the opening price of the security on the Ex-Dividend date will be 23½. Throughout the day the price will fluctuate because of other factors but always reflecting the amount of the dividend. If the cash dividend is in the amount that is not within the trading range of an ⅛ of a point, the price of the security will be reduced by the next ⅛ of a point.

EXAMPLE: If the dividend is for 30 cents a share, the next trading fraction is ⅜; therefore, the price will be reduced by ⅜ on the Ex-Dividend date. If the dividend is 10 cents a share, the price will be reduced by an ⅛, and so on. The broker may advise the Specialist not to reduce the price on the Ex-Dividend date. This is done only for a cash dividend. The order must be marked as DNR — Do Not Reduce.

Price Adjustments on Stock Dividends and Splits

On the Ex-Dividend or the Ex-Distribution date, the order and the price are adjusted to reflect the stock dividend.

The prices on the open order are adjusted by dividing the price on the order by 100 percent and adding the percentage of the stock dividend or the stock distribution.

EXAMPLE: A corporation declares a 50 percent stock dividend; a customer has an open order to buy 100 shares at 52. On the Ex-Dividend or the Ex-Distribution date, the price of 52 will be reduced by 34 cents (52 ÷ 150%). If the calculation does not correspond with the trading fraction of ⅛ of a point, the price will be reduced by the next ⅛ of a point.

If the corporation declares a 2 percent stock dividend, the price on the open order will be reduced by 50 cents (52 ÷ 102%).

In the case of a 2 to 1 split or a 100 percent stock dividend, the shares on open orders are increased by 100 percent. Therefore, an open order for 100 shares will be for 200 shares. The share adjustments are done by the following formula:

$$\left(\begin{array}{c} \text{Old amount} \\ \text{on the order} \end{array} \right) \times \left(\begin{array}{c} \% \text{ of stock} \\ \text{distribution} \end{array} \right) = \left(\begin{array}{c} \text{New shares to be} \\ \text{added to the order} \\ \text{only in round lots.} \end{array} \right)$$

Therefore, a 200 share order becomes 300 shares on a 3 to 2 split or 50 percent stock dividend. A 600 share order becomes 700 shares on a 6 to 5 split or 20 percent stock dividend.

All open orders and stop orders are cancelled immediately when the corporation declares a reverse split.

CHAPTER SEVEN

THE SPECIALIST SYSTEM OF THE NEW YORK STOCK EXCHANGE

The Specialist on the floor of the Stock Exchange is the market maker of a group of securities assigned to him by the administration of the Exchange. He has the responsibility to maintain a fair and reasonable market for the securities in his jurisdiction. The Stock Exchange has three important characteristics: continuity, liquidity, and depth. *Continuity* refers to the continuous trading of securities on the floor of the Exchange. *Liquidity* is the Exchange's ability to convert a security into cash at any time that the security owner wishes to sell. *Depth* indicates the ability of the Stock Exchange to handle any type of volume transactions. The Specialist is the center of these three activities. He has to make sure that the three elements are always functioning in an efficient manner. His skill and capital are necessary to assure liquidity and depth. If there are no buyers of the security on the floor, he is obligated to buy; and if there are no sellers, he is obligated to sell. To perform these functions, the Specialist may either act as an agent or as a principal in the transaction.

THE SPECIALIST AS AGENT

The Specialist has the responsibility to receive the order to buy or sell the security on the Exchange floor when the firm's floor broker or the Two-Dollar broker is unable to execute the order. These orders are usually limit orders to buy or stop orders to sell the security. These orders will also include limit orders to sell and stop orders to buy at prices above the current market level. After receiving the orders, the Specialist will enter them in his book as a reminder to execute the trade when the market price comes to that level.

When the Specialist executes the order as an agent, he will charge a brokerage fee for his services. The Two-Dollar broker acting on behalf of the firm will also charge a fee. Both fees may be negotiated between the firm and the Specialist or the Two-Dollar broker. In this transaction, the Specialist is acting as an agent. But if the Specialist's book does not have any customer orders, he is obligated to buy or sell the security from his inventory, acting as a dealer or a principal. As an agent, the Specialist must confirm all open limit orders to the brokers twice a year.

THE SPECIALIST AS PRINCIPAL

The Specialist is responsible for maintaining a two-sided market for the securities in his jurisdiction. He is required to bid and offer when the public is reluctant to do so. He is expected to maintain a fair, equitable, and consistent market for the securities based on the concept of supply and demand. He will maintain the price by selling or buying the security. He may even sell the security in off-hours, after receiving the floor governor's approval.

This can be illustrated in the following manner:

1. The Specialist is bidding to buy 100 shares of Bee Corp. at $60 a share for his account and at the same time he is offering to sell the same security at 60⅜.

2. If someone sells him 100 Bee Corp. at 60, he may then bid 59¾ for 100 Bee Corp. and offer to sell at 60⅛.

3. If someone else sells him another 100 Bee Corp. at 59¾, he may then lower his bid to 59½ and the offer to 59⅞. In this example, the Specialist is continually maintaining the market for the security even at personal expense to himself.

The Specialist is allowed to maintain two types of accounts to enable him to conduct a fair market for the security. He will maintain both a *trading account* and an *investment account*. He will, however, keep these accounts separate. The investment account will enable the Specialist to take advantage of long-term capital gains and the trading account will enable him to arrange financing for the securities in the account. This financing is exempted under Federal Reserve margin requirements, and the Specialist generally obtains a credit up to 90 percent of the market value of the securities pledged.

The Specialist is also allowed to do wash sale—a practice denied to other investors. Under a wash sale, a Specialist may repurchase stocks sold at a loss within the past 30 days and still be able to use the loss to offset profits in calculating his income tax. In selling the security short, however, he must not depress the price of the stock. This means he must sell the stock short at ⅛ point above the previously priced transaction.

Rules for Specialists

1. A Specialist cannot buy the stock as a principal until a customer's market order to buy has been satisfied.

2. A Specialist cannot sell the stock until a customer's market order to sell has been completed.

3. A Specialist may not have priority of time over any customer's limit order in his book.

4. A Specialist may not be a party to a principal transaction if the trade picks up a customer's stop order in his book.

5. A Specialist may not act as broker and dealer in the same transaction. This will be a conflict of interest.

6. A Specialist is not allowed to guarantee any member's personal account or execution price, thus enabling the person to avoid a market risk.

7. A Specialist may not participate in any proxy contest of the company in whose stock he maintains a market.

8. A Specialist may not serve as officer or director of the company in whose stock he is the Specialist.

9. A Specialist is not allowed to have any control in the security or be the principal stockholder of the company.

10. A Specialist may not accept any compensation from the company in which he acts as Specialist.

11. A Specialist is not allowed to engage in business transactions of any kind with the company in which he acts as Specialist. This restriction also applies when doing business with the directors and the principal stockholders of the corporation.

Illustrations of the Specialist's Trading Activities

EXAMPLE 1

Buy		Sell
	35	
500 Paine Webber	$\frac{1}{8}$	
100 Blair & Co.	$\frac{1}{4}$	
100 Lazard		
400 Ludlow & Co.	$\frac{3}{8}$	
	$\frac{1}{2}$	200 Prudential
		1,000 Drexel
	$\frac{5}{8}$	100 Shearson
		600 Tucker
	$\frac{3}{4}$	
	$\frac{7}{8}$	

The Specialist's Book of Bee Corp.

1. Let us assume that a broker comes to a post and asks for a quotation. The Specialist looking at his book will give the highest bid and the lowest offer with the number of shares represented. Therefore, the Specialist will say: "35⅜ to 35½, 500 by 1,200." This quotation is the highest bid for 500 shares and the lowest offer for 1,200 shares as noted in the Specialist's book.

2. If the broker likes the quotation, he will simply say, "Take 100."

3. This means the broker is buying 100 shares of the 1,200 shares offered at 35½.

4. The Specialist will give up the name of Prudential-Bache to the broker buying the security. Prudential's order was entered in the Specialist's book first, therefore, it has priority over Drexel.

5. The Specialist will write a report to Prudential-Bache announcing the sale of 100 shares at 35½ to the broker.

But if this was a sale trade and the broker seeking the quotation says, "Sold 200," this means that the broker is selling 200 shares at 35⅜, which is the highest bid in the Specialist's book. The Specialist in this case will give up Lazard and Ludlow to the broker for 100 shares each. The Specialist will write an execution report to Lazard and Ludlow.

EXAMPLE 2:

Buy		Sell
	23	
	⅛	
	¼	
	⅜	
100 Dean Witter	½	
400 Merrill Lynch	⅝	
	¾	100 Stop-Lazard
	⅞	1,000 Shearson
		1,000 Tucker

The Specialist's Book of Cee Corp.

1. Broker A will go to the post and ask for a quotation of Cee Corp.

2. The Specialist will respond by saying "23⅝ to 23⅞, 400 by 2,000." The Lazard's "Stop" order will not be considered by the Specialist because this is a private arrangement between Lazard and the Specialist.

3. Broker A says "Sold 100." That means the broker is selling it at 23⅝. This price level, 23⅝, elects the stop order (at or below 23¾). Now Lazard's memorandum order becomes a market order and must be executed immediately by the Specialist at 23⅝. The Specialist will earn three floor commissions on these transactions.

EXAMPLE 3:

1. Broker A wants to sell 100 shares short of Dee Corp. stock.

2. Let us assume that the previous transaction on this security was at 21⅜ on a plus tick.

3. The Specialist can offer Broker A's stock as low as 21⅜ changing the current offer from 21½ to 21⅜.

4. If somebody buys the security as 21⅜, this will be a zero plus tick and is acceptable under SEC regulations.

Buy		Sell
100 Shearson	21	
200 Merrill	$\frac{1}{8}$	
100 Tucker	$\frac{1}{4}$	
300 Lazard		
	$\frac{3}{8}$	
	$\frac{1}{2}$	500 Paine Webber
		500 Drexel
	$\frac{5}{8}$	
	$\frac{3}{4}$	
	$\frac{7}{8}$	

The Specialist's Book of Dee Corp.

EXAMPLE 4:

Buy		Sell
100 Merrill Lynch	35	
100 Prudential		
200 Advest		
200 Shearson	$\frac{1}{8}$	
100 Paine		
100 Oppenheimer		
400 Lazard	$\frac{1}{4}$	
	$\frac{3}{8}$	200 Stop-Tucker
	$\frac{1}{2}$	
	$\frac{5}{8}$	300 Goldman
		100 First Boston
	$\frac{3}{4}$	1,000 Johnson Lane
		500 Piper Jaffray
	$\frac{7}{8}$	300 Dain Bosworth
		700 Morgan Stanley

The Specialist's Book of Bee Corp.

1. By looking in his book, the Specialist will announce the following quotation for Bee Corp.:

35¼ to 35⅝, 400 by 400

This is the highest bid and the lowest offer. You'll notice the Specialist has ignored Tucker's "Stop" order for 200 shares at 35⅜. Stop orders are only memorandum orders that will be activated by the Specialist.

2. Let us assume that the previous sale transaction of this security was 35½, plus tick.

3. Let us assume that the Specialist has 100 shares long in his account.

4. At this point, Broker A enters the crowd and asks to be "stopped" at 35¼ on the 100 shares to be sold.

5. How should the Specialist handle a situation like this? If all the bids in his book are cancelled, he will be obligated to purchase Broker A's 100 shares at 35¼. If the Specialist purchases Broker A's stock at 35¼, this will activate Tucker's stop order. This is, therefore, not allowed. If the Specialist wishes to treat this order in this manner, he needs to have the Exchange floor official's approval. Because this will be an involved process, the Specialist will not stop Broker A's order. Broker A will simply sell his 100 shares to Shearson at 35¼ as indicated in the Specialist's book.

6. When Broker A sells 100 shares to Shearson at 35¼, this transaction at 35¼ will elect Tucker's stop order.

7. Tucker's stop order will now be activated and will be a market order in the Specialist's book.

8. The Specialist at this point will cross Tucker's market order at 35¼ pairing it off with 100 shares remaining to be bought by Shearson and 100 shares for Paine Webber.

9. At this point the Specialist will announce:

"35¼ for 200, 200 at 35⅜ sold."

ODD-LOT TRADING

Units of trading on the floor of the New York Stock Exchange and other exchanges are 100 share lots for most of the securities and 10 shares lots for some preferred issues. An odd-lot is a number of shares less than the trading unit. An odd-lot for most of the securities are shares from 1 to 99 and from 1 to 9 for preferred issues.

Orders for odd-lot trades on the floor of the New York Stock Exchange are executed through a computerized procedure taking the Specialist's trading account as the inventory location to buy or sell the odd-lots.

In executing the odd-lot orders, the Specialist on the floor acts as a dealer–principal for the broker who is acting as agent for an odd-lot customer. It is the Specialist's responsibility, along with maintaining a fair market for the securities in his inventory to buy all odd-lots offered to him for sale and to sell odd-lot when a broker wishes to purchase. Because the Specialist is acting as principal in the transaction and cannot charge a commission, the Exchange has allowed him to charge a service fee for executing odd-lot orders. This service fee is called the odd-lot differential, which is added to the customer's odd-lot purchase or deleted from the customer's odd-lot sale. It will be part of the execution price and not a separate item. If the odd-lot purchase order is executed at 37¼, it will include the ⅛ of a point odd-lot differential. In addition to the odd-lot differential charged by the Specialist, the broker acting as agent for the odd-lot customer would charge a commission for the trade. This commission, of course, will appear as a separate item in the customer's confirmation ticket.

After receiving an odd-lot order, the Specialist will consider the last round-lot order transaction as the base to execute the odd-lot trade. This last round-lot trade is known as *the effective sale*. The amount of the odd-lot differential that the Specialist will charge is usually an eighth of a point above or below the price of the security in the effective sale. The odd-lot buyer pays an eighth of a point more, and the odd-lot seller gets an eighth of a point less than the price of the round-lot trade in the effective sale. The odd-lot differential for high-priced securities on the floor of the American Stock Exchange is ¼ of a point above or below the price of the corresponding round-lot trade.

The Specialist will not charge any odd-lot differential if the odd-lot trade is entered before the day's trading session starts and the Specialist executes the trade at the opening transaction. The reason for this is that the Specialist will have ample time to combine all odd-lot trades and pair them off before the trading starts.

All odd-lots entered as part of round-lots through the Exchange's Designated Order Turnaround System (DOT) are executed without an odd-lot differential. Through the DOT system all orders, up to a designated number of shares, are sent directly to the Specialist for execution, thus saving the broker a floor brokerage fee. And if the order through this system contains odd-lot numbers together with round-lots, the broker would also save the odd-lot differential. Such orders as 295 shares or 311 shares, etc. are executed through the DOT with no floor brokerage fee and no odd-lot differential for the odd-lot portion. Single odd-lot orders, such as 35 shares, 67 shares, etc. are, therefore, charged an odd-lot differential.

The odd-lot orders are automatically executed by the Specialist based on the effective sale of the last round-lot trade. A broker on the floor cannot bid or offer on an odd-lot. After receiving an odd-lot ticket, the Specialist waits until a round-lot order is executed and then executes the odd-lot based on the round-lot sale.

Buying and Selling Odd-Lots Long

Buy Long	Effective Round-Lot Transactions	Odd-Lot Execution Price
38 shares	27	$27\frac{1}{8}$ $(27 + \frac{1}{8})$
62 shares	$35\frac{1}{8}$	$35\frac{1}{4}$ $(35\frac{1}{8} + \frac{1}{8})$
Sell Long		
38 shares	27	$26\frac{7}{8}$ $(27 - \frac{1}{8})$
62 shares	$35\frac{1}{8}$	35 $(35\frac{1}{8} - \frac{1}{8})$

Selling Odd-Lots Short

If the customer wishes to sell an odd-lot short, the execution price will be higher than the last round-lot transaction at a different price. The regulatory requirement will prevent the odd-lot short seller to depress the price of the security.

EXAMPLE:

The customer wishes to sell an odd-lot short, and the security has round-lot transactions in the following sequence: $25\frac{1}{4}$, $25\frac{3}{8}$, $25\frac{1}{4}$, $25\frac{1}{8}$. The Specialist will consider $25\frac{3}{8}$ as the effective sale to execute the odd-lot short sale. The execution price for the odd-lot will, therefore, be 25¼ (25⅜ − ⅛). Because it is a sale, the odd-lot differential is deducted from the effective sale price. The reason the Specialist must take 25⅜ as the effective sale is because it is higher in value than the other transactions.

Odd-Lot Limit Orders

In instructing his broker to buy or sell odd-lots at limit prices, the customer must consider the odd-lot differential.

On the buy side, the Specialist will consider the first round-lot transaction *below* the customer's limit price; while on the sell side, he will consider the first round-lot transaction *above* the customer's limit price. This is done so that when the odd-lot differential is added or deducted from the round-lot transaction price, the odd-lot execution price will comply with the customer's limit order.

For limit orders on short sale of odd-lots, the Specialist will consider the effective sale of the first round-lot transaction that is both higher in value than the last different price and above the limit order of the customer.

The customer's limit odd-lot order will not be executed until there is a round-lot trade low enough for the buy side and high enough for the sell side to be considered as an effective sale transaction. The customer may, of course, enter a GTC limit order for the odd-lot. But unlike the round-lot GTC limit orders, the odd-lot GTC limits do not have to be reconfirmed every three months by the broker.

Odd-Lot Stop Orders

A stop order is only a memorandum order that the Specialist will hold as a notice in his book. He will activate the stop order only when a round-lot transaction occurs at or through the stop order price. In this situation, the Specialist is considering a round-lot transaction to activate the odd-lot stop order. This round-lot transaction is referred to as "electing sale." The electing sale, therefore, will be the round-lot transaction executed at or through the odd-lot stop order memorandum. The Specialist will consider the effective sale immediately after the electing sale to execute the odd-lot stop order.

EXAMPLE 1:

1. The customer enters an order

"Buy at 25⅞ stop."

2. Round lot transactions are executed in the following sequence:

25¾, 25⅞, 26, 26⅛.

3. The electing sale in this example is *25⅞*, and the effective sale on which the odd-lot will be taken as a basis for execution is *26*.
4. The odd-lot trade will, therefore, be executed at 26⅛ (26 + ⅛).

EXAMPLE 2:

1. The customer enters an order

"Sell at 20¾ stop."

2. The round-lot transactions are executed in the following sequence:

21, 20⅞, 20¾, 20⅝.

3. The electing sale is 20¾ and the effective sale will be 20⅝.
4. The odd-lot order will be executed at 20½ (20⅝ − ⅛).

Odd-Lot Stop Limit Orders

A stop limit order is treated as a limit order as soon as the Specialist chooses the electing sale of the round-lot transaction. This order is not necessarily executed based on the value of the subsequent round-lot transaction. If the subsequent round-lot trade is at a price at least ⅛ of a point lower than the customer's buy limit order or an ⅛ of a point higher than the sell limit order, the odd lot order will not be executed.

EXAMPLE 1:

1. Customer enters an order

"Buy 67 Bee Corp. at 30¼ stop. Limit 31."

2. The round-lot transactions have occurred in the following sequence:

30¼, 30⅜, 30½, 30⅝.

3. The electing sale transaction is 30¼ and the effective sale
is *30⅜*.

4. The odd-lot will be executed at

30½ (30⅜ + ⅛).

EXAMPLE 2:

1. The customer enters an order:

"Sell 67 Bee Corp. at 27⅛ stop. Limit 27."

2. The round-lot transactions have occurred in the following sequence:

27, 26⅞, 27, 27⅛.

3. The effective sale is 27⅛.
4. The odd-lot will be executed at 27 (27⅛ − ⅛).

On-The-Quotation Odd-Lot Orders

In order to accommodate a customer's odd-lot order the Specialist is allowed to sell the security short from inventory at a price
below the last different price. The on-the-quotation odd-lot orders
are executed at the prevailing offering or the bid price of the security on the floor rather than at a price of a round-lot transaction.
In order to expedite the transaction, the customer may instruct his
broker to enter the odd-lot order as on-the-quotation odd-lot
order. This method is not too popular on the floor, but it is available for the customer to consider.

At-the-Close Odd-Lot Orders

If the customer prefers to buy or sell the odd-lot near the end of the trading day, he will instruct his broker to enter the order as *at-the-close odd-lot order*. The Specialist will execute this order based on the final quotation of the day. After the bell rings, indicating the conclusion of the trading session, the Specialist will consider the prevailing highest bid and the lowest offer in his quotation book to execute at-the-close odd-lot orders. This means the buy order will be executed at the offering price plus the odd-lot differential, and the sell order will be executed at the bid price minus the odd-lot differential. Short sales at the close are not allowed.

Basis Price Odd-Lot Orders

If the spread between the bid and the asked prices is too wide, particularly for some inactive issues, the Specialist is allowed to create an artificial price to execute the odd-lot. This artificial round-lot price is referred to as the *basis price*, which is somewhere between the bid and the offer. After establishing the basis price, the Specialist must receive the approval of the Exchange floor official before executing the odd-lot order.

In this case, the customer will instruct his broker to mark the ticket "on basis."

Bunching of Odd-Lot Orders

Customers or brokers are allowed to bunch odd-lot orders and execute as round-lots to avoid the odd-lot differential.

When a broker bunches various customers' odd-lot orders, he must make sure to allocate proper quantities among the customers involved.

Off-Board Odd-Lot Trading

Some brokerage houses execute their customers' odd-lot orders directly from their trading account. Procedures vary from firm to firm. Generally only market orders are executed through this method. The firm will bunch all similar odd-lot customers' orders, and buy and sell from the firm's inventory account.

CHAPTER EIGHT

TRANSACTIONS ON THE OVER-THE-COUNTER MARKET

The securities market has many facets and components. The market is identified as Primary, Secondary, Third, and Fourth.

The Primary Market is for securities primarily listed at a stock exchange. The New York Stock Exchange is the Primary Market for IBM, the Midwest Stock Exchange or the Pacific Stock Exchange is the Secondary Market for IBM.

Non-NYSE broker–dealers may trade NYSE-listed securities in the over-the-counter market. This is known as the Third Market.

Institutional accounts may trade NYSE-listed securities with other institutions through a computerized network known as Instinet. The trade will bypass the floor of the exchange without any broker intermediary. This is known as the Fourth Market.

The over-the-counter securities market does not have a centralized place for trading securities. The transaction is consummated over a computer terminal or by telephone. The transactions are done on a negotiated basis as opposed to the auction trading at a securities exchange. A broker in Denver, for instance, will sell a security over the telephone to a broker in Milwaukee. He will simply say, "I sell 100 shares," and the other will say," I buy 100 shares," and the trade will be confirmed. The securities in the over-the-counter market are corporate stocks, bonds, municipal securities, U.S. government obligations, foreign securities, and money market instruments. There are over 60,000 securities traded in this market, as opposed to approximately 5,000 on all securities exchanges. Most bank and insurance company stocks are traded on the over-the-counter market, as well as mutual fund shares and American Depositary Receipts (ADRs).

THE MECHANICS OF TRADING ON THE OVER-THE-COUNTER MARKET

The customer instructs his account executive to purchase a security. The account executive will write a ticket and forward it to the Order Room.

The Order Room clerk will try to locate a market maker of the security to effect the transaction. The market maker is a broker–dealer who has made an inventory of the security in his position and will stand ready to provide continuing bids and offers for that security. The market makers may be listed in one of the two components of the over-the-counter market — The National Quotation Bureau (NQB) and the National Association of Securities Dealers Automated Quotation System (NASDAQ).

A. The National Quotation Bureau (NQB)

The NQB publishes and distributes daily lists of securities and bids and offers of the market makers on the over-the-counter market. There are three types of lists, Pink sheet, the Yellow sheet, and the Blue list. The Pink sheet is for stocks, the Yellow sheet for corporate bonds, and the Blue list is for municipal bonds. The Pink sheet contains approximately 10,000 different securities with several market makers for each security. The quotations on the Pink sheet are those at the close of business of the previous day.

After checking the sheets, the Order Room clerk will canvass different market makers to try to get the best possible price for the customer. He will simply contact a market maker and ask for his market on the security. The market maker discloses his "trading market" by saying, "26½ to 27," meaning he will buy at 26½ from a seller or sell at 27 to a buyer. By revealing this quotation, the market maker is making a "firm market," which means he stands ready to trade at those prices at that point in time.

The Order Room clerk may contact another market maker of the same security. The second market maker may quote "26⅜ to 27½ subject." A "subject" market means this market maker is not ready to trade the security at these prices. He would like to verify the quotation before he firms up the market.

For inactively traded securities, the market maker may qualify his prices on a security as "work-out market." A work-out market means that the broker–dealer is not aware of an actual market of the security but can execute the order in a reasonable period of time. He will respond to the inquiry from the Order Room clerk by saying "26 to 27 work-out" — meaning he will try to work out a price somewhere in between.

After shopping the street, the Order Room clerk will select the market maker with the most favorable quotation. The transaction is done by the Order Room clerk simply saying, "I'll take 100 at 27½," and the market maker will respond, "Sold to you."

B. The National Association of Securities Dealers Automated Quotation System (NASDAQ)

NASDAQ is a computerized trading system developed in 1971 for the NASD. Market makers and their quotations are linked through an electronic data terminal system. CRT devices located in the Order Room of brokerage houses will provide the facility of trading through this system. Unlike the Pink or the Yellow sheets, NASDAQ provides an on-line quotation system.

1. Only NASD members are allowed to be market makers on NASDAQ.
2. The bids and offers are continuously updated. There is no reason to shop the market.
3. NASD supervises the activities on NASDAQ and the capital requirements of the market makers.
4. NASDAQ will display only the firm market prices for securities.
5. Trading volume is reported daily to a computer center.

All quotations on NASDAQ must represent bona fide bids and offers. If it is a "nominal price," it must be clearly stated that it is a "nominal" quotation. Nominal quotations are for information purposes only. These nominal quotations cannot be disseminated to the news media. No quotes will appear on NASDAQ until the issue has been traded on NASDAQ for 30 calendar days.

NASDAQ provides three levels of service:

Level One: This is available to any member-firm authorized by the NASD. This level indicates inside bids and offers in each security with a minimum of two market makers entering the quote.

Level Two: This level indicates all quotes of the market makers.

Level Three: This level will allow the market maker to change the quotation. The change is reflected in five seconds. This level is available only to market makers.

In making the quote, the broker–dealer is making the commitment that he will be prepared to buy or sell the security at the price he is indicating. All registered market makers must report their daily volume with regard to securities for which they are maintaining a market.

NASDAQ operates every business day of the week. The broker–dealer may continue to trade on NASDAQ even if the market of a particular issue is halted or suspended.

A broker–dealer is not allowed to do "front-running"—the practice of buying or selling a security for the firm inventory in advance of important news on the security. It is also a violation to execute an order for the firm inventory at a price equal to or better than the price in a customer limit order. A broker–dealer may not accept a stop order for a security booked on NASDAQ. Stop limit orders may be accepted if the stop price and the limit price are the same.

All orders must be executed at the best possible available price that may be based on the volatility, the liquidity of the security and the size of the market.

In effecting a transaction for his customer, a broker–dealer may either act as broker–agent or dealer–principal.

A. Broker as Agent

When acting as agent in a transaction, the broker must advise his customer that he acted as a broker between the customer and the market maker. The broker will charge a commission. The commission must appear as a separate item on the confirmation ticket.

B. Broker as Principal

When acting as a principal in a securities transaction, the broker must advise the customer that he is acting as a dealer. This means the broker becomes the contra side of the trade. The broker purchases the security from a market maker, places it in his inventory, and later sells it to his customer. He will be acting as a dealer in this transaction. The broker will buy it at one price and sell it at a higher price. The difference will be his profit. The broker will charge his customer the net price. He will not be allowed to charge commissions in this transaction.

Regulations prohibit the broker from acting as agent and dealer in the same transaction. The market makers report these transactions daily to the NASD, and it then reports them to the press.

5 PERCENT MARK-UP RULE

The broker must exercise care to comply with the NASD *mark-up* and *mark-down* policy. The mark-ups and mark-downs must be fair and reasonable. NASD has imposed a 5 percent mark-up and mark-down rule for broker–dealers to follow. The broker-dealer must be ready to defend his pricing structure if it exceeds the 5 percent mark-up of the prevailing offering price and the 5 percent mark-down of the prevailing bid price. Mark-ups and mark-downs may not be justified on the basis of expenses incurred by the broker–dealer.

The mark-up is calculated by taking the difference between the net price to the customer and the "inside" price of the security, and dividing the difference by the inside price.

EXAMPLE:

The customer buys the security at 12¼. The quoted bid was 11½ and the inside offer was 12. The mark-up percentage will be: 2 percent (¼ divided by 12).

The broker–dealer may not establish a pattern of habitual mark-ups or downs even at 5 percent or less. The percentage of mark-ups or downs must be based on:

- The type of security
- The availability of the security in the marketplace and the broker's inventory
- The price of the security
- The size of the transaction

The broker will only be required to disclose the commission to the customer, not the mark-ups and mark-downs; unless the broker has assumed a degree of risk in the transaction (this applies to dealers and not market makers).

The mark-up policy does not apply to public offerings of mutual funds, variable contracts, and registered offerings, where the securities are sold at an established price.

EXAMPLE:

The customer buys the security from the broker at $10 a share. If the broker acts as agent, he will charge a commission.

But if the broker, in turn, buys the security from a market maker at $10 a share, he will sell it to the customer at $10\frac{1}{2}$. In this case, he will act as a dealer and charge no commission.

CORRESPONDENT BROKER–DEALER

A correspondent broker–dealer is a broker located in another city that has a relationship with a broker in the first city. He will execute the orders of the broker in the first city. The correspondent network is important for over-the-counter trading.

SWAP TRANSACTIONS

When a customer sells a security and uses the proceeds to purchase another security, the broker must take two separate orders from the customer. But if he decides to act as a principal or agent, he must treat the transaction as a single order for the purposes of determining the total profit/commission.

SIMULTANEOUS TRANSACTIONS

This is also known as a riskless transaction — the broker–dealer takes a position only after receiving the customer's order. The broker–dealer in this case is not a market maker. He will buy the security from the market maker after he receives the customer's order. He will charge a mark-up or mark-down that must be disclosed to the customer.

INTERPOSITIONING

NASD considers Interpositioning unethical and unfair. Interpositioning refers to double mark-ups or mark-downs. The broker will channel the customer's order to another non-market maker broker. The first broker will have a mark-up, and the second broker will have his own mark-up. Interpositioning is allowed if the intent is to save the customer money and if an agreement is reached between broker–dealers at different locations.

THE OVER-THE-COUNTER MARKET AND THE NASD

The over-the-counter market is governed and supervised by the National Association of Securities Dealers. The NASD establishes operating standards to promote just and equitable principles of trade.

The Organization of NASD

The Board of Governors is the ruling body of the NASD. There are 25 standing committees assigned for a specific area and 13 district committees in various parts of the United States.
The standing committees are:

1. Arbitration
2. Automation
3. Bonding
4. Business Conduct
5. Capital Standards

6. Corporate Financing
7. Direct Participation
8. Entry Standards
9. Executive
10. Finance
11. Financial Reporting
12. Foreign
13. Gold Regulations
14. Information
15. Investment Companies
16. Long-Range Planning
17. Margin
18. Municipal Securities
19. NASDAQ
20. Options
21. Qualifications
22. Real Estate
23. Third Market Rules
24. Uniform Practice
25. Variable Contracts

The chairman of each district committee serves on the Advisory Council to the Board of Governors. The district committees are empowered to formulate local practice codes and resolve disputes arising between members of the same district.

To oversee and monitor member firm operations, the Board of Governors has established various licensing requirements for persons associated with a member organization. The following is a list of these licensing requirements:

Series 2 — (SECO)

This is for non-NASD members. The license is for broker-dealers and their registered representatives dealing in securities involving interstate commerce. The examination for licensing is governed by the SEC.

Series 3 — National Commodity Futures Examination

This is for commodity brokers. It enables the licensee to deal in futures contracts.

Series 4 — NASD Registered Options Principal

This enables the licensee to deal in and supervise registered representatives dealing in options.

Series 5 — Interest Rate Options

This enables the licensee to deal in interest rate options.

Series 6 — NASD Investment Company Products/Variable Contracts Limited Representative

This will enable the licensee to sell investment company products, mutual funds, unit trusts, variable annuities, etc.

Series 7 — NASD General Securities Registered Representative

This will enable the licensee to sell stocks, bonds, options, government and municipal bonds, tax shelters, real estate syndications, mutual funds — except commodities and interest-rate options. This license supersedes series 2, 6, 22, and 52.

Series 8 — Limited Principal General Securities Sales Supervisor

This license is for branch office managers in general securities organizations. It serves as a substitute for Series 4, 12, 24, and 53 for persons whose duties involve sales supervision only.

Series 12 — Branch Office Manager

This license will enable the person to supervise a branch office as required by the New York Stock Exchange.

Series 22 — NASD Direct Participation Programs Registered Representative

This license will enable the person to sell tax shelters, such as oil and gas, real estate syndications, etc.

Series 24 — NASD General Securities Principal

This license is for registered principals. The Series 7 exam is a prerequisite. The registered principal will supervise Series 7 licensees.

Series 26 — Investment Company Products/Variable Contracts Principal

This licensee will supervise Series 6 licensee. Series 6 examination is a prerequisite.

Series 27 — Financial and Operations Principal

The licensee will be responsible for the firm's net capital computations.

Series 39 — Direct Participation Programs Principal

The licensee will supervise Series 22 licensees in the area of tax shelters.

Series 52 — Municipal Securities Rulemaking Board Registered Representative

The licensee will deal in municipal securities.

Series 53 — Municipal Securities Rulemaking Board Supervisory Principal

The licensee will supervise Series 52 licensees.

Series 54 — Municipal Securities Rulemaking Board Financial Principal

The licensee will be responsible for the firm's net capital computations.

*Series 63 — Uniform Securities Agent State Law Exam
(National Uniform Blue Sky Exam).*

The licensee will meet the Blue Sky requirements of the states.

Exemptions from Registration with NASD

The following persons are exempt from NASD registration requirements:

1. Limited partners, non-voting stockholders, and employees with no active duties in the management of the brokerage organization

2. Floor brokers and Specialists on an exchange

3. Brokers dealing in exempt securities, such as U.S. government obligations

4. Brokers dealing in commodities

5. The clerical staff of the brokerage firm

6. Foreign associates of the brokerage firm. These associates are not U.S. citizens but operate outside of the country conducting securities activities with non-U.S. citizens in foreign jurisdictions.

THE UNIFORM PRACTICE CODE OF THE NASD

The Uniform Practice Code regulates the mechanics of executing and completing securities transactions between member firms of the NASD. The following are the sections of the code presented in simplified terms:

Sec. 1.

a. All over-the-counter transactions in securities between members, except transactions cleared through a clearing agency and securities exempted under the Securities Exchange Act of 1934, shall be subject to the provisions of this code.

b. In trades between members, failure to deliver or receive securities on or after the settlement date does not affect a cancellation of the contract, unless the parties mutually consent to cancel the trade.

Sec. 2.

The National Uniform Practice Committee shall have the power to issue interpretations or rulings with respect to this code.

Sec. 4. Delivery Dates

a. *For "Cash."*
In a transaction for "cash," delivery shall be made to the purchaser on the day of the transaction.

b. *Regular Way.*
For a "regular way" transaction, the delivery shall be made to the purchaser on the fifth business day after the trade day.

c. *Seller's Option.*
For a "seller's option" transaction, delivery shall be made to the purchaser on the day on which the option expires. But prior to the expiration of the seller's option, the seller may deliver the security any time after the fifth business day after the trade date, provided the seller gives 24-hour notice to the buyer.

d. *Buyer's Option.*
For a "buyer's option" transaction, delivery shall be made on or before the date on which the option expires. If delivered before expiration date of the buyer's option, arrangement must be made for the buyer to accept the security.

e. *"When, as and if issued."*
For a transaction in a security, "when, as and if issued," delivery shall be made to the purchaser on the business day after the seller had given a written notice to the buyer to accept the security.

f. *"When, as and if distributed."*
For a transaction in a security "when, as and if distributed," delivery shall be made to the purchaser on the business day following the date on which the seller had given a written notice to the buyer to accept the security.

Accrued Interest

"When, as and if issued and distributed" transactions in interest-bearing securities shall be with accrued interest to the date of settlement. Interest shall be computed on the basis of the expired portion of the coupon current at the time of the settlement, and all due and past due coupons must be detached.

Marks to the Market for "When, As and If Issued and Distributed" Transactions

The broker who is partially unsecured by reason of a change in the market value of the "when issued" security may demand from the other broker a deposit equal to the difference between the contract price of the "when issued" transaction and the market price of the security. This mark to the market procedure may be necessary because during the life of the "when issued" contract, it is possible that the quoted price of the proposed new security may fluctuate widely.

Sec. 5. Transactions in Securities "Ex-Dividend," "Ex-Rights," or "Ex-Warrants."

  a. Designation of ex-date.
    1. In respect to cash or stock dividends, the ex-dividend date shall be the fourth business day before the record date. In the case of stock dividends or splits that are 25 percent or greater, the ex-dividend date shall be the first business day following the payable date. In respect to dividends or splits of ADRs and foreign securities, the ex-dividend date is designated by the NASD.
    2. Late dividend announcement. If dividend information is not received sufficiently in advance of the record date, the ex-dividend date shall be determined by the NASD.
    3. Ex-dividend dates for mutual fund shares shall be designated by the issuer or its principal underwriter.

  b. Ex-right date.
    1. In respect to subscription rights, the ex-right date shall be the first business day after the effective date of the Registration Statement.
    2. Late rights announcement. If information is not received sufficiently in advance of the effective date of the Registration Statement, the ex-right date shall be the first practical business day.

c. Ex-Warrant date.
1. In respect to the issuance of warrants, the ex-warrant date shall be the fourth business day before the record date.
2. Late warrant announcement. If information is not received sufficiently in advance of the record date, the ex-warrant date shall be the first practical business day.

Sec. 6. Transactions "Ex-Interest" in Bonds which are dealt in "flat."

a. Transactions except for cash.
All transactions, except for "cash," in bonds which are traded "flat" shall be "ex-interest" in the following manner:
1. On the fourth business day before the record day.
2. On the fifth business day preceding the date on which an interest payment is to be made if no record date has been declared.
3. If notice of the record date is not made public sufficiently in advance, the "ex-interest" date shall be the first business day following the public notice of the record date.

Sec. 7. "Ex-Liquidating" Payments.

Sec. 8. Transactions in "Part-Redeemed" Bonds.

This section deals in transactions in bonds that have been redeemed in part. The settlement price of contracts in "part-redeemed" bonds shall be determined by multiplying the contract price by the original principal amount.

Sec. 9. Comparisons and Confirmations.
"Don't Know" Notices.

a. Sent by Each Party.
1. Each party in a transaction, other than a cash transaction, shall send a comparison on or before the first business day following the date of the transaction.
2. Comparisons for cash transactions shall be exchanged on the day of trade.

3. Each party must check discrepancies on the comparison ticket if they exist.
4. These rules do not apply to transactions cleared through a clearing agency.

b. The comparison ticket must be a uniform ticket.

c. "DK" Procedure.

When a party in a transaction does not receive a comparison or a signed "DK" from the contra-broker by the close of business day following the trade date, the following procedure may be utilized:

1. Not later than the fifteenth calendar day after the trade date the confirming broker shall send a "DK" notice to the contra-broker.
2. The contra-broker after receiving the "DK" notice has four business days to either confirm or "DK" the transaction.
3. If the confirming broker does not receive a response from the contra-broker by the close of business of the fourth business day after the receipt of the "DK" notice, the confirming broker has no further liability.
4. "DK" notices must be signed manually by authorized personnel of broker–dealers.

Sec. 10. Proper Description of Securities and Notices and Comparisons.

Sec. 11. Confirmations on "When, as and if issued and distributed" Contracts.

Confirmation or comparisons on these types of transactions must identify the plan under which the security is proposed to be issued or distributed.

Sec. 12. Time and Place of Delivery of Securities.

The delivery shall be made at the office of the purchaser between the hours established by rules or practice.

Sec. 13. Payment.

Payment against the security may be made by certified check, cashier's check, bank draft, or cash.

Sec. 14. Stamp Taxes.

a. The seller shall furnish to the buyer at the time of delivery a ticket to which shall be affixed state transfer tax stamp if the state in which the sale occurred required such a tax. The seller may pay the tax through a clearing organization.

Sec. 15. Part Delivery.

The buying broker shall be required to accept a partial delivery on any contract, provided the position remaining undelivered is not an amount that includes an odd-lot.

Sec. 16. Units of Delivery — Stocks.

1. If the transaction is for 100 shares, the certificates can be for the exact number of shares or certificates totaling 100 shares.
2. If the transaction is greater than 100 shares, multiples of 100 shares may be used. If odd-lots are used, the broker must make sure that the combination of the odd-lots is equal to a 100 share unit. For example: A transaction for 200 shares can be delivered in the following manner:

$$2 \times 100$$
$$4 \times \ \ 25, 1 \times 100$$
$$2 \times \ \ 50, 1 \times 100$$
$$5 \times \ \ 20, 1 \times 100 \ \text{etc.}$$

In using odd-lots, the odd-lots combined must make up a 100 share unit. A delivery in certificates of 1×95, 1×55, and 1×50 to cover the above example cannot be accepted even though the combination covers the trade for 200 shares.

3. If the transaction is for an odd-lot, the exact amount of the contract must be delivered.
4. A uniform delivery ticket must be used in all cases.

Sec. 17. Units of Delivery — Bonds.

a. Coupon bonds. Coupon bonds must be delivered in denominations of $1,000, $100, or multiples aggregating $1,000.

b. Registered bonds. Registered bonds must be delivered in denominations of $1,000 or multiples of $100 aggregating $1,000. Denominations larger than $100,000 cannot be accepted.

c. Bonds issued in both coupon and registered form. If the bonds are issuable in both coupon or registered form, either one may be delivered provided there will be no charge by the transfer agent to interchange one form to the other.

d. The units of delivery may be agreed upon by brokers at the time of the trade.

Sec. 18. Units of Delivery — Certificates of Deposits for Bonds. The same as in Sec. 17.

Sec. 19. Delivery of Securities with Draft Attached. Acceptance of Draft.

Drafts accompanying shipments of securities must be done between the hours established by rule or practice.

Sec. 20. Acceptance of Draft Prior to Settlement Date.

This will be accepted at the option of the drawee.

Sec. 21. Acceptance of Draft Containing Irregularities Shall Be at the Option of the Drawee.

Sec. 22. Expense Due to Shipment.

Expenses of shipment, insurance, postage, draft collection charges, etc. shall be paid by the seller.

Sec. 23. Expenses Due to Delay.

Failure to accept the draft with no irregularities shall make the drawee liable for the payment of interest to the date the draft is paid. The drawee will also be liable for other incidental expenses due to the delay.

Sec. 24. Claims for Irregularities.

Claims for irregularities, such as price, interest, fees, etc. shall be presented not later than 10 days after payment. This limitation does not cover other reclamation problems discussed in Sections 51–57.

Sec. 25. Delivery of Temporary Certificates.

A temporary certificate shall not be a good delivery when permanent certificates are available.

Sec. 26. Delivery of Mutilated Securities.

a. A mutilated certificate must be first authenticated by the transfer agent before the delivery is made.

b. A delivery of a bond with a mutilated coupon attached to it shall not be a good delivery unless the coupon is authenticated by the transfer agent or the paying agent.

Sec. 27. Delivery of Securities Called for Redemption.

If the security is called for redemption, the certificate shall not be a good delivery, except if the entire issue is called for redemption.

Sec. 28. Delivery Under Government Regulations.

a. If a governmental agency requires a special document for a security, the delivery of that security must accompany the specific document.

b. If the certificate has any restriction or stop and that restriction cannot be removed by a simple request, that certificate shall not be a good delivery. The broker can reclaim that certificate without any time limit.

Sec. 29. Assignments and Powers of Substitution.

a. Any registered security to be a good delivery must be endorsed by the registered owner.

b. The endorsement can be done on the certificate itself or

on a separate stock or bond power. There must be separate stock or bond powers for each certificate.

c. The signature must be exactly as the name appears on the face of the certificate.

d. Any alteration or correction on the assignment must be guaranteed.

e. The power of attorney in the assignment space must be executed in blank.

f. The signature guarantee to the endorsement must be accepted by the transfer agent.

g. Except for Canadian securities and ADRs, the signature requirements for foreign securities must be based on the jurisdiction of the foreign authority.

h. Broker–dealers must use a Uniform Transfer Form in requesting securities for transfer.

Sec. 30. Witnesses to Assignments.

A certificate with a signature by a person since deceased is not a good delivery.

Sec. 31. Certificates of Company Whose Transfer Books are Closed.

The endorsement on a certificate of a corporation whose transfer books are closed indefinitely for any reason shall be acknowledged before a notary public.

Sec. 32. Certificate in Name of Corporation.

A certificate in the name of a corporation or an institution shall be a good delivery if the certificate has the following statement; "Proper papers for transfer filed by assignor."

Sec. 33. Certificate in the Name of a Firm.

Sec. 34. Certificate in Name of Dissolved Firm Succeeded by New Firm.

A certificate endorsed by a dissolved firm must have the statement "Execution Guaranteed" placed by the new firm.

Sec. 35. Certificate in Name of Married Woman.

When laws of some states and foreign countries restrict the rights of a married woman to transfer certificates, the woman's signature must accompany her husband's signature. If the woman is single, the following phrase must appear after her signature "_____ feme sole."

Sec. 36. Certificate in Name of Deceased Person, Trustee, etc.

a. A certificate shall not be a good delivery endorsed by one of the following:
   1. A person since deceased
   2. Infant
   3. Receiver in bankruptcy
   4. Agent
   5. Attorney

b. A certificate shall be a good delivery if endorsed by one of the following:
   1. Domestic individual executor or administrator
   2. Domestic individual trustee
   3. Domestic guardian, committee, conservators, and curators.

Sec. 37. Joint Tenants, etc.

A certificate is a good delivery if signed by all co-tenants.

Sec. 38. Two or More Names.

A certificate is a good delivery if signed by all registered owners.

Sec. 39. Delivery of Bonds. Liability of Expenses.

A failure to deliver by the seller shall make the seller liable for any expense incurred as a result of failing to deliver.

Sec. 40. Coupon Bonds.

a. A coupon bond must have proper coupons attached to it. Acceptance of check in lieu of missing coupons shall be at the option of the buyer.

b. Endorsed bonds. A coupon bond bearing an endorsement of a person or firm shall not be a good delivery unless sold specifically as an endorsed bond.

c. Interest in default. A bond upon which interest is in default shall carry all unpaid coupons.

Sec. 41. Registrable as to Principal.

A coupon bond registrable as to principal shall be a good delivery only if registered to bearer.

Sec. 42. Endorsements for Banking and
Insurance Requirements.

A coupon bond bearing an endorsement indicating that the bond was deposited in accordance with a governmental requirement pertaining to banking institutions or insurance companies shall not be a good delivery.

Sec. 43. Coupon Detached Prior to Delivery.

a. A bond dealt in "and interest," for delivery on or after the date on which interest is due and payable, shall be delivered without the coupon payable on such date.

b. Late delivery. If transactions in bonds dealt in "and interest" where delivery is due prior to the interest payable date but is made on or after the interest payment date, the bonds may be delivered without coupons payable on such date. The seller may present detached, unpaid coupons to the buyer for payment. The buyer will bear the risk of nonpayment.

Sec. 44. Stamped Bonds.

Corporations during the period of reorganization will stamp their bonds to reflect the adoption of a new plan. Bonds so stamped are good delivery.

Sec. 45. Certificates of Deposit.

Certificates of deposit issued by depositories other than those specified at the time of trade shall not be a good delivery.

Sec. 46. Computation of Interest.

a. Interest to be added to the dollar price. On the settlement of contracts of bonds and interest-paying securities, there shall be added to the dollar price accrued interest computed up to, but not including, the day of settlement of the trade.

b. Accrued interest is computed on the basis of 30 days each month.

c. Registered bonds traded "and interest." When a delivery of a registered bond traded "and interest" is made between the record date and the payable date, a deduction equal to the full amount of the interest to be paid by the issuer shall be made upon settlement.

d. Registered bonds traded "flat." When delivery of a registered bond traded "flat" is made after the record date and if the trade is made prior to the "ex-interest" date, a due bill check for the full amount of the interest shall accompany the delivery.

e. Income bonds. Income bonds are dealt in "flat" even though such bonds may pay interest.

f. Fraction of a cent. In payments involving interest, fractions of a cent above five mills shall be regarded as one cent, below five mills must be disregarded.

Sec. 48. Due Bills and Due Bill Checks.

a. A security sold before the ex-dividend or ex-right date and delivered too late for transfer on or before the record date shall accompany a due bill. If the due bill obligates the seller to deliver stock, the buyer will prorate the value of the contract and shall make payment of the balance upon redemption of the due bill. This requirement to prorate the value of the contract shall not apply to stock dividends less than 10 percent.

b. Due bill checks for cash distribution and interest. Due bill checks shall accompany securities delivered too late for transfer.

c. Redemption of due bills. Due bills are redeemable on the payable date.

d. Default upon redemption of due bills. A due bill presented for redemption and not honored by the seller may be treated as fail to receive from the seller.

Sec. 49. Claims for Dividends, Rights or Interest, etc.

a. A buyer of stock who has the certificate in his possession prior to the record date has no claim on the seller for the dividend. But the seller must help the buyer to collect the dividend.

b. All claims for dividends must be substantiated by letters from transfer agents.

Sec. 50. Transfer Fees.

All transfer fees to the transfer agent must be paid by the party requesting such transfers.

Sec. 51. Uniform Form.

A Uniform Reclamation form must accompany securities being reclaimed.

Sec. 53. Time and Manner of Reclamation.

When a security is reclaimed, the receiving broker must give the delivering broker another security or the proceeds of the contract.

Sec. 54. Minor Irregularities.

Domestic securities must be reclaimed within 15 days after the original delivery and foreign securities within 45 days.

Sec. 55. Wrong Form of Certificate.

If a wrong form of the certificate is delivered, this may be reclaimed not later than 15 days after the original delivery.

Sec. 56. Irregular Deliveries — Lost or Stolen Securities etc.

Reclamations for any irregularity shall be within 30 months after the settlement of the contract. This will include lost or stolen securities, rejected items from transfer agents, etc.

Sec. 57. Called Securities.

Reclamations of called securities may be made without limit of time.

Sec. 58. Marking to the Market.

A broker who is partially unsecured by reason of a change in the market value of the security may demand a deposit equal to the difference between the contract price and the market price. Failure to comply with this demand shall entitle the broker making the demand to close the contract without notice.

Sec. 59. Buy-In Procedures.

A contract that has not been completed by the seller may be closed by the buyer not sooner than the third business day following the settlement date.

a. Notice of buy-in. A buy-in notice shall be delivered to the seller not later than 12 noon two business days before the execution of the buy-in. The buy-in notice must accompany a copy of the comparison.

b. The buy-in notice must have detailed information about the trade. The broker receiving the buy-in notice may retransmit the notice to another broker.

c. Seller's failure to deliver after receipt of buy-in notice. If the seller fails to deliver the security, the buyer may close the contract by buying the security for cash. Or he may buy the security for guaranteed delivery not later than five business days after the trade. The buy-in is executed for the account and the liability of the party in default.

d. Partial delivery by seller. Prior to the execution of the buy-in, the buyer shall accept any portion of the securities called by the buy-in notice.

e. Securities in transit. If the securities are in transfer or in transit, the seller may ask for an extension for the buy-in for seven calendar days. The seller is required to give the certificate numbers of the securities in question. NASD may grant another seven calendar days of extension if requested.

f. Notice of executed buy-in. The broker executing the buy-in must immediately notify the broker in default.

g. "Close-out" under Committee or Exchange Rulings. When a stock exchange or the NASD rules that all open contracts of a particular broker should be closed-out immediately, brokers may close out as directed.

h. Buy-in for warrants, rights, convertible and called securities. Contracts for these securities that have been called for redemption may be bought-in without notice.

i. Contracts made for cash. Contracts made for cash or for guaranteed delivery may be bought-in without notice on the day following the due day.

j. Buy-in desk required. Brokers are required to have a buy-in section staffed to process and research all buy-ins.

Sec. 60. Selling Out.

a. Conditions permitting sellout. If the buyer does not accept a delivery of a security, the seller may, without notice, sell-out the security for the account and liability of the broker in default.

b. The broker executing a sellout must immediately notify the broker in default.

Sec. 61. Rights, Warrants.

Rights-unit of trading. Transaction in rights shall be on the basis of one right accruing to each share of stock. The unit of trading in rights shall be 100 rights.

Warrants-unit of trading. Unit of trading shall be 100 warrants.

Sec. 62. CUSIP Number.

The CUSIP number must be used on Transfer, Delivery, Comparison, and Confirmation Tickets.

CHAPTER NINE

STOCK MARKET TICKER TAPE AND FINANCIAL TABLES

All transactions on an exchange are reported on the ticker tape. Transactions of exercise and assignments of options are not.

Stocks traded on the stock exchange are assigned a letter symbol to identify each security.

Amer. Tel & Tel	T
Exxon Corp.	XON
General Electric	GE

The symbols are either one, two, or three letters. Sometimes a fourth letter is used to indicate preferred stock, classified voting, etc. ADR issues have five-letter symbols ending with a Y. The symbol of a listed stock under bankruptcy proceedings has the letter Q preceding the symbol of the stock.

THE CONSOLIDATED TAPE

The consolidated tape is a computerized ticker tape system that reports securities transactions at the following marketplaces:

- Regional exchanges
- Instinet
- The third market
- The New York Stock Exchange
- The American Stock Exchange

All NYSE issues traded at these marketplaces are reported on the NYSE ticker tape. All Amex issues and issues exclusively traded on regional exchanges are reported on the Amex ticker tape.

THE TICKER TAPE

The ticker tape has two lines: the top is the symbol of the stock traded and the bottom, and slightly to the right, is the number of shares and the execution price. If the tape does not indicate any shares with the price, it is assumed that a 100 share round lot is traded.

```
XON              GE
      56½              72¼
```

Here an 100 share unit of Exxon has been transacted at 56½ and a 100 shares unit of GE at 72¼.

Trades between 200 and 9,900 shares are reported by the quantity without the zeroes and with a letter s preceding the price.

```
XON              GE
      2s 56½           6s 72¼
```

Here 200 shares of EXXON is traded at 56½ and 600 shares of GE at 72¼.

Trades of 10,000 and up are reported in full with zeroes included.

```
XON              GE
      15,000s 56½        52,000s 72¼
```

Certain preferred stocks on the exchange trade on the basis of 10 share units. The round lot is 10 shares and the odd-lot are shares between 1 and 9. The ticker tape reports the trading activity of these preferred stocks by reporting the shares with no zeroes deleted followed by two s letters placed vertically.

XEPR   YLPR

10 s 56½   70 s 72¼

Here 10 shares are traded at 56½ and 70 shares traded at 72¼.

Sequential Transactions

The exchange may delete the whole number or the price of a security when a series of trades occur in the same issue at the same time with different fractional change.

XON

10,000s 56½   ¾   3s ⅞   5s 57

1   2   3   4

Here there are four different trades. The exchange has dropped the whole amount — 56 — in trades number 2 and 3; but when the whole number is changed, it reports again.

The first trade:	10,000 shares at 56½
The second trade:	100 shares at 56¾
The third trade:	300 shares at 56⅞
The fourth trade:	500 shares at 57

Delayed Transactions

When the selling broker on the floor of the stock exchange forgets to report the transaction or delays the reporting, the ticker tape will display this error by the letters SLD (sold) after the symbol of the stock. This means this trade is out of sequence.

```
XON. SLD
          4s 56½
```

Sold Last Sale

When a stock rises or declines sharply, one or two points above or below the last transaction, the ticker tape will report this as "SLD LAST SALE," on the bottom line of the tape next to the price of execution.

```
XON
    2,000s 56½ SLD LAST SALE
```

When this sharp price fluctuation occurs at the opening of the trading session, the tape will report this as OPD after the symbol of the stock.

```
XON . OPD
          2,000s 56½
```

Stopped Trade

A "stopped" trade means that a broker will be guaranteed a price for a security while trying to seek a better price. The execution price will be guaranteed by the Specialist. This stopped trade is reported on the ticker tape as $\frac{s}{t}$ following the execution price.

```
┌─────────────────────────────────────┐
│                                     │
│   XON                               │
│         2s 56½  s                   │
│                 ─                   │
│                 t                   │
│                                     │
└─────────────────────────────────────┘
```

Bids and Asked Prices on the Tape

In some cases when the trading of an issue has been affected by lack of liquidity in the marketplace, the exchange, in order to improve the issue's trading pattern, will report the Bid and Asked prices of the issue on the ticker tape. The Bid and Asked prices are separated by a dot.

```
┌─────────────────────────────────────┐
│                                     │
│   XON                               │
│         B 56.57                     │
│                                     │
└─────────────────────────────────────┘
```

This means there is a Bid price at 56 and Asked price at 57.

When Issued, When Distributed Stock

When a security by the corporation has not been issued yet, the exchange starts the trading of the security on a *When Issued* or *When Distributed* basis until the security is made available to the public. WI or WD letters will appear on the tape in vertical order next to the execution price.

```
┌──────────────────────────────────────────────┐
│                                              │
│   XON                  GE                    │
│         3s 56½  w           2s 76¼  w        │
│                 ─                   ─        │
│                 I                   D        │
│                                              │
└──────────────────────────────────────────────┘
```

Ex-Dividend, Ex-Right, Ex-Warrant, Ex-Distribution Trades

When a security is traded on the basis of ex-dividend, ex-right, ex-warrant and ex-distribution, these transactions are reported on the ticker tape as XD, XRT, XW and XDIS respectively. The tape will report this only during the initial trading hours of the *ex*-date. After a few transactions on that day XD, XRT, XW and XDIS are dropped, even though the trading continues on the basis of ex-dividend, ex-right, etc.

Late Tape

Due to heavy market activity, the tape at times falls behind the activity on the floor. To save time, the ticker tape will report only the last digit and the fraction of the execution price. The tape will display "DIGITS DELETED."

DIGITS DELETED XON

3s 6½

This means 300 shares executed at 56½. The tape reports only the last digit of the whole number and the fraction. But if the whole price ends with a zero, the entire figure is reported. Example: 50½ is not reported as 0½ but as 50½. When conditions improve, the whole digit reporting is resumed. The tape will indicate this by "DIGITS RESUMED." The tape may also delete the volume figure:

VOLUME DELETED XON

6½

In this case, both volume and digits are deleted. When conditions change, reporting of the volume is resumed. The tape will report this as "VOLUME RESUMED."

If the activity on the floor is hectic, the exchange may decide to omit repeat prices of a security on the ticker tape. This will be reported on the tape as "REPEAT PRICES OMITTED." This means that sequential execution prices of the same security at the same prices are omitted until the tape catches up with the trading activity. Exceptions are: opening trades, stopped trades, and trade corrections.

HOW TO READ FINANCIAL TABLES

The market prices of securities are published in the newspapers as they are reported by the exchanges, the NASD, government bond, and municipal bond dealers.

Stock Tables of NYSE and ASE Securities

The financial tables report the trading activities of securities listed on the exchanges. The tables have 11 columns in the following order:

52 weeks				YLD	P-E	Sales				Net
High	Low	Stock	Div.	%	Ratio	100s	High	Low	Close	Chg
84¼	49⅞	IBM	3.44	4.0	13	14,887	u85½	84¼	85¼	+3⅜
1	2	3	4	5	6	7	8	9	10	11

Let us study each column separately.

Columns 1 and 2. These are the high and the low of the security's price during the last 52 weeks preceding the current week.

Column 3. The name of the security.

Column 4. Dividend distribution. This stock pays $3.44 a share dividend annually to stockholders of record.

Column 5. Yield is the percentage return on investment. If an investor wishes to purchase IBM at the current market price with $3.44 a share annual dividend, his investment would yield 4.0 percent. It is determined by:

$$\frac{\text{Dividend per share}}{\text{Price per share}}$$

Column 6. P-E Ratio. The price-earning ratio is computed by comparing the current price of the security with the annual earnings per share of the corporation. It is determined by:

$$\frac{\text{Market price of the security}}{\text{Earnings per share}}$$

No figure will appear in this column if the security is a preferred stock or the corporation has not declared any earnings.

Column 7. Trading volume in 100 share units. The figure has shown 14,887, which means 1,488,700 shares are traded. If the security, such as a preferred stock, is traded on the basis of a 10-share trading unit, the trading volume is reported in full with a letter Z in the front of the figure, Z200. If the security is traded ex-dividend or ex-right, there will be a letter X appearing in front of the volume figure.

Column 8. High. The highest price of the security on that day. You notice the letter u in front of 85½. This indicates that 85½ is a new high for the year.

Column 9. Low. This is the lowest price of the security on that day. If that price is a new low for the year, the letter d will appear in front of the price in column 9.

Column 10. Close. This is the final sale price of the security.

Column 11. Net change is the difference between yesterday's closing price and today's closing price. Ex-dividend prices are taken into consideration when calculating the net change.

THE OVER-THE-COUNTER TABLES

The NASDAQ National Market issues are reported by the press in the following manner:

1982				Sales				Net
High	Low	Stock	Div.	Hds	High	Low	Last	Chg
21	11	Color Tile	0	500	20	19⅝	20	+⅜

These columns are self-explanatory.

The remaining over-the-counter issues are reported as:

Stock & Div.	Sales 100s	Bid	Asked	Net Chg
AEC .40	38	5	5½	+¼
1	2	3	4	5

Let us study these columns.

Column 1. This is the name of the stock and the annual dividend rate. This corporation pays 40 cents a share dividend annually.

Column 2. Total volume in 100 share units traded by the market maker. 3,800 shares are traded in this example.

Column 3. This is the Bid price; somebody is bidding to buy at $5.

Column 4. This is the Asked price; somebody is asking to sell at $5½.

Column 5. Net change. This is the difference between yesterday's closing bid price and today's closing bid price.

Issues are added and deleted on NASDAQ by the board of the NASD.

THE CORPORATE BOND TABLES — BONDS LISTED ON THE STOCK EXCHANGE

The market quotations of bonds listed on the stock exchanges are reported in the following manner:

Bonds	CUR YLD	VOL	High	Low	Close	Net Chg
ATT 8¾s00	11.	375	82¾	82¼	82½	+⅛
1	2	3	4	5	6	7

There are seven columns used for reporting.

Column 1. The name of the bond. These are Amer. Tel & Tel bonds maturing in the year 2000. Only the last 2 digits of the year are printed. 1997 will appear as 97. 8¾% is the interest rate. This means the corporation pays an annual interest of 8¾% per each $1,000 face value of a bond.

Column 2. The current yield is the investor's percentage of return on his investment. It is computed by:

$$\frac{\text{Annual interest}}{\text{Current market value of the bond}} = \text{Current yield}$$

Using the above quotation:

$$\frac{(8\frac{3}{4}\% \text{ of } \$1,000 \text{ bond}) \text{ as reported in Column 1}}{(82\frac{1}{2} \text{ of } \$1,000 \text{ bond}) \text{ as reported in Column 6}} = 11\%$$

The security will yield 11%.

If the bond is a convertible corporate bond, the current yield is not calculated.

Column 3. Number of bonds traded. This is expressed in $1,000. In this case, there were $375,000 bonds traded.

Column 4. High. This is the highest execution price on that day. It is reported in two digits or in three digits. 82 means one has to pay $820 to purchase a bond with a face value of $1,000. 105 means one has to pay $1,050 to purchase a bond with a face value of $1,000. The fractions for bond trading are the same as in the stock market, except $\frac{1}{8}$ of a point in the stock market is $12\frac{1}{2}$ cents and in the bond market it is $1.25. One point in the bond market is $10.

$$\frac{1}{8} = \$1.25 \qquad\qquad \frac{5}{8} = \$6.25$$
$$\frac{1}{4} = \$2.50 \qquad\qquad \frac{3}{4} = \$7.50$$
$$\frac{3}{8} = \$3.75 \qquad\qquad \frac{7}{8} = \$8.75$$
$$\frac{1}{2} = \$5.00$$

$82\frac{1}{2}$ for a bond means $825.00 for $1,000 bond. $105\frac{7}{8}$ means $1,058.75 for $1,000 bond.

Column 5. Low. The lowest price for the day.

Column 6. The closing price of the day.

Column 7. Net change is the difference between yesterday's closing price and today's closing price. It is expressed as a percentage of the bond's $1,000 face value. In this example the net change is $+\frac{1}{8}$. This means the bond's price has gone up $1.25 per $1,000 bond.

U.S. GOVERNMENT AND AGENCY SECURITIES

The securities of the United States government and agency obligations are reported in the financial pages in the order of type and maturity. The early maturity dates come first. Because these securities are traded in the over-the-counter market, the market reporting is done on the basis of Bid and Asked prices.

U.S. TREASURY BILLS

The market quotation for U.S. Treasury Bills is expressed in terms of percentage from the face value. These securities are sold at a discount price from the face value. They are non-interest bearing issues maturing in three months, six months, or one year. They are issued in minimum denominations of $10,000. An investor interested to purchase these bills will pay a discount price. At maturity, he will redeem the bill at the full face value. The difference between the cost of purchase and the redemption price is considered as interest income.

The newspaper quotation of the market price will be:

Bid	Asked
15	14

In this case, the Bid is higher than the Asked price, which means the Bid has a higher percentage discount from the face value and, therefore, a lower dollar price. To convert this into dollars, the investor will subtract the yield from 100:

$$\text{Bid} \qquad 100 - 15 = 85$$

Somebody is bidding $8,500 to purchase a $10,000 face value of a bill.

$$\text{Asked} \qquad 100 - 14 = 86$$

Somebody is offering $8,600 to sell a $10,000 face value of a bill. The same percentages are used for other denominations. This means $85,000 and $86,000 respectively for bills in denominations of $100,000.

U.S. TREASURY NOTES AND BONDS

Notes and bonds issued by the U.S. Treasury Department are interest-bearing securities. They are issued in minimum denominations of $1,000. A Treasury Note matures anytime between one year and 10 years of issuance, whereas bonds mature between 10 years and 30 years.

The market activity of these securities is reported in the following manner:

Rate	Maturity Date	Bid	Asked	Bid Chg.	Yld
13⅛s	1994 Jul	104.27	105.11	.1	9.71
1	2	3	4	5	6

Column 1. This is the interest rate of the bonds. These bonds pay an annual interest rate of 13⅛%.

Column 2. Maturity date. These bonds will mature in July of 1994. If this column contains two different years for maturity, such as 1992–1994 Jul, this means that the Treasury Department may redeem these bonds anytime between July 1992 and July 1994.

Column 3. The Bid price. Somebody is bidding to buy a $1,000 face value of U.S. Treasury Bond at $104.27. The price is expressed in percentage of $1,000. One point is $10, and the fractions used for Treasury and federal agency obligations are ⅟₃₂ of $10 or ⅟₆₄ of $10. This is computed in the following manner. Bid price 104.27 means:

104 is $1,040
.27 is ²⁷⁄₃₂nd of $10

Whatever you see after the decimal point, whether one digit or two digits, you put that figure over 32 and calculate as to $10. In this case, it is ²⁷⁄₃₂nd of $10. The result is then added to $1,040.

Column 4. The Asked price. Somebody is offering to sell $1,000 bond at 105.11. This means

1,050 + ¹¹⁄₃₂

Column 5. Bid Change. The Bid price of this bond today is up .1 or ⅟₃₂nd of $10 from yesterday's Bid.

Column 6. This is the yield. This means if one wanted to purchase these bonds at the current asked price of 105.11 and holds the bonds until maturity, July of 1994 at 13⅛% annual interest rate, the yield on his investment will be 9.71%.

The trading of federal agency securities is reported in the same manner.

MUTUAL FUNDS

The market quotations of open-end investment companies or mutual funds are published daily and weekly in the financial pages of major newspapers. The Bid price is the Net Asset Value of the fund (NAV). This is the price that the investor will receive when the shares are redeemed by the company. The Asked price includes the maximum sales charge imposed by the fund when one purchases the shares. If there is a designation N.L., it means *no load*; the fund will not charge a sales fee. In that case, the Asked price and the Bid price will be the same.

Name of Fund	*NAV*	*Offer Price*	*NAV CHG.*
Chemical Fd.	10.82	11.82	+.37
1	2	3	4

Column 1. The name of the fund.

Column 2. NAV. This is the price that the investor will receive when he redeems the shares through the fund.

Column 3. The offer price is the sales charge plus NAV. In this case, the sales charge is $1 a share.

Column 4. The net change in NAV is the price change of Net Asset Value.

Some publications also may publish the investment company yield and expense ratio for mutual funds. The investment company yield is determined by:

$$\frac{\text{Annual dividend}}{\text{Current offering price}}$$

and the expense ratio is determined by:

$$\frac{\text{Annual operating expense}}{\text{Average annual net asset}}$$

There are basically two types of investment companies —
open-end and closed-end. The market price of the closed-end fund
is not linked to the Net Asset Value. Closed-end funds generally
sell at a discount from the Net Asset Value and are traded in the
same way as equity securities.

LISTED OPTIONS

Unlike the stock exchanges, there is no consolidated tape system
for options. Dually listed options are reported separately by individual option exchanges. The listing of options is done vertically
as to the name of the underlying security and horizontally as to
the class of option, put or call, and different expiration month.

Option & N.Y. Close	Strike Price	CALLS			PUTS		
		Jan.	Apr.	July	Jan.	Apr.	July
Bee Corp. 62¾	45	r	17	s	⅛	r	s
62¾	50	12¼	12½	s	⅛	r	s
62¾	55	7¾	7½	r	½	1¹⁄₁₆	1½
62¾	60	3¾	4½	5	1⅛	2¾	4
62¾	65	1½	2⅝	2¾	r	3½	r
1	2	3	4	5	6	7	8

Column 1. The name of the underlying security and the closing price of the stock on the stock exchange.

Column 2. The strike prices established by the option
exchanges. Columns 3, 4, 5, 6, 7, 8 are the expiration months of
the option.

Letter designation r in the price box of the option means the
option is not traded and s means the option is not offered. o
means old.

The options exchanges also report the volume of the option
transactions. This is expressed by *total volume* and *open interest*.

Total Call Vol: 383,907   Call open Int: 3,651,161

Total Put Vol: 110,301   Put open Int: 1,815,379

The total call volume means the aggregate number of call contracts traded on the exchange on that day. The total put volume is the volume reporting for puts 387,897 call contracts corresponds to 38,789,700 shares of underlying securities. The open interest is the number of outstanding contracts still open in the books of the Options Clearing Corporation. All opening transactions, whether buys or writes, will add to the number of open interest, and all closing transactions will reduce the number of open interests.

CHAPTER TEN

THE SECURITY ORGANIZATIONS

A securities firm can either be a partnership or a corporation. The partnership form of business prevailed in the industry until the 1950s, when the securities exchanges amended their rules to allow corporate entities as members. The advantages of one over the other are similar to those in other industries as discussed earlier. There are some differences, however, which characterize the brokerage industry as a whole.

The period between the start of the Great Depression and the end of World War II is known as an inactive and dormant period for the securities industry. Brokerage firms were organized as partnerships, and each partner had his own area of activity. Although some decisions originated from a managing partner, the firm was run as an entity of autonomous groups based on customs and practices unique only to the securities industry. Because of low volume, there was no need for expansion; therefore, there was no demand for capital. The resources of each partner were sufficient to raise the necessary funds to run the organization.

As the character of the securities industry started to change in the early part of the 1950s, so did the organizational needs of partnerships. Because of a general rise in business activity, firms sought to acquire a more permanent form of organization. The corporate form offered this perpetuity of business. Here responsibilities of each officer were clearly defined with an organizational structure based on a chain of command. It also provided an added advantage as manifested in other corporations — liabilities of corporate officers were limited.

Corporation or partnership, the securities firms represent an important segment in the nation's economic structure. They finance the birth, formation, and growth of new ventures and serve the ever-growing population of investors.

TYPES OF SECURITIES ORGANIZATIONS

A securities firm is organized upon precepts adopted decades ago. Its composition depends upon the type of business activity it has elected to conduct. Some firms specialize in bonds; others in a group of listed securities. Some are investment bankers dealing in securities flotations; some specialize in commodities and others specialize in options or short-term obligations. They all have common characteristics, however. Their essential business is that of investing for themselves or for the public and offering a multitude of services that characterize their particular mode of operation.

Commission Houses

These are brokerage houses that render financial services for retail as well as institutional customers. They are members of principal securities and commodity exchanges, and the organization generally has a branch office format. They also are known as "wire houses" because of branch-home-office communication systems. From the administrative standpoint, the operation is centered in the home office with branches acting as servicing, income-producing, or supplementary support posts. Their revenue is largely derived from commissions in executing orders for customers. If the brokerage house is a corporation, the principal officers — voting stockholders — should be qualified to be regular or allied members of the Exchange. The general partners of the partnership firm should also be qualified for this status.

Investment Banking Houses

These are security underwriters primarily involved with flotations of new issues, offering of financial services to institutions, underwriting private placements, and so on. Their clients are mostly corporations and governments that seek the services of an investment banker for their financial needs. The investment banker acts as a middleman between the corporation and prospective investors. He plays an important economic role in financing the capital requirements of corporations, whether public or private.

Over-the-Counter Dealers

These are broker–dealers who are engaged in transactions of unlisted securities. They are generally commission brokers or market makers of over-the-counter securities. The market itself contains a wide range of securities from stocks and bonds to financial papers and U.S. Treasury obligations. The over-the-counter market has over sixty thousand different issues, compared to only a few thousand that are listed on all securities exchanges. Most of the trading in government, municipal, and corporate bonds occur in this market. The broker–dealers are brought together by means of various communications systems, telephone, telegraph, teletype, mail, and so on, with no facilities for a centralized marketplace.

After the creation of the security, a public corporation may decide not to have the issue listed on an exchange or because of the listing requirements of an exchange, the issue might not be eligible for listing. These securities will find their home in the over-the-counter market. The term "over-the-counter" has its origin from the time when brokers used to do the trading of this type of security "over their counters."

The broker–dealers may act as agents buying and selling for their customers or as dealers for their own account. Unlike listed securities, broker to broker transactions are not reported to a central room for publication. Quotations are obtained by direct communication between traders.

The Third Market Dealers

These are broker–dealers who transact trades of listed securities in the over-the-counter market. The trading activity in this area has increased tremendously over the past few years, particularly since the inauguration of NASDAQ, which allows trading of listed securities throughout its system.

The third market serves a purpose in providing negotiated trading and competition among traders. It is particularly beneficial to an institutional investor in facilitating block transactions without disrupting the securities market.

The third market dealer must comply with the requirements of the SEC to qualify him to participate in off-board trading.

Mutual Fund Dealers

These are securities firms primarily involved in the sale and redemption of investment company securities. Most mutual fund shares are sold in the over-the-counter market. Some closed-end funds are listed on the New York Stock Exchange.

Discount Brokers

Discount brokers execute trades without offering investment advice to customers. They generally charge a lower commission rate than a full service brokerage organization.

The Specialist Firm

The Specialist is a market maker of securities. His customers are mainly the members of an exchange who come to him to buy or sell securities. He can either be a broker or a dealer. As a broker, he transacts business with other brokers on a commission basis. As a dealer, he buys and sells for his own account, thus maintaining an orderly market. He is not expected to prevent a stock from declining or rising; rather, his function is to try to keep the rises and declines fair and orderly.

Commodity Brokers

These are brokers who deal in commodity futures contracts for themselves or for their customers. The commodity department is usually a division of the general stock brokerage operation. As members of commodity exchanges, they are governed by various laws, rules, and regulations. The trading in mercantile and agricultural commodities, such as wheat, cotton, rice, eggs, butter, etc., are federally regulated by the Commodity Futures Trading Commission.

Bond Houses

These are firms primarily engaged in underwriting, distributing, and dealing in bonds. Some may be specialized in municipal bonds, others in U.S. government obligations, federal agency instruments, corporate bonds, tax exempt notes, and so forth.

Mainly involved in underwriting of bonds, they act as middlemen between lenders and borrowers. They bid for a new issue on a competitive basis or as a private arrangement; and if the deal is accepted, they underwrite it themselves or act as the manager of a syndicate. After the underwriting negotiations are completed, the bond house will sell the issue to the public. Among other divisions, support areas for the bond house include: the trading room, purchase and sales department, and the cashiers operation.

Note Brokers

These are generally commercial paper houses acting as middlemen between the issuer of commercial paper and institutional or private investors. This type of borrowing is a means to finance the seasonal inventory requirements of a corporation. The dealers buy these short-term instruments from the issuers at one rate and sell them at another. The difference between the two is their profit. These brokers may constitute a division of a general brokerage operation or a subsidiary organization.

Option Dealers

With the inauguration of the Chicago Board Options Exchange in 1973, the popularity of options trading has increased tremendously. The option exchanges provide an auction market for options of listed securities and indexes, and members transact business for their account or for the account of their customers.

Options are purchased and sold through brokers who are members of an exchange where such options are listed. The auction market determines the price or the premium of the option to be paid by the purchaser and received by the seller.

Members charge commissions at the time of trading and upon the exercise of an option. Commissions are based on the amount of money in the transaction and the aggregate exercise price of the underlying security. The purchaser pays a commission at the opening purchase transaction, at the closing sale transaction, at the liquidation of his position, and upon exercise of the option. The writer, in turn, pays a commission at the opening sale transaction, in a closing purchase transaction and upon exercise of the option if he is required to deliver or purchase the underlying security.

Primary Government Bond Dealers

These are dealer organizations registered with the Federal Reserve Bank. The Fed executes transactions of U.S. Treasury obligations with the primary dealers through the Federal Open Market operations.

Registered Traders

These are members of the Exchange who buy and sell securities for their own account. They do not deal with the public. Their transactions give the market greater liquidity.

Two-Dollar Brokers

Two-Dollar brokers are independent floor brokers who execute orders for other members or member organizations. They are called Two-Dollar brokers because they once received $2 in floor brokerage commissions for every 100 shares of stock they executed.

MEMBERSHIP IN THE SECURITIES EXCHANGES

There are nine securities exchanges throughout the country registered with the Securities and Exchange Commission. Among them, six play a large role in the securities business: the New York, American, Midwest, Pacific, Philadelphia, and Boston Stock Exchanges. Much of the securities trading in the country is done on these exchanges. The New York Stock Exchange, in particular, occupies a position of unique importance in the field of finance.

The exchanges operate on an auction concept. Bids and offers are made openly on the floor. Buyers and sellers compete with one another. The highest bidder buys the stock, and the person with the lowest offer sells. Orders are executed and prices are determined on the basis of supply and demand for a given security.

The exchanges provide the mechanism for the transfer of securities ownership from one person to another. They are responsible for the liquidity and marketability of listed securities, and furnish a barometer of business conditions throughout the world.

THE NATIONAL ASSOCIATION OF SECURITIES DEALERS

The over-the-counter market is regulated by the National Association of Securities Dealers (NASD), which was organized in 1938 upon the enactment of a legislation known as the Maloney Act. The Act established a mechanism for regulating the over-the-counter securities market. The NASD is national in scope with an organizational plan similar to a corporation. It has districts and branches throughout the country operating under a central direction of a board of governors, president, and vice-presidents. It is a membership corporation. Members are broker–dealers who have met the statutory requirements for membership. The rules of the Association regulate business practices and establish criteria for members on how to conduct their business with one another.

Membership in the Association is not a requirement, but broker–dealers find it to their advantage to apply for membership.

Rules of Fair Practice

These rules are a series of regulations adopted by the NASD to enforce equitable principles of trade and ethical conduct in the securities business. The articles in the Rules of Fair Practice include rules pertaining to such members' business activities as:

1. Business conduct of members
2. Maintenance of books and records and disclosure of financial condition
3. Dealings with members and nonmembers
4. Handling of customers' accounts, securities, and funds
5. Margin accounts
6. Requirements for members' "failed to deliver" and "failed to receive"
7. Handling of complaints
8. Schedule of penalties

Uniform Practice Code

The Uniform Practice Code of the NASD establishes uniformity of customs and practices among members; defines various terms and prescribes methods of execution; regulates settlement and delivery of securities, handling of payments, computation of interest, and so on.

An Association committee called the National Uniform Practice Committee is empowered to issue interpretations or rulings with respect to the applicability of the Code. The Code deals with the following:

1. Modes and units of securities delivery
2. Procedures with respect to dividends, ex-dividends, ex-rights, ex-warrants, and due bills
3. Comparisons, confirmations, and "Don't Know" (DK) trades
4. Procedures for non-transferable securities
5. Reclamation and rejection of securities
6. Mark to market
7. Procedures for buy-ins and sellouts.

ORGANIZATION OF THE SECURITIES FIRM

Structure

The classification of different types of securities firms leads us to the organization and composition of the securities firm itself. Basically all securities firms have similar organizational structures, with variations as to the functions and staffing of different areas.

A securities firm has many departments, units, and divisions — all integrated and interdependent to each other. As in any other organization, it requires a division of responsibility to function as an entity. Whether partnership or corporation, it must have a line of authority manifested on an organizational chart, a managing partner, administrative partner, partner in charge of underwriting, operations partner, and so forth — each with his own area of responsibility and reporting to an executive or a policy committee.

In the case of a corporation, the organization chart includes a board of directors, an executive committee, the chairman of the board, a vice chairman of the board, a president, and divisional or administrative vice presidents. The policy committee or the board of directors formulates the operating and financial policies of the firm. The administration of those policies is the responsibility of the chief executive officer — the chairman of the board or the president, or the managing partner in a partnership.

The firm's activities, in the main, are separated into two large divisions. The first is the administrative area or service departments with their support functions. Within this division is included the registered representative who represents the liaison between the firm and its customers. The second division is the production or income-producing departments. These two areas are colloquially referred to as the "Front Office" and the "Back Office."

The Income-Producing Department or the "Front Office"

The production department has many divisions, units, and sections. Depending on the firm's activities, it can be divided into different groupings. The most important sections in this area are the sales force, and the underwriting and trading departments.

Each division is headed by a partner or a vice president who exercises supervision over his department's activities. The following are the various sections in the income-producing area of a typical brokerage organization:

- Branch offices division. This includes the sales representatives, branch managers, and other income-producing activities on the regional level.
- Foreign Division
- Mutual Fund Sales
- Underwriting
- Institutional Sales
- Block Trading
- Commodity Division
- Options Sales

To support the income-producing department and as an adjunct to it, the firm will have the following departments:

- The Research Department
- The Trading Department
- Exchange Floor Department
- OTC Trading Department
- Bond Trading Department
- Options Trading Department

Detailed explanations of each of these departments are made in other chapters of this book.

The Operations Department

The second division in a brokerage firm is the Operations or the "Back Office" Department. The organization of the operations area depends upon the firm's activities, methods used for electronic data processing, and general bookkeeping functions. There are many divisions and sections assigned for specific functions. Although this is the non-income-producing area of the firm, experience has shown that it is one of the most important. Its main purpose is to provide service to the firm's customers. It maintains the record keeping and paperwork to handle customer's securities and cash and establishes credit requirements. Additionally it handles order room, purchase and sales functions, cashiering activities, internal controls, and so forth.

The following are the various segments of the Operations Department:

The Order Room

The main function of this department is to process the paperwork necessary to execute an order. It can be subdivided into other units such as corporate bond orders, NYSE orders, Amex orders, OTC orders, round-lots, odd-lots and so forth. The staff in this department receives orders and directs them to the appropriate market for execution.

The Purchase & Sales Department

After the order is executed, data is sent to the Purchase & Sales Department for computation, matching, and comparison. All transactions are verified with the contra-brokers and clearing corporations, and advisory notices are presented to the Cashiers Department for the eventual settlement of the transaction.

The Cashiers Department

This department prepares the certificates for delivery in accordance with instructions received from the Purchase and Sales Department. If the transaction is a purchase, the cashiers will accept the security delivered by the selling broker. The department is the custodian of all securities; and its activities are geared to the proper safeguarding, record keeping, adequate controls, and movement of these securities. The staff prepares certificates for transfer of title; processes securities for tender offers, subscriptions, redemptions; handles the disbursement and receipt of checks; and performs other financial activities for the firm and its customers.

The Customer Credit Department

The Customer Credit Department, popularly known as the "Margin Department," oversees the customer's activities. The staff checks the customer's transactions, the debits, the credits, longs, shorts, standing instructions, and so forth. It complies with various statutes and regulations with respect to proper segregation of customers' securities and extension of credit to customers.

The New Accounts Department

Data of all new accounts are presented to the New Accounts Department for processing. The staff checks the accuracy of the documents submitted with the new account card and assigns numbers for each customer.

The Electronic Data Processing Department

All records are submitted to the firm's computers for processing. A firm may have computers on its premises or be a subscriber to a service organization. In either case, data is submitted from the Order Room, P & S, Cashiers, Margin, and other operating divisions to generate various data, statements, and management reports.

The Commodity Department

Like the Customer Credit Department, the staff in the Commodity Department supervises commodity transactions, vis-a-vis various rules and regulations in this field.

The Accounting Department

This department is charged with general accounting and record keeping functions in conjunction with financial reporting. All financial data is submitted to the Accounting Department, and it is the staff's responsibility to record and interpret the data and present meaningful reports to management.

Internal Audit & Compliance Department

The main purpose of this department is to safeguard the firm from fraudulent activities; maintain audit controls on all procedures; prevent violations of rules, regulations and firm policies; and supervise the activities of the firm's personnel.

In addition to these departments, the non-income-producing area will also include the Personnel Department, the Communications Department, the Mail Room, the Purchasing Department, and the Payroll Section.

The following chapters will cover a more detailed examination of all the facets of these operating departments.

EMPLOYMENT REQUIREMENTS

Employment practices in the securities business are governed by various rules, particularly the statutes of the state where the organization conducts its business. All employees are subject to a thorough background investigation. In filing an application for employment, an applicant must disclose full information with regard to his background, medical history, education, citizenship, and so forth. It is the requirement of certain states (New York is one of them) and the SEC that employees be fingerprinted, and the prints examined by the Attorney General's office. Particular attention is given to employees hired for sensitive areas, such as the Cashier's Department.

The securities firm must maintain a file of every employee during his employment and for a minimum period of three years after his termination.

The New York Stock Exchange may disapprove the employment of any person if the Exchange has determined that the employee has violated any provision of the Exchange Constitution and rules and has acted in detriment to the interest or welfare of the Exchange. It may fine, censor, or revoke his registration.

After his employment, the employee continues to be under the scrutiny of his employer. The Exchange must be notified whenever an employee of a member organization is arrested, indicted, convicted, is being investigated by a regulatory agency, or has violated the Exchange Constitution and rules.

THE INVESTOR AND THE MARKETPLACE

There are basically two types of investors: retail and institutional. They both enter the securities market with the hope to make a profit or preserve their investments based on their objectives and particular needs.

The institutional investors are investment companies, pension funds, insurance companies, trust companies, trust accounts, and so on. They generally trade in blocks of securities.

The marketplace has several types of agents that serve these investors:

1. *Brokers.* Brokers act as agents between the seller and the buyer. They earn a commission in offering their services and are responsible to execute orders properly, maintain records, and provide investment services to their customers. The regulatory authorities have strict regulations regarding the broker's business conduct. They require him to have intricate knowledge of all phases of the securities industry; skill in the elements of securities marketing, finance, and market analysis; and above all, ethical and irreproachable conduct.

2. *Dealers.* Dealers also act as agents, but they don't repre-

sent buyers and sellers. As principals, they purchase securities for their own inventory and sell them to customers hopefully at a higher price. Dealers are not allowed to charge a commission for the trade. The difference in money between the cost of purchase and the sale will be their profit or loss. They may act as market makers of a security or a group of securities.

3. *Investment Adviser.* The investment adviser also acts as an agent for the investor. His role is to make recommendations of what securities to purchase or sell and the type of broker the investor must select.

4. *Custodian Bank.* The custodian bank acts as the safe-keeper of securities for the investor. It may occasionally buy and sell securities for the account of the investor. It is responsible for maintaining the investor's accounts properly and forwarding corporate mailings and reports on a timely basis.

CHAPTER ELEVEN

CUSTOMER ACCOUNT SUPERVISION

In opening a new account, the account executive's most important consideration is to know his customer. The New York Stock Exchange Rule 405, the American Stock Exchange Rule 411, and Sections 2 and 21 of the NASD's Rules of Fair Practice place specific requirements for the account executive to apply due diligence and gather essential facts on the customer's background upon initiation of the account.

Certain forms and procedural requirements aid the account executive in this task. The account forms executed by the customer must be signed by the account executive and approved by the branch manager of the brokerage firm.

The account forms call for all the pertinent information on the customer's background — name, address, Social Security number, occupation, financial status, bank and credit references, investment objectives, and so on. Care must be exercised to ascertain whether the customer is suitable for the type of investment he is proposing. The account will be denied if the branch manager feels that the customer is unsuitable for a specific trading practice or type of security. No customer accounts will be accepted in jurisdictions where the account executive does not have a currently effective registration license, even if the securities firm is licensed to conduct business in that jurisdiction.

The initial transaction of a new account must be approved by the branch manager before it is sent to the order room for execution.

INFORMATION NECESSARY TO OPEN AN ACCOUNT

The Legal Name of the Customer

The account form must have the full legal given name of the customer. If the customer wishes to open a numbered account or an account with a code name, he must submit a special authorization to that effect. The authorization will disclose the full identity of the account and must be kept in a permanent file at the securities firm. The broker must never use initials or nicknames. If the customer wishes to use initials, such as "W.T. Jones," the broker must receive a certification from him to that effect. The broker must remove all honorary and professional titles from the title of the account, and use acceptable abbreviations in describing ownership.

Address

The account executive must obtain the permanent address of the customer. An address containing only a post office box number may not be accepted. A post office box number may be used for mailing purposes only. In the event of a trip or vacation, the customer may instruct the account executive to hold the mail for up to two months for domestic travel and three months for foreign trips.

Telephone Numbers

The account form must include the customer's business and home telephone numbers.

Social Security Number

It is a federal requirement for securities firms to obtain the customer's Social Security or tax identification number. The number is used to mail notification to the Internal Revenue Service regarding dividends, interest, and sales of securities. The customer must give his Social Security number or tax identification number, as required by the Currency and Foreign Transactions Act and Tax Equity and Fiscal Responsibility Act (TEFRA). For custodian accounts, the broker must obtain the minor's Social Security number — not the custodian's. For foreign accounts, he must have the foreign tax identification number of the customer.

Occupation

The account executive must know his customer's occupation. Investment objectives are generally based on the customer's income level. From a regulatory standpoint, customers associated with various financial institutions require approval from their employers before opening a brokerage account at a securities firm.

1. Employees or officers of brokerage firms wishing to open accounts at a securities firm must receive approval from their employer. Copies of trade confirmations and statements will be forwarded to the customer's employer.

2. Employees of securities exchanges and affiliated companies must obtain prior approval from the exchange before opening accounts at a securities firm.

3. Employees of banks, trust companies, insurance companies, and other financial institutions must obtain prior approval from their employers to open a margin account at a securities firm. Cash accounts are acceptable without approval.

4. Employees of the securities firm must receive approval of their branch or division manager before opening an account.

5. The aforementioned restrictions are also directed to the spouses of the employees. Exceptions are made in the event of a legal separation. The account executive must receive a certification to the effect that the employee has no financial interest in the account of his spouse.

Citizenship

The account form must disclose the customer's nationality. Certain U.S. corporations restrict or forbid ownership of their securities by foreign nationals, and U.S. citizens are not eligible to purchase foreign securities that have not met the SEC registration requirements.

Age

The account executive must know the age of his customer. Minors are not allowed to make securities transactions or have direct ownership of securities. The age of majority varies from state to state. The statute of the customer's state of domicile must be examined to ascertain the state's definition of an "adult." Exceptions are made when a court order has emancipated the minor and considers him an adult, or when a judge has certified the minor as a head of household.

Bank and Credit References

The security firm must verify the customer's bank and credit references before accepting the account.

Account Referral

The account form must indicate the manner in which the customer was introduced to the account executive. If the person is a "walk-in" customer, a thorough investigation must be conducted before approving the account.

Agents and Fiduciaries

Verification of the agent's or fiduciary's authority must be done through examination of the required documents.

Discretionary Accounts

In opening a discretionary account, the customer authorizes the account executive to buy or sell securities in his account at the account executive's discretion. The discretionary accounts require special handling and treatment. The securities firm requires an authorization form to be signed by the customer. This form must be kept in a permanent file for at least six years after the account has been closed.

WHAT TO DO WHEN THE CUSTOMER IS
REPORTED TO HAVE PASSED AWAY

Upon notification that the customer is deceased, the account executive:

1. Must cancel all open orders and instructions from the customer.
2. Must change the title of the account to read "Estate of John Brown."
3. Request the necessary documents to establish the authority of the legal representative of the estate.

TYPES OF ACCOUNTS

The following is an alphabetical listing of different types of securities accounts. The abbreviations used to describe the title of the account are the acceptable abbreviations in the securities industry. For the interest of uniformity, care must be exercised to open the account by using these standardized formats:

Administrator of Estate

Title of the account:
"John Brown ADM EST Mary Brown."

Documents required:

Cash Account
1. A new account form.
2. A certificate of appointment of administrator or letters of administration evidencing the appointment of the administrator.

Margin Account: Not permissible. Fiduciaries are generally not allowed to trade securities on margin.

Administrator of Estate with Will Annexed

Title of the account:
"John Brown ADM CTA EST Mary Brown."

Documents required:

Cash Account
1. A new account form.
2. A certificate of appointment of administrator.

Margin Account: Not permissible.

Administrator (Successor) of Estate with Will Annexed

Title of the account:
"John Brown ADM CTA EST Mary Brown."

Documents required:

Cash Account
1. A new account form.
2. Certificate of appointment of administrator.

Margin Account: Not permissible.

Administrator (Special) of Estate

Title of the account:
"John Brown SPL ADM EST Mary Brown."

Documents required:

Cash Account
1. A new account form.
2. Certificate of appointment of administrator.

Margin Account: Not permissible.

Administrator (Temporary) of Estate

Title of the account:
"John Brown TEMP ADM EST Mary Brown."

Documents required:

Cash Account
1. A new account form.
2. Certificate of appointment of administrator.

> *Margin Account:* Not permissible.

Association (Unincorporated)

Title of the account:
"ABC Association."

Documents required:

Cash Account
1. A new account form.
2. Trading authorization granting authority to one of the officers or a member to effect securities transactions in behalf of the association.

> *Margin Account:* In addition to the documents mentioned above, the following are required:

1. Customer's agreement.
2. Loan consent agreement.
3. Credit agreement.
4. Bylaws authorizing the association to deal in margin trading.

Bank

Title of the account:
"City National Bank."

Documents required:

Cash Account

1. A new account form.
2. Trading authorization granting authority to certain officers of the bank to deal in securities transactions.
3. Corporate resolutions and/or bylaws.

> *Margin Account:* In addition to the documents mentioned above, the following are required:

1. Customer's agreement.
2. Loan consent agreement.
3. Credit agreement.
4. Bylaws authorizing the bank to engage in margin trading.

Bank as a Fiduciary with an Individual in a Testamentary Trust

Title of the account:
"City National Bank and John Brown TR UW Mary Brown."

Documents required:

Cash Account

1. A new account form.
2. A certificate of appointment of trustee or letters of trusteeship.
3. Trading authorization granting authority to bank officers to act in behalf of the trust.

> *Margin Account:* Not permissible for fiduciaries unless the will creating the trust specifically authorizes the trustee to engage in margin trading.

Church

Title of the account:
"The First Presbyterian Church."

Documents required:

Cash Account

1. A new account form.
2. Trading authorization executed by the board of trustees or the governing body of the church. It may also be signed by the bishop or the rector if they are empowered to do so.

> *Margin Account:* In addition to the documents mentioned above, the following are required:

1. Customer's agreement.
2. Loan consent agreement.
3. Credit agreement.
4. Bylaws authorizing the church to engage in margin trading.

College and Schools

Title of the account:
"Dartmouth College."

Documents required:

Cash Account

1. A new account form.
2. Trading authorization signed by the board of trustees.
3. Bylaws.

> *Margin Account:* In addition to the documents mentioned above, the following are required:

1. Customer's agreement.
2. Loan consent agreement.
3. Credit agreement.
4. Bylaws authorizing the school to deal in margin transactions.

Committee

Title of the account:
"John Brown COMM Mary Brown an Incompetent."

Documents required:

Cash Account
1. A new account form.
2. A certificate of appointment of committee.

> *Margin Account:* Not permissible for a fiduciary.

Community Property

Title of the account:
"John Brown and Mary Brown Community Property."

The words "community property" may not be abbreviated in the account title.

Documents required:

Cash Account
1. A new account form.
2. A community property agreement signed by the parties in the agreement.

> *Margin Account:* In addition to the documents mentioned above, the following are required:

1. Customer's agreement.
2. Loan consent agreement.
3. Credit agreement.

Conservator

Title of the account:
"John Brown CONS Mary Brown."

Documents required:

Cash Account
1. A new account form.
2. Certificate of appointment of conservator or letters of conservatorship.

Margin Account: Not permissible.

Corporation

Title of the account:
"ABC Corp."

Documents required:

Cash Account
1. A new account form.
2. Trading authorization authorizing an officer to act in behalf of the corporation.

> *Margin Account:* In addition to the documents mentioned above, the following are required:

1. Customer's agreement.
2. Loan consent agreement.
3. Credit agreement.
4. Bylaws authorizing the corporation to deal in margin transactions.

Curator

Title of the account:
"John Brown Curator Mary Brown."

Documents required:

Cash Account
1. A new account form.
2. Certificate of appointment of curator.

> *Margin Account:* Not permissible for fiduciaries.

Custodian to a Minor

Title of the account:
"John Brown Cust for Mary Brown, a Minor under Unif Gifts to Min Act (State of Residence)."

Documents required:

Cash Account
1. A new account form.

    Margin Account: Not permissible.

Executor to Estate

Title of the account:
"John Brown EX EST Mary Brown."

Documents required:

Cash Account
1. A new account form.
2. Certificate of appointment of executor or letters testamentary.

    Margin Account: Not permissible.

Foundation

Title of the account:
"John Brown Foundation."

Documents required:

Cash Account
1. A new account form.
2. Trading authorization granting power to an officer to deal in securities transactions in behalf of the foundation.
3. Bylaws.

    Margin Account: In addition to the above documents, the following are required:

1. Customer's agreement.
2. Loan consent agreement.
3. Credit agreement.
4. Bylaws authorizing the foundation to engage in margin trading.

Guardian

Title of the account:
"John Brown GDN Mary Brown, a Minor."

Documents required:

Cash Account
1. A new account form.
2. Certificate of appointment of guardian or letters of guardianship.

   Margin Account: Not permissible.

Independent Executor to Estate

Title of the account:
"John Brown IND EX EST Mary Brown."

Documents required:

Cash Account
1. A new account form.
2. Certificate of appointment of executor.

   Margin Account: Not permissible.

Individual

Title of the account:
"John A. Brown."

The account should have the full legal given name of the customer. For female customers, the account should indicate either Miss or Mrs. The account must be opened as Mrs. Mary Brown and not as Mrs. John Brown.

Documents required:

Cash Account
1. A new account form.

Margin Account: In addition to the above documents, the following are required:

1. Customer's agreement.
2. Loan consent agreement.
3. Credit agreement.

Inter-vivos Trust or Living Trust

Title of the account:
"John Brown TR UA November 10, 1971
MB Mary Brown FBO William Brown."

Documents required:

Cash Account

1. A new account form.
2. Copy of the trust agreement. The full text of the agreement is required and not some excerpts.

Margin Account: In addition to the above documents, the following are required:

1. Customer's agreement.
2. Loan consent agreement.
3. Credit agreement.
4. Trust agreement specifically authorizing the trustee to engage in margin trading.

Investment Club

Investment clubs are not recognized as legal entities. It is advisable to open the account as a partnership, in which case regular partnership account requirements will apply.

Title of the account:
"ABC Investment Club."
(A partnership)

Joint Tenants

Title of the account:
"John Brown and Mary Brown JTTEN."

Documents required:

Cash Account

1. A new account form.
2. Joint tenancy agreement signed by all the tenants.

> *Margin Account:* In addition to the above documents, the following are required:

1. Customer's agreement.
2. Loan consent agreement.
3. Credit agreement.

Life Tenant

Title of the account:
"John Brown LIFE TEN UW Mary Brown."

Documents required:

Cash Account

1. A new account form.
2. The instrument establishing the life tenancy.

> *Margin Account:* Not permissible.

Nominee

Title of the account:
"Brown & Co."

Documents required:

Cash Account

1. A new account form.
2. A certificate establishing the nominee.
3. Bylaws, if applicable.

> *Margin Account:* In addition to the above documents, the following are required:

1. Customer's agreement.
2. Loan consent agreement.
3. Credit agreement.
4. Bylaws authorizing the nominee to deal in margin transactions.

Partnership

Title of the account:
"ABC & Co. (A Partnership)."

Documents required:

Cash Account

1. A new account form.
2. A copy of the partnership agreement.

> *Margin Account:* In addition to the above documents, the following are required:

1. Customer's agreement.
2. Loan consent agreement.
3. Credit agreement.
4. Partnership agreement must specifically authorize the partner to deal in margin trading.

Pension Trust

Title of the account:
"John Brown TR XYZ Corp. Pension
Fund UA November 10, 1971."

Documents required:

Cash Account

1. A new account form.
2. A copy of the pension agreement.

> *Margin Account:* In addition to the above documents, the following are required:

1. Customer's agreement.
2. Loan consent agreement.
3. Credit agreement.
4. The pension agreement must specifically authorize the pension trust to deal in margin transactions.

Pledgee

Title of the account:
"Brown Trust Co. Pledgee UA
John Brown November 10, 1971."

Documents required:

Cash Account
1. A new account form.
2. A copy of the pledgee agreement.

> *Margin Account:* In addition to the above documents, the following are required:

1. Customer's agreement.
2. Loan consent agreement.
3. Credit agreement.
4. A pledgee agreement must specifically authorize margin trading.

Power of Attorney

Title of the account:
"John A. Brown."

The account must be opened in the name of the principal only, with no power of attorney designation in the title of the account.

Documents required:

Cash Account
1. A new account form.
2. A copy of the power of attorney signed by the principal.

Margin Account: In addition to the above documents, the following are required:

1. Customer's agreement.
2. Loan consent agreement.
3. Credit agreement.
4. The power of attorney signed by the principal must specifically authorize the attorney-in-fact to engage in margin trading in behalf of the principal.

Receiver

Title of the account:
"John Brown Receiver XYZ Corp."

Documents required:

Cash Account

1. A new account form.
2. A certificate of appointment of receivership.

Margin Account: Not permissible.

Sole Proprietorship

Title of the account:
"XYZ & CO. (a sole proprietorship)."

Documents required:

Cash Account

1. A new account form.
2. Trading authorization.

Margin Account: In addition to the above documents, the following are required:

1. Customer's agreement.
2. Loan consent agreement.
3. Credit agreement.
4. A trading authorization for opening a margin account.

Tenants in Common

Title of the account:
"John Brown and Mary Brown TEN COM."

Documents required:

Cash Account

1. A new account form.
2. A joint account agreement signed by all the tenants.

   Margin Account: In addition to the above documents, the following are required:

1. Customer's agreement.
2. Loan consent agreement.
3. Credit agreement.

Tenants by Entirety

Title of the account:
"John Brown and Mary Brown TEN ENT."

Documents required:

Cash Account

1. A new account form.

   Margin Account: In addition to the above documents, the following are required:

1. Joint consent agreement.
2. Credit agreement.

Testamentary Guardian

Title of the account:
"John Brown Testamentary GDN Mary Brown."

Documents required:

Cash Account

1. A new account form.
2. Certificate of appointment of guardian.

Margin Account: Not permissible.

Testamentary Trustee

Title of the account:
"John Brown TR UW Mary Brown."

Documents required:

Cash Account

1. A new account form.
2. Certificate of appointment of trustee or letters of trusteeship.

Margin Account: Not permissible.

Trustee in Bankruptcy

Title of the account:
"John Brown TR in Bankruptcy Mary Brown."

Documents required:

Cash Account

1. A new account form.
2. Certificate of appointment of trustee in bankruptcy.

Margin Account: Not permissible.

Usufructuary

A type of joint ownership applicable only in the state of Louisiana.

Title of the account:
"John Brown Usufruct Mary Brown Naked Owner."

Documents required:

Cash Account

1. A new account form.
2. A usufructuary agreement signed by both the usufruct and the naked owner.

   Margin Account: In addition to the above documents, the following are required:

1. Customer's agreement.
2. Loan consent agreement.
3. Credit agreement.

ACCOUNTS OF INVESTMENT ADVISERS

Investment advisers registered with the Securities and Exchange Commission under the Investment Advisers Act of 1940 may open a securities account in behalf of their customers. There are two types of accounts: the special omnibus account and the adviser's client account.

Special Omnibus Account

This is a single account for the investment adviser. Securities transactions are done in this account, and the investment adviser allocates the transactions to his customers.

The required document is a special omnibus account agreement signed by the investment adviser.

Adviser's Client Account

This account is opened on a fully disclosed basis. A separate account is opened and maintained for each customer of the investment adviser. In this case, the securities firm obtains all necessary documents to support the customer's account.

OPTION ACCOUNTS

No branch office shall conduct any options business unless the branch office manager has been qualified as a Registered Options Principal.

No account executive shall transact option trades unless he is qualified to do so. The account executive is qualified if he has passed the NASD options examination.

Individuals who are qualified as registered options representatives or registered option principals will be asked to take the qualification examination when the compliance registered options principal and the senior registered options principal concur that the person in question lacks competence to handle option accounts.

1. All new option accounts must be approved by the branch manager, the registered options principal (ROP), and the senior registered options principal (SROP).

2. A current prospectus of the Options Clearing Corporation must be mailed to the customer at the time of the opening of the account.

3. The option account of all fiduciaries, such as executors, administrators, trustees, and the like, must be approved by the compliance registered options principal (CROP) in addition to the approval by individuals mentioned above.

4. No option account will be opened for entities or associations, such as investment clubs and partnerships, except where written evidence specifically authorizing the entity to do option trading has been obtained.

5. The customer must submit an account agreement to the securities firm within 15 calendar days of the opening of the option account. This written agreement, signed by the customer, will state that the customer is aware of the rules of the Options Clearing Corporation and has received a current OCC prospectus. If the customer fails to submit the account agreement, only closing options transactions will be allowed in his account.

CHAPTER TWELVE

SETTLEMENT OF CONTRACTS

THE PURCHASE AND SALES DEPARTMENT

The primary functions of the Purchase and Sales (P & S) Department are to process, compare, match, and confirm the trade after it is executed either on the floor of the stock exchange or in the over-the-counter market. The P & S Department resolves all the discrepancies of the trade, if there are any, and notifies the Cashiers Department to settle the trade. The P & S Department, therefore, is the midpoint between the Order Room and the rest of the operations division of the securities firm. Without its intervention, the trade remains uncompared, and, therefore, unsuitable for processing by other segments of the securities organization.

Functions

The P & S Department prepares all necessary notices pertaining to the transaction and sends confirmation of the trade to the customer. To verify the accuracy of the trade reports, it delivers and receives statements to and from brokers and the clearing corporations. It is in the P & S Department that the trade is formally entered in the books of the firm and becomes a part of what is known as the Trade Blotters.

In preparing the trade confirmations, the Purchase and Sales Department computes the commission, taxes, and fees (if any), the price of the security, and the net and gross amounts involved. It mails the confirmation of the trade to the customer immediately after the execution of the trade. If the security is listed on a stock exchange, the P & S Department verifies the trade with the contra-broker through the facilities of a clearing corporation. On the day of the trade, it notifies the respective clearing corporation of the transaction data — the number of shares, the name of the security, the name of the contra-broker, the execution price, and so on — and the clearing corporation, in turn, will prepare the contract lists. After receiving the Contract Lists from the clearing corporation, the P & S Department will make all necessary adjustments and present the corrected data to the clearing corporation for final processing.

In the case of a non-NASDAQ, over-the-counter transaction, the selling and buying brokers generally compare and verify the trade directly with each other.

Operation

The overall operation of the P & S Department varies from one firm to another, depending on whether the firm is on a manual operation or utilizes electronic data centers to process trades. In the latter case, computers do the issuance and maintenance of the ledgers. The operation also depends upon the size of the firm and the nature of its business activity.

Whether automated or manual, the operation follows this standard pattern:

Trade Day. After the execution of the trade, the Order Room submits the order copy to the P & S Department. The P & S clerk checks the order copy, prepares the figuration if necessary, and sends the confirmation to the customer and the comparison to the contra-broker. The P & S clerk also prepares the Exchange Ticket for the clearing corporation and the Trade Day Blotters.

Trade Day Plus One. On the business day following the trade day, the P & S clerk receives the floor report and compares it with the order copy. He makes the necessary adjustments on the Trade Day Blotters and delivers the Exchange Tickets to the clearing corporation.

Trade Day Plus Two. On the second business day after the trade day, the P & S clerk receives the contra-broker's comparisons. He compares and reconciles them with the firm's blotters.

Trade Day Plus Three. On this day the P & S Department receives the P & S contract sheets from the clearing corporation. The list summarizes the trades in the following categories:

- Matched trades. This means the information submitted to the clearing corporation by both selling and buying brokers are matched. Both brokers had submitted identical information.
- Uncompared and Advisory trades. This means one of the brokers had failed to submit an Exchange Ticket to the clearing corporation or had submitted erroneous data.

After receiving the Purchase and Sale contract sheets, the P & S clerk reconciles and adjusts all discrepancies, and submits corrected information to the clearing corporation.

Trade Day Plus Four. On this day, the clearing corporation sends the respective brokers the Delivery Lists and Receive Lists. The selling broker is instructed to deliver the security and the buying broker is instructed to receive the security.

Trade Day Plus Five. The P & S Department has done its job. Now it is up to the Cashiers Department to settle the transaction by delivering or receiving the securities in question.

OVER-THE-COUNTER TRANSACTIONS

Over-the-counter transactions between brokers not participating in a clearing facility are settled on a trade-by-trade basis. Each trade becomes a contract in itself, and the brokers will receive and deliver securities against payment without the intervention of a clearing organization. The trades are not paired off.

Each broker will prepare a comparison ticket that states the terms of the transaction and will send it to the contra-broker no later than the business day following the trade date. The contra-broker will sign the comparison ticket, agreeing to the terms of the contract, and return it to the sender prior to the settlement date of the transaction.

This method, also known as "Window Settlement," is done infrequently as more firms seek the aid of the clearing corporation to settle their transactions.

PREPARATION OF THE CONFIRMATION TICKET

The confirmation tickets sent to customers are prepared by the P & S Department immediately after the execution of the trade. The confirmation ticket will indicate the following information:

1. Name and amount of security.
2. Sold or purchased.
3. Whether the firm had acted as a principal or an agent in the transaction.
4. The trade date and the settlement date. The date and time of execution must be disclosed or furnished on request.
5. CUSIP.
6. Customer's account number.
7. Name of customer.
8. Name of the account executive.
9. Commissions. (No commissions will be charged if the firm had acted as a principal in the trade.)
10. The ticket must disclose whether the broker had acted as a principal or as broker–agent. If the broker had acted as a principal, the ticket must disclose the amount of any mark-up or mark-down.
11. Any odd-lot differential must be indicated on the ticket.
12. The confirmation ticket must disclose if there is any control relationship between the brokerage organization and the issuing corporation of the security.
13. For new issues, the ticket must disclose whether the firm is part of the underwriting or the selling team.
14. Stock transfer taxes and SEC fees, paid by the seller.
15. For bond transactions, the yield and the dollar price must be disclosed. If the trade is made on the basis of the dollar price, the confirmation ticket must disclose the price and the lowest of the following figures:
    a. Yield to premium call
    b. Yield to par option
    c. Yield to maturity

For trades made on yield basis, the ticket must indicate the yield and the lowest of the following figures:
    a. Price to premium call
    b. Price to par option
    c. Price to maturity

In addition, the option or the redemption date and the price used in the calculation must be disclosed.

For trades made at par, the confirmation ticket discloses the dollar price.

16. For bond transactions, the ticket must disclose the *dated date* and the first interest payment date; and whether the bond is in bearer form, registered form, or registered as principal only.
17. If the bond is called or pre-refunded, the date and the amount must be disclosed.
18. For callable securities, the confirmation ticket must disclose the fact that the yield may be affected by the call provision.
19. The ticket must show any specific qualifications of the security such as "flat" or default.
20. Accrued interest on bonds, if any.

The customer is required to make prompt payment to the broker on all purchases even if he has not yet received a confirmation ticket. Any information about the trade requested by the customer must be sent within five business days for new trades or within 15 business days for trades 30 days or older.

Delivery of Confirmations

The broker to broker comparisons must be delivered on the trade date or the day after.

Customer confirmations must be sent on the trade day as required by SEC Rule 10b-10.

The SEC Fee

The SEC registration fee is charged to the selling customer on all equity securities listed on stock exchanges except for the following transactions:

1. Sale of a stock through a prospectus
2. Sale of a stock through a private placement
3. Sale of a stock through a tender or an exchange offer
4. The exercise of warrants and rights

5. Conversion of securities

6. Trades executed outside the United States

The broker will charge the SEC fee even if the trade of the security listed on the stock exchange is executed on the over-the-counter market.

No SEC fees are charged for bond transactions.

Accrued Interest on Bonds

For most bond transactions, the confirmation ticket must also indicate the accrued interest on the bond. The buying customer must give accrued interest to the selling customer on the settlement date. It is an expense to the buyer that will be added to the proceeds of the sale. This expense is only temporary, however, because the buyer will eventually receive the interest from the issuer on the interest payable date.

The following bond transactions will not carry accrued interests:

1. Income bonds

2. Bonds in default status

3. Transactions in municipal and corporate bonds executed five business days prior to an interest record date

Bonds generally pay interest to the bondholders every six months on a designated date. The interest payment will cover the last six-month period. Therefore, if a person sells a bond during a six-month period, the new buyer will receive the full interest from the issuer on the following payment date. But since the new buyer was not the owner of the bond during the entire period of the previous six months, part of that interest belongs to the seller. In anticipation of his receiving the full interest, the buyer must give the seller a portion of that interest on the trade settlement date. This may be illustrated by the following example:

1. Customer A sells $1,000 Bee Corp. 6 percent 1/1/2000 to customer B on settlement date, Oct 19.

2. Bee Corp. pays 6 percent interest on January 1 and July 1 as indicated by the maturity date of the bond.

3. The bondholder will, therefore, receive 6 percent of $1,000 every year in two installments — $30 in January and $30 in July.

4. On January 1 following this trade, the new buyer will receive $30 in interest from the issuing corporation.

5. This $30 interest covers the last six-month period, but due to the fact that he was not the owner of the security during the entire period of time, part of the $30 interest belongs to the seller representing the period of his ownership.

6. The buyer, therefore, must give the seller a portion of the interest payment. This portion is called the accrued interest.

Calculation of Accrued Interest

For corporate and municipal bonds, the accrued interest is calculated on the basis of 30 calendar days in each month. The seller will receive accrued interest calculated from the last day that he received his last interest check until the day of the settlement of the trade, but not including the day of settlement. In the above example, the customer sells $1,000 Bee Corp. 6 percent 1/1/2000 on Oct. 19. The last time he received his interest check from the issuer was July 1. Therefore, July has 30 days, August has 30 days, September has 30 days, and October in this example has 18 days, up to but not including the day of settlement. Altogether, therefore, the seller must receive from the buyer accrued interest on the basis of 108 days.

The formula for calculating interest is:

$$\text{Interest} = \text{Principal} \times \frac{\text{Rate}}{100} \times \frac{\text{Time}}{360}$$

$$\left(1 = P \times \frac{R}{100} \times \frac{T}{360}\right)$$

In this example:

$$I = 1,000 \times \frac{6}{100} \times \frac{108}{360} = \$18.00$$

This amount is due the seller and will be charged to the buyer as part of his cost.

If the transaction was for a cash trade, the accrued interest will again be calculated in the same way. In this case, the settlement date of the trade will be the day of the trade. Therefore, the calculation will be from the last day the seller received his interest check until the day of the settlement (which is the trade day), but not including the day of settlement.

For U.S. government obligations, the accrued interest is calculated not on the basis of 30 days each month, but rather on the basis of the actual days of the actual months involved: 365 days in a regular year or 366 days in a leap year.

EXAMPLE:

The customer sells $1,000 U.S. Treasury Bond 6 percent 1/1/2000 on Oct. 19 (settlement date).

This bond pays interest every January 1 and July 1.

The accrued interest will be calculated on the basis of the *actual* days from the last time the seller received his interest check until the day of the settlement of the trade, but not including the day of settlement.

> July has 31 days
> August has 31 days
> September has 30 days
> October has 18 days
> Total = 110 days

For greater accuracy, the following formula is used for U.S. government obligations.

$$I = P \times \frac{R}{2} \times \frac{1}{100} \times \frac{T}{181} \text{ for regular year, and}$$

$$I = P \times \frac{R}{2} \times \frac{1}{100} \times \frac{T}{182} \text{ for leap year.}$$

For the above trade, the accrued interest that the seller would receive:

$$I = 1,000 \times \frac{6}{2} \times \frac{1}{100} \times \frac{110}{181} = \$10.93$$

The following table may be used for settlement dates of various securities:

SETTLEMENT DATES

Type of Security	Cash Trade	Regular Way Trade	Seller's Option
Stocks Corporate bonds Municipal bonds ADRs	T	T + 5	8–60 Calendar days
U.S. government and federal agency securities	T	T + 1	2–60 Calendar days
Commercial papers Certificates of deposit Bankers' Acceptances	T	T + 1	None
Options and futures contract	T	T + 1	None
Repurchase agreements	T	T	None
Eurodollar instruments	No set time	No set time	No set time

T denotes trade date

If the corporate bond is sold five business days before the interest record date, the seller will get the full six months of interest and his confirmation ticket will indicate the interest as "flat."

EXAMPLE:

The customer sells $1,000 Bee Corp. 6 percent 1/1/2000 on June 24. The settlement date will be July 1, which is also the interest payable date. Using the above formula, the accrued interest calculation will be:

January = 30 days
February = 30 days
March   = 30 days
April   = 30 days
May   = 30 days
June   = 30 days (up to but not including the
                   settlement date)
         180 days of interest

This is the full six months (half of 360 days a year). No accrued interest will be credited to the seller's account. He will receive his full interest check directly from the issuer.

If the maturity date of the bond is 1/15/2000, the month of January will have 16 days for accrued interest calculation purposes. In this example, if the customer sells the bond on March 20, the settlement date, he will receive accrued interest from the buyer calculated on the basis of 65 days — January has 16 days, February, 30, and March, 19.

Other Functions

In addition to these functions, the P & S Department is also responsible for monitoring the floor brokerage commissions. These are commissions owed to Specialists for transacting business or to Two-Dollar brokers for executing orders on behalf of the firm. They also include commissions payable or receivable resulting from give-ups.

The utilization of electronic equipment is becoming increasingly important in brokerage organizations where the economics of cost and the necessity to process trades within a limited time schedule are replacing manpower with machines. The trend is toward automation with computerized floor operation, floor reports, more reliance on technological devices and less reliance on messengers carrying trade tickets from the exchange to the Order Room and the P & S Department. In most firms, the electronic data processing department has taken over most of the functions of the P & S Department.

Customer Statements

Active customers must receive statements at least quarterly. The customer may request the broker to hold the mail for a maximum of two months if he is traveling within the states and for three months for foreign travel. Customer statements may never be mailed to the account executive.

CHAPTER THIRTEEN

SECURITIES PROCESSING

THE CASHIERS DEPARTMENT

The Cashiers Department, also called the Securities Cage, plays an important role in the organization of a securities firm. As its name suggests, its role is financial. It maintains the financial records and is responsible for the movement of securities. Fundamental to its operation are these functions: delivery of securities and checks to brokers and customers and receipt of securities and checks from brokers and customers. Around these rather simple facets, there exists a chain of complex practices and procedures governed by stringent rules and regulations.

The department is the center of activity. After being notified of a transaction by the Purchase and Sales Department, it sets its mechanism in motion to settle the trade. On the settlement date, it has to either receive the security from the selling broker and pay out the money or deliver the security to the buying broker versus payment.

The department usually consists of 10 sections that are all interrelated. The division of responsibilities and the number of different sections and units depend upon the size of the firm and its business activity.

Box and Vault

This is the focal point of all the traffic of securities. It is a central depot of fungible certificates grouped in accordance with the mode of operation of the firm. Generally, the securities are filed in alphabetical order in a box container, and clerks known as "box persons" are responsible for a segment of the alphabet. All types of delivery instructions originating from the Margin, Purchase and Sales, or Dividend Departments are forwarded to this section. The section operates on instructions from another department.

The vault of the firm is also located in this section. It contains securities registered in the name of the firm and held for its customers and securities registered in the name of the customer.

At the time of the purchase, the customer may give one of the following instructions to his broker:

a. Deliver the security to the customer's bank against a predetermined amount of money, which is usually the purchase price. This is known as COD or DVP.

b. Transfer the security in the name of the customer and deliver it to him.

c. Transfer the security in the name of the customer and hold the security in the firm's vault for the customer.

d. Leave the security in "Street" name for the customer.

After being instructed by the registered representative, the Margin Department issues the appropriate instruction and submits it to the Box and Vault section. To deliver the security to the customer's bank, the box person matches the certificate with the instruction and forwards it to the Receive and Deliver section of the Cashiers Department for processing. The movement of the security is properly recorded, and the Stock Record is updated by the data processing center. Under Rule 387 of the New York Stock Exchange and similar rules of other exchanges and the NASD, all COD or DVP deliveries must be made through a book-entry system of a depository if the security is eligible at the depository and if the receiving and delivery institutions are members of the depository. If the instruction is to register the security in the name of the customer, the box person matches a certificate with a transfer instruction and delivers it to the Transfer section. The brokerage firm does not issue or register certificates. The primary function for the Transfer section is to prepare the certificate for transfer. The registration and issuance of new certificates is made by the transfer agent.

Another type of instruction is to transfer the shares and hold the certificate. This custodial arrangement is common in the financial community and is done for several reasons: the customer wants to sell the stock within a short period of time and tries to avoid the redelivery of the certificate; the customer has some sort of indebtedness to the firm and the Margin Department is instructed to hold the certificate until payment is received; or the customer simply wants the security registered in his name and held at the brokerage firm.

The fourth type of instruction involves all the intricacies of a brokerage operation. Leaving the securities in "Street" name entails a series of procedures, record keeping, and maintenance. After making the payment for the purchase, the customer instructs his broker to leave the certificate in "Street" name. The word "Street" denotes the financial district in New York. The practice is to have certificates endorsed in blank by the registered owner, fully negotiable and fungible in nature with appropriate certifications and guarantees, ready to be used for delivery to fulfill brokerage commitments without the necessity of transfer. This is a requirement for margin accounts where securities of this nature are collateralized for bank loan purposes. Certificates in "Street" name may be used as many times as desired until a final transfer into the name of a bona fide purchaser is accomplished.

In safeguarding these securities, the Box and Vault section is charged with a custodial responsibility. It makes certain that the fully-paid-for securities held in "Street" name are properly segregated and not used for brokerage purposes. The same is true, of course, for the securities registered in the name of customers and held in the vault. These securities, too, are segregated from normal operational procedures. The requirements of the securities exchanges and the regulatory agencies are stringent with respect to these practices and procedures at the brokerage firm. They call for strict control of these certificates, proper record keeping, and tight maintenance. As discussed above, instructions are originated from the Margin Department. The Cashiers Department is not authorized to use the securities held in segregation without the express approval of the Margin Department.

Segregation Control

This is a rather small section in the Cashiers Department. Its primary function is to control the segregation of securities. The segregation clerk approves the removal of the certificate from segregation when it is accompanied by a release of segregation instructions from the Margin Department. He plays the role of a watchdog to see that the segregation procedures are within the rules of the regulatory bodies and that record keeping and the security movements are in compliance with those rules.

Within the purview of the rules, there are two methods in segregating securities. The first is the Individual Identification System in which certificates are properly identified as to the name and the account number of the customer. The Margin clerk places the certificates in segregation if the security is wholly owned by the customer or places that portion of securities in a margin account that is in excess of the amount necessary to collateralize a debit balance. When conditions are reversed, the Margin clerk submits instructions to release the security from segregation. Under the Individual Identification System, the certificates are placed in separate envelopes bearing the name of the customer or are identified by attaching tags or labels to the certificates with the name or the account number of the customer. The envelope or the tag will also bear the date of entry into segregation.

The second and more popular method of segregating securities is the Bulk System. The segregated shares do not bear identification tags and are not placed in envelopes. In fact, certificates in "Street" name are filed in alphabetical order without any sort of identification. The control of segregation and safeguarding of securities is accomplished by means of cards indicating the total number of shares of a particular stock in segregation. This method is again controlled by the Margin clerk who issues instructions to segregate and to release. The modern method of bulk segregation has replaced the cards with security listings published by the data processing department and updated daily.

In most of the brokerage offices, the EDP listings are used extensively to determine securities allotments for purposes of segregation and to establish excess security positions. The listing, in a summary form, is a by-product of the stock record and indicates various house accounts with security positions and their interrelations. Analyzing one position at a time, the listing reflects the amount of shares deposited in each house account. It indicates the number of shares deposited in the Box and Vault accounts at various depositories and presented for transfer into the firm's name, various in-transit accounts, and shares deposited in the branches. All these are properly identified by house account numbers representing the total amount of shares of a given stock available on a given day. The EDP listing also will indicate the amount of shares segregated by instructions from the Margin Department. By simple arithmetic, the segregated amount is subtracted from the total amount of shares, indicating the amount considered as excess. These excess shares are derived principally from margin accounts in which the firm is financing the customer's indebtedness. The securities firm may use these excess securities at its discretion for purposes deemed necessary for the conduct of its business.

The daily segregation listing also reflects various brokerage commitments or anticipated receipts from brokers and customers. It shows the amount of shares in Fail To Deliver, Fail To Receive, Stock Borrow, Stock Loan, Bank Loan As Collateral, Customer Short Sales, Firm Short Sales, Customer Fail To Receive, and so on. These are shown for informational purposes to enable the box person to use the excess shares as advantageously as possible or to remedy a deficit condition, by either borrowing or recalling from Stock Loan and Bank Loan.

Under the Bulk method, the listing is an important tool for the Cashiers Department. It provides the necessary controls in security movements and a daily report of segregation requirements.

SEG LISTING

Vault	Box	DTC	TFR	Branches	In Transit	SEG	Excess	Deficit	FD
100	200	300	0	100	100	500	300		100

FR	SL	SB	BL	CFR	Suspense A/C
100	200	0	100	100	50

SEC Rule 15c 3-3 on Segregation

To provide protection for customer funds and securities deposited with a brokerage firm, the Securities and Exchange Commission adopted Rule 15c 3-3, effective January 15, 1973.

The Rule was adopted under the Securities Exchange Act of 1934. Its origin goes back to the Securities Investors Protection Act of 1970 when Congress issued directives to the SEC to adopt rules for the protection of customer funds and securities.

The rules cite specific instructions to the securities firm as to its mode of operation with respect to customers' assets. It tries to accomplish, with the use of a formula, the following objectives:

1. To ensure that the customers' free credit balances and the funds realized through the use of the customers' securities are retained in safe areas or held in a reserve bank account.

2. To ensure that the fully-paid-for securities are accounted for by the broker and that they are in the broker's possession and control.

3. To separate the brokerage operation from the firm's trading and underwriting operations.

4. To ensure that the brokers' records are maintained on a current basis.

5. To ensure that the processing of securities is done in an expeditious manner.

6. To prohibit the use of customer funds except for designated purposes.

7. To broaden the broker's financial responsibility.

8. To protect the customers' assets in the case of a brokerage liquidation.

The rule provides regulatory safeguards over customers' assets, and its operation is carefully monitored by the SEC. The following is the operation of Rule 15c 3-3 and its principal highlights:

1. Once a week, the broker (preferably a responsible person in the Controllers Department) must compute the SEC formula specified in this rule and determine whether or not monies must be deposited in the "Special Reserve Bank Account for the Exclusive Benefit of Customers." The computation is done as of the close of business on Friday night. Deposits into the account must be made not later than 10:00 o'clock the following Tuesday morning.

2. Under the rule, the broker's proper maintenance of the "Reserve Bank Account" is important. The bank in which the account is held must be cognizant of the fact that cash and/or qualified securities deposited in the account are for the exclusive benefit of the customer. The broker may make withdrawals from the account provided that it is in conformity and compliance with the rule.

3. The broker must maintain the physical possession or control of all fully paid for and excess margin securities for the account of customers.

The word "control" has a specific definition, and the SEC has determined the following to be acceptable control locations for securities:

a. Securities that are in a clearing corporation or depository

b. Securities in special omnibus account held by another broker

c. Securities at the transfer agent

d. Securities held at foreign banks or depositories acceptable to the SEC

e. Securities in transit between offices of the broker

4. In order to reduce the number of securities in his possession and control, the broker must make daily determination of fully paid for and excess margin securities. If these securities are being used as collateral for bank loans, the broker should recall them or substitute them with other securities within two business days. If these securities are being used for stock loan purposes, they must be recalled within five business days.

If these securities are in "Fail to Receive" from another broker past the prescribed number of days, the broker must close out the contract through the normal buy-in procedures. The same is true for securities receivable by the broker as stock dividends, stock splits, and so on.

5. All records pertaining to the computation of the formula or the broker's action with respect to the possession and control of fully-paid-for securities must be maintained properly for examination by the SEC. These records, depending on the area of activity, are kept in the Cashiers, Stock Record or Accounting Departments.

6. The rule provides some latitude for the broker–dealer to seek an extension of time in which he is required to buy-in securities for various reasons. Applications for extensions are made to the appropriate regulatory agency.

THE STOCK TRANSFER SECTION

Processing securities for transfer is done by stock transfer personnel. As noted above, the brokerage office does not effect registration and issuance of certificates; they merely process the items by affixing the necessary certifications and guarantees and submitting them to the transfer agents.

The conveyance of securities to and from transfer agents is generally done through the facilities of a clearing corporation where items transferable to one agent are grouped together and delivered to the agent via the service. Various practices at the brokerage level control the movement of these securities. In New York, items submitted for transfer generally are accompanied by a brokers-originated ticket, a copy of which is retained by the transfer section. Copies of the transfer instructions are also kept until the item is returned from the transfer agent and is registered in the requested name.

In general, the transfer section performs two principal functions:

a. It provides a financial service to the customer in requesting security registrations evidencing his proportionate ownership in the corporation.

b. By the use of documents, certifications or guarantees, it converts nonnegotiable items into negotiable instruments for delivery.

The movement of certificates in and out of transfer is recorded and updated in the stock record.

Because of the complexities of security transfers, it is customary and a sound business practice to monitor the age of transfer items periodically to alleviate possible irregularities and delays.

REGULAR TRANSFER

Generally items are not placed in transfer into the customer's name until the security is fully paid for. The issuance of the transfer instructions (known as transfer fanfolds) by the Margin Department is done after establishing the fact that the customer has sufficient credit in his account to cover the purchase of the security to be transferred.

The transfer instruction serves many purposes. One of its copies is attached to the certificate and serves as the transfer agent's copy; another may be used to update the stock record; a third may be sent to the Margin Department or the branch office advising as to the status of the item; and the master copy is retained by the transfer section with the numbers of the certificates properly recorded. When the new certificate is received, the clerk matches it with the master copy and proceeds with the instruction, either delivering it to the customer or holding it in safekeeping.

The internal systems and procedures of the brokerage transfer section differ from one house to another. A wire house with heavy transfer activity and serving a large number of retail customers will have different sets of controls and practices with the emphasis on transfers into the customer's name. It is customary to divide the staff into two groups: one to prepare the certificates for transfer and another to process the new certificates received from transfer. This provides audit control. Items transferable at out-of-town locations are handled by still another group that relies largely on regular mail or insured carriers to transport the securities to and from non-local agents.

Fanfolds used in this section are limited in number. They consist largely of forms necessary to process securities for transfer. One of these, the Private Name Fanfold, is either issued manually by the Margin Department or is generated by the computer.

Another form used by the transfer section is the fanfold for securities to be registered in the name of the firm. This is similar to the Private Name Transfer Fanfold. After the certificates are processed and ready to go to the agents, the transfer clerk prepares a window ticket called Brokers Originated Window Ticket (BOWT) to accompany the certificates. This is a three-ply form, one to be retained by the broker and the other two to be submitted with the certificate. When the new certificates are issued, the agent delivers them to the broker with the third copy of the BOWT. This is a standard form used primarily in the New York area.

REGISTRATION OF CERTIFICATES

Registering certificates of stocks and bonds in the name of investors is governed by various rules and statutes.

The following are the requirements for registration:

1. The investor's full legal given name must be used.
2. References such as "Special Account," "Account Number Ten," etc. must be omitted.
3. For fiduciary accounts, the relationship of the fiduciary must be disclosed properly. Example: John Brown EX EST of Mary Brown.
4. For business accounts, the legal status of the business organization must be disclosed. Example: Brown & Co. (A partnership), Brown & Co. (A sole proprietorship) etc.
5. Registering securities in the name of minors, persons since deceased, or fictitious entities is not permissible.

Transfer agents use generally acceptable abbreviations in describing ownership of securities. The following is a list of certificate registrations:

Individuals

1. *John Doe ADM EST Mary Doe.* Used for an administrator for an estate.
2. *John Doe COMM Mary Doe Incompetent.* Used for a person acting as committee for an incompetent person.
3. *John Doe CONS Mary Doe.* Used for a person acting as conservator for another person.
4. *John Doe CUST Mary Doe Under the UNIF GIFTS TO MIN ACT.* Used to describe ownership of a security by a minor under the Uniform Gifts to Minor's Act.
5. *John Doe EX EST Mary Doe.* Used for an executor to an estate.
6. *John Doe GDN Mary Doe a Minor.* Used for a guardian to a minor.
7. *John Doe TR UA Nov. 10, 1984 MB Mary Doe FBO Charles Doe.* Used to describe a living trust or an inter-vivos trust.
8. *John Doe TR Bee Corp. Pension Trust UA Nov. 10, 1984.* Used to describe a pension trust.
9. *John Doe Receiver Bee Corp.* Used for a receiver of a corporation.
10. *John Doe Testamentary GDN Mary Doe UW Charles Doe.* Used for a person acting as guardian under a last will and testament.

11. *John Doe TR UW Mary Doe.* Used for a trustee acting under a last will and testament.

12. *John Doe TR in Bankruptcy Mary Doe.* Used for a trustee in bankruptcy.

Joint Accounts

1. *John Doe and Mary Doe Community Property.* Used to describe a joint account under the community property law acceptable in certain states.

2. *John Doe and Mary Doe JTTEN.* Used to describe a joint tenency with right of survivorship.

3. *John Doe LIFE TEN UW Mary Doe.* Used to describe a life tenancy under a will.

4. *John Doe and Mary Doe TEN COM.* Used to describe a tenancy in common.

5. *John Doe and Mary Doe TEN ENT.* Used to describe a joint account under the tenancy by entirety acceptable in certain states.

6. *John Doe USUFRUCT Mary Doe Naked Owner.* Used to describe a joint ownership under a Usufructuary law adopted by the state of Louisiana.

Business Entities and Associations

1. *Bee Association.* Used for an unincorporated organization.

2. *Bee Corporation or Bee Inc.* For corporate accounts.

3. *Bee Investment Club.*

4. *Bee and Co. (A Partnership).* Used for entities operating under a partnership.

5. *Bee & Co. (A sole proprietorship).* Used for an entity operating as a sole ownership.

6. *Bee & Co.* Used for a nominee name.

THE FUNCTION OF THE TRANSFER AGENT AND REGISTRAR

A corporation will assign a transfer agent to prepare certificates for transfer and to maintain records of ownership. These are generally commercial banks acting on behalf of the corporation in recording the ownership of securities. When the transfer agent receives the security for transfer, the agent will cancel the certificate and issue a new one in the name of the new owner and update the record of ownership. The transfer agent will then send the cancelled certificate and the newly issued certificate to the registrar. The registrar is another agency, usually a commercial bank, designated by the corporation. The registrar's sole function is to make sure that for every cancelled certificate another certificate is issued with the same number of shares. Upon receipt of the cancelled and the new certificate from the transfer agent, the registrar will compare the number of shares and, if satisfied, will validate the issuance of the new certificate. Both the cancelled and the new certificates are then returned to the transfer agent. The transfer agent will keep the cancelled certificate in its archives and will forward the new certificate to the presenter.

A corporation may act as its own transfer agent or may designate several transfer agents around the country. If multiple transfer agents are designated for the same issue, it is important for the corporation to assign one as the principal transfer agent and the others will be the co-agents. The principal transfer agent will distribute financial reports, proxies, and other information to stockholders as directed by the corporation. The co-transfer agents may cancel and issue new certificates but must report all transactions to the principal transfer agent.

TRANSFER OF BONDS

The requirements for transfer of registered bonds are similar to those of stocks. The assignment form of a bond is a "bond power" and the transfer agent is called the "Bond Registrar."

There are no transfer requirements for bearer bonds. These are negotiable instruments with no record of ownership; whoever is the holder of the bond is the owner of the bond.

THE CUSIP NUMBER

The CUSIP Service Bureau of the Standard & Poor's Corp. assigns a unique CUSIP number for each security usually on request. There are over two million CUSIP numbers. They each identify a class of security. If an issuer has three classes of securities, that means there will be three separate CUSIP numbers. CUSIP numbers are accepted by all financial institutions, banks, and stock exchanges; and as such they are valuable tools in processing securities transactions. Short-term securities, such as commercial papers, CDs, and options, do not have CUSIP numbers.

The CUSIP number consists of nine characters in the following manner:

1. The first six digits identify the issuer.
2. The next two digits identify the class of the security. Stocks of the issuer are identified by two numeric digits, and bonds are assigned two alphabetical characters or one alphabetical character and one numeric digit.
3. The last character is the check digit. This will provide a method of checking the accuracy of the numbers transmitted.

THE FINS NUMBER

FINS is an acronym for Financial Industry Numbering System. The FINS number identifies an individual financial institution, such as a bank or a securities firm. The FINS system is administered by the Depository Trust Company.

TRANSFER AGENT TURNAROUND RULES

The SEC Rules 17 Ad-1 through 17 Ad-7 require that transfer agents transfer securities within three business days from the day of receipt. The rules apply to routine transfers only. They do not apply to non-routine transfers. Non-routine transfers are transfer items that require documents or counsel's opinion to transfer tender offers, conversions, reorganizations, redemptions, and exchanges.

Specifically, the SEC rules require transfer agents turnaround within three business days of receipt of at least 90 percent of all routine items for transfer during a month. Transfer agents that fail to comply with the turnaround schedule are required to file with the SEC within 10 business days following the end of the month.

The notice to the SEC must indicate the number of items that the transfer agent failed to turnaround, the reasons for such failures, and the steps taken to prevent a future failure.

The SEC turnaround rules do not apply to transfer agents that receive fewer than 500 items for transfer during any six consecutive months. Open-end redeemable securities, such as mutual funds and CDs, are also exempt from these requirements.

According to these rules, all written inquiries concerning the status of transfer items must be answered by the transfer agent within five business days of the receipt of the inquiry.

The transfer agents also are required to maintain all receipts, logs, and schedules showing the date each routine and non-routine item is received from the presenter.

REQUIREMENTS FOR TRANSFER

Endorsements of Certificates

1. The stockholder must sign his name exactly as it appears on the face of the certificate.

2. The signature may be placed either on the reverse side of the certificate or on a stock power or a bond power.

3. A certificate registered in the names of two or more people is acceptable only if signed by all the stockholders.

4. A certificate registered in the name of a fiduciary, such as a custodian, guardian, or executor, must be endorsed in the capacity of the fiduciary.

5. A certificate registered in the name of two people is acceptable if one signs the certificate and the other a stock or bond power.

6. Signatures in pencil are not acceptable.

7. Signatures pasted on the reverse side of the certificate are not acceptable.

8. The stockholder may place an "X" mark on the line of the signature. This will be acceptable if the certificate bears the signatures of two witnesses and their addresses, with a certification that "the assignment was read to the assignor in our presence and he signified his intention to transfer the security." This certification must be signed by both witnesses.

9. The endorsement by a person since deceased is not acceptable.

10. A certificate registered in the maiden name of the registered owner may be signed by the new name. The broker must furnish a certification to that effect.

11. The stock power, the bond power, and the reverse side of the certificate contain a space for a power of attorney designation. To make the security a nonnegotiable item, it is customary to place the name of the organization to which the security is being sent. The receiver organization will then release the power of attorney, thus making the security a negotiable instrument.

12. The signature of the registered holder must be guaranteed. This is an indispensable requirement for transfer of securities. To guarantee signatures on certificates, the authorized institutions must be commercial banks that are members of the FDIC and/or the Federal Reserve System, and brokerage houses that are members of stock exchanges.

Legal Transfer Requirements

Custodian to a Minor

1. A certificate registered in the name of John Doe Custodian for Mary Doe under the Uniform Gift to Minors Act, requires the signature of the custodian.

2. When the minor comes of age, he may transfer the security into his individual name by presenting the certificate with a certified copy of his birth certificate.

Sole Proprietorship

A certificate registered in the name of a sole proprietorship requires the signature of the sole proprietor and a certification from the securities firm that the stockholder is a sole proprietorship and the person signing is the sole proprietor.

Given a certificate registered in the name of a sole proprietorship, the following documents are required upon the death of the sole proprietor:

1. Signature of the executor or the administrator
2. A certified copy of the certificate of appointment

3. An affidavit of domicile
4. Inheritance tax waivers if required by the state

Partnership

A certificate registered in the name of a partnership requires the signature of one of the general partners. The securities firm must provide a certification to the transfer agent that the stockholder is a partnership and the person signing is a general partner.

Given a certificate registered in the name of the partnership and a request to transfer to the name of one of the partners, the transfer agent would require:

1. Signatures by all the partners
2. A list of all the partners of the firm

Investment Clubs

A certificate registered in the name of an investment club requires the signature of the authorized member of the club and a club resolution signed by the secretary of the club authorizing the person who has signed the certificate.

A certificate registered in the name of a disbanded investment club requires the endorsement of an authorized member and a copy of the instrument of disbandment.

Corporations

A certificate registered in the name of a corporation requires the signature of the authorizing officer and a resolution signed by another officer. The resolution must have the corporate seal and must have a recent date.

Given a certificate registered in the name of the corporation and a request to transfer to the name of an officer of the corporation, the transfer agent would require:

1. An endorsement by an authorized officer
2. A resolution signed by another officer specifically authorizing the transfer to the individual name of the officer

A certificate registered in the name of a corporation that has been dissolved requires the endorsement by an authorized officer, a resolution signed by another officer, and a copy of the instrument of dissolution.

Unincorporated Associations

A certificate registered in the name of an unincorporated association requires the signature of an authorized person and a resolution of the governing body signed by another officer.

Churches and Religious Orders

A certificate registered in the name of a church or a religious organization requires the signature of an authorized trustee and a resolution signed by another trustee.

Power of Attorney

A certificate registered in the name of a person who has given another person a power of attorney to act in his behalf requires the following:

1. The certificate will be signed by the agent acting as attorney-in-fact
2. It will be accompanied by a copy of the power of attorney

Bankruptcy and Receivership

A certificate registered in the name of a bankrupt requires the signature of the receiver and a certified copy of the certificate of appointment of receivership.

Given a certificate registered in the name of a bankrupt and a request to transfer to the name of the receiver in bankruptcy, the transfer agent would require:

1. An endorsement by the bankrupt person
2. A certificate of appointment of receivership dated within 60 days

Living Trusts

A certificate registered in the name of "John Doe TR UA dated Jan. 2, 1984 MB Mary Doe FBO William Doe" requires the signature of John Doe as trustee. If there is more than one trustee, all of them must sign the certificate.

When a certificate is registered in the name of trustees and one of them has resigned, the transfer agent would require:

1. An endorsement by all the presently acting trustees
2. A certification by the securities firm that the trustees signing the certificate are the presently acting trustees

When a certificate is registered in the name of trustees and one of them is deceased, the transfer agent would require:

1. An endorsement by the presently acting trustees
2. A certification by the securities firm that the trustees signing the certificate are the presently acting trustees

Testamentary Trust

A certificate in the name of "John Doe TR UW Mary Doe" requires the signature of John Doe as trustee. If there is more than one trustee, all of them must sign the certificate.

When a certificate is registered in the name of trustees and one of them resigns or is deceased, the transfer agent would require:

1. An endorsement by the successor trustee
2. A certificate of appointment of successor trustee dated within 60 days

Guardianship

A certificate registered in the name of "John Doe GDN for Mary Doe" requires the signature of John Doe as guardian.

When a certificate is registered in the name of a deceased guardian, the transfer agent would require:

1. An endorsement by the successor guardian
2. A certified copy of death certificate
3. A certificate of appointment of a successor guardian dated within 60 days

Committee and Conservatorship

A certificate registered in the name of "John Doe Conservator for Mary Doe" requires the signature of John Doe as conservator.

Joint Tenants with Right of Survivorship

When a certificate registered in the name of "John Doe and Mary Doe JTTEN" and John is deceased, the transfer agent would require:

1. A certified copy of the death certificate
2. Signature by Mary Doe
3. Affidavit of domicile
4. Inheritance tax waiver, if required by state

When a certificate registered in joint tenants with right of survivorship and both tenants are deceased, the transfer agent would require:

1. An endorsement by the legal representative of the last decedent
2. A certificate of death of the first decedent
3. An affidavit of domicile for the last decedent
4. A certificate of appointment for the last decedent
5. Inheritance tax waivers for both decedents, if required

Tenancy in Common

When a certificate is registered in the name of "John Doe and Mary Doe TEN COM" and John is deceased, the transfer agent would require:

1. Signature of Mary Doe
2. Signature of the legal representative of John's estate

3. A certified copy of the certificate of appointment
4. An affidavit of domicile
5. Inheritance tax waiver, if required by state

When a certificate is registered in tenancy in common and both tenants are deceased, the transfer agent would require:

1. An endorsement by the legal representatives of both tenants
2. Affidavit of domicile for both tenants
3. Two certificates of appointment for both tenants
4. Inheritance tax waivers for both decedents, if required

Tenants by Entirety

The requirements are the same as in joint tenants with right of survivorship.

Life Tenancy

A certificate registered in the name of a life tenant requires a signature by the life tenant and a certified copy of the will.

A certificate registered in the name of a deceased life tenant, the transfer agent would require:

1. An endorsement by the legal representative of the prior decedent
2. A certificate of appointment of the legal representative dated within 60 days
3. The death certificate of the life tenant

Community Property

The same requirements as in tenants in common.

Decedents

When a certificate is registered in the name of a deceased person, the transfer agent would require:

1. A signature by the legal representative of the estate
2. A certified copy of the certificate of appointment dated within 60 days
3. Affidavit of domicile
4. Inheritance tax waiver, if required by the state

Executor to Estate

A certificate registered in the name of "John Doe EX EST of Mary Doe" requires only the signature of John Doe as executor. If there is more than one executor, all of them must sign the certificate.

When a certificate registered in the name of an executor who is deceased, the transfer agent would require:

1. An endorsement by the successor executor
2. A certificate of appointment of successor executor dated within 60 days

Administrator to Estate

A certificate registered in the name of "John Doe ADM EST of Mary Doe" requires only the signature of John Doe as administrator. If there is more than one administrator, all of them must sign the certificate.

RECEIVE AND DELIVER SECTION

This is one of the most important sections in the Cashiers Department. It has the responsibility for receiving and delivering securities and checks to and from customers and brokers. The operation revolves around a series of balancing procedures, usually completed before the end of the day.

Unlike the Box, Vault, and Transfer sections, the Receive and Deliver section, because of its very nature, plays a financial role in the department. It advises the cashier and the cash manager as to money positions on a given day. This is an important factor to determine the firm's overall financial condition on a day-to-day basis.

In general, the section is divided into two rather distinct groups: Customer Receive and Deliver and Broker Receive and Deliver. As the names suggest, the first is responsible for handling only customer securities and checks, and the second for broker securities and checks.

Customer Receive and Delivery Section

All customer items, with the exception of stock transfers, are channeled through this section for delivery to customers. The certificates are received from the Box and Vault section with delivery instructions and are mailed to the customer after a routine verification of shares and negotiability. There are two types of deliveries. One is a free delivery to the customer or to his designated agent, and the other is a delivery versus payment (a C.O.D. delivery) where the purchases by the customer are consummated by the delivery of the instrument against the payment of the purchase price. This section is responsible for both, and the operational procedure involves the recording of the number of certificates delivered and the receipt of the check for the items.

The receipt of securities from the branches or customers is done in the same manner — recording the certificates received, and if there are payments to be made, submitting the check to the customer.

Again, as in the case of the other sections of the Cashiers Department, the instructions to receive and deliver securities to and from customers originate from the Margin Department.

Broker Receive and Deliver Section

The Broker Receive and Deliver section has a different role to play. It is in this area that the broker to broker commitments are accomplished and financial obligations fulfilled. A trade between a buying and a selling broker is settled by this section when notified by the Purchase and Sales Department. The section's primary functions are to effect deliveries and receive securities on the trade settlement date; compare, verify and balance the monies received or presented; and advise the money cashier as to disbursements and receipts.

As discussed above, on the day before the settlement date, the Purchase and Sales department submits the blotters and summaries to the Broker Receive and Deliver sections. The Receive Balance Orders, prepared by the clearing corporation, are also sent to the section to prepare the staff to receive the security from the selling broker against a specified amount of money established by the clearing corporation. (On the sale side, the Deliver Balance Orders are sent to the Box and Vault section to prepare items for delivery.) The broker who has sold the security on the trade date is charged to deliver the instrument on the settlement date in accordance with the rules of the exchange on which the stock was traded. At a prescribed time, the security is sent to the Broker Receive and Deliver section and monies are exchanged. For securities listed on stock exchanges, the clearing corporations play a significant role in settling the trades. Most exchange trades are obviated by the clearing process where sales of the security are off-set by purchases of the same security. This process will be discussed in detail in a later chapter.

The mechanics of receiving and delivering securities by the Broker Receive and Deliver section are generally the same. They all place heavy responsibilities on the operating clerk (the R & D clerk) to deliver the proper instruments with the exact number of shares and receive the proper certificates in good deliverable form. The receive and deliver forms originate either from the P & S department or have come from the clearing corporation via the P & S. The R & D clerk's function is usually transient in nature; he does not hold certificates or maintain an inventory supply of securities. He receives the certificates and immediately deposits them in the Box and Vault section or receives certificates from that section and delivers them immediately. In doing this and controlling the traffic of securities, he is charged with certain attendant procedures of record maintenance and stock record update. The security position in "Fail to Deliver" and "Fail to Receive" accounts are kept in balance daily by the personnel in this section. Monies payable or receivable to and from brokers or clearing corporations are verified and checked daily. The control of aged fails and the procedures of buy-ins are also performed by this section.

Fail to Deliver or Receive

If the security is not received or delivered on the specified time and date, the trade will not be consummated, and settlement remains unfulfilled. This is a condition important to the cashiering function. On the sale side, if the security is not delivered on the settlement date, the stock record reflects an open "Fail to Deliver" as a receivable. The firm will not receive the payment because the securities are not delivered. This causes a financial problem. To meet its obligations, the firm will be forced to borrow money by depositing collateral securities made available by margin accounts.

The "Fail to Deliver" figure is one of the most important barometers for the efficiency of the Cashiers Department and is a significant criterion for its money management operation. The proceeds of the sale generally are paid to the customer on the trade settlement date, and the broker should retrieve his money from the buying broker by delivering the security in a timely fashion. It is this factor that has caused financial and operational problems for many brokerage firms during recent years. The regulatory agencies frown upon an abnormal increase in the "Fail to Deliver" figure. The exchanges have imposed mandatory rules to force the contract settlement of items over a specified period of time, usually 30 days. The rules threaten the execution of a buy-in against the defaulting broker. This is a procedure whereby the buying broker or the floor department of the exchange buys the security against the account of the selling broker who has failed to deliver the security.

The same is true for items purchased by the firm but not yet received. Accordingly, a "Fail to Receive" condition is reflected in the stock record as a payable. Although the burden is on the failing broker to complete the delivery, an unusual increase in the "Fail to Receive" figure may also be considered as a sign of operational difficulty. The firm might have purchased the security for a customer who is in need of the certificate. The mandatory buy-in rules also apply to these situations. A failure to close an aged contract is a violation of exchange rules.

Reclamations

If securities being received do not match with existing instructions or if they are not in good deliverable form, the R & D clerk will return the certificates to the sender through the clearing house. This is known as Reclamation. After the completion of all these receipts, the R & D clerk will indicate on the money settlement sheet the amount of money due other brokers against the receipt of securities.

Before the end of the day, the Receive and Deliver section will receive a check from the clearing corporation, if deliveries exceed the receives, or will deliver a check to the clearing house, if receives exceed the deliveries.

OTC Transactions

Over-the-counter transactions not handled through a clearing entity are settled individually. The selling broker will deliver over the window to the buying broker, and separate checks are exchanged.

Delivery to Clearing Corporations

Up-to-date knowledge of different systems and procedures of various clearing organizations is important. The staff in the R & D section must be able to handle delivery and receipt through any method, no matter how cumbersome it may seem to appear. The operation of this section requires a proper valuation of all these procedures and an understanding of the underlying concept.

Delivery to Out-of-Town Brokers

Deliveries for out-of-town destinations are generally processed through a bank. This is known as bank drafting. The delivering broker will forward the securities to his bank with instructions to deliver them to an out-of-town broker or institution. The Receive and Deliver clerk will prepare a bank draft to accompany the securities. There are two ways of accomplishing these deliveries:

1. The bank forwards the securities to its correspondent bank, and the bank's messenger delivers them to the receiving organization. If the certificates are in order, the receiving firm draws a check to the order of the bank effecting the delivery. The money is then transmitted to the delivering broker's bank and credited to his account. For this service, the bank charges a fee that includes the cost of transporting the security and the attendant insurance expense.

2. The broker may select bank drafts on an immediate-credit

basis. Again, the certificates are forwarded to the bank. Upon receipt of the securities, the bank credits the broker's account for the amount of money on the delivery bill. This is a type of bank loan, and the broker is charged interest at the prevailing rate.

Fail Control

This is a small section in the Cashiers Department born into existence primarily as a result of the paperwork crisis of the securities industry in the late 1960s. The section is charged with controlling fails of any nature and to comply with the requirements of the regulatory agencies in this area. Aging of both "Fails to Deliver" and "Fails to Receive," handling and processing of buy-in notices to and from brokers, and a routine inspection of all customer and broker deliveries are the principal functions of this section.

TYPES OF DELIVERIES

Principally there are three types of deliveries to satisfy a contract: deliveries for cash contracts, for regular way contracts, and for seller's option.

Cash Contracts

Deliveries of securities to honor a cash contract must be made before 2:30 p.m. if the transaction is made at or before 2:00 p.m. Deliveries against transactions made for "Cash" after 2:00 p.m. are due within 30 minutes. Cash transactions are generally made in unusual circumstances—a buyer wants immediate delivery of the certificate, or a seller sells to dispose of his ownership. Reasons for this emergency procedure are many: taxes, tender offers, conversions, rights, privileges, and so on.

Regular Way Contracts

A majority of securities contracts are made in a regular way. This is the standard type of delivery where the securities sold in the securities market must be delivered on the fifth business day after the transaction. If the trade is executed on Monday, the delivery must be made on T + 5 — the following Monday — assuming that there are no holidays between the trade date and the settlement date. The trade settles regular way on T + 5. All contracts that would otherwise fall on a holiday will mature on the succeeding business day, unless otherwise directed by the exchange.

Seller's Option

This is a special contract that allows the seller to effect delivery of the security on a delayed basis. The delivery is made on the expiration day of the option. It can also be made prior to the expiration date if the seller submits one day's written notice to the buyer.

Under this arrangement, the seller has up to 60 calendar days to effect a delivery. If the expiration day falls on a non-business day, the delivery is made on the succeeding business day.

Unless otherwise directed by the clearing corporation, broker to broker securities deliveries must be effected before 11:30 a.m., or the selling broker will fail to deliver and the buying broker will fail to receive. The rules are very specific as to the consequences of unaccomplished deliveries. The contract may be closed by the buyer as provided by the rules. In every case of non-delivery, the party in default is liable for any damages.

For "When, As, and If issued" trades, the settlement date will be the date agreed upon by both parties, but cannot be earlier than the fifth business day following the mailing of the confirmation ticket. Confirmation to broker-dealers must be sent within two days after the trade day.

Acceptable Denominations for Delivery

For Stocks

To settle an exchange contract, stock certificates must be in the exact amount of the trading unit if the trading unit is 100 shares or in any multiple of the trading unit or smaller amounts aggregating the trading unit. If the unit of trading is less than 100 shares, the delivery must be in the exact amount of stock sold or for smaller amounts aggregating the amount sold.

For Bonds

If the unit of trading is $1,000 or $5,000, the denominations of the bonds must be either $1,000 or $5,000. Bonds in lower denominations are also acceptable if they are exchangeable without charge for $1,000 or $5,000 certificates.

If the unit of trading is more than $5,000, the delivery must be made in the denominations of the trading unit. Bonds in larger denominations are acceptable if they can be exchangeable without charge for bonds in the unit of trading.

Contracts in bonds may be settled by delivering bonds in coupon or registered form, provided that these bonds are interchangeable without charge and are prepared in accordance with the engraving requirements of the exchange.

In all cases, the buyer must accept partial deliveries from the seller if delivered in lots of one trading unit or multiples of the unit.

The broker will not be concerned with these denominational delivery rules if the deliveries are being made through a book-entry system of a depository organization.

Good Delivery

All certificates must be in good deliverable form when used for delivery. A temporary certificate is not considered as a good delivery when permanent certificates are available. All certificates and registered bonds must have proper assignments to effect delivery.

If the name of an individual or a member organization is inserted in the assignments as attorney, a power of substitution executed by the individual or the member organization in blank must be obtained.

It is an indispensable requirement that the signatures be guaranteed before a delivery can be effected. The guarantor of the signature may be one of the following:

1. A member organization of a stock exchange
2. A commercial bank or trust company, member of the Federal Reserve System whose signatures are on file with and acceptable to the transfer agent of the security.

Generally, securities requiring documents to effect transfers are not considered as good deliverable items. Care must be exercised to differentiate items "good for transfer" from items "good for delivery." A certificate accompanied by a proper document may be considered as "good for transfer," but under the rules of the exchange and the NASD it may not be a "good for delivery." The NYSE, the American Stock Exchange, and the NASD have amended their rules to accept securities registered in fiduciary names as good delivery items provided that the documentation is not necessary to effect transfers. This would be certificates registered in the names of executors, administrators, trustees, guardians, etc.

The delivery ticket must accompany the certificate. For municipal bonds, the buyer is not required to accept a partial delivery regarding a single trade in a security.

Delivery Requirements for Municipal Bonds

For bearer bonds, the unit of delivery is $1,000 or $5,000 principal value; for registered bonds the unit of delivery is $1,000 and multiples of $1,000 — up to $100,000.

If the municipal bond is semi-mutilated it will be considered as a good delivery if the certificate is validated by the trustee, the registrar, the transfer agent, the paying agent, or the issuing entity.

All coupons must be attached to the coupon bond for delivery.

For bonds in default, the deliverer must include all unpaid or partially paid coupons with the delivery.

If the settlement date of the trade is after the interest payment date, the delivery of the security will not include the coupon.

If the delivery is being made 30 days prior to the interest payment date, the deliverer may attach a due-bill or a bank check in lieu of the coupon.

If the coupon attached to the bond is mutilated, the delivery will be a good delivery if the coupon is endorsed or guaranteed by the bank or the issuer.

If the coupon attached to the bond is cancelled, the bond will be accepted for delivery if the coupon is endorsed or guaranteed by the trustee, the paying agent, or the issuer.

A "called" bond is not a good delivery if the call notice was published on or prior to the delivery date, unless the trade is executed as "called" or the entire issue is being called.

A municipal bond without a copy of the legal opinion is not a good delivery, unless the trade is executed as "ex-legal."

For insured municipal securities, a document of insurance must accompany the certificates.

A due-bill or a bank check must accompany the certificate if the transfer of the security cannot be accomplished on or before the interest payment date. The same is true for securities traded "flat."

All expenses of shipment of the security is borne by the seller.

The delivery cannot be rejected for insignificant money differences with the following schedule taken as a guideline:

- A money difference of $10 for trades between $1,000–$24,999.

- A money difference of $25 for trades between $25,000–$99,999.

- A money difference of $60 for trades between $100,000–$249,000.

- A money difference of $250 for trades between $250,000–$999,999.

- A money difference of $500 for trades over $1 million.

- The differences must be solved by both parties within 10 business days after the settlement date. The accrued interest payment must be calculated with the contract price.

The receiving organization may reclaim the item within one business day after the delivery for interest checks missing, mutilated certificates, and no legal opinion; within three business days following the receipt of the notice that the bank refuses to honor the interest check; within 18 months following the delivery for wrong issue, duplicate delivery, over-delivery, and rejection by the transfer agent.

The receiving party may reclaim the item at any time for counterfeit or stolen securities and for partially called bonds if the call notice was published on or before the delivery date, and the trade was not identified as "called."

All rejections and reclamations must accompany a notice explaining the rejection or the reclamation.

MARKING TO THE MARKET

Brokers may demand the difference between the contract price and the market price of the security at any time. The exchanges and the NASD have special rules setting up the mechanics of marking to the market. The broker who is partially unsecured by reason of the change in the market value of the security may demand the difference in money from the other broker. Payment must be made directly to the broker or through the clearing corporation.

BUY-INS

Failure to deliver securities at the prescribed day and time as directed by the clearing house will subject the clearing member into a situation where undelivered securities may be bought in by the purchasing broker at the expense of the selling broker. The rules of the clearing corporations with respect to buy-ins are based on the rules of the securities exchanges to which they are affiliated.

Buy-In Procedures at the New York Stock Exchange

A. Regular Buy-Ins

In order to close out a contract, a member–broker should submit a buy-in form to the defaulting broker prior to 45 minutes after the time the securities were to be delivered. The delivery time at NYSE is 11:30 a.m. Eastern Standard Time. That means the buy-in notice should be submitted before 12:15 p.m. If the broker continues to fail to deliver, the buying broker will then present the buy-in notice to the Exchange. This should be done between 2:15 and 2:30 p.m. The actual execution of the buy-in is not done until after 2:30 p.m.

The rules provide the postponement of buy-ins in the event that there is no fair market on the floor or if the party in default has physical possession of stock in good deliverable form and has notified the originator of the buy-in. If the defaulting broker is failing to receive the security from another broker, he may retransmit the buy-in notice to that broker, acting, therefore, as a middle man between the two brokers. After the buy-ins are executed, payment representing the difference between the original contract and the new buy-in value is sent to the broker before 3:00 p.m. on the day following execution.

If the broker wants to buy the defaulting broker in on a cash basis, the procedure differs slightly. Because such trades require delivery of the security on the same day as the trade, the buy-in notice is presented to the Exchange between 2:30 and 2:45 p.m. for trades executed before 2:00 p.m., or within 45 minutes for transactions after 2:00 p.m.

One problem that the purchasing broker should always bear in mind is that when the buy-in notice is presented, the party in default may deliver the security in question even after the 11:30 a.m. cut off time and, of course, before the execution on the floor. The delivery must be accepted if it is in good delivery form.

B. Mandatory Buy-Ins

In order to control fails and the related financial impact on the securities firms, the exchanges and the regulatory agencies have established various schedules for the brokers to close out old contracts.

In the case of the New York Stock Exchange, a broker should not have "Fails to Receive" over 30 days. He must present the Notice of Intent of the Mandatory Buy-In to the defaulting broker before 1:00 p.m. on the fourth business day prior to the 31st calendar day after settlement date. The response to this notice should be presented to the originator before 5:00 p.m. on the third business day after the effective date of the notice.

The buy-in order is then submitted to the Exchange by 9:30 a.m. on the 31st calendar day with instructions as to the type of order desired — "Cash," "Next Day," or "Regular Way."

THE STOCK RECORD DEPARTMENT

This is one of the nerve centers of a securities firm where the activities of all segments of the operations division are recorded and controlled. The stock record department plays an extremely critical role for the entire organization in providing the necessary tools of accountability for securities transactions. The principal functions of the department are to maintain the records, summarize the reports, and reconcile security positions.

Operation of Stock Record Department

When a customer makes a purchase, the firm's ledgers record the transaction by crediting the customer's account in the amount of shares purchased. The record will maintain that position until the item is either delivered to the customer or sold.

The basic accounting principles of debits and credits apply in the stock records. The purchased security held by the firm for the customer will reflect a "Long" position in the records with a corresponding "Short" position indicating the location of the security in the house. The "Long" represents the debits and accounts payable that will be securities the firm owes to customers, institutions, or other brokers. The "Short" positions are the credits and accounts receivable that are securities held in custody by the firm in various locations, and depositories and securities due from customers or brokers.

On the trade settlement date, if the selling broker has failed to deliver the security, the buying broker's record will indicate a "Long" position for the customer with a corresponding "Short" position as "Fail to Receive" from the broker.

EXAMPLE

Selling Broker		Buying Broker	
Long	*Short*	*Long*	*Short*
100 FD	100	100	100 FR
The broker fails to deliver.	Customer sells 100 shares but fails to deliver to broker.	Customer buys the security.	The broker fails to receive.

In summarizing the security movements, the stock record department applies the principle of dual entries — credits are offset by debits. For every "Long," there should always be a "Short" position. If not, the stock record will reflect a discrepancy, and a stock record clerk will be assigned to resolve it. The ultimate objective of the department is to have a balanced record without any "breaks" or differences. The dual entry procedure originates from the operating departments. To record a security movement, for instance, a section of the Cashiers Department makes an entry-debit or credit, with a corresponding entry to be made by another section of the same department. If the Receive and Deliver section accepts a certificate from a customer, a "Long" position is created; but when the same certificate moves to the Vault to be held for the customer, a "Short" position is established. If either of the sections fail to generate the entry, the stock record will reflect an out-of-balance condition or a "break."

The day's activity starts with the gathering of all reports and data. Depending upon the size of the firm and its operating mode, this may be either a manual documentation or listings produced by the Data Processing Center. In the latter case, it is a common practice to publish only those security positions that had activity on the previous day. The daily stock record "take-off" is scrutinized by the staff of the stock record department to review the security movements and to resolve the "breaks."

The verification of source documents and corresponding entries is done through the use of record retention procedures, such as microfilming. Because of the complexities of the operation, it has become the practice of most securities firms to microfilm all security movements and the documents accompanying the securities. This has become a valuable aid in resolving stock record differences.

Stock Record Reports

Although the format of the stock record or the securities ledger varies from one firm to another, the frequency of security reports is generally the same. There is a daily "take-off" and a complete printout of the entire stock record every week. The daily "take-off" reflects the securities received in or delivered out on the previous day. To maintain proper accountability of records, it is customary to assign separate stock record positions to each segment of the operation. Each repository of securities has a distinct house account number that provides easy identification of the location of the item. The stock record daily "take-off" identifies the movement of a particular security by indicating a debit or a credit of a house account. If the Transfer Department delivers a security to a customer, the stock record will indicate a movement of the item out of the transfer house account and a reduction in the customer's security position. The weekly stock record, on the other hand, reflects the aggregate security positions in all account numbers where securities are lodged.

Stock Record Positions

Long Positions

Long positions in the stock record are on the debit side and are considered as payables. These are securities held for customers or owed to brokers.

Short Positions

Short positions in the stock record are on the credit side and are considered as receivables. These are securities either physically held by the firm or expected to be received from the customers or brokers. Securities held by the firm are lodged in a well-defined location, such as a "Box" properly indicated in the stock record. A Box is a location where securities are placed either permanently or temporarily. This is reflected in the stock record as a "Short" (credit) position. Manual or automatic entries are made whenever there is security movement through the Box location. A credit entry increases the quantity in the Box, and a debit entry decreases it. It is an invalid condition if a short side location has a net "Long" position in the stock record. This is an error and must be corrected. It means that an entry is made taking away securities from the location in excess of the securities on hand. If the Vault has 200 shares and a debit entry is made for 300 shares, the stock record would indicate an invalid condition (Long) of 100 shares for the Vault location.

The following is a list of Short and Long firm locations:

> Short (Credits)
>> Vault
>> Box
>> Safekeeping
>> Depository Location
>> Private Name Transfer
>> Firm Transfer
>> Legal Transfer

Exchange–Reorganization
Fails to Receive
CNS (within a clearing corporation)
Stock Loan
Bank Loan
Lost Securities Account
In-Transit

Long (Debits)
Fails to Deliver
CNS (within a clearing corporation)
Stock Borrow

RECORD RETENTION

Rule 17a-4 of the Securities and Exchange Commission specifies the records that broker-dealers are required to maintain. The following is the schedule for retention of various documents and records:

A. Broker-dealers must preserve for a period of six years, the first two in an easily accessible place, the following records:

1. Blotters for securities purchased or sold.
2. Receipt and delivery of securities with certificate numbers.
3. Receipts and disbursements of cash.
4. Records for debits and credits.
5. Records reflecting the firm's assets and liabilities, income and expense, and capital records.
6. Customer accounts and the itemized transactions in each account.
7. The firm's stock record or position book.

B. Broker-dealers must preserve for a period of at least 3 years, the first 2 years in an easily accessible place, the following records:

1. Records reflecting the securities in transfer, dividends and interests received, securities borrowed and loaned, monies

borrowed and loaned, securities used for collateral, securities in fail to receive and fail to deliver.

2. Memoranda of customers' orders.
3. Memoranda of the firm's orders for its own account.
4. Confirmations and notices to customers.
5. Records of cash and margin accounts.
6. Records of options transactions.
7. All check books, bank statements, cancelled checks and bank reconciliations.
8. Copies of all bills payable and receivable.
9. Copies of all communications sent or received by the broker-dealer relating to business.
10. All trial balances, computations of aggregate indebtedness and net capital, financial statements, branch office reconciliations, internal audit papers.
11. All documents and power of attorney authorizing a person to act in behalf of the account.
12. All written agreements of the broker-dealer.
13. Copies of Focus Reports and the annual financial statements.
    (a) Money balance positions, long and short
    (b) Amount of secured note, description of collateral securing such note
    (c) Description of futures commodity contracts
    (d) Description of option positions
    (e) Detail relating to information for possession or control requirements under SEC Rule 15c3-3 and reported in the Focus Report.

C. Broker-dealers must preserve for a period of at least 6 years after the closing of any customer account.

D. Broker-dealers must preserve during the life of the firm articles of incorporation, minute book and stock transfer books.

E. Broker-dealers must preserve in an easily accessible place:

1. The registration application of the account executives.
2. The fingerprint records of employees.
3. All copies of notices reporting lost, stolen, missing or counterfeit securities under SEC Rule 17f-1.

F. All records required under SEC Rule 17a-3 and 17a-4 may be kept in microfilm format instead of hard copy documentation format.

G. If the records required to be maintained under SEC Rules 17a-3 and 17a-4 are prepared by an outside service bureau in behalf of the broker-dealers, the outside service bureau must file with the SEC a report to the effect that all records are the property of the broker-dealers and will be subject to SEC audit and examination.

RECORD RETENTION IN THE BRANCH OFFICE

The branch office must maintain and keep current the following records:

1. Customer account information records.
2. List of third party accounts.
3. List of persons authorized to trade for corporations and partnerships.
4. List of employee and employee related accounts.
5. Copies of all correspondence to customers.
6. Copies of customer complaints.
7. Daily order review records.
8. Copies of extensions, margin calls, and house calls.
9. Copies of security receipt and transmittal forms.
10. Month-end customer statements.
11. Copies of executed and unexecuted order tickets.

CHAPTER FOURTEEN

MONEY CASHIERING

Proper cash utilization and competent management of money are essential for a successful securities operation. On a given day, substantial amounts of money representing receipts from customers or brokers against the purchase or delivery of securities and disbursements to customers, brokers, clearing corporations, and institutions flow through the Cashiers Department. The proper employment of these vast amounts of money is extremely vital in maintaining the department as a profit center. Cost of money is an important factor in any brokerage operation. Therefore, one of the most important functions of the Cashiers Department is to reduce the need to borrow money and, consequently, to reduce the attendant interest costs — and that's the responsibility of the money management team.

There are many elements affecting this — all centered around the main goal of proper utilization of cash and securities. It is the responsibility of the Cashier to see that certain strategies are employed to meet all goals and objectives on a daily basis.

SECTIONS OF THE MONEY MANAGEMENT DEPARTMENT

There are three sections in the cashiering operation that form the money management organization: Money Cashier, stock loan, and bank loan. The money management department is not a distinct group separated from other areas, but rather a group with interrelated activities.

The Money Cage

The Money Cashier is the manager of the Money Cage. The Money Cage is the clerical side of money management where certain routine functions are performed. Its primary responsibility is to receive and disburse checks. Requests to issue checks may originate from any section of the operations division — the Accounting Department to make payments for general expenses; the Margin Department to pay customers; the Receive and Deliver section to pay brokers on their receipt of securities; or the Dividend Department for payment of dividends and interests.

Deposit of checks and monies is also done in much the same way. The Accounting Department receives an income check and sends it to the Money Cage for deposit in the appropriate account; the Margin Department receives checks from customers and forwards them to the Money Cage for deposit, and so on. It is, therefore, the only area in the organization where all cash representing firm or agency activities is mobilized and centralized. This is the melting pot of all unsegregated funds.

From an operational standpoint, the day starts with an opening balance at the operating bank. This is the Money Cashier's starting point. He increases and decreases this balance by deposits and disbursements as the day progresses. He will mobilize funds from various segments of the organization and will either pay off bank loans or transmit the funds to other areas. There is a constant change in the money position. If the opening balance is not large enough to accommodate a payout or a disbursement, the Money Cashier requests a day loan from a bank. For this purpose, a day loan agreement, which calls for the return of money on the same day, is executed.

Throughout the day, the Money Cashier will mechanically or manually compile all money figures from customer payments and receipts, payments to or from the clearing houses, over the window deliveries, syndicate pickups or deliveries. It is the practice of the Money Cage to categorize these disbursements and deposits to facilitate reconciliation of the bank balances. After this compilation is concluded, which will be sometime in the afternoon, the Money Cashier will make a final determination to either borrow additional funds or to pay off existing loans. To help him arrive at an early decision as to his money position, the manager of the Money Cage requires the assistance not only of the people immediately around him, but also personnel in the Dividend Department, the Exchange and Reorganization section, the Margin Department, Receive and Deliver section, Stock Loan and Bank Loan sections, Accounting Department, Syndicate Department, and the branch cashiers. It is the successful mobilization of cash from these areas or the recognition of their financial requirements that enables the Money Cashier to make his final determination.

As part of the mobilization of funds, all checks directed to the organization are forwarded to the Money Cage. Customer checks payable directly to the firm are deposited at the operating bank. Caution must be exercised in accepting third-party checks. These are checks drawn by a third party and payable to the firm. The maker of the check must execute a release form holding the brokerage firm free and harmless from any liability and authorizing the broker to deposit the check in the customer's account.

Checks drawn by a corporation cannot be accepted in an individual customer's account unless supported by corporate bylaws specifically authorizing the broker to accept the check.

Checks drawn on a trade name where sole proprietorship by the customer can be established are acceptable by the broker for the individual account of the customer. Checks drawn by the customer in a fiduciary capacity, however, cannot be accepted for his personal account.

It is not customary for a client to make payments to the broker in cash, although it is legal tender. Cash received by the brokers over a certain amount must be reported to the Federal Reserve Bank of the district. Disbursements to customers are made under instructions from the Margin Department. It is the responsibility of this department to request that checks be issued in the name of the customer exactly as it appears in the books of the firm. Checks issued to the order of the customer as fiduciary should be so indicated. In accepting checks from customers or brokers, the Money Cashier must question post-dated, unsigned checks, and checks indicating an incorrect amount of money.

The day's receipts and disbursements are totalled in journals or blotters, and a summary is prepared indicating the various control accounts in the general ledger. This summary should agree with the totals of all source documents prepared during the course of the day. This summary is eventually forwarded to the Accounting Department for reconciliation and control.

The Bank Loan Section

A securities firm is engaged in bank loan activities for many reasons. The demands for funds to operate the brokerage business are many, and an intelligent borrowing program is important for the successful conduct of business. A heavy demand for funds starts primarily from the need to service the customer's margin transactions. The broker has extended credit to the margin account, and he must borrow money to meet the demand.

The nature of a particular brokerage business is another consideration for loans. If the broker is engaged in investment banking activities, he usually relies on substantial bank borrowings to carry the inventory until it is distributed. Capital funds in the firm are available, but they are not employed for investment banking purposes because most of the time the demand exceeds the supply. The investment bankers first borrow the funds from a bank, then give them to the client corporation against delivery of the securities. The certificates are then distributed to the buyers, funds are received, and the loan is paid off.

Market-making activities of the firm may be another reason for loans. If the firm is engaged in making markets in over-the-counter issues, they generally rely on bank borrowing to carry the inventory even for a short duration.

From the cashiering standpoint, loans are made to satisfy payments against receipt of securities on a continuous basis. The cashier checks his money position daily. If his operating bank shows a deficit, he borrows money to meet that deficit. If it indicates excess funds, the bank loan is paid in that amount. There are several kinds of loans that are available to the cashier. The first is the "Day Loan," which is a convenient arrangement between the bank and the broker. Day loans are unsecured loans and are repaid before the end of the day. Because the lending bank's reserve position is not affected, the broker is usually charged a low interest rate. The broker and the bank execute a Day Loan Agreement against which funds are extended to the broker.

The "Overnight Loan" is a secured loan. The broker is charged the prevailing broker's loan rate and is obligated to support it by collateralizing securities at the bank.

Before the end of the day if there is need for borrowing money, the cashier delivers certificates to the lending bank and requests a loan based on the market value of the securities. This is called a collateral loan. Depending on the quality of the collateral, the bank lends from 70 percent to 95 percent of the value of the securities. These certificates are kept at the bank until the loan is paid. The Bank Loan clerk works closely with the Money Cashier, recognizes the need for funds, and deposits collateral to secure the loan. If these securities are needed for delivery or other reasons at a later date, the loan clerk will substitute them with other securities. He is in constant touch with lending institutions.

The practice in the financial community is to seek reciprocity in this area. By mutual agreement, a bank may allow the borrowing broker to keep the collateral in his vault. This eliminates the clerical procedure of delivering and receiving collaterals constantly and it saves the inherent cost of borrowing "Day Loans" to pay off the "Overnight Loans" if the collateral securities are needed for deliveries. The broker executes an "Agreement to Pledge" and holds the certificates in his vault properly identified for the lending bank. During the period of the loan, the securities are subject to the bank's audit.

The interest rate of the call loan, which is payable on demand, is the broker's loan rate. This might be different from the prime rate that the bank charges to its preferential customers. The broker executes a "loan agreement," which can be on a continual basis, and eliminates the necessity of signing daily promissory notes.

An important function of the Bank Loan Manager of a brokerage firm is to make a distinction between loans to brokers for firm activities and loans based on customers' collateral. This is a requirement of the Federal Reserve Board.

The Stock Loan Section

This unit in the Cashiers Department, where the staff is primarily involved in processing securities for a loan or borrowing securities from institutions, is a principal source of revenue if promoted and managed properly. Excess securities in margin accounts may be used for loans. This is done through the express authorization of the customer. The mechanics are simple: available certificates are delivered either through the clearing house or directly against a specified amount of money that will be the current market price of the shares. In lending the excess securities, the firm is attempting to utilize the cash for its financial needs.

This is a temporary condition until the security is returned against the same funds. The stock loan and stock borrowed may be done through a depository organization.

During recent years, the business of stock loans has become increasingly important to the securities industry. It has become a significant vehicle in financing the customer indebtedness, which is, in fact, the lending of money to customers in the process of their securities trading. This is, by far, a better medium of financing than the bank loan where the money received against a collateralized security may not be the full market value of the shares as in the case of stock loan.

Securities are borrowed to satisfy immediate needs. To borrow the stock is, of course, a requirement when the customer is executing a short sale. The transaction is consummated by the delivery of the borrowed certificates. Immediate availability of the instruments is the key to success. If the requested shares are scarce, the lending broker may demand a cash premium over the market value. During the life of the loan, the lending or borrowing broker may "mark the item to the market" by making an adjustment in the original amount of money if there is a reasonable fluctuation in the market value of the security.

Sources for borrowing securities are many — among them are securities firms, banks, insurance companies, universities, and so on.

IMPORTANCE OF MONEY MANAGEMENT

In recent years, money management has become an important feature in brokerage operations because of increased public and institutional participation in the stock market. Therefore, large sums of money are at the disposal of the securities firm. It is the intelligent employment of these funds that makes a successful money management operation. The cash utilization program is dependent upon the cashier's operating procedures and the firm's financial condition. It calls for the use of all resources to effect securities delivery — CODs, "Fails to Deliver," or return of borrowed securities. It also calls for the optimum use of excess securities for stock loans. Funds derived from these sources are used for paying off loans, thus reducing the interest expense that is a significant cost factor in the brokerage business. The management of money, therefore, has become an important exercise in economics.

In order to be successful, all areas of the money management team must work efficiently and together. Speeding cash inflows and slowing cash outflows is one way to achieve a successful program. To accomplish this, the firm's operating and sales forces are coordinated with the account executive. The mailing of the confirmation to the customer immediately after the trade is executed assures prompt payment by the customer. Immediate mobilization of funds from all branch operations to a central Money Cage is important. Therefore, a request is made for the branch managers to draw down their local deposits on a continuous basis.

An effective stock loan program is another area for the money management team. Techniques used to attain an effective program may include speedy delivery of securities to the borrowing firm, incentive programs for the staff of the Stock Loan section, and mark to market.

CHAPTER FIFTEEN

TRADING SECURITIES ON MARGIN

The term "margin" refers to the amount of money deposited by a customer in a brokerage account to protect the broker against unfavorable fluctuations of security prices. Margin trading provides the mechanism to increase the investor's purchasing power when dealing in securities transactions.

MARGINABLE SECURITIES

Not all securities may be purchased on margin. Marginable securities, under Regulation T of the Federal Reserve System, are the following:

1. Securities, rights, and warrants listed at a registered stock exchange and the National Market System of NASDAQ.
2. Over-the-counter securities approved by the Federal Reserve.
3. Convertible securities listed at a stock exchange if they can be converted into marginable stocks.
4. Bonds listed at a stock exchange that carries rights or warrants allowing the holder to subscribe to a marginable security.

The Regulation T of the Federal Reserve imposes initial margin requirements in trading marginable securities. Regulation T's current requirement is 50% for long purchases and short sales. That means that the customer must deposit either cash equal to 50% of the cost of the purchase or the proceeds of the sale in short sales. The current loan value of marginable securities is 50%. The loan value is the complement of the percentage of the margin requirement. If the Regulation T margin requirement is 65%, the loan value of the marginable security is 35%. The loan value of a security is the amount of money the broker is allowed to lend to the customer, based on the type of security.

TABLE 15.1. INITIAL MARGIN REQUIREMENTS AND LOAN VALUES OF MARGINABLE SECURITIES.

Marginable Securities	*Required Initial Margin*	*Loan Value*
1. Stocks, rights, and warrants listed at a national stock exchange and on NASDAQ.	50% of the cost of the transaction.	50% of the market value of the security.
2. Over-the-counter securities approved by the Federal Reserve Board.	50% of the cost of the transaction.	50% of the market value of the security.
3. Convertible bonds listed at a national stock exchange that can be converted into a marginable security. Convertible bonds in the OTC market approved by the Federal Reserve Board.	50% of the cost of the transaction.	50% of the market value of the security.
4. Bonds listed at a national stock exchange that carries rights or warrants allowing the holder to subscribe to a marginable security. OTC bonds carrying warrants approved by the Federal Reserve Board.	50% of the cost of the transaction.	50% of the market value of the security.

EXEMPT SECURITIES

Securities exempt from Regulation T margin requirements are the following:

1. Securities of the United States.
2. Obligations of states and municipalities.
3. Nonconvertible bonds listed at a stock exchange, and certain qualified unlisted bonds.

The customer may purchase exempt securities on margin. The margin requirements will be based on regulations of the stock exchanges, the NASD, and the policies of the brokerage house. (See Table 15.2.)

TABLE 15.2. MARGIN REQUIREMENTS FOR EXEMPT SECURITIES.

Security	Required Initial Margin
1. U.S. government and federal agency securities.	5% of the face value of the security.
2. Municipal securities.	15% of the face value or 25% of the market value, whichever is the lesser amount.
3. Nonconvertible bonds listed at a national stock exchange and certain unlisted bonds in the over-the-counter market.	25% of the market value of the bond.

Under current New York Stock Exchange requirements, exempt securities have the following loan value:

1. U.S. government and federal agency securities.	95% of the face value of the security.
2. Municipal securities.	85% of the face value or 75% of the market value, whichever is the greater amount.
3. Nonconvertible bonds listed at a stock exchange and certain unlisted bonds in the over-the-counter market.	75% of the market value of the bond.

REGULATORY REQUIREMENTS

Margin transactions are governed by the following regulatory agencies: the Federal Reserve System, the securities exchanges, the National Association of Securities Dealers, the Securities and Exchange Commission, and the policies of the brokerage house.

The Regulations of the Federal Reserve System

The Fed is authorized to establish margin regulations by Section 7A of the Securities Exchange Act of 1934. The Fed's Board of Governors determines the margin percentage based on general economic considerations and the condition of the securities market. It has gone as high as 100% and as low as 10% during the halcyon days of the 1920s. "Fifty percent" means that on a $10,000 transaction, the customer must pay the broker at least $5,000 in cash or deposit marginable securities worth $10,000; $10,000 worth of marginable securities has a loan value of $5,000. Cash or securities must be deposited with the broker by the settlement date of the transaction or no later than seven business days after the trade date. The Fed imposes penalties if more credit is extended to the customer.

How to Satisfy a Regulation T Call. The customer may use one of three methods to meet a "Reg T" call by the broker.

1. Deposit cash equal to the call.
2. Deposit marginable securities with a loan value equal to the call. This is determined by applying the following formula:

$$\text{Market value of the security} = \frac{\text{Regulation T call}}{\text{Loan value percentage}}$$

If the loan value percentage is 35% and the Reg T Call is for $2,450, the customer must deposit marginable securities worth $7,000 ($2,450 ÷ .35).

3. Sell securities long in the account to meet the call. This last method should be done only in unusual circumstances. Regulatory authorities do not approve of customers selling securities long in the account to meet Reg T calls as a habit. Selling securities long in the account may be done to meet margin maintenance call and not the Reg T requirement.

If the customer has more than one Reg T call, his funds are applied on a first-in and first-out basis. The broker must retain the funds until the customer's checks are cleared.

The broker must maintain a daily record of all margin calls issued and the manner in which the calls were satisfied. The records must be made available for review by NYSE and NASD examiners.

In addition to Regulation T, Federal Reserve Regulations U, G, and X control customer margin transactions.

Regulation U regulates loans extended by a bank for securities trading. The customer must sign a statement of purpose and deposit securities as collateral for the loan if the loan is for the purpose of buying marginable securities. This is called *purpose loan.* The customer must comply with the Fed's maximum margin limitations. If after collateralizing the securities the customer uses the loan for purposes other than securities trading, the bank extends credit based on the bank's credit policies. This is a *non-purpose loan* and not subject to the Fed's credit limitations.

Regulation G regulates credit by persons other than banks and broker–dealers. The lender must obtain a statement of purpose signed by the customer. These loans, if used for purchasing marginable securities, are again subject to the Fed's maximum credit limitations. If the loans are for other purposes, the lender may extend credit to the customer as he sees fit. The customer may deposit nonmarginable securities for collateral with the lender.

Regulation X defines requirements for the borrower of funds.

Stock Exchange and NASD Margin Requirements

The New York Stock Exchange requires a minimum initial equity in the account. At the initiation of the margin account, the customer must deposit cash no less than $2,000 or its equivalent in marginable securities. If the cost of the purchase is under $2,000, the customer is not required to deposit funds greater than the purchase cost. The $2,000 initial equity is not affected by the market depreciation of securities in the account. This means, if the account's equity falls below $2,000 due to market depreciation, the broker will not issue a margin call as long as the equity in the account is above the margin maintenance requirement. The customer is not required to deposit more cash or securities. The $2,000 initial equity is affected by cash or security withdrawal by the customer. The customer may not withdraw cash or securities from his account if, after the withdrawal, the account's equity falls below $2,000.

MARGIN MAINTENANCE

After the initiation of the margin account, the customer must comply with the margin maintenance requirements of the securities exchanges and the NASD. The Federal Reserve does not have margin maintenance regulations. The New York Stock Exchange requires that the equity in the margin account be at least 25% of the market value of the securities held in the account, or $2,000, whichever is the greater amount. The equity cannot be lower than 25% or $2,000 at any time. When the security in the account declines in value, the broker will issue a margin call requesting additional cash or marginable securities to bring the equity in the account to an acceptable level.

$$\begin{pmatrix} \text{Margin} \\ \text{maintenance} \\ \text{call} \end{pmatrix} = \begin{pmatrix} \text{Margin} \\ \text{maintenance} \\ \text{requirements} \end{pmatrix} - \text{Margin equity}$$

How to Satisfy a Margin Maintenance Call. To meet a maintenance call, the customer may either deposit cash equal to the call, deposit marginable securities equal to ⁴⁄₃ the call, or sell securities long in the account equal to four times the call.

EXAMPLE

$$\begin{pmatrix} \text{Margin} \\ \text{maintenance} \\ \text{call} \end{pmatrix} = \begin{pmatrix} \text{Maintenance} \\ \text{requirement} \end{pmatrix} - \text{Margin equity}$$

$$\$1,500 = \$14,500 - \$13,000$$

The broker will issue a margin call for $1,500.

1. The customer may deposit $1,500. This will reduce his debit balance, thereby increasing his equity and, therefore, maintenance requirement will be satisfied.

2. The customer may deposit marginable securities with a market value of $2,000 ($1,500 × ⁴⁄₃) to meet the maintenance call. The deposit of $2,000 worth of securities will increase the long market value by $2,000; the equity will, therefore, also increase by $2,000. By depositing securities, however, the customer will also increase the margin maintenance requirements by $500 (25% of $2,000).

3. The customer will sell a security long in the account to meet the maintenance call of $1,500. He must sell securities worth $6,000 (four times the call). The sale of the securities will reduce the long market value and the margin debit, each by $6,000.

The customer may determine a margin maintenance call in advance by multiplying the margin debit by ⅓. Anytime the long market value of the security falls below this amount, a maintenance margin call is issued. According to stock exchange and NASD rules, the customer must satisfy a maintenance margin call promptly and within a reasonable period of time; for some brokers this means between one and five business days.

The Policies of the Brokerage House

The aforementioned margin regulations are only minimum requirements by the Fed, NYSE, and the NASD. Broker–dealers may require higher initial margin than the Fed's 50%, higher initial equity than the NYSE's $2,000 minimum, and higher margin maintenance than 25% equity. Some require 30%, others 40% or higher, and so on.

PURCHASE OF SECURITY IN A CASH ACCOUNT

In purchasing a security in a cash account, a customer may give any one of the following instructions to the broker:

1. Transfer the security in the name of the customer and ship.

2. Transfer the security in the name of the customer and hold. The broker will keep the certificate in the name of the customer. The customer will receive the dividends directly from the corporation.

3. Keep the security in Street Name. The security will be registered in the name of the brokerage firm. The broker will act as nominee for the customer who remains the beneficial owner of the security. The broker will receive all dividends and credit them in the customer's account.

4. Cash on delivery or deliver vs. payment (COD or DVP). The customer will instruct the broker to deliver the purchased security in Street Name to a bank or a financial institution and receive payment for the security.

For all margin accounts, the purchased securities must be kept in Street Name. No other instructions are allowed.

Methods of Payment

1. The customer may use clearing house funds to make payment for securities purchases. Clearing house funds generally mature into federal funds overnight. The customer may use checks, cashier's checks, or cash. Brokers discourage the use of currency for securities transactions. Customer cash received by brokers in excess of $10,000 is reported to the Federal Reserve Bank. Payments to cover purchases of U.S. government obligations and agencies must be made in federal funds. Payments to cover options transactions are made in clearing house funds.

2. For COD or DVP transactions, the broker will deliver the customer's purchased security to a designated financial institution. The delivery must be made within 35 calendar days after the trade date. The bank is obligated to make payment upon receipt of the security. The broker has the right to liquidate the account if the bank rejects the delivery due to lack of instructions. If the COD delivery is made to another broker–dealer designated by the customer, the delivering broker must secure a letter of free credit from the receiving broker certifying that adequate funds are available in the account to pay for the security.

3. Third party checks — partnership checks payable to an individual, corporate checks for an individual account, checks for a fiduciary (executor, administrator, trustee, etc.) for an individual account — are not acceptable.

4. *Cancellations and Liquidations.* A broker–dealer shall promptly cancel or liquidate a transaction for which the customer has not made full payment within the required time. A broker–dealer may, at his option, disregard any sum due from the customer not exceeding $500.

5. *90-Day Freeze.* If the purchased security is sold without having been previously paid for in full by the customer, the account will be frozen for 90 calendar days. During this period the customer is required to have sufficient cash in his account to meet the purchase cost of another security. A regulatory agency may grant a waiver from the 90-day freeze.

6. *Extensions of Time Periods.* If the customer does not make full payment for the cost of the transaction within the required time, the broker–dealer may apply for an extension. Applications for extension shall be filed with a regulatory agency prior to the end of the seven business day period. If the broker–

dealer does not have any direct electronic access to the regulatory agency, the application may be considered as timely filed if it is postmarked no later than midnight of the last day of the seven business day period.

SALE OF SECURITY IN A CASH ACCOUNT

In selling a security, the customer may give any one of the following instructions to the broker:

1. Send the proceeds of the sale.

2. Remit periodic payments to the customer representing the proceeds of the sale.

3. Leave the proceeds of the sale in the customer's account. This generally earns no interest for the customer.

4. In a receive versus payment (RVP) arrangement, the customer will instruct his bank to deliver the sold certificate to the broker and receive payment. The bank will credit the amount in the customer's bank account. This is the reverse of COD on the purchase side.

Under Rule 387 of the New York Stock Exchange and the similar rules of the NASD and other securities exchanges, this trade must be consummated by a book-entry method through a depository organization, provided that both the receiving and delivering institutions are participating members of depositories and the security is eligible at the depository.

5. Invest the proceeds of the sale in money market funds. The customer will earn interest and may withdraw the funds whenever he wishes.

Delivery of Certificates

When the customer sells a security, he must deliver the certificates to the broker by the trade settlement date. The delivery must be made in good deliverable form. The customer may not be paid if the certificates lack endorsement or require legal documents to transfer. Certificates subject to a reverse split, restricted or legend certificates, and certificates not in proper deliverable units must be transferred first before they are considered as good deliverable instruments.

Under SEC Rule 15c3-3, a broker is required to liquidate the account if securities sold by the customer are not received by the tenth business day after the settlement date. The broker may apply for an extension to the stock exchange or the district office of the NASD, requesting more time. Upon completion of the extension period, the broker must liquidate the account. Exempt securities, such as U.S. government and municipal securities, are not subject to this rule.

The proceeds of the sale may not be remitted to the customer prior to the settlement date. This type of prepayment is allowed only in an extreme emergency.

The customer may direct the broker to issue checks in other names; he must complete the proper authorization forms and submit them to the broker, authorizing the broker to issue the check.

The proceeds of the sale of mutual fund shares are generally remitted to the customer only after the broker has received the liquidation payment from the fund.

BUYING POWER IN A MARGIN ACCOUNT

The *buying power* is the amount of securities that the customer may purchase, or sell short, using the credit balance of the excess equity in the margin account. The Regulation T excess represents the amount of money available for use as down payment for the customer to purchase new securities on margin.

EXAMPLE

Long market value	$10,000
Margin debit	−3,000
Margin equity	$ 7,000
Margin required	$ 5,000 (50% of $10,000)
Regulation T excess	$ 2,000 ($7,000 − $5,000)

At 50% Regulation T margin requirement, the customer's buying power is $4,000, with a $2,000 Regulation T excess in the account. The customer may purchase another marginable security worth $4,000 without any additional margin requirement.

The computation of the buying power is done by dividing the excess into the margin required:

$$\frac{\$2,000}{.50} = \$4,000$$

At 65% Regulation T requirement, the buying power will be:

$$\frac{\$2,000}{.65} = \$3,076$$

$$\text{Buying power} = \frac{\text{Regulation T excess}}{\text{Margin required}}$$

INTEREST CHARGES ON MARGIN DEBIT

At the opening of the account, the broker is required to explain to the customer the method in which he charges interest on margin debit. This is a requirement under the Truth in Lending Law and SEC Rule 10(b)-16. Brokers are free to increase or reduce interest rates, as the money market conditions dictate. The interest rates may vary from one customer to another. The larger the margin debit, the less the interest charge will be and vice versa. The broker must indicate the interest charge on the customer's statement. He computes the charges by using the following formula:

$$\frac{\text{Interest}}{\text{charge}} = \frac{\text{Margin}}{\text{debit}} \times \frac{\text{Interest rate}}{100\%} \times \frac{\text{Number of days}}{360 \text{ days}}$$

For interest calculation purposes, the broker considers every month to have 30 calendar days.

EXAMPLE

The customer's margin debit is $10,000 and the interest rate is 12%. The interest charge for the month will be:

$$\frac{\text{Interest}}{\text{charge}} = \$10,000 \times \frac{12\%}{100\%} \times \frac{30}{360 \text{ days}} = \$99.99$$

This will appear as a separate charge in the customer's statement. If the customer does not pay this amount, the broker will increase the customer's margin debit by this amount for the interest charge computation of the following month.

TRANSFER OF A CUSTOMER ACCOUNT
TO ANOTHER BROKER

When a customer instructs his broker to transfer his account to another broker, the broker must:

1. Cancel all open orders.
2. Deliver securities long in the account to the other broker.
3. Calculate interest charges up to the date of the securities delivery.
4. Deliver the Regulation T letter to the other broker regarding the status of the account, including the balance in the customer's SMA. This letter must state that there are no outstanding and unsatisfied Regulation T margin calls. The receiving broker will accept the letter in good faith, without requesting additional margin as collateral. Open short positions may also be transferred to the other broker. The two brokers' cooperation is essential in transferring margin accounts.

The New York Stock Exchange Rule 412 requires brokers to follow specific procedures to expedite the transfer of accounts.

MARGIN ACCOUNT

A customer may have more than one margin account with a broker–dealer provided that each margin account is supervised by a different account executive.

The following transactions will be done in a margin account:

1. Buying securities on margin.
2. Selling securities short.
3. Writing uncovered options.

When Additional Margin Is Required

1. *Computing deficiency:* All transactions on the same day shall be combined to determine whether additional margin is required by the broker–dealer.
2. *Satisfaction of deficiency:* The additional required margin may be satisfied by a transfer from the SMA or by a deposit of cash, marginable or exempt securities.
3. *Time limits:* A margin call shall be satisfied within seven business days after the margin deficiency was created or increased. This seven business day period may be extended for one or more limited periods upon application by the broker–dealer to a regulatory agency.

Liquidation in Lieu of Deposit

If the margin call is not met in full within the required time, the broker–dealer shall liquidate securities sufficient to meet the margin call. If the margin deficiency is $500 or less, no action need be taken by the broker–dealer.

Withdrawal of Cash or Securities

Cash or securities may be withdrawn from an account, except if:

1. Additional cash or securities are required to be deposited into the account for a transaction on the same or a previous day. Or:
2. The withdrawal would create or increase a margin deficiency.

Margin excess may be withdrawn or transferred to the SMA by debiting the margin account and crediting the SMA.

Interest and Service Charges

A broker–dealer may debit the following items in the customer's margin account:

1. Interest charged on margin debit.
2. Premium on securities borrowed in connection with short sales or to effect delivery.
3. Dividends or interest on other distributions due on borrowed security.
4. Any other service charges that the broker–dealer may impose.

A customer may withdraw interest and dividends on any distributions from his margin account, if the withdrawal does not create or increase a margin deficiency in the account, or if the current market value of any securities withdrawn does not exceed 10% of the current market value of the security with respect to which they were distributed.

UNRESTRICTED ACCOUNTS

The customer's margin account is unrestricted if the equity is equal to or greater than the Regulation T margin requirement. The customer may withdraw cash or securities representing the excess equity in the account below the minimum margin maintenance requirement. No cash withdrawals are allowed, other than cash dividends, from an unrestricted account if the margin equity in the account is less than $2,000. The customer may withdraw a fully paid-for nonmarginable security long in an unrestricted account at any time. To withdraw a marginable security long in the account, the customer must make sure that the security's loan value is equal to or less than the margin excess in the account.

RESTRICTED ACCOUNTS

The customer's margin account becomes restricted if the margin equity is below the initial margin requirement of the securities in the account. To withdraw cash or securities from a restricted account, the customer may withdraw:

1. Cash from his SMA.
2. Excess cash generated as a result of a purchase transaction of a marginable security to cover a short sale.

3. Cash dividends or interests provided that the SMA is equal to or greater than the dividends or interests.

4. A marginable security, provided that the customer deposits *either* marginable security with a loan value equal to 50% of the market value of the security to be withdrawn *or* cash equal to the loan value of the security to be withdrawn.

5. A stock dividend credited in the account, provided that the stock was not used as margin in the interim.

SPECIAL MEMORANDUM ACCOUNT (SMA)

This is used as a general reservoir for excess funds. The customer is allowed to withdraw cash or securities, which he might not otherwise be permitted to do in a margin account. The SMA may contain the following entries:

1. Dividend and interest payments.

2. Proceeds of sale of securities or cash no longer required on any expired or liquidated security positions that may be withdrawn by the customer.

3. Margin excess transferred from the margin account.

ILLUSTRATION OF A MARGIN TRANSACTION

Bee Corp. stock is $100 a share. The customer buys 100 shares in a margin account. The customer deposits $5,000 to comply with the Regulation T requirement and borrows $5,000 from the broker. His account will read:

Long	Current Price	Market Value	Reg T Call Margin Required
100	$100	$10,000	$5,000
	Long market value	$10,000	
	Margin debit	−5,000	
	Margin equity	$ 5,000	

The margin clerk will monitor the status of the account on a daily basis. He will make sure that the equity in the account is at least 25% of the market value of the security long in the account. If the equity reaches the 25% level, the margin clerk will issue a margin maintenance call. To satisfy the call the customer may deposit either cash equal to the call or marginable securities with a market value equal to ⅓ of the call. If the call is for $1,500, he must deposit marginable securities with a market value of $2,000 (⅓ × $1,500). Or the customer may sell some shares in the account to satisfy the call. When the security declines in price to a point where the margin equity falls below 25%, the account is considered to be undermargined.

Bee Corp. declines to $60 a share. The account will read:

Long	Current Price	Market Value
100	$60	$6,000
	Long market value	$6,000
	Margin debit	−5,000
	Margin equity	$ 1,000

Twenty-five percent of $6,000 is $1,500. The margin equity is $1,000; the account is, therefore, undermargined by $500. The customer must deposit $500 or marginable security worth $6,667 (⅓ × $5,000).

The customer may determine a margin maintenance call in advance by simply dividing the margin debit by 3 and adding the result to the margin debit.

$$\$5,000 \div 3 = \$1,666$$

$$\$5,000 + \$1,666 = \$6,666$$

If the stock falls below $6,666, the account will be undermargined by the difference between $6,666 and the current market value.

At this point the margin equity in the account is $2,000 and the long market value of the security is $6,000. The equity represents 33% of the long market value, adequate enough to satisfy the minimum margin maintenance requirement. The equity, however, is below the Regulation T 50% margin requirement. Fifty percent of $6,000 is $3,000, and the equity is $2,000. And since the equity is below 50% of the current market value of the security, the margin account is considered to be restricted.

When the account becomes restricted the customer may

withdraw excess funds from his special memorandum account (SMA), provided that the withdrawal does not bring the account below the minimum margin maintenance requirement. SMAs are used as reservoirs of excess funds. The broker will place profits and other funds generated as a result of customer transactions, dividends, interests, proceeds of sale of securities, and so on. The funds in the SMA are available to the customer at all times. He may use them to purchase more securities or withdraw them in cash. The SMA account does not have a debit balance and does not reflect the depreciation of the market value of the security long in the account. Brokers treat SMAs as memo accounts.

If the customer has nothing in his SMA and wishes to withdraw cash from his restricted account, he must deposit marginable securities with a loan value equal to the cash withdrawn. If he wishes to withdraw $1,000, he must deposit $2,000 worth of marginable securities, with a loan value at a 50% level. If the loan value is 40% (with the Regulation T requirement being 60%), the customer must deposit marginable securities worth $2,500 to be allowed to withdraw $1,000 in cash from the restricted account ($1,000 ÷ 40 = $2,500). Forty percent of $2,500 is $1,000.

If the customer wishes to withdraw securities from his restricted account, he must deposit cash equal to 50% of the market value of the security to be withdrawn. If he wishes to withdraw 100 Cee Corp. valued at $100 a share, he must deposit $5,000 in cash (50% of $10,000).

With his account in a restricted condition, the customer may sell securities long in his account and purchase new securities without depositing margin ordinarily required for securities purchases, provided that both the sale and the purchase transactions occur on the same day. This is called *same-day substitution*.

The customer sells 100 Dee Corp. long in the account at $85 a share. Using the proceeds of the sale, he purchases 100 shares Tee Corp. at $85 a share. If both transactions are made on the same day, the customer is not required to deposit 50% margin for the purchase of 100 shares Tee Corp.

If, on the other hand, the cost of the purchase of the second security is greater than the proceeds of the sale of the first, the customer is required to deposit 50% of the difference between the two amounts. For example, he sells 100 shares for $8,500 and buys, on the same day, another security worth $10,000. The customer must deposit 50% of the difference.

$$\$10,000 - \$8,500 = \$1,500 \ (50\% \text{ of } \$1,500 = \$750)$$

If the purchased security has less value than the proceeds of the sale of the other security, only 50% of the difference is credited to the customer's SMA. For example, the customer sells a security for $10,000 in a restricted account and buys, on the same day, another security for $5,000. The customer's SMA will reflect a credit of $2,500.

$$\$10,000 - \$5,000 = \$5,000 \ (50\% \text{ of } \$5,000 = \$2,500)$$

SELLING SECURITIES SHORT

A *short sale* is the sale of a security with the understanding that it will be purchased and delivered at a later date. The broker lends the security to the customer who will sell it with the anticipation that it will be purchased later at a lower price. The difference in money between the proceeds of the sale and the cost of the purchase will be the customer's profit in the transaction. An important factor is the availability of the security in the marketplace. The security must be borrowed before a short sale transaction is consummated. Borrowing the security is an indispensable requirement. The proceeds of the sale are not made available to the customer until he buys the security to cover his short position. After the purchase transaction, the customer's account will reflect the net difference — profit or loss — between both transactions.

Short selling is an important factor for the general well-being of the stock market. Even though, by selling the security short, the short seller creates an artificial supply in a particular security, his activity is important to provide the necessary liquidity for the security. This becomes apparent in periods of falling prices. When the price of the security starts falling, the demand to purchase the security will be scarce. Yet the short seller will purchase the security at this point to cover his short. This activity will, therefore, provide a built-in buying interest. This buying activity in a declining period will help cushion the decline in a down market. The same is true in a rising market. When the security rises, the short seller sells the security short. This will cushion the optimism in a rising market.

TYPES OF SHORT SALES

There are basically three types of short sales:

1. A bona fide short sale or "sale first and purchase next"
2. "Short against the box"
3. "Arbitrage short"

In a *bona fide short sale*, the customer will cover his short position by purchasing the security. If the purchase cost is higher than the proceeds of the short sale, the investor will consider the difference in money as capital loss. If the purchase cost is less than the proceeds of the short sale, the investor will consider this as capital gain. The short-term tax treatment is applied in both cases regardless of the time period involved in the short sale and purchase transactions.

In *short against the box*, the customer owns the security but elects to sell it short without altering his long position. His primary objective is to defer the payment of taxes until a later date. Let us assume that the current market value of the security is higher than the original cost of the purchase. If the customer decides to sell the security, he would incur a tax on capital gains for that year. To defer the tax to the following year, he would sell the stock short against his long position. He becomes liable for capital gains taxes only after his long position is delivered off to cover the short sale. The broker simply pairs off and cancels both positions in the customer's margin account. If the customer's long position was held more than six months, the resulting profit or loss will be long term.

In an *arbitrage short*, the customer takes advantage of the disparity of prices of a given security at different exchanges. He will sell the security short at one exchange and buy it back at another.

The customer in selling the security short is bearish on the security. He believes the price will decline. He would sell it at a high price and hope to purchase it at a lower price. There is risk, however, if the security rallies instead of declines. Because of the risk, it is a regulatory requirement to effect the short sale in a margin account under a broker's constant supervision. In short against the box, the risk is limited — or rather protected. Since the customer is long and short the same security, future price fluctuations will not affect his profit or loss status.

Whether bona fide short sale, short against the box, or arbitrage short, the trades must be executed in accordance with regulatory requirements. Under SEC Rules 10a-1 and 10a-2, a person selling a stock exchange security short may not execute the trade at a price that would depress the price of the security in the general market.

To explain this we must first discuss the trading mechanism of securities on an exchange. Brokers identify each transaction on the floor as uptick, downtick, zero plus tick, zero minus tick, and so on. Let us assume that the price of a security declines to 39⅞ immediately after trading at 40. This price (39⅞) is ⅛ of a point lower than 40. The transaction at 39⅞ is called a *minus tick*. If the succeeding transaction is again at 39⅞, the transaction is known as *zero minus tick*. If after this the stock is traded at 40, the trade will be called a *plus tick*. If the succeeding transaction is again 40, it is called a *zero plus tick*. And so on.

First sale	40
Minus tick	39⅞
Zero minus tick	39⅞
Plus tick	40
Zero plus tick	40
Minus tick	39⅞
Zero minus tick	39⅞

Using this as a guideline, a short seller must make sure that the short sale is made at a price identified as a plus tick or zero plus tick. If the plus tick or the zero plus tick is not available at the time, the short seller may offer to sell the stock at a price that would be designated as zero or zero plus when the trade is accepted by the buyer.

If the price of the last sale is 39⅜ immediately after trading at 39½, the transaction is a minus tick. The short seller may offer to sell the stock at 39½ or 39⅝. This offer, if accepted by the buyer, would be identified as a plus tick.

On the ex-dividend dates the trade designations are adjusted to reflect the dividend distribution. On the ex-dividend date the price of the security is reduced by the amount of the dividend. If the stock pays 50¢ a share in dividends, the price of the security is reduced by 50¢ on the ex-dividend date. Minus and plus tick designations take the dividend into consideration.

EXAMPLES OF PLUS TICK AND MINUS TICK

The very first transaction of a security in the stock exchange will be designated as plus tick without any consideration as to whether it is a short sale or a long sale. Subsequent transactions will then be designated as zero plus, plus minus, or zero minus as the case may be. These designations will continue on a consecutive basis from day to day.

1. Minus Tick:
Quotation on the Floor — 48⅝ to 48⅞

The security has the following trades on the floor:

48⅜
48⅝ minus tick

The short seller offers to sell the stock at 48¾ or 48⅞. If accepted by the buyer, this transaction will represent a plus tick. The short sale will comply with the SEC regulation.

2. Plus Tick:
Quotation on the Floor — 43⅜ to 43⅝

The security had the following trades on the floor:

43⅞
43½ plus tick

The short seller may offer to sell at 43½ (zero plus tick) or 43⅝ (plus tick). If the buyer accepts, the trade will be designated as zero plus tick or plus tick. This will also comply with the SEC regulation. The uptick rule does not apply to transactions in the over-the-counter market.

MARGIN REQUIREMENTS FOR SHORT SALE

Short sales are subject to the margin requirements of Regulation T, the NYSE, other exchanges, and the NASD. The trade is done in a margin account, and the broker marks the short security position to the market daily, weekly, or periodically. It is a requirement that the proceeds of the sale be kept in the account as a credit balance, together with additional margin requirements. The purpose is to hold the credit balance as collateral against the short position. It will be used to cover the cost of purchasing the security.

SELLING SHORT IN A MARGIN ACCOUNT

Pursuant to stock exchange and NASD rules, the margin account must have a minimum of $2,000 in equity. This is a requirement for marginable securities. Short sale margin requirements for marginable securities are set by Regulation T of the Federal Reserve Board and for exempt securities by the stock exchanges and the NASD. A nonmarginable security may also be sold short, provided the broker is able to borrow the security on behalf of the customer.

TABLE 16.1. SHORT SALE MARGIN REQUIREMENTS

Security	Required Initial Margin	Margin Maintenance Requirement
1. Stocks, rights, and warrants listed on a national stock exchange.	50% of the net proceeds of sale.	1. If the price per share is above 16¾, the maintenance requirement is 30% of the market value.
2. Over-the-counter securities approved by the Federal Reserve Board	50% of the net proceeds of sale.	2. If the price per share is between 5 and 16⅝, the maintenance requirement is $5 a share.
		3. If the price is between $2½ to $5 a share, the maintenance is 100% of the market value.
		4. If the price is under $2½ a share, the requirement is $2½ a share.
3. Convertible bonds listed at a national stock exchange that can be converted into a marginable security. Convertible bonds in the OTC market approved by the Fed.	50% of the net proceeds of sale.	5% of the face value or 30% of market value, whichever is the greater amount.

TABLE 16.1. SHORT SALE MARGIN REQUIREMENTS (Continued)

Security	Required Initial Margin	Margin Maintenance Requirement
4. Bonds listed at a national stock exchange that carry rights or warrants allowing the holder to subscribe to a marginable security. Approved (by the Fed) OTC bonds carrying warrants.	50% of the proceeds of sale.	5% of the face value or 30% of the market value, whichever is the greater amount.
5. Nonconvertible bonds listed at a national stock exchange and certain unlisted bonds in the over-the-counter market.	50% of the proceeds of sale.	5% of the face value or 30% of the market value, whichever is the greater amount.
6. U.S. government obligations and federal agency securities.	5% of the face value of the security.	5% of the face value of the security.
7. Municipal securities.	15% of the face value or 25% of the market value, whichever is the lesser amount.	15% of the face value or 25% of the market value whichever is the lesser amount.

SELLING A MARGINABLE STOCK SHORT

The customer sells 100 Bee Corp. short at $50 a share. Let us assume that Bee Corp. is a marginable stock listed at a stock exchange. The total proceeds of the sale is $5,000. The broker will deduct commissions, taxes, and fees, crediting the customer's account with the net proceeds. The proceeds of the sale will be kept in the account until the customer buys the security to cover the short position. Without considering the commissions, taxes, and fees, the customer's account will read:

Short	Current Price	Total Market Value	Credit Balance
100 Bee Corp.	$50	$5,000	$5,000

Regulation T requires the customer to deposit cash equal to 50% of the net proceeds of the sale as margin within seven business days. The broker will issue a Regulation T call for $2,500 (50% of $5,000). After the cash deposit is made, the account will reflect the new credit balance as follows:

Short	Current Price	Total Market Value	Credit Balance
100 Bee Corp.	$50	$5,000	$7,500

To determine equity in a short account, the broker subtracts the current market value of the short security from the credit balance in the account. (Equity in a long account is determined by the long market value minus the debit balance.)

$$\text{Equity in short account} = \text{Credit balance} - \text{Short market value}$$

In the preceding example, the equity is $2,500 ($7,500 − $5,000 = $2,500). This equity of $2,500 is sufficient to comply with NYSE's minimum initial margin requirement of $2,000.

To determine the NYSE margin maintenance requirement, the broker will consider 30% of the market value of the short security or $5 a share, whichever is greater:

$$30\% \text{ of } \$5,000 = \$1,500$$

$$100 \times 5 = \$500$$

Therefore, $1,500 is the margin maintenance requirement, or to use the more specific guideline: The stock is priced over $16¾ a share. The broker will consider 30% equity for margin maintenance. The account will read:

Short	Current Price	Total Market Value	Credit Balance
100 Bee Corp.	$50	$5,000	$7,500
Margin equity		$2,500	($7,500 − $5,000)
Margin maintenance requirement		$1,500	(30% of $5,000)

The equity of $2,500 is sufficient to cover both the initial margin requirement of $2,000 and the maintenance margin of $1,500.

The broker's margin department will mark the account to the market and determine the equity and maintenance when the price of the security rises or declines. Since this is a short sale, the equity will increase when the security declines in value. If Bee Corp. stock declines to $40 a share, the short account will be calculated as follows:

Short	*Current Price*	*Total Market Value*	*Credit Balance*
100 Bee Corp.	$40	$4,000	$7,500
Margin equity		$3,500 ($7,500 − $4,000)	
Margin maintenance		$1,200 (30% of $4,000)	

There is an increase of $1,000 in equity and a reduction of $300 in margin maintenance.

The mark to the market procedure will also determine the excess equity in the account. The account will have an excess when the equity exceeds the Regulation T margin requirement. To determine the excess, let us go back to our example:

Short	*Current Price*	*Total Market Value*	*Credit Balance*
100 Bee Corp.	$40	$4,000	$7,500
Margin equity		$3,500 ($7,500 − $4,000)	
Margin required (50%)		−2,000 (50% of $4,000)	
Regulation T excess		$1,500	

When the security declined to $40 a share, the equity in the account had increased to the point that it exceeded the Regulation T margin requirement. The excess of $1,500 may be withdrawn by the customer in cash or applied for future purchases or short sales. With $1,500 cash the customer may purchase securities worth $3,000 at 50% margin requirement. The $3,000 represents the customer's buying power. Another term in this connection is the *short selling power*. This represents the maximum amount of securities one may sell short by using the Regulation T excess without having to deposit more margin. The formula for both is the same:

$$\frac{\text{Buying power or}}{\text{Short selling power}} = \frac{\text{Regulation T excess}}{\text{Required margin}}$$

The Regulation T excess is determined by:

$$\text{Reg T excess} = \text{Equity} - \text{Required margin}$$

The Regulation T excess is credited in the customer's SMA. It may be withdrawn by the customer provided the withdrawal does not reduce the equity below $2,000 or place the account on a maintenance call. In determining Regulation T excess, consideration is given to the amount of equity needed for margin maintenance. In the preceding example, the equity is $3,500, the Regulation T excess is $1,500, and the margin maintenance is $1,200 (30% of $4,000). In allowing the customer to use the excess, the margin clerk will compare Regulation T excess with maintenance excess and authorize the lesser amount to be used by the customer:

Total Market Value	Margin Required	Equity	Margin Maintenance
$4,000	$2,000	$3,500	$1,200
Regulation T excess		$1,500	($3,500 − $2,000)
Maintenance excess		$2,300	($3,500 − $1,200)
The lesser amount is $1,500.			

If the customer uses the excess of $1,500 his account will read:

Total Market Value	Margin Required	Equity	Margin Maintenance
$4,000	$2,000	$2,000	$1,200
Regulation T excess	0		
Maintenance	0		

Let us now determine equity in a rising market. Using the same example, let us see what happens if Bee Corp. stock rallies to $60 a share. The short account will be marked to the market.

Short	Current Price	Total Market Value	Credit Balance
100 Bee Corp.	$60	$6,000	$7,500
Margin equity		$1,500	($7,500 − $6,000)
Margin maintenance		$1,800	(30% of $6,000)
Maintenance call		$ 300	($1,800 − $1,500)

The equity in the account is not sufficient to maintain the account at a 30% market value of the security. The customer must deposit cash or equivalent securities immediately.

To demonstrate margin maintenance requirement, let us consider a security with a market price of $10 a share. The customer sells 500 shares of Cee Corp. short. His account will read:

Short	Current Price	Total Market Value	Credit Balance
500 Cee Corp.	$10	$5,000	$7,500 (proceeds of the sale plus Reg T margin)
Margin equity		$2,500	($7,500 − $5,000)
Margin maintenance		$2,500	($500 × 5)

Since the price of the stock is between $5 and $16⅝, the broker will consider $5 a share for margin maintenance purposes instead of 30% of the market value of the security.

For lower-priced securities the margin maintenance requirement is higher. Since lower-priced securities tend to be more speculative in nature, the NYSE requires more collateral for greater protection and security.

EXAMPLE 1

The customer sells 1,000 Tee Corp. short at $3 a share. His account will read as follows:

Short	Current Price	Total Market Value	Credit Balance
1,000 Tee Corp.	$3	$3,000	$4,500
Margin equity		$1,500	($4,500 − $3,000)
Margin maintenance		$3,000	(100% of $3,000)
Maintenance call		$1,500	($3,000 − $1,500)

The price of the stock is between $2½ and $5 a share. The NYSE margin maintenance requirement will therefore be 100% of the market value of the short security. The broker will issue a maintenance call for $1,500. The customer must deposit this in cash or in equivalent securities immediately.

EXAMPLE 2

The customer sells 2,000 Dee Corp. short at $2 a share. His account will read:

Short	Current Price	Total Market Value	Credit Balance
2,000 Dee Corp.	$2	$4,000	$6,000 (proceeds of the sale plus Reg T margin)
Margin equity		$2,000	($6,000 − $4,000)
Margin maintenance		$5,000	($2,000 × $2.50)
Maintenance call		$3,000	($5,000 − $2,000)

Since the security is trading under $2½ a share, the margin maintenance is calculated on the basis of $2.50 a share. The broker will issue a maintenance call for $3,000, and the customer must deposit this in cash or in equivalent securities immediately.

CHAPTER SEVENTEEN

PROCESSING OF DIVIDENDS AND INTERESTS

The Dividend Department of a financial organization performs specific bookkeeping functions related solely to processing of dividends and interests. It is responsible for allocating, paying, crediting, and claiming dividends and interest distributions on securities. Its operation is dependent upon the accuracy of security positions in the securities firm. There may be underpayment or overpayment of dividends due to a variety of errors.

Underpayments of dividends may be attributed to the following:

1. Errors made by the disbursing agent

2. Errors in the security positions of the firm

3. The transfer department's failure to transfer the shares over the record date

4. The failure of the selling broker to deliver the securities sold on the settlement date.

The selling broker's records will then indicate a fail to deliver and the buying broker's records will indicate a fail to receive. In the event of a dividend distribution, the buying broker will impose a condition for the settlement of the trade. The Dividend Department will advise the Receive and Deliver Section of the Cashier's Department to make sure that when the security is eventually

A DUE BILL CHECK

Due Bill Check	*No. 1234*

Consider this check as Due Bill until payable date as shown below.

New York _____ 19_____

ABC Bank

Pay to the order of _____ $ _____

_____ Dollars.

in payment of dividend or interest

Dividend Account
Interest Account

On _____ Not payable before _____

Record Date _____

A DUE BILL FOR STOCK DIVIDEND OR STOCK DISTRIBUTION

For value received, the undersigned hereby assigns transfers, and sets over to _____ the stock distribution of _____ ( ) shares of _____ stock of _____ to be issued on _____ to the registered holder of _____ ( ) shares of _____ _____ stock of _____ represented by _____ to which the undersigned is entitled as a stock dividend, and hereby irrevocably constitutes and appoints _____ attorney to transfer the shares representing said stock dividend on the books of said corporation, with full power of substitution.

Dated _____ Official Signature _____

delivered by the selling broker, a Due Bill is attached to the delivery. The Due Bills obligate the selling broker to deliver the dividends to the buying broker soon after the corporation distributes them to the holders of record.

Due Bills are promissory notes. They provide assurances that the broker delivering the security will honor his obligation to pay the dividend to the buying broker when the dividends are distributed by the corporation. The Due Bill practice also expedites the trade settlements of securities sold on the day before the dividend date. When the selling broker delivers the security too late for the buying broker to effect the transfer on the record date, he must issue a Due Bill and deliver it to the buying broker with the security. The trading period between the ex-dividend date and the record date is called "the Due Bill period." On the payment day, the buying broker endorses the Due Bill and presents it to the selling broker for payment.

FOUR DATES FOR DIVIDENDS

There are four dates associated with dividend distributions: the Declaration date, the Ex-dividend or Ex-interest date, the Record date, and the Payable date.

1. *The Declaration Date.* The board of directors of a corporation decides to distribute a portion of the net earnings to stockholders. This may be in the form of cash disbursements, share distributions, or stock dividends. Dividends are usually announced to the public through newspapers or, more specifically, through financial service publications. The financial section of newspapers carries a daily schedule of board of directors' dividend meetings. It is at these meetings that dividends are voted upon.

2. *The Ex-dividend or Ex-interest Date.* When a dividend is declared for distribution, the stock exchange where the security is listed for trading will set aside a day for the security to trade on the basis of ex-dividend or ex-interest. On a regular way trade when the settlement of the trade is the fifth business day after the trade day, the ex-dividend date is the fourth business day before the record date. On the ex-dividend day, the buyer of the security will not be entitled to receive the dividend. This is because he becomes the legal owner of the security on the fifth business day, which means that over the record date, the security is still in the name of the seller. The seller will receive the dividend from the disbursing agent and not the buyer. In order not to penalize the buyer, the stock exchange will reduce the market price of the security on the ex-dividend date to reflect the amount of the dividend.

3. *Record Date.* Simultaneously with the declaration of dividends, the board of directors also determines the record date and makes proper notification to the transfer agents. The transfer agent, on that day, will close the books of the corporation and

gather the names of eligible stockholders entitled to receive dividends.

4. *Payable Date.* The disbursing agent must make sure that the dividend check is mailed to the stockholder by the payable date.

EXAMPLE

1. The record date for dividend is Friday, which means the ex-dividend date is Monday — four business days before the record date.

2. On Monday if the customer purchases the security, he will be the legal owner of the security on the following Monday, the fifth business day after the trade day.

3. The buyer will not be entitled to receive the dividend because over the record date he was not considered the legal owner of the security.

4. The stock exchange will reduce the market price of the security on Monday, the ex-dividend date, to reflect the amount of the dividend.

   For cash trades, where the trade settles on the day of the trade, the ex-dividend date will be the day after the record date. A person buying the stock in a cash trade on any day up to and including the record date may have the security transferred into his name and receive the dividend.

Stock Distribution

For stock dividends and stock splits the ex-dividend date, or the ex-distribution date, is set after the payment date. Generally, the ex-distribution date for stock dividends and stock splits is the business day following the payment date. This also applies to subscription rights. The ex-distribution date for these rights is the business day following the day when the rights start trading.

For stock dividends and stock splits, the Due Bills are redeemable beginning on the fifth business day after the payment date.

EXAMPLE

The corporation declares a 5 percent stock dividend.

Declaration Date	Record Date	Payable Date
March 7	March 18	March 30

March–April

S	M	T	W	Th	F	S
		1	2	3	4	5
6	7	8	9	10	11	12
13	14	15	16	17	18	19
20	21	22	23	24	25	26
27	28	29	30	31	1	2
3	4	5	6	7	8	9

If a person purchases this security on trade date March 14, his trade will settle on March 21, the business day following the record date.

All regular way contracts in the stock market will trade with Due Bills attached from March 14 through March 30.

On March 31, the business day after the payable date, the security will trade on the basis of ex-distribution and the outstanding Due Bills are redeemed for the stock dividend on April 6, which is the fifth business day after the payable date.

When delivering a security to the buying broker after the record date, March 18 through April 6, the selling broker must attach a Due Bill to the security.

TYPES OF DIVIDEND DISTRIBUTION

1. *Cash dividends.* The corporation declares a cash dividend on the basis of earnings per share.

2. *Stock dividends.* The corporation disburses dividends in the form of the company's own shares. The distribution is made out of the unissued portion of the company's stock, or a new authorization is sought from the Secretary of State of the state of incorporation.

3. *Stock split.* The corporation may decide to alter the price of the company's stock in the marketplace. This may be done through a stock split.

In a stock split the company will distribute a set number of shares to stockholders of record. If the split is 2 to 1, each stockholder will receive another share for each share he holds. The book value of the corporation will be cut in half together with the market value of the shares. The total market value of the shares would remain the same, however. For 5 to 4 stock splits or less (25 percent), the stock split is handled as stock dividend and not as a stock split. The 5 for 4 stock split or less will not affect the par value of the stock.

4. *Reverse split*. The corporation may decide to do a reverse split to increase the market value of the security.

5. *Scrip dividend*. These are dividends paid in the form of scrips. Scrips are certificates or promissory instruments issued by the corporation to be exchanged for cash at a later date. A company trying to conserve its cash elects to issue scrips in lieu of cash dividends.

6. *Commodity dividends*. On rare occasions, a company may elect to distribute a commodity or goods as dividends to stockholders.

7. *Liquidating dividends*. This is done at the time of the dissolution of the corporation when the assets are distributed as liquidating dividends to the company's stockholders.

ALLOCATION OF DIVIDENDS

A publication of Standard & Poor's Corporation provides all statistical information about dividends. This publication is sent to the Dividend Department of the securities firm, which, in turn, advises the Cashier Department to make certain that all certificates placed in various depository accounts are registered in the name of the firm or its nominee. This is an important first step for the accountability and allocation of dividends. Between the record date and the payable date, the Dividend Department completes the proportionate allocation of dividends to customers and brokers, and, on the payable date, proceeds to credit the accounts accordingly.

The allocation of dividends are made in the following way:

1. *Cash dividends*. Let us assume that a corporation declares to distribute 50 cents a share dividend to stockholders of record, and the securities firm is holding a certificate in its nominee name

for 2,600 shares. The stock record of the firm will indicate the beneficial owners of the security to be:

Customer 1		200 shares
Customer 2		500 shares
Customer 3		1,000 shares
Customer 4		600 shares
Customer 5		300 shares
	Total	2,600 shares

On the payable date, the disbursing agent will send the securities firm a check in the amount of $1,300. The Dividend Department will immediately credit each customer's account accordingly:

	Shares	*Cash dividend of 50 cents a share*
Customer 1	200	$ 100
Customer 2	500	$ 250
Customer 3	1,000	$ 500
Customer 4	600	$ 300
Customer 5	300	$ 150
Total	2,600 shares	$1,300

If, in error, the Dividend Department receives a check in the amount of $1,200, $100 less, it will still credit each customer's account proportionately and will conduct research to resolve the error. Conversely, if the Dividend Department receives a check in the amount of $1,400, $100 more, it will place the $100 in a suspense account and will give it to the owner upon presentation of a proof of ownership.

2. *Stock dividend.* Let us assume that the corporation declares a 2 percent stock dividend. That means it will distribute 2 additional shares for every 100 shares owned. Taking the same example, the securities firm will receive 52 shares from the disbursing agent as stock dividend. The Dividend Department will update the position of each customer in the following manner:

	Shares	*2% Stock Dividend*
Customer 1	200	204 shares
Customer 2	500	510 shares
Customer 3	1,000	1,020 shares
Customer 4	600	612 shares
Customer 5	300	306 shares
Total	2,600 shares	2,652 shares

3. *Stock split.* Let us assume that the corporation declares to split 4 to 3. That means for every 3 old shares, the corporation will distribute 4 new shares. The securities firm holding 2,600 shares will now have 4/3 × 2,600 = 3,466.66. The fraction (.66) of the shares will be sent to the securities firm in cash. The Dividend Department, in turn, will give the customer cash in lieu of fractional shares after crediting each customer's account proportionately:

	Shares	4 to 3 Stock Split
Customer 1	200	266.66 shares
Customer 2	500	666.66 shares
Customer 3	1,000	1,333.33 shares
Customer 4	600	800.00 shares
Customer 5	300	400.00 shares
Total	2,600 shares	3,466.66 shares

4. *Reverse splits.* 1 to 5. This means for every 5 old shares, the stockholder will receive 1 new share. The corporation is splitting down the shares in a corporate reorganization. At this time, the securities firm must surrender the certificate for 2,600 shares to the transfer agent. The transfer agent will then issue a new certificate in the amount of 520 shares (1/5 × 2,600). The Dividend Department will then update the records of each customer accordingly:

	Shares	1 for 5 Reverse Split
Customer 1	200	40 shares
Customer 2	500	100 shares
Customer 3	1,000	200 shares
Customer 4	600	120 shares
Customer 5	300	60 shares
Total	2,600 shares	520 shares

DIVIDEND CLAIMS

The Dividend Department prepares claim letters in cases where the dividend declared by the corporation rightfully belongs to the firm. Letters claiming dividends are standard throughout the financial community. They simply state the reasons for the claim, the security description, the dividend rate, the amount, the record date, the payable date, the certificate number, and the registration.

Before instituting the claims, however, the Dividend Department must receive a confirmation from the transfer agent that the certificate in question was outstanding in the books of the corporation over the record date.

INTEREST ON DEBT INSTRUMENTS AND ACCRUED INTEREST

Debt instruments generally pay interest at specified dates. The interest may be paid monthly, quarterly, semi-annually, or annually. If the security is registered in the name of the customer, the paying agent will mail an interest check to the bondholder of record.

The description of the bond will indicate the amount of interest to be paid and the dates of interest payment.

EXAMPLE

$1,000 Bee Corp. 6% due Jan 1/2000.

This means on January 1, 2000, the corporation must pay the stockholder the principal face value of the bond. In the meantime, it must pay an interest of 6 percent of $1,000 every year. Six percent of $1,000 is $60. The corporation will pay the interest in two installments — $30 one month and six months later another $30. In this example, the interest payment dates are January 1 and July 1.

DIVIDEND REINVESTMENT

The Dividend Reinvestment Program is an inexpensive way to raise equity capital. Instead of receiving cash dividends, the stockholder will advise the corporation to reinvest the dividend by buying more shares in his account. There are basically two different plans:

1. *Market purchase plan.* Under this plan, the company's shares are purchased on the open market at the prevailing price.

2. *Original issue plan.* The company will issue the share from the authorized but unissued stock. This will generate additional capital for the company.

COUPON COLLECTION

Coupon bonds are generally issued in bearer form. Bearer certificates do not disclose the owner's name and there are no records of ownership. It is the responsibility of the owner of the security, therefore, to clip the coupons attached to the instrument and present them to the paying agent to collect the interest. Coupons also may be presented to any bank that will act as the collection agent.

The presentation of the coupon is done through the use of envelopes, called "shells." The shells are presented to the bank for collection. The coupons will indicate the following information:

- Name of the issuer
- Name of the paying agent
- Interest due date
- Amount of interest
- Coupon number
- Bond serial number
- Authorized signature

The bank may refuse to honor the coupon for any one of the following reasons:

1. Mixed coupons are in the same envelope.
2. The bonds have already been called.
3. Stops are placed on coupons.

The coupon payments for U.S. Treasury securities are handled through the Federal Reserve System. The Fed credits the amount of interest in the account of the participating financial institution.

CHAPTER EIGHTEEN

MERGERS, TENDER OFFERS, AND PROXIES

The Exchange-Reorganization Department of a securities firm performs certain specific functions for conversions, redemptions, exchanges, and tender offers of securities.

Similar to other areas of securities operation, the procedures in this department are clerical and generally routine in nature.

REDEMPTION OF SECURITIES

Callable bonds or preferred stocks may be called by the corporation at the discretion of the board of directors. When the security is called, the holder will surrender the security and receive cash in lieu. There are two types of calls: absolute and partial. Absolute or full call redeems the entire security issue; a partial call redeems only a portion of the issue.

In a partial call, it will be the function of the Exchange-Reorganization Department to submit the certificate numbers being called if the certificates are kept in bulk form, where one certificate represents the ownership of several customers. The securities firm must adopt a system of an impartial lottery in which the selection is made based on customers' proportional holdings. No interests are paid after the bond is called.

CONVERSIONS AND EXCHANGES

The Exchange-Reorganization Department will also process the conversion and the exchange of a security from one type to another.

The convertible security will have the term of the conversion, such as the conversion price and ratio. The conversion price is the price at which one share of common stock will be valued if the security is converted. The conversion ratio establishes the number of shares that can be obtained for each convertible security.

The conversion privileges may extend throughout the life of the issue or for a fixed period of years. Occasionally, the conversion price and the ratio may change in later years. To convert the security, the broker or the bank will forward the certificates to the conversion agent.

In exchanging the security, the Exchange-Reorganization Department must make sure to send the offering circular and letters of transmittal to solicit customers' instruction before proceeding to effect the transaction. The exchange of the security will be made according to the terms of the merger agreement. After the exchange is completed, the records are updated and the customers are notified. If the merger is an outright acquisition for cash, the amount of money will be credited in the customer's account.

SUBSCRIPTION OF RIGHTS

The board of directors of a corporation may give preemptive rights to the stockholders to subscribe to new shares. The Exchange-Reorganization Department will use the subscription rights with appropriate funds from the customer's account to acquire new shares and credit the shares in the customer's account. If the customer does not wish to subscribe to new shares, the securities firm will sell the rights for the customer and credit the proceeds of the sale in the customer's account.

Subscription warrants are handled in the same manner. The customer will subscribe to new shares by exercising the warrant. Warrants are usually issued at the time of issuance of a new security to make the security more attractive to the investor. Warrants carry no voting rights, and the holder will receive no dividends.

EXAMPLE

RIGHTS

4 Rights are needed to purchase 1 new share of Bee Corp. at $35 a share.

WARRANT

1 Warrant is needed to purchase 3 new shares of Bee Corp. at $35 a share.

TENDER OFFERS

A corporation or an individual interested in acquiring another corporation will file a proxy statement with the Securities and Exchange Commission. The purchaser will announce that he is interested in purchasing the shares of another corporation at a set price.

The purchaser has basically three methods to accept the security being tendered:

1. *Outright purchase of all the shares of the corporation at a set price.*

2. *First-come-first-served basis.* The purchaser will accept the shares tendered on a first-come-first-served basis. The purchaser intends to purchase, for instance, only 3 million shares of a corporation's stock, therefore, he will only accept the first 3 million shares tendered.

3. *Pro Rata allocation.* Here the purchaser will apply a ratio by taking all the shares tendered and comparing them with the total number of shares he intends to purchase. If the tender offer is for 3 million shares and the stockholders present 4 million shares, the purchaser will apply a ratio formula in the following manner:

$$\frac{\text{Total number of shares to be purchased}}{\text{Total number of shares tendered}} = \frac{\text{Proportion of each}}{\text{tenderee's shares}}$$

In our example above:

$$\frac{3,000,000}{4,000,000} = 0.75 \text{ or } 75\%$$

This means the purchaser will accept 75 percent from each tenderee's security position. If the stockholder had submitted 100 shares, only 75 shares will be accepted and the remaining 25 shares will be returned to the customer.

The securities firm will benefit by soliciting customers to tender their securities. Even though there are no brokerage commissions involved in tender offers, the intended purchaser will offer tender fees to the broker who induces the customer to tender the stock. The Securities Exchange Act of 1934 prohibits short tender. That means the investor responding to the tender offer must own the security. A customer who has sold the security "short" against the box has a zero position. He cannot tender the security long in his account.

The Procedures for Tender Offers

1. On the notification date of the tender offer, the Exchange-Reorganization Department requests a current stock record listing of the security in question.

2. The certificates in the Cashiers Department are counted and turned over to the Exchange-Reorganization Department.

3. The department will notify the customers who are the beneficial owners of the security.

4. A few days before the expiration date of the tender offer, the Exchange-Reorganization Department will send a follow-up to those customers who have failed to respond to the first request.

5. On the day of the expiration, the Exchange-Reorganization clerk will count all the certificates and resolve differences, if any. He will scrutinize the original stock record to ensure that all customers have responded.

6. Certificate with proper documentation will be submitted to the tender offer agent.

7. If certificates are not available at the time of the tender offer, the Exchange-Reorganization Department will issue a letter of guarantee to the agent-bank. This means that the physical certificates will be delivered at a prescribed time in the future.

PROXY DEPARTMENT

The Proxy Department of a securities firm is responsible for handling and processing corporate reports and proxy materials.

The board of directors of a public corporation invites the stockholders of the company to participate in the management of the company at least once a year. This is done by voting on such issues as approval of company goals and objectives, election of directors, and issuance of additional shares. This is an inherent right of the stockholder if he is the holder of shares with voting privileges. The directors announce the date of the stockholder meeting and send each stockholder proxy material to be used in the event that the holder is unable to attend.

Proxies are authorizations granted by the stockholder empowering a company representative to act in his behalf at the company meeting. Proxies are standard forms containing the name of the corporation, the date and the nature of the meeting, the name of the agent representing the stockholder, and the authorization clause. The stockholder will sign the form and mail it to the corporation prior to the meeting. In the event that the certificates are held by the securities firm for the customer, the corporation sends the proxy material to the securities firm that, in effect, is the stockholder of record.

The Procedure in the Proxy Department

The operating procedure in the Proxy Department is similar to that of the Dividend Department. It starts with the announcement of the record date for the meeting. All "Street" name certificates are sent to the transfer agent on or before the record date for transfer to the nominee name of the securities firm. This will ensure the receipt of the proxy material.

The Proxy Department tallies the number of shares held beneficially for customers. After the receipt of the proxy material, the tallies are sent to the customers for response. If the proxy card is signed by the customer with no special preferences, the assumption is that the shares owned by the customer will be voted as recommended by the management on all matters to be considered at the meeting.

There are stringent rules and regulations in this area. In some cases, the stockholder is not allowed to vote by proxy, and in other cases, the life of the proxy authorization is limited. Various rules of the Securities and Exchange Commission define the manner in which proxy statements are disclosed and proxies are solicited.

If the customer fails to respond to the proxy notification, the securities firm is allowed to vote according to its judgment. It is allowed to vote only on routine items, such as election of auditors, certain routine company proposals, etc.

The SEC regulations in this area are as follows:

1. The SEC rules require that corporations ask brokers and other nominees 20 days in advance of the record date of the annual meeting for the sets of the proxy materials needed for each beneficial owner.

2. The rules require that brokers respond no later than seven business days after receipt of inquiry from the corporation, and mail proxy materials and annual reports to the beneficial owners no later than four business days after the receipt from the corporation.

3. The SEC rule allows a corporation to stop sending annual reports or proxy materials to the shareholder if the material has been returned as undeliverable for two consecutive annual meetings, unless state law requires otherwise.

Securities depositories and custodian banks generally process the proxy cards through an *Omnibus Proxy* Plan. The depository or the bank will send a list of beneficial owners to the proxy agent of the corporation and the agent will mail the proxy cards directly to the beneficial owners, thus bypassing the depository.

CHAPTER NINETEEN

OPTIONS TRADING

An option is a contractual instrument that gives the buyer or the holder the privilege to take advantage of the contract terms or to exercise the purchase or sale of a particular security at a set price, within a specified period of time. The buyer of the option has the right to exercise this privilege. This must be done before the option expires. After the expiration date, the option ceases to exist.

There are two instruments in the options market: a *call* and a *put*. The call is so named because the buyer is "calling for the stock." A call option gives the holder the privilege to buy a security at a specified price within a specified period of time. A put means the buyer is "putting the stock to the writer." The put option gives the holder the privilege to sell the security at a specified price within a specified period of time. Put and call options are used for two diverse investment objectives. The buyer of the call expects the price of the underlying security to go up, while the buyer of the put expects the price of the underlying security to go down.

Behind these two investors are the writers or sellers of the option. An investor will write or sell a call option promising to sell his security to the buyer of the call at the exercise price. In turn, he will write or sell a put option promising to buy the security from the buyer of the put at the exercise price. In either case, the investor expects the price of the underlying security to stay the same during the life of the option.

The option buyer pays a premium to the option writer and has the privilege to buy or sell the underlying security. The option writer has the commitment to either sell or buy the security.

CHARACTERISTICS OF OPTIONS

1. Options provide an inexpensive way to buy the security.
2. Options provide more leverage to the investor. For instance, he would buy a call option at a premium of $5 a share for 100 shares of the underlying security and at an exercise price of $50 a share. This would give the investor the privilege to purchase 100 shares at $50 a share anytime during the life of the option. If the market price of the underlying security goes up to $60 a share, he would exercise his call, which means he would buy the security at $50 a share and turn around and sell it in the open stock market at $60 a share, with a minimum cost of $500 for the option plus commissions. In contrast, had he purchased the same security outright, 100 shares would have cost him $5,000 plus commissions. He would have then sold it at $60 a share, earning $1,000 less commissions. For an outlay of $5,000, a gain of $1,000 is only 20%. The options transaction, however, would give him a return of 100% for his money. With the rise of the underlying security to $60 a share, the premium of the call would have risen from $5 to $10. Instead of exercising his option, the investor would have simply sold the option at $10.

EXAMPLE

	Debit	Credit
a. Cost of purchasing 1 call at $5	$500	
b. Proceeds of sale of 1 call at $10		$1,000
	$500	$1,000

Net gain:	$500
Outlay of funds:	$500
Percentage of profit:	100%

3. Options provide minimum risk and exposure. The extent of the loss will only be the premium that the investor will pay to buy the option.
4. Options provide unlimited rewards. The potential for profit is unlimited in an options trade. Taking the above example,

it is possible for the price of the underlying security to go up to $85 a share. With an exercise price of $50 a share, the buyer of the call would make a substantial profit by selling or exercising the option.

5. Options provide versatility to the investor. It is possible for an investor to purchase options with different exercise prices, all expiring at the same time. The investor may purchase or write options of Bee Corp. at exercise prices 50, 60, 70, and so on — all expiring in the month of October. The investor may even purchase or write options with the same exercise price expiring in different months. He may purchase options with an exercise price of 50 expiring in January, another one expiring in April and another expiring in July — all with the same exercise price.

6. The options exchanges provide liquidity. With the creation of a fungible options instrument, the investor in buying an option was not obligated to exercise his option. With the liquidity offered by the organized marketplace, the investor instead of exercising the option was able to sell the option or close out his contract anytime during the life of the option. Just like trading in securities, the investor would buy an option at a low price and would sell it at a higher price. The difference in money would be his profit. On the other hand, a writer of an option increases profit on his investment of the underlying security by writing a call option on it. For example, he will buy 100 shares of Bee Corp. at $50 a share and write a call option on it. If the premium of the option is $5, he will receive $500 (5 × 100) less brokerage commission. This $500 is his, whether or not the call is exercised. For the writer, this is a hedge against a possible decline in the security's price. By writing the call, he is making the commitment to sell his security to the buyer of the call if the buyer exercises his call. In the event of an exercise, the writer will deliver 100 shares and the call buyer will give him funds equal to the aggregate exercise price. With an exercise price of $50 a share, the call buyer will give the call writer $5,000. This $5,000 will have nothing to do with the first $500 that the writer received from the call buyer at the time when the call was written.

As with the option buyer, the option writer has the flexibility to close out his written contract anytime during the life of the option. He will do so by simply buying the identical option back. Again, the difference in money will be his profit or loss, as shown in these two examples.

EXAMPLE

	Debit	Credit
a. Investor A writes 1 call Bee Corp. 50 at 5		$500
b. Investor A buys back 1 call Bee Corp. 50 at 6	$600	
The investor in this example will lose $100.	$600	$500

EXAMPLE

	Debit	Credit
a. Investor B writes 1 call Cee Corp. 50 at 5		$500
b. Investor B buys back 1 call Cee Corp. 50 at 4	$400	
	$400	$500

The investor in this example will make a profit of $100.

The writer is able to close out his contract anytime before the expiration date of the option or before the option has been exercised. This closing transaction will terminate the writer's commitment to sell or buy the security. This does not, however, affect the option buyer's right to exercise his option.

The Options Clearing Corporation acts as an intermediary between the buyer and the writer. In fact, the clearing corporation is the entity that sells to the option buyer and buys from the option writer. The option buyer and writer have no direct relationship. The clearing corporation acts as the sole obligor.

Opening transaction	Closing transaction
Buy Option — Long	Sell Option — Zero position
Write Option — Short	Buy Option — Zero position

The forces of supply and demand in the options market dictate the price of the option. The supply and demand are generally based on whether the price of the underlying security is rising or falling in the stock market. If the price of the underlying security is on the rise, there will be increased demand to buy calls on that security, but less interest to write calls. With less writers and more buyers, the price of the call will go up. The reverse is true for a put option. A rising stock market will reduce the demand to buy puts; therefore, the price of the put will go down.

EXPIRATION CYCLE

Listed stock options have standardized expiration dates. They expire three times a year and for certain securities once every month. The expiration dates are established by the options exchange. An option expires in 3 months, 6 months, or 9 months. The investor has the choice to pick any one of the three.

After selecting the security, the options exchange will assign an expiration cycle to the put and call options. The year is divided into three cycles:

> First cycle: January, April, July, October
> Second cycle: February, May, August, November
> Third cycle: March, June, September, December

The exchange will assign any one of the three cycles. Once a cycle has been assigned, however, the expiration months of that option will always be in that cycle.

Let us assume that the options exchange after receiving the regulatory approval selects Bee Corp. for options trading. They will assign any one of the three expiration cycles. Let us say they select the first cycle. Therefore, the call and put options of Bee Corp. will always expire in January, April, July, or October. But since the life of an option may not exceed 9 months, only options expiring in 3 consecutive months of the cycle are traded at a given time.

In this example, there will be a call and a put option of Bee Corp. expiring in January, April, and July. The October option will not be introduced until the January options expire. On Monday, after the January options have expired, a new call and put option will be opened with an expiration date of October, and of course, trading in options expiring in April and July will continue.

The standardized expiration time of all listed options are:

Eastern Time Zone: 11:59 P.M. Saturday following the third Friday of the expiration month.

Central Time Zone: 10:59 P.M. Saturday following the third Friday of the expiration month.

Pacific Time Zone: 8:59 P.M. Saturday following the third Friday of the expiration month.

If an option is not exercised prior to these datelines, it becomes worthless.

Even though the options expire on a Saturday, brokers need to have exercise instructions from their customers no later than the Friday afternoon prior to the expiration Saturday.

SELECTING THE EXERCISE PRICE

After assigning the expiration cycle, the options exchange will assign different exercise or strike prices for the put and call options. The rule of thumb for the exercise prices of stock options are:

- If the price per share of the underlying security is between $10 and $100, the exercise prices will have increments of $5. That will be 45, 50, 55, 60, and so on.
- If the price per share of the underlying security is above $100 a share, the exercise prices will have increments of $10. That will be 110, 120, 130, 140, and so on.

In establishing different strike prices, the exchange will take the volatility of the underlying security into consideration. The greater the volatility, the more strike prices the options will have. Strike prices are made to surround the current market price of the underlying security. For instance, if the market price of the underlying security is $47, the exchange may establish two strike prices, one at $45 and the other at $50. A security with a price per share of $35 may have options with strike prices of $30, $35, and $40. The exchange may assign two, three, or more strike prices.

The objective is to provide liquidity and depth in the options market.

New exercise prices may be introduced anytime during the life of an option. When a new exercise price is introduced, the other options with old exercise prices will continue to trade.

CLASSIFICATIONS OF OPTIONS

Options of an underlying security have three categories: *type*, *class*, and *series*. There are two types — all calls are one type, and all puts are another type. The class denotes the expiration months of the option. All January calls are one class; all April calls are another class; all July calls a different class, all January puts a different class, and so on. Series denotes the expiration month and the strike price of the option. For example, a call of Bee Corp. January 50 is a series; a put of Bee Corp. January 60 is another series.

Table 19.1 shows two different types of options for Bee Corp., calls and puts. There are six different classes: Jan. calls, Apr. calls, July calls, Jan. puts, April puts, and July puts. This constitutes 15 different series of calls and 15 different series of puts. The investor has 60 different choices. He may buy 15 different calls and 15 different puts or write 15 different calls and 15 different puts on the same underlying security. When January options expire, the chart will show April, July, October options. April options will then be identified as near-term, the July options as mid-term and October options as far-term. When April options expire, the three months in the chart will be: July, October, January, and so on.

TABLE 19.1

Bee Mkt	Str	Calls			Puts		
		Jan	Apr	July	Jan	Apr	July
55	45	9	10	11	1	2	3
55	50	4	5	6	1½	2½	3½
55	55	2	3	4	2	2½	3
55	60	1½	2½	3½	4	5	6
55	65	1	2	3	9	10	11
↑	↑	↑	↑	↑	↑	↑	↑
Market price of the underlying security	Strike prices of options set by the exchange	Near-term calls	Mid-term calls	Far-term calls	Near-term puts	Mid-term puts	Far-term puts

Table 19.1 shows the prices of option series. Jan. 45 call is $9. Since 1 call represents 100 shares of the underlying security, the value of 1 call Jan. 45 is, therefore, $900 (9 × 100). The Jan. 45 put is $1. It will cost the buyer $100 to buy 1 put Jan. 45.

Prices of options are determined through an auction process between the buying broker and the selling broker. The prices are not negotiated as they were in the over-the-counter trading.

As previously mentioned, one of the most important features of the options exchange lies in its ability to provide liquidity. The organized marketplace provides a forum for continuous trading of options in a secondary market. This was practically nonexistent in the over-the-counter trading. The option buyer now has the ability to sell his option at any time during the life of the option. At the present time, less than 3% of options are actually exercised. The majority of investors simply sell the options before the expiration date.

When buying an option, the investor has three choices:

1. He may exercise his option.

2. He may sell the option in a closing transaction. He must do so before the option expires.

3. He may let the option expire, in which case he will lose no more than the cost of purchasing the option plus commissions.

Over 97% of investors take the second choice because it is economically more advantageous to them than the first choice. The following will illustrate the differences between the two:

EXAMPLE

CHOICE 1

	Debit	Credit
a. Investor A buys 1 call Bee Corp. Jan. 50 at $5	$500	
b. Commission to broker	$25	
c. The market price of Bee goes up to $65. The investor wishes to exercise his call		
d. Investor buys 100 at $50 a share	$5,000	
e. Investor sells 100 Bee at $65		$6,500
f. The investor pays $75 to exercise the call and $75 to sell the security	$75 $75	
	$5,675	$6,500

The investor will have a net profit of $825 (6,500 − 5,675). On an investment of $5,675 the percentage of profit will be 14.5%.

$$\left(\frac{825}{5,675} \times 100\right)$$

EXAMPLE

CHOICE 2

	Debit	Credit
a. Investor A buys 1 call Bee Corp. Jan. 50 at 5	$500	
b. Commission to broker	$25	
c. Value of Bee Corp. goes up to 65, the price of Jan. call will go up to 15		
d. The investor sells (close) 1 call Jan. 50 at 15		$1,500
e. Commission to broker	$25	
	$550	$1,500

The investor will have a profit of $950 (1,500 − 550). On an investment of $550, the percentage of profit will be 172%.

$$\left(\frac{950}{550} \times 100\right)$$

It is, therefore, much more economical and practical to consider the second choice.

On the last day of trading the options are usually sold to the market makers or the specialists on the floor of the exchange. The market maker will buy the option and when the trading stops he will be the holder of the option with the privilege to exercise. On the last day of trading — a Friday — the market maker will have until 11:59 P.M. Eastern Standard time the following day to exercise his option. Through this exercise he will either buy the security on the call side or sell the security on the put side. The market makers usually buy or sell the security on that given Friday in anticipation of their exercising the option the following day.

Transactions of listed options settle on the business day following the trade (T + 1). Options traded on the last day are usually settled on the day of the trade.

POSITION LIMITS

There are position limits imposed by options exchanges. This means the investor may not buy or write as many options as he wishes. If the position limit imposed by the options exchange is 8,000, this means an investor or a group of investors acting together, may not have option positions exceeding 8,000 puts and calls on the same side of the market for the same underlying security.

The buy and sell side of the options trade are:

Buy side	Sell side
A. Buy call	C. Write call
B. Write put	D. Buy put

Investor A, in buying a call will have the option to buy the security. Investor B, in writing a put makes the commitment to buy the security in the event of an exercise. Investor C, in writing a call makes the commitment to sell the security in the event of an exercise. Investor D, in buying a put, will have the option to sell the security.

If the position limit is 8,000, that means all option contracts, put and call, on the same underlying security on the same side of the market, buy or sell, may not exceed 8,000 for an investor or a group of investors acting together.

> Buy calls (open transaction)
> Write puts (open transaction)
> (on the same underlying security)

This is the same (buy) side of the market, therefore, the number of option contracts may not exceed 8,000 if that is the position limit imposed by the options exchange.

> Write calls (open transaction)
> Buy puts (open transaction)
> (on the same underlying security)

Again, this is the same (sell) side of the market, therefore, the number of option contracts may not exceed 8,000 for a customer or a group of customers acting together.

THE VALUE OF AN OPTION

There are many theories and calculations to determine the value of a call and a put. The formulas are mostly mathematical interpretations of various factors that govern the price or the premium of an option. In the over-the-counter market the prices were determined through a negotiated arrangement between the buyer and the writer. The price of an option was usually structured on the basis of 5% or 10% of the market value of the underlying security, plus such factors as dividends, the price-earning ratio, the rating of the underlying security, the availability of option writers, the total number of shares outstanding, the financial outlook of the company, and the life of the option.

The price of a listed option is determined in a different manner from the OTC market, although the factors are generally the same, namely: 1) the life of the option, 2) the volatility of the security in the stock market, 3) dividends and the financial standing of the underlying security, 4) the current interest rates in the economy, and 5) the relationship between the strike price of the option and the market price of the underlying security.

Before buying or writing an option, the investor must analyze the market value as well as the theoretical value of the option contract. There are various services that provide a computerized and sophisticated analysis as to the value of an option. Several standards and parameters are used to arrive at a fair value of an option. The fair value or the theoretical value may not be the same as the market value, however. The market value of the option is generally based on the forces of supply and demand. The parameters that one uses to determine the theoretical value are usually based on the risk-reward feature of the option and its relationship to the underlying security.

The following are some of the factors that would influence the price structure of an option:

1. *The life of the option.* The longer the life of the option, the higher the price. An option expiring in January will be worth less than an option on the same underlying security expiring in April. The April option will be worth less than the July option and so on. The holder of the option will have more time to exercise his option.

TABLE 19.2

Mkt	Str	Calls			Puts		
		Jan	Apr	July	Jan	Apr	July
55	50	4	5	6	1	2	3
55	55	2	3	4	2	3	4
55	60	1	2	3	4	5	6

The near-term options are worth less than the mid-term options; and the mid-term options are worth less than the far-term options for both calls and puts.

2. *The volatility of the underlying security.* The more volatile the security is in the stock market, the higher the price will be of the option. The holder of a call or a put has a greater opportunity to exercise the option if the price of the underlying security has been fluctuating upward or downward over a period of time. Conversely, if there is not too much movement in the price of the security, the option holder has less chance to exercise his option; therefore, the value of the option will be comparatively low.

3. *Dividends on the underlying security.* Another factor that influences the price of an option is the rate of cash dividends on the underlying security. The higher the dividend, the lower the price of the option.

4. *Current short-term interest rates.* Higher interest rates in the economy tend to push the option prices upward.

5. *The relationship of the price of the underlying security with the strike price of the option.* Perhaps this is the most important factor that affects the price of an option. The correlation between the price per share of the underlying security and the strike price of the option is characterized by the following terms:

   a. *In-the-money call.* When the strike price of a call is lower than the price per share of the underlying security, that call option is known as in-the-money call.

   b. *Out-of-the-money call.* When the strike price of a call is higher than the price per share of the underlying security, that call option is called out-of-the-money call.

   c. *In-the-money put.* When the strike price of a put is higher than the price per share of the underlying security, that put option is identified as in-the-money put.

d. *Out-of-the-money put.* When the strike price of a put is lower than the price per share of the underlying security, that put option is referred to as out-of-the-money put.

e. *On-the-money option.* When the strike price is the same as the price per share of the underlying security, both the call and the put options are identified as on-the-money options.

TABLE 19.3. THE RELATIONSHIP BETWEEN THE PRICE OF THE UNDERLYING SECURITY AND THE STRIKE PRICE OF THE OPTION

	Call	*Put*
Strike Price < Market Price	In-the-money	Out-of-the-money
Strike Price > Market Price	Out-of-the-money	In-the-money
Strike Price = Market Price	On-the-money	On-the-money

In trying to identify an option, whether it's in-the-money or out-of-the-money, one has to compare only the strike price of the option against the market price of the underlying security. The price of the option is not taken into consideration.

THE INTRINSIC VALUE OF AN OPTION

The intrinsic value of an option is the amount of money in in-the-money options. Only in-the-money options have intrinsic value. On-the-money and out-of-the-money options do not have any intrinsic value.

If the market price of Bee Corp. is 50 and the strike price of the call is 45, the intrinsic value of the option is 5. The aggregate intrinsic value is determined by multiplying the intrinsic value times the number of shares representing the options. The intrinsic value of 2 calls Bee Corp. Jan. 45 is $1,000 (5 × 200).

PARITY

If the price of an option equals the intrinsic value of the option, that option is said to be trading at parity with its underlying security. Only in-the-money options have parity since only in-the-money options have intrinsic value.

Parity in a call option is determined by the following formula:

$$\left(\begin{array}{c}\text{Market Price of}\\\text{Underlying Security}\end{array}\right) = \text{Strike Price} + \text{Call Premium}$$

$$(M = S + C)$$

Parity in a put option is determined by:

$$\left(\begin{array}{c}\text{Market Price of}\\\text{Underlying Security}\end{array}\right) = \text{Strike Price} - \text{Put Premium}$$

$$(M = S - P)$$

TABLE 19.4

Mkt	Str	Calls			Puts		
		Jan	Apr	July	Jan	Apr	July
55	50	4	5	6	1	2	3
55	55	2	3	4	2	3	4
55	60	1	2	3	4	5	6

In this table April 50 call has parity. April 50 call is an in-the-money option. The intrinsic value is 5 and the premium is 5. The market price of the security is equal to the strike price of the option plus the premium of the call.

The April 60 put also has parity. The market price of the security is equal to the strike price of the option minus the premium of the put. The April 60 put is an in-the-money put.

TIME VALUE PREMIUM

The time value premium is the amount by which the option premium exceeds the intrinsic value. For in-the-money options, the time value premium is the excess portion over parity. For on-the-money and out-of-the-money options, it is the premium of the option.

For instance, the market price of Bee Corp. is $28, the strike price of Jan. call is 25, the premium of the call is 4, the time value premium of Jan. 25 call is $1. Jan. 25 call is an in-the-money option and its premium exceeds the intrinsic value. For an in-the-money call, the time value premium is determined by:

$$\left(\begin{array}{c} \text{Call Time} \\ \text{Value Premium} \end{array} \right) = (\text{Call Premium} + \text{Strike Price})$$

$$- \text{Stock Price}$$

$$\$1 = (4 + 25) - 28$$

For an in-the-money put, the time value premium is determined by:

$$\left(\begin{array}{c} \text{Put Time} \\ \text{Value Premium} \end{array} \right) = (\text{Put Premium} + \text{Stock Price})$$

$$- \text{Strike Price}$$

Here again, it is the excess over the intrinsic value of the put.

The market price of Bee Corp. is $55, the strike price of the July put is 60 and the premium of the put is 7. The time value premium of July 60 put is $2. July 60 put is an in-the-money put, and its premium exceeds the intrinsic value. Using the above formula:

$$\$2 = (7 + 55) - 60$$

The summit or the high point of the time value is when the stock price is equal to the strike price of the option. As the option moves away from this summit in either direction, whether in-the-money, or out-of-the-money, the time value premium loses its value correspondingly.

The time value premium decays gradually as the option comes closer to its expiration day. This erosion of the time value is not uniform throughout the life of the option. The time value premium decays much faster as the option comes closer to its final day of trading, which is the third Friday of the expiration month. At closing, the time value premium becomes zero. All on-the-money and out-of-the-money options will expire worthless and all in-the-money options will close at parity.

MARGIN REQUIREMENTS FOR OPTIONS

In an options transaction, the term *margin* refers to the amount of money or collateral the broker receives from the option writer to ensure that the customer will honor his obligation to sell or buy the underlying security. This may be in the form of cash or marginable securities.

LONG PURCHASES

Options are not marginable. The customer may not purchase options on margin; all purchases must be paid for in full. Options do not have collateral loan value. For all purchases the customer must make full payment plus the commissions to the broker within 7 business days after trade. A transaction in a listed option settles on the business day following the trade day (T + 1). This is only for clearing purposes.

The customer may use a margin account or a cash account to purchase options. In either case he is required to make full payment, and the value of his long option position is not calculated as part of his margin equity. There are no margin requirements if the customer exercises his call option and sells the underlying security on the same day. The customer must pay any difference in money between the transactions.

COVERED OPTION WRITING

There are no margin requirements for covered option writing. When the customer writes a covered call, he has a long position of the appropriate number of shares of the underlying security. To cover his call writing, he may use:

1. Fully paid-for securities.
2. A convertible security exchangeable for an equivalent number of shares of the underlying security.
3. A warrant granting him the privilege to subscribe to the equivalent number of shares of the underlying security.
4. The purchase of the underlying security on margin.

In all cases his call writing will be considered covered and there will be no need for margin collateral. He may use either his cash account or a margin account to write the covered option. For a covered call against a security purchased on margin, it will be more appropriate, of course, for the customer to use a margin account instead of a cash account.

In purchasing the security on margin, the customer is using leverage. He must deposit sufficient collateral to maintain the required margin equity in his account. As long as the margin requirements are satisfied in full, the status of the covered call will not change.

EXAMPLE

The customer purchases 200 shares of Bee Corp. at \$50 on margin and writes 2 calls Bee Corp. Jan. 50. The customer must deposit margin for the purchase and his call writing is considered covered — no need for margin on the call option. Regulation T requires 50% margin or \$2,000 in the account and a margin maintenance of 25% of the market value of the security at all times. The broker may require more than 25% for margin maintenance if he chooses. The account will read:

SECURITY POSITION

Long	Current price	Total market value	Reg T requirement
200 Bee Corp.	\$50	\$10,000	\$5,000
Total market value		\$10,000	
Margin debit		−5,000	
Margin equity		\$5,000	
Margin maintenance (25% of \$10,000)		\$2,500	

OPTION POSITION

2 calls Bee Corp. Jan. 50 covered

The broker will mark the security account to the market and demand additional margin should the security price fall in value. This will not alter the covered status of the call. If he sells the security before the expiration of the option, however, his call will be uncovered and the customer must deposit the required margin for the call.

The customer may deposit his security or money at a bank and write either a covered call or a put with his broker. The broker will demand an escrow receipt executed by the bank to protect the broker in the event of an assignment. This must be a commercial bank acceptable to the broker and approved by the Options Clearing Corp. In issuing an escrow receipt, the bank guarantees the broker that the certificate or the money order will be delivered in the event of an exercise of the option.

When the customer is said to have written a covered put, he has deposited cash equal to the aggregate exercise price of the put option or equivalent collateral. He writes 1 put Bee Corp. Jan. 50 covered. His broker's account must have a credit balance of a minimum of $5,000, the total aggregate exercise price. This will insure his obligation to pay for the underlying security if the put option is exercised. Some brokers allow customers to invest the cash in a money market fund earning interest for the customer. The money market fund must not have any short-term or long-term maturities, and it must not have any check writing privileges by the customer. It must be in the custody of the broker, and it may be liquidated at the broker's discretion to honor the customer's commitment if the put option is exercised.

A put option writing is considered covered when the customer sells the underlying security short, provided he has deposited sufficient collateral as margin to cover his short security position. The put writing does not require margin. Since the short selling of the security is done in a margin account, it is advisable for the customer to write his put option also in a margin account. A short seller anticipates a decline in the value of the security, and he is obligated to purchase the security to cover his short. Writing a put option will satisfy his obligation. A put writer purchases the underlying security when his option is exercised.

Should the security rise in value, the broker will mark the short account to the market and demand more margin collateral. The market fluctuations of the underlying security will not change the covered status of the put option. If the customer covers his short position by purchasing the security before the expiration of the put option, he must leave sufficient cash in his account to maintain his covered put. Otherwise his put option will be uncovered, or *naked*.

UNCOVERED OPTION WRITING

When the customer writes an uncovered option, he must deposit margin collateral to protect the broker in the event the option is exercised. The broker must ensure that there is sufficient collateral to honor the writer's commitment to either buy or sell the security when the buyer of the option exercises his privilege.

The following are the regulatory margin requirements for uncovered options.

1. The transaction must be done in a margin account.

2. The customer's account must have a minimum of $2,000 equity at the time of the transaction. He may deposit $2,000 in cash or marginable securities with a loan value of $2,000, at 50% Regulation T requirement, that will represent a marginable security valued $4,000.

3. The minimum margin for each uncovered stock option contract is 100% of the premium plus 5% of the market value of the underlying security.

4. The customer must deposit and maintain margin equal to 15% of the market value of the underlying security. Fifteen percent is the regulatory minimum. Some brokers may require a higher percentage if they choose.

5. The customer must also deposit margin equal to 100% of the premium of the option contract.

6. In the event the option contract is out-of-the-money, the broker will subtract the amount of the money in out-of-the-money.

7. The broker will mark the account to the market and demand additional margin to maintain the account in compliance with regulatory requirements. The customer may apply the premium of the option towards his margin requirement. If the margin requirement is $3,500, a $500 premium received as proceeds of the writing of the option may be deducted from $3,500.

Uncovered Call Writing

When the customer writes an uncovered call, he must deposit margin equal to 15% of the market value of the underlying security plus 100% of the premium of the option. The broker will subtract the amount of money in out-of-the-money. Minimum margin is 100% of the premium plus 5% of the market value of the underlying security.

EXAMPLE

The customer writes 1 call Bee Corp. Jan. 30 at 5, uncovered. The market price of Bee Corp. is $30. His margin requirement will be:

a.	15% of $3,000	$450
b.	Plus the premium	+500
c.	Minus the amount in out-of-the-money	− 0
d.	Margin required	$950

The customer may use the proceeds of the sale of the option, $500, towards his margin.

$$\begin{array}{r} \$950 \\ -500 \\ \hline \$450 \end{array}$$

The customer must make sure there is a minimum of $2,000 equity in his account to comply with the initial margin requirement.

Bee Corp. stock rises to $40 a share. The broker will mark the account to the market in the following manner:

a.	15% of $4,000	$600
b.	Plus the premium	+500
c.	Margin required	1,100
d.	Previous margin deposit	−450
e.	Margin call	$650

EXAMPLE

The customer writes 1 call Cee Corp. Jan. 30 at 4. Cee Corp. stock is $25 a share. His margin requirement will be:

a.	15% of $2,500	$375
b.	Plus the premium	+400
		$775
c.	Minus the amount in out-of-the-money	
	($3,000 − $2,500)	−500
		$275

The broker must make sure that this $275 margin is not lower than the minimum regulatory requirement. The margin may not be lower than the premium plus 5% of the market value of the underlying security:

a. Premium $400
b. 5% of $2,500   +125
                                                                     ─────
                                                                     $525

Since the amount calculated is less than $525, the broker will consider $525 as the required margin.

Again, the customer must make sure that his margin account has a minimum of $2,000 initial equity.

EXAMPLE

The customer writes 1 call Dee Corp. Jan. 30 at 1. The market price of Dee Corp. is $17. His margin requirement will be:

a. 15% of $1,700 $255
b. Plus the premium   +100
                                                                    ─────
                                                                    $355
c. Less the amount in out-of-the-money
   ($2,000 − $1,700)   −300
                                                                    ─────
                                                                     $55

The broker will use the minimum margin:

a. Premium $100
b. 5% of $1,700   + 85
                                                                    ─────
                                                                    $185

The broker will issue a margin call for $185. Again the amount of equity in the account must be a minimum of $2,000.

Uncovered Put Writing

When the customer writes an uncovered put, he must deposit margin equal to 15% of the market value of the underlying security, plus the premium of the option, less the amount in out-of-the-money. The customer may use the proceeds of the sale towards his margin requirement. The account must have a minimum of $2,000 in equity at the time of the transaction.

EXAMPLE

The customer writes 3 puts Bee Corp. Jan. 50 at 5. Bee Corp. stock is $47 a share. His margin requirement will be:

a. 15% of ($4,700 × 3) $2,115
b. Plus the premium of the option   +1,500
c. Margin required $3,615
d. Premium received   (3 × $500)   −1,500
e. Margin call $2,115

Bee Corp. stock declines to $44 a share. The broker will mark the account to the market and issue a margin call, if needed.

a. 15% of ($4,400 × 3) $1,980
b. Plus the premium of the option   +1,500
c. Maintenance margin requirement $3,480

The premium received in writing an option may be used only once.

Fifteen percent is the regulatory requirement. Brokers may require a higher percentage if they wish. Some brokers require as high as 30% of the market value of the security. Other brokers require that option writing customers maintain an equity higher than $2,000 in the account at all times. This may range from $3,000 to as high as $15,000.

The broker's daily mark to the market procedure is essential. If the underlying security should fall, in a put writing, the broker must make sure that the customer has enough margin collateral to purchase the security at market price and sell it at the strike price in the event of the exercise of the put.

WRITING PARTIALLY UNCOVERED STRADDLES

A straddle is a combination of a call and a put of the same underlying security with the same strike price and expiration date. If the customer owns the underlying security and deposits the aggregate exercise price of the put, there will be no margin requirements in writing a straddle. This will be a covered straddle writing for both the call and the put side of the combination. When the customer owns the underlying security and writes a straddle, no margin is needed on the call side. The put, however, is considered uncovered, and he must place the required margin to protect the put portion of the combination.

Straddle	Coverage
Call	Customer owns the underlying security, a convertible bond or warrant that can be converted into the appropriate number of shares.
Put	Customer has deposited the aggregate exercise price of the put.
Call	Customer owns the underlying security or has an escrow receipt from an acceptable bank.
Put	Customer owns a put of an equal or greater strike price with at least equal life.
Call	Customer owns another series of calls of the same class equal to or lower than the strike price with at least equal life.
Put	Customer has the aggregate exercise price deposited in his account.

The following are varieties of partially covered, or partially uncovered, straddle writing:

Straddle	Coverage
Call	Customer owns the underlying security, or other securities discussed above.
Put	Uncovered. Needs necessary margin for the put portion.
Call	Uncovered. Needs necessary margin for the call portion.
Put	Full aggregate exercise price on deposit with the broker.
Call	Uncovered. Needs necessary margin for the call portion.
Put	Customer has sold short the underlying security. Needs margin for the short account.
Call	Uncovered. Needs necessary margin for the call portion.
Put	Customer owns a put of equal or greater strike price with at least equal life.

EXAMPLE

The customer writes 1 straddle Bee Corp. Jan. 40. The market price of Bee Corp. stock is $35. The premium of the call is $5, and that of the put is $4. The customer owns 100 shares of Bee Corp. The call side of the straddle, therefore, is covered — no need for margin. For the uncovered put portion of the straddle, the broker will calculate:

a.	15% of $3,500	$525
b.	Plus the premium of the put	+400
c.	Margin required	$925

The customer may use the proceeds of his option writing toward his margin requirement.

EXAMPLE

The customer writes 1 straddle Bee Corp. Jan. 30. The market price of Bee Corp. is $35. The premium of the call is $5, and that of the put is $4. The customer does not own the underlying security but owns a long put Bee Corp. Jan. 45. The call side of the straddle is uncovered and the put side is covered. For the uncovered call of the straddle, the broker will require the following margin:

a. 15% of $3,500		$525
b. Plus the premium		+500
c. Required margin		$1,025

EXAMPLE

The customer writes 1 straddle Bee Corp. Jan. 30. The market price of Bee Corp. is $35. The premium of the call is $5, and that of the put is $4. The customer does not own the underlying security but deposits the aggregate exercise price of the put. The put portion of the straddle is, therefore, covered; there is no need for margin. The call portion is uncovered. The broker will calculate margin:

a. 15% of $3,500		$525
b. Plus the premium		+500
c. Required margin		$1,025

EXAMPLE

The customer writes 1 straddle Bee Corp. Jan. 30. The market price of Bee Corp. is $35. The premium of the call is $5, and that of the put is $4. The customer has sold short 100 shares of Bee Corp. at $35. The call portion of the straddle is uncovered, but the put side is covered. The customer is required to meet the margin requirement for the short sale in addition to the margin requirement for the uncovered call.

SHORT ACCOUNT

Short	Current price	Total market value	Margin required	Credit balance
100 Bee Corp.	$35	$3,500	$1,750	$5,250
Credit balance		$5,250		
Current short market value		−3,500		
Margin equity		$1,750		
Margin maintenance (30% of $3,500)		$1,050		

Regulation T margin requirement will be $1,750.

Uncovered call	
15% of $3,500	$525
Plus the premium of the call	+500
Required margin	$1,025

Combined margin requirement for the straddle and the short sale: $1,750 + $1,025 = $2,775.

WRITING TOTALLY UNCOVERED STRADDLES

If both the call and the put in the straddle combination have no coverage, the margin requirement is as follows: The broker calculates each side separately based on the margin requirements already discussed. Whichever option requires the greater margin, that option determines the margin requirement for the straddle.

EXAMPLE

The customer writes 1 call Bee Corp. Jan. 30. Both the call and the put are uncovered. The premium of the call is $4, and that of the put is $3. The market price of Bee Corp. is $35. The broker will calculate each side separately and consider the greater amount for margin requirement:

Call margin calculation	
15% of $3,500	$525
Plus the premium of the call	+400
Required margin for call	$925

Put margin calculation	
15% of $3,500	$525
Plus the premium of the put	+300
	$825
Minus the amount in out-of-the-money: ($3,500 − $3,000)	−500
Required margin	$325

Since the margin requirement for the call side is the greater of the two, the broker will consider $925 as the required margin for the straddle. The customer may deduct the total premium received from the margin requirement.

a. Required margin		$925
b. Premium received	($300 + $400)	−700
c. Margin call		$225

EXAMPLE

The customer writes 1 straddle Bee Corp. Jan. 50 uncovered. The market price of Bee Corp. is $40. The premium of the call is $2, and that of the put is $7. The margin requirement will be:

Call margin calculation	
15% of $4,000	$600
Plus the premium of the call	+200
	$800
Minus the amount in out-of-the-money ($5,000 − $4,000)	−1,000
Required margin:	
Premium	$200
Plus 5% of $4,000	+200
	$400

Put margin calculation	
15% of $4,000	$600
Plus the premium of the put	+700
Margin required	$1,300

The broker will consider $1,300 as the required margin for the straddle. The customer may apply the premium received toward the margin requirement:

a. Required margin		$1,300
b. Premium received	($200 + $700)	−900
c. Margin call		$400

WRITING SPRADDLES

A spraddle is a combination of a call and a put of the same underlying security with the same expiration date but different strike prices. Types of fully covered and partially covered spraddles are the same as straddles. If the customer owns the underlying security and has deposited the aggregate exercise price of the put, he will write a fully covered spraddle and no margin is needed. If the customer has sold the underlying security short and writes a spraddle, this will be partially covered. The call side requires margin and the put side will be considered covered provided the customer has complied with the margin requirements for the short sale. If the customer owns the underlying security and writes a spraddle, the call side will be covered but the put side will be uncovered and requires margin. The margin calculation for partially uncovered spraddles is the same as for partially uncovered straddles.

When the customer writes a totally uncovered spraddle in which both the call and the put have no coverage, the margin requirements are as follows:

1. The broker will calculate each side separately based on the margin requirements, as discussed.
2. He will consider the side with the greater amount and ignore the other side with the lesser amount.
3. He will add the amount in in-the-money of the side he ignored to the greater amount.

EXAMPLE

The customer writes 1 spraddle Bee Corp. Oct. uncovered. The call has a strike price of $50 with a premium of $4, and the put has a strike of $60 with a premium of $3. The market price of Bee Corp. is $58. The broker will calculate each side separately and consider the greater amount for margin. To the greater amount he will add the amount in in-the-money of the side he ignored.

Call margin calculation	
15% of $5,800	$870
Plus the premium of the call	+400
Margin required	$1,270

Put margin calculation	
15% of $5,800	$870
Plus the premium of the put	+300
Margin required	$1,170

The margin calculation for the call is the greater of the two. The broker will consider $1,270. To this amount he adds the amount in in-the-money of the put side.

a. Margin required		$1,270
b. Put in-the-money	($6,000 − $5,800)	+200
		$1,470
c. The customer may deduct the amount of premium received		−700
d. Margin call		$770

EXAMPLE

The customer writes 1 spraddle Cee Corp. July uncovered.

Price of Cee Corp. Stock	Call strike	Put strike	Call premium	Put premium
$45	$40	$50	$3	$2

Call margin calculation	
15% of $4,500	$675
Plus the premium of the call	+300
Margin required	$975

Put margin calculation	
15% of $4,500	$675
Plus the premium of the put	+200
Margin required	$875

The broker will consider the greater amount, $975, to which he will add the amount in in-the-money of the other side.

a. Margin required		$975
b. In-the-money amount		+500
		$1,475
c. The customer may deduct the amount of premium received	($300 + $200)	−500
d. Margin call		$975

EXAMPLE

The customer writes 2 spraddles Dee Corp. April uncovered.

Price of Dee Corp. stock	*Call strike*	*Put strike*	*Call premium*	*Put premium*
$36	$35	$30	$3	$1
Call margin calculation				
15% of ($3,600 × 2)				$1,080
Plus the premium of the call				+600
Margin required				$1,680
Put margin calculation				
15% of ($3,600 × 2)				$1,080
Plus the premium of the put				+200
				$1,280
Minus the amount in out-of-the-money				
($3,600 × 2) − ($3,000 × 2)				−1,200
Margin required				$80

The broker will consider the greater amount, $1,680. The put side is out-of-the-money. The broker will add nothing to $1,680.

a.	Margin required	$1,680
b.	Minus premium received	−400
		$1,280

MARGIN ON SPREAD

A spread is a combination of long and short options. It is a simultaneous purchase and write of a different series but the same class of options. In establishing a spread position, the customer is required to deposit margin collateral to cover the written or the short side of the combination if the short side has any risks associated with it. All spreads are established in a margin account, and the account must have a minimum of $2,000 in equity at the time of the transaction.

For margin purposes the broker classifies spreads into "qualified" and "unqualified." In a *qualified spread*, the short option expires at the same time, or before, the long option. In an *unqualified spread*, the short option is not covered by the long side.

Unqualified Spread

Both options are treated as separate contracts. The customer pays for the long option in full and deposits the necessary margin to cover the short side.

EXAMPLE

The customer establishes the following spread position:

Long: 1 call Bee Corp. Jan. 50 at 4
Short: 1 call Bee Corp. April 50 at 6

The short side is uncovered because it expires after the long option. The customer must deposit margin based on calculations as discussed.

Price of Bee Corp. stock	Long	Premium	Short	Premium
$52	1 call Bee Corp. Jan. 50	$4	1 call Bee Corp. April 50	$6

The customer must make a payment of $400 for the long side.

Margin calculation for the short call	
15% of $5,200	$780
Plus the premium of the call	+600
Margin required	$1,380
Less premium received	−600
	$780

Qualified Spread

In establishing a *qualified spread,* the customer may offset the cost of the purchase of the long side by the premium received in writing the short option.

The options are not treated as separate contracts. The long option expires no earlier than the short option. If any risks are associated with the short side, the customer is required to deposit the necessary margin.

Margin requirements for qualified spreads are the following:

Call Spreads

The margin requirement is the lesser of the two amounts:

1. The margin requirement for an uncovered call calculated as discussed.

Or:

2. The excess, if any, of the aggregate exercise price of the long call over the aggregate exercise price of the short call.

Put Spreads

The margin requirement is the lesser of the two amounts:

1. The margin requirement for an uncovered put as discussed.

Or:

2. The excess, if any, of the aggregate exercise price of the short put over the aggregate exercise price of the long put.

EXAMPLE

	Debit	Credit
a. Long 1 call Cee Corp. April 40 at 4	$400	
b. Short 1 call Cee Corp. Jan. 40 at 3		$300
c. Market price of Cee Corp. is $40	$100	

This is a *debit spread*: The cost of the long exceeds the premium of the short. The customer will simply pay the debit amount to the broker, $100. The short side is covered because it expires before the long option. There is no need to deposit margin because no risks are associated with the spread. By writing the short call the customer is committed to deliver 100 shares of Cee Corp. at $40 a share if the option is exercised by the January expiration date. If he is assigned, he will simply exercise his long call. He will purchase the stock at strike price $40 and deliver it against the assignment notice.

Calculating on the basis of the requirement discussed, the margin will be the lesser of the following two amounts:

Margin for uncovered short call	
15% of $4,000	$600
Plus the premium of the call	+300
Margin required	$900

Or:

Excess of aggregate exercise price of long call over aggregate exercise price of short call.

$$\$4,000 - \$4,000 = 0$$

No need for margin.

EXAMPLE

The customer establishes the following spread. The price of Dee Corp. is $35.

	Debit	Credit
a. Long 1 put Dee Corp. Jan. 40 at 3	$300	
b. Short 1 put Dee Corp. Jan. 30 at 2		$200
	$100	

This is a *debit spread*. The cost of the long option is more than the premium for the short. The customer will pay the difference to the broker, $100.

By writing 1 put Dee Corp. Jan. 30, the customer is making a commitment to buy 100 shares of Dee Corp. at exercise price $30, if the option is exercised by the January expiration date. Upon assignment, he will simply exercise his long put option — that is, sell 100 shares of Dee Corp. at the exercise price of $40 and buy 100 shares at $30 against the assignment notice. There is no risk in this spread. Therefore there is no need for margin. It will cost the buyer less money to buy the shares than to sell.

The margin requirement will be the lesser of the two:

Margin for uncovered short put	
15% of $3,500	$525
Plus the premium of the put	+200
	$725
Minus the amount in out-of-the-money ($3,500 − $3,000)	−500
Margin required	$225

Or:

The excess of the aggregate exercise price of the short put over the aggregate exercise price of the long put. Since the excess is zero, there is no need for margin.

EXAMPLE

The customer establishes the following spread position (Credit Spread):

	Debit	Credit
a. Long 1 call Tee Corp. Jan. 60 at 3	$300	
b. Short 1 call Tee Corp. Jan. 55 at 4		$400
The price of Tee Corp. is $58 a share		$100

The cost of the purchase is less than the premium of the short option. Some risk is associated with this combination. By writing the Jan. 55 call the customer is committed to sell 100 shares of Tee Corp. at $55 a share. Upon assignment he will exercise his long call. He will buy the stock at the strike price of $60 and deliver it against the assignment notice at $55 a share. By buying at $60 and selling at $55, the customer experiences a loss of $500. To cover this the broker requires margin of $500. The customer may apply the $100 credit in the spread toward the margin requirement.

The margin requirement will be the lesser of the two:

Margin for the uncovered short call	
15% of $5,800	$870
Plus the premium of the call	+400
Margin required	$1,270

Or:

The excess of the aggregate exercise price of the long call over the aggregate exercise price of the short call:

$$\$6,000 - \$5,500 = \$500$$

The broker will consider $500 as the margin requirement. The customer may apply the credit of $100 toward his margin:

a. Margin	$500
b. Premium received	−100
c. Margin call	$400

EXAMPLE

The customer establishes the following spread position, with the market price of Bee Corp. at $85.

	Debit	Credit
a. Long 1 call Bee Corp. July 100 at 15	$1,500	
b. Short 1 call Bee Corp. July 90 at 18		$1,800
		$300

The margin requirement will be the lesser of the two:

Margin for the uncovered short call:	
15% of $8,500	$1,275
Plus the premium of the call	+1,800
	$3,075
Minus the amount in out-of-the-money ($9,000 − $8,500)	−500
Margin required	$2,575

Or:

The excess of the aggregate exercise price of the long call over the aggregate exercise price of the short call:

$$\$10,000 - \$9,000 = \$1,000$$

The broker will consider $1,000 as the required margin. The customer may apply the amount of credit, $300, toward his margin requirement:

a. Margin requirement	$1,000
b. Credit	−300
c. Margin call	$700

Margin Requirement for Butterfly Spreads

A *butterfly spread* is a combination of two short options, one long option in-the-money and one long option out-of-the-money. In establishing a butterfly spread, the customer must deposit sufficient margin to cover any risks associated with the position. If there are no risks—that is, if the long option covers the short option—there is no need for margin deposit.

EXAMPLE

The customer establishes the following butterfly spread, with the market price of Bee Corp. at $35.

Long	Price	Long	Price	Short	Price
1 call Bee Corp. Jan. 40	$3	1 call Bee Corp. Jan. 30	$5	2 calls Bee Corp. Jan. 35	$2

In a butterfly combination, the customer writes 2 calls on-the-money, buys 1 call in-the-money, and buys 1 call out-of-the-money.

	Debit	Credit
a. Buys 1 call Jan. 40 at $3	$300	
b. Buys 1 call Jan. 30 at $5	$500	
c. Writes 2 calls Jan. 35 at $2		$400
	$800	$400

The customer must deposit $400 since the debit exceeds the credit by $400. Let us now consider if any risks are associated with this combination.

In the event his two short calls are assigned, he is required to deliver 200 shares of Bee Corp. at $35. To be able to deliver 200 shares, he must exercise his long options with the following results:

	Debit	Credit
a. Buys 100 Bee Corp. at $40	$4,000	
b. Buys 100 Bee Corp. at $30	$3,000	
c. Sells 200 Bee Corp. at $35		$7,000
	$7,000	$7,000

Since there are no risks to the broker, there is no need for margin.

EXAMPLE

The customer establishes the following butterfly position, with the market price of Bee Corp. at $45.

Long	Price	Long	Price	Short	Price
1 call Cee Corp. April 55	$1	1 call Cee Corp. April 40	$7	2 calls Cee Corp. April 45	$3

	Debit	Credit
a. Buys 1 call April 55 at $1	$100	
b. Buys 1 call April 40 at $7	$700	
c. Writes 2 calls April 45 at $3		$600
	$800	$600

The customer must deposit $200 since debit exceeds credit by $200.

In the event of an exercise against his short calls, the customer will exercise his long options with the following result:

	Debit	Credit
a. Buys 100 Cee Corp. at $55	$5,500	
b. Buys 100 Cee Corp. at $40	$4,000	
c. Sells 200 Cee Corp. at $45		$9,000
	$9,500	$9,000

It will cost the customer $500 more than the proceeds of the sale to exercise his long option. Therefore, the broker will require margin in the amount of $500.

OPTION STRATEGIES

There are many advantages in trading options. The investor may apply a variety of strategies to achieve investment objectives. The following is a brief discussion of some of the strategies.

Buying Calls

One obvious strategy is to buy calls and invest the difference. The investor buys calls on the same number of shares that would otherwise have been purchased outright and invests the difference in money market instruments.

EXAMPLE

If the investor purchases 100 shares of Bee Corp. at $50 a share, he would invest $5,000 to own the security. Instead he buys 1 call of Bee Corp. 50 at $5. This costs him $500. (1 call represents 100 shares, $100 \times 5 = 500$.) He then invests the remaining $4,500 in money market instruments earning interest. The interest that he earns reduces the cost of purchasing the call. This is leverage with a limited risk. From an investment point of view, this arrangement is more advantageous than an outright investment of $5,000.

Writing Options

The strategy for the option writer is to receive additional income on his investment. He buys a security at $50 a share and writes 1 call option on it. If the option premium is $5, he will receive $500. Writing a call option on the security does not affect his ownership in the security. He continues to receive dividends and has full voting rights. By writing a call option, he is making the commitment to sell his security at the strike price in the event of an exercise. If the call is exercised prior to the ex-dividend date for a cash dividend, the call holder will be entitled to the dividend. Conversely, the holder of the put who exercises his put prior to the ex-dividend date and delivers the security to the writer of the put after the ex-dividend date must also deliver the dividend on that security.

If the writer owns the security and writes a call option on it, it's called covered call writing. If without owning the security he writes a call option on it, that call writing is called uncovered or naked. For an uncovered call, the writer must deposit margin with his broker to assure the delivery of the security in the event of an exercise. The margin can be either in the form of cash or securities.

Buying Put Options

In the case of put options, these strategies are reversed. Put options on options exchanges were introduced on June 3, 1977.

Today, with both a put and a call, the investor has a wide range of strategies from which to choose. The buyer of the put expects the price of the underlying security to go down. Buying a put is similar to selling the security short. In both cases, the anticipation is for the price of the security to fall. The short seller sells the security first and when or if the market price of the security goes down, he then buys the security to cover his short position. The difference in money will be his gain. In selling the security short, he is making the commitment to ultimately buy the security back. He has, in effect, sold a borrowed security. He eventually buys it back.

When the investor buys a put, he has the option to sell the security. He does not have to own the security at the time he purchases the put. When the market of the underlying security falls, he will buy the security in the open stock market and exercise his put, selling the security at the higher strike price. The put buyer has no exposure for margin calls or payment of dividends as he would have had in a short sale. As in the case of buying a call, his risk is limited. He loses no more than the cost of purchasing the put.

As in the case of calls, the buyer of the put, instead of exercising his put, simply sells it in a closing transaction. The difference in money is his gain or loss.

EXAMPLE

	Debit	Credit
a. Investor A buys 1 put Bee Corp. Jan. 50 at 5 (open transaction)	$500	
b. Investor A sells 1 put Bee Corp. Jan. 50 at 6 (closing transaction)		$600
His profit is $100 less commissions	$500	$600

Another strategy commonly used in put options is buying the underlying security and the put option on it. This combination protects the investor against a possible drop in the market value of the underlying security. For example, the investor buys a stock at $50 a share and buys a put with an exercise price of 50. If the stock goes down, the investor exercises his put, selling the security at $50. This is an added insurance against a possible decline in the value of the security.

Writing Put Options

In writing a put option, the investor agrees to buy the under-lying security from the buyer of the put if the buyer exercises his put. Again, by writing the put, the investor increases his income with the hope that the put will not be exercised. He must main-tain sufficient funds with his broker to assure that the security is purchased in the event of an exercise. As with the call writer, a writer of a put may also terminate his obligation by simply buy-ing back the identical put, as long as the option has not yet been exercised. His profit or loss will be the difference between the two premiums.

EXAMPLE

	Debit	*Credit*
a. Investor A writes 1 put Bee Corp. Jan. 50 at 5 (open transaction)		$500
b. Investor A buys 1 put Bee Corp. Jan. 50 at 4 (closing transaction)	$400	
The investor makes a profit of $100 less commissions.	$400	$500

Buy a Call and Sell the Security Short

A popular strategy used by short sellers is a combination of a short sale and a long call. The investor sells the security short and buys a call on it. This combination protects him against a pos-sible rise in the market value of the underlying security. When he sells the security short, he is expecting a lower price of the secu-rity to cover his short position. To protect himself against a rising market, he buys a call on the security, and when the security rises in value, he will exercise his call, buying the security at the strike price. This covers his short position in the underlying security.

Straddles

In another strategy known as *straddle*, the investor buys a call and a put on the same underlying security with the same strike price and the same expiration month. He will have a locked-in profit in either direction of the price of the underlying security.

EXAMPLE

The investor buys 1 call Bee Corp. Jan. 50 and simultaneously buys 1 put Bee Corp. Jan. 50. Both in an opening transaction.

Buy 1 call Bee Corp. Jan. 50
Buy 1 put Bee Corp. Jan. 50

When the price of Bee Corp. security goes up, he will exercise the call position and let the put portion expire; but when the price of the security drops, he will exercise the put portion and let the call portion expire. He profits from either direction of the price movement of the security. The only time he loses is when the price of the security remains the same during the life of the combination, but he loses no more than the cost of the combination. If, for instance, the call is worth $500 and the put is worth $400, the combination will cost him $900 plus commissions. His maximum exposure will be the cost of the transaction.

The investor may decide to write a straddle. He will write a call and write a put with the same exercise price, the same expiration month, and the same underlying security. His objective in this case will be to receive the premium. If he constructs the combination discussed above, he receives a combined premium of $900 less commissions. By writing the straddle he hopes the price of the underlying security will remain relatively the same.

In a combination known as *spraddle*, the investor buys 1 call and buys 1 put on the same underlying security with the same expiration month but different strike prices.

Buy 1 call Bee Corp. Jan. 50
Buy 1 put Bee Corp. Jan. 60

Spreads

Undoubtedly the most popular strategy in the options market is a combination known as *spread*. Here the investor buys and writes the same type (call or put) but different series of options. For example, he buys a call and writes a call of different series on the same underlying security.

Buy 1 call Bee Corp. Jan. 50
Write 1 call Bee Corp. Jan. 60

This is a simultaneous purchase and write in opening transactions. In making this combination, the investor maximizes his potential for profit and at the same time reduces his risk. He does not mix the two types, taking either the calls or the puts. In either case, the objective is the same. There are many different types of spread combinations. The following are some of the more popular ones.

1. *Vertical spread.* The investor buys a call or a put and writes a call or a put. Both options have the same expiration month but different strike prices. This is also known as perpendicular spread or price spread.

Buy 1 call Bee Corp. Jan. 50
Write 1 call Bee Corp. Jan. 60

2. *Horizontal spread.* The investor buys a call or a put and writes a call or a put. Both options will have the same strike price but different expiration months. This combination is also known as calendar spread or time spread.

Buy 1 call Bee Corp. Jan. 50
Write 1 call Bee Corp. Apr. 50

3. *Diagonal spread.* The investor buys a call or a put and writes a call or a put. The options have different strike prices and different expiration months.

Buy 1 call Bee Corp. Jan. 50
Write 1 call Bee Corp. Apr. 60

CHAPTER TWENTY

CLEARANCE OF SECURITIES

One of the most important aspects in the operation of the securities business is the clearance of shares — a simple matching process of securities transacted and the ultimate delivery or receipt of net balances. This clearing process obviates most of the transactions in the marketplace, eliminates unnecessary paperwork, and reduces the traffic of certificates from one broker to another. Without the clearance of shares and money, it would be difficult for the brokerage business to cope with the growing volume of securities transactions.

HISTORY OF THE CLEARING HOUSES

Attempts to organize a successful clearing operation at the New York Stock Exchange did not materialize until 1892, exactly 100 years after its organization. The concept originated in Europe and was adopted by the Philadelphia Stock Exchange prior to its implementation in New York.

It started as a pilot operation for certain selected securities, and participation by member firms was voluntary. It was not until 1920 that this pilot operation gave birth to a formal organization called the Stock Clearing Corporation.

Before the adoption of this process, the mechanics of securities handling was a tedious one. Each transaction had to be taken separately. A security that was sold had to be delivered to the purchasing broker against payment, and a security that was bought had to be received in against the purchase price. Insurmountable problems were caused by the process of delivering and receiving certificates and checks by messengers, depositing the checks, and turning the securities around to deliver them to other brokers. To complete the transaction, the buying broker had to receive the stock and make payment to the selling broker. If he could not get his payment in time, he was forced to borrow the money to satisfy the selling broker on a "Day Loan" basis. The cost of this loan reduced his profitability.

EXAMPLE:

> Broker A sells 100 shares to Broker B.
> Broker B sells 100 shares to Broker C.

Broker A delivers a stock certificate for 100 shares to Broker B and collects money due him. Broker B delivers the 100 shares to Broker C and receives money in return.

It is apparent from this illustration that Broker B's interest in the shares is transient even though he might have been representing two customers. He has simultaneously purchased and sold the security on the same day, and not withstanding the contract prices, his involvement in the activity is temporary. He would receive the certificate from Broker A and make payment, but immediately would relinquish his interests by delivering it to Broker C and receive payment. Operationally, this step seems unnecessary. Broker B's problem, however, is more financial than operational.

At the time when Broker A was presenting the certificate to him, Broker B might not have had sufficient funds to make payment. Because he did not have title to the shares, he could not deliver the certificate to Broker C and receive his money in return. He was forced, therefore, to go to a commercial bank and borrow money on a temporary basis until the transaction with C was consummated.

This lack of immediate funds was one of the main reasons for the creation of the clearing corporation. In spite of the secrecy surrounding the industry when one broker's transactions were kept in complete confidentiality from another, the idea of a clearance of shares and money achieved immediate popularity after a successful experiment with a group of brokers and with certain specified securities. Today, there are four clearing corporations in the country. Transactions on the New York, American, and the over-the-counter NASDAQ market are handled by the National Securities Clearing Corp. Trades on the Midwest Stock Exchange are handled by the Midwest Clearing Corp. Trades on the Pacific Stock Exchange are handled by the Pacific Clearing Corp., and trades on the Philadelphia Stock Exchange are processed by the Stock Clearing Corp. of Philadelphia.

NET BY NET SETTLEMENT

As discussed earlier, the clearing corporation obviates most of the transactions executed on the floor of the exchange by a netting process. Sales are offset by purchases.

Different exchanges have different clearing principles and, therefore, different operating procedures. The oldest method that is presently in use on a limited basis is done on a net-by-net settlement in which the clearing corporation mandates the delivery of the security to a specified broker for a specified price.

Immediately after the trade has been executed, the clearing corporation puts the mechanism in motion to settle the trade. It starts with a comparison of the contracts between the two firms, the summarization of the total sales and purchases, the determination of settlement prices, the printout of the deliver and receive balance orders, and finally the actual delivery and receipt of the security in question.

The intricacies of the clearing process are many, and the obviation of the transactions involves a series of complex procedures. The following is a simple illustration of a clearing activity where a transaction or transactions have been eliminated through the process. On the same day, three transactions are made in the same security issue:

> Broker A sells 100 shares to Broker B.
> Broker B sells 100 shares to Broker C.
> Broker C sells 100 shares to Broker D.

These transactions involve four different brokers, each representing a different customer. Each trade was probably made at a different contract price.

Since Brokers B and C have relinquished their interests in the shares, they will be relieved of the actual involvement in the delivery and receipt of the certificates. The clearing corporation directs Broker A to deliver 100 shares to Broker D, even though Broker A had nothing to do with Broker D on the floor of the exchange. The following diagram shows why this was done:

BROKER A	BROKER B	BROKER C	BROKER D
Sells	Buys		
	Sells	Buys	
		Sells	Buys

For Brokers B and C, the buys and sells cancel each other out, so Broker A with a "Sell" Delivers to Broker D who has a "Buy."

Because contract prices vary for a given security from trade to trade, the clearing corporation establishes a standard price for all participating firms at which transactions are settled. This price is called the *Settlement Price*.

At the conclusion of each trading session, the clearing house determines the settlement prices of all the securities traded by simply taking the closing price of each stock and dropping the pennies. The settlement price of a security last traded at $27\frac{5}{8}$ will be 27. There is no monetary loss or gain. The transactions are settled with the contra-broker through the clearing corporation.

EXAMPLE

BROKER A

Sales		Purchases	
100 at 27 $\quad$ = \$ 2,700.00		200 at $27\frac{3}{8}$ = \$5,475.00	
200 at $27\frac{1}{2}$ = $\quad$ 5,500.00		100 at 27 $\quad$ = $\quad$ 2,700.00	
300 at $27\frac{1}{8}$ = $\quad$ 8,137.50			
$\quad\quad\quad$ \$16,337.50		$\quad\quad\quad$ \$8,175.00	

The broker has sold a total of 600 shares of this stock at varying contract prices for an aggregate amount of \$16,337.50. In the meantime, however, he has purchased a total of 300 shares for \$8,175.00. After offsetting the sales with the buys, the clearing corporation advises the broker to deliver only 300 shares to a designated brokerage house against the settlement price of that particular security ($27). The brokerage firm will receive $8,100 against the delivery of 300 shares. Since the difference between the sale money ($16,337.50) and the purchase money ($8,175.00) is $8,162.50, the remaining $62.50 which was temporarily obviated in the clearing process is paid to the brokerage firm in the form of a *Settlement Differential*.

The payment to or from the clearing corporation is not done on an individual security basis. All securities delivered and received on a given settlement day are netted by the clearing corporation so that at the end, the brokerage firm either receives a check from the corporation or submits one to the corporation as a final settlement of all transactions for that day.

The following is the procedure for clearing after the execution of the trade.

The floor clerk notifies the Order Room as to the number of shares, the name of the security, the customer involved, the name of the contra-broker, and the price per share. The Order Room, in turn, advises the Purchase and Sales Department of the brokerage firm.

On Trade Date +1, the Purchase and Sales Department submits the buy and sell data to the clearing corporation that prepares a list indicating the compared and uncompared trades.

On Trade Date +2, the P & S Department makes the necessary adjustments and resubmits data to the clearing corporation that prepares supplementary lists indicating the adjusted data.

On Trade Date +3, the clearing corporation prepares the Receive and Deliver Balance orders and a clearance and settlement statement for each clearing member. These are the actual forms by which the securities are delivered and received.

On Trade +5, which is the due day for delivery, the Cashiers Department prepares the item and delivers it to the buying broker via the clearing organization. This delivery is accompanied by a credit list indicating the value of the items.

After comparing the values of the receipts and deliveries by each clearing member, the clearing corporation effects the money settlement and advises the participants.

CONTINUOUS NET SETTLEMENT (CNS)

The clearing corporation has introduced a more technological and modern approach that affords the securities firms more flexibility and less clerical involvement in processing securities transactions.

The new clearance method updates the security and money positions of the participating brokers continuously. Therefore, the concept came to be known as Continuous Net Settlement (CNS). The prototype for CNS was originally introduced by the Pacific Stock Exchange Clearing Corporation. The Continuous Net Settlement is a method of clearance and settlement of securities transactions whereby open security positions and money balances are brought forward daily on a perpetual basis. Only one net position is shown for each security. This position is constantly updated by settling trades, deliveries, stock dividends, receipts and transfers. After a comparison process, the contra-side of all trades becomes the clearing corporation itself. Deliveries are made directly to the clearing corporation and the securities are sent to the broker by the clearing corporation. An important part of the system is the daily adjustment of the price of the open securities positions (Mark to Market) to reflect the current market price of the security in question.

EXAMPLE

Monday *Feb. 1*	*Tuesday* *Feb. 2*	*Wednesday* *Feb. 3*	*Thursday* *Feb. 4*	*Friday* *Feb. 5*
Buys 100 shares		Buys 200 shares		Sells 100 shares
Monday *Feb. 8*	*Tuesday* *Feb.9*	*Wednesday* *Feb. 10*	*Thursday* *Feb. 11*	*Friday* *Feb. 12*
Long 100 shares		Long 300 shares		Long 200 shares

On February 1, the broker buys 100 shares of Bee Corp. On the settlement date, February 8, the broker's account will be "Long" in the clearing corporation's record. On February 3, the broker buys 200 shares of Bee Corp. On February 10, the settlement date of that trade, his position will be updated in the clearing corporation's records with a long position of 300 shares. On February 5, the broker sells 100 shares of Bee Corp., again on the settlement date of that trade, February 12. His position will be reduced by 100 shares, leaving him with a long position of 200 shares. In the Continuous Net Settlement system the broker's position is being updated every time he makes a trade.

Dividends and Interest

Because the clearing corporation is the contra-side for all net positions, it is a relatively simple matter to control cash and stock dividends due to and from member-brokers. The clearing corporation establishes a cut-off date for stocks on which a dividend is payable. This will permit stocks to be transferred by the record date.

Mark to Market

Under a net-by-net balance order system, members whose contracts are partially unsecured because of price fluctuations must mark such contracts individually with contra-brokers. In the CNS procedure, all contracts are automatically marked to the market when the current market price of the security differs from the previous price.

BOOK-ENTRY SETTLEMENT

The security transactions are settled through a book-entry procedure that is a computerized accounting system. The seller advises the depository company to debit his account the number of shares sold and credit the buyer's account without any physical delivery of securities.

NATIONAL SECURITIES CLEARING CORPORATION

The National Securities Clearing Corporation clears the trades on the New York and the American Stock Exchanges, and the NASDAQ over-the-counter trading. Its continuous net settlement system is linked to the Depository Trust Company (DTC), with interface arrangements with other depositories and clearing corporations.

Operation of the Clearing System at NSCC

The operation begins with trade reporting and comparison. On Trade Day +1, members submit all trade data to the clearing corporation. The clearing corporation compares the purchases and sales and produces a "Contract List." All uncompared trades must be resolved by members, and any additions, deletions, or corrections must be submitted to the clearing corporation on Trade Day +2 and Trade Day +3.

The accounting operation groups all CNS securities that have been compared on Contract Lists between Trade Day +1 and Trade Day +3 by date of settlement and produces the "Compared Trade Summary," which indicates the trades and net totals for each security.

On Trade Day +4, each member receives a "Projection Report" indicating the anticipated positions for Trade Day +5, the settlement day. This report shows the current position, net trading activity due to settle on Trade Day +5, net stock dividends due for payment and the resulting projected net position. The projected net positions are valued at the current market price.

The brokerage Cashiers Department reviews the "Projection Report" and determines what securities should not be delivered. These exemptions are indicated on the "Projection Report" and submitted to the clearing corporation on the evening of Trade Day +4. Its recycling procedure provides two levels of exemptions:

Level 1. It may withhold a position from the entire settlement cycle to be netted with the following day's trades.

Level 2. It keeps the position from being automatically settled against the member's security positions at DTC but allows settlement when new depository activity, such as new deposits, releases from collateral loan, or securities received from a bank against payment, occur. For the cashiering operation, this is an excellent tool for same-day turnaround of securities.

The settlement process at CNS is certificateless. As mentioned above, the operation is linked to DTC, and automatic bookkeeping entries are made between CNS and DTC. CNS takes a member's previous day's closing positions and creates a single net position per security by taking new settling trades and stock dividends into consideration. The net position may be a "Short" (shares owed to the broker by the Clearing Corporation). The net position may then be settled by a book-entry movement from DTC to CNS. Certificates are immobilized within DTC; only journal entries reflect the movement of securities.

THE MIDWEST CLEARING CORPORATION

The Midwest Clearing Corporation (MCC), a wholly owned subsidiary of the Midwest Stock Exchange, is the clearing arm for the Exchange. Its purpose is to provide clearing and settlement services for trades made on the Midwest Stock Exchange as well as for trades made on other exchanges. Together with the Midwest Securities Trust Company, MCC provides a wide range of integrated services through utilization of a computer and operational facility known as the MST System.

Through the MST System, which utilizes the concept of Continuous Net Settlement, trades are netted daily into one position, short or long, for each security traded. On settlement day, all trades settling that day are netted into a Pay or Collect Settlement figure, payable either to MCC or to the participant. Throughout the settlement process (T + 1 − T + 5), MCC provides each participant with computer-generated reports that keep the participant abreast of the status of his trades made through the MST System, as well as all deliveries, deposits, and dividends. Other reports itemize the Free, Value, Depository, and Pledge positions each participant currently holds, as well as the current status (netted shares and value) of all trades settling within the next four days for each security.

Operation of the Clearing System at MCC

1. *Trade Comparison and Recording.* Trades may be entered into the MST System from many sources. Trades made on the Midwest Stock Exchange, whether through CNS or trade for trade, are entered into the system. Trades made on other exchanges such as the New York, American, Cincinnati, Philadelphia, Boston, and the Pacific Stock Exchanges may be routed to MCC through One Account Settlement system for settlement in the MST System. After these trades are compared, they are reflected on the "Purchase and Sales Report" issued to each participant.

The P & S Report offers a comparison tool for transactions between participants and reflects all trades entered into the MST System as transacted on the previous day. Listing of each security issue is by ticker symbol and is in CUSIP number order. The contra participant's account symbol is listed with each trade, as well as trade type, and the gross and net value of the shares bought or sold in the security issue. A notation is made for trades transacted on exchanges other than the Midwest Stock Exchange. Each participant is responsible for comparing his trade blotter with the entries on the P & S Report and reporting any discrepancies to his floor broker.

2. *Settlement.* Each day, all sales are netted against all buys within a given issue. This netted figure becomes the participant's position within MCC and consists of a share balance, either short or long, and a debit or credit money figure. The stock position is valued at the current market price based on the previous day's closing. This price is marked to the market, and a cash adjustment either credits or debits the participant's account. Net buyers of securities are charged the current market value, and net sellers are credited for the current market value of the shares they deposit to fill short positions.

On Trade Day +1, and on each day in the settlement cycle, MCC provides an "Activity Report" to each participant. The "Activity Report" details all stock and cash movements occurring within the participant's account on that day, and indicates the daily Pay or Collect Settlement figure.

As stated above, the "Activity Report" details all stock and cash movements and changes in security positions occurring within each account on a given day. These movements and their corresponding effect on money values and share positions are listed by security issue in CUSIP number order. The "Activity Report" is broken down into six sections, each covering a different aspect of movement within the MST System:

a. Trade for Trade Activity

b. Deposits, deliveries, book-entry movements submitted to the MST System by the participant

c. Activity within Continuous Net Settlement, including positions with corresponding marking to the market of security prices

d. Itemization of special services applied to the participant's account. These include the OTC Envelope Service, Special Security Movements (receipts and deliveries), as well as other special services provided through MCC.

e. Miscellaneous cash adjustments, including corrective adjustments made to the account

f. Summary of Pay or Collect Settlement figure

Additionally, each participant receives the "Net Position Report," which reflects the results of all security movements and settling transactions listed on the "Activity Report." The "Net Position Report" details all of the participant's positions and keeps track of all total shares pending future processing.

Within the MST system, there are various positions in which the security may be held. These positions have been established to meet the particular needs of the participant. These are Free positions that represent fully paid for stock and may be used to complete short transactions (Clearing Free) or to provide stock for loans (Loan Free). The Depository Free position may be used to segregate stock by customer account. The Value positions reflect trades not yet settled (MCC Value) or stock that has been loaned out (Loan Value).

BOOK-ENTRY CLEARANCE AT THE FEDERAL RESERVE BANK

The Federal Reserve Bank, acting as the fiscal agent of the United States government, clears transactions in U.S. Treasury securities through its book-entry method.

This method eliminates the need for physical receipt and delivery of certificates. The participating members advise the Fed to credit or debit their account and settle the money payments through adjustments in the reserve accounts at the Fed. These settlements may be made for members in the same federal district or for members located in other districts.

CHAPTER TWENTY ONE

SECURITIES DEPOSITORIES

The predominant feature of the capital markets in the United States is the existence of registered securities. From the time of the Revolutionary War, the American investor has insisted on having an actual certificate registered in his name. This practice has continued through the centuries to the detriment of the securities operation.

Because of the existance of the stock certificate, the capability of the marketplace to handle large volume transactions is limited. Unlike Europe or Asia where practices and procedures are different, there is a constant traffic of certificates among the securities firms. Legislation has not provided flexibility in this area; on the contrary, it has continued to rely on the certificate as evidence of ownership. Throughout history, the stock certificate has come to represent the American productive resources and wealth.

Is it necessary for corporations to issue stock certificates? If it is an instrument to furnish information as to the identity of the registered owner, it can be done in ways other than issuance of securities.

A trade executed on the floor of the exchange may transmit data to the transfer agent to effect the change of ownership in the books of the corporation. This may be done simultaneously, removing all obstacles between the marketplace and the transfer agent. It would have real time processing system, eliminating the necessity of physical securities and establishing an electronic share transfer operation.

Various studies have indicated that the certificate is not an indispensable instrument. Corporations may adopt alternative means to record and transfer title. There are, however, legal constraints that govern the issuance of certificates. The Uniform Commercial Code and state statutes will have to be modified to legislate the certificate out of existence.

In the meantime, there has been increased activity in the financial community to immobilize the stock certificate. Immobilization ignores the certificates and focuses attention only on the interests it represents. Thus, instead of constantly delivering, receiving, transferring, and processing stock certificates, the securities firm handles only the transfer of the interest from one owner to another through a bookkeeping medium.

The idea of immobilizing the stock certificate originated in Europe. Immediately after World War II, the French adopted a central depository system taught to them by the Germans during the occupation. The system, called SICOVAM, disregards the certificate entirely and transfers ownership by book-entry debits and credits.

In this country, the New York Stock Exchange took the initiative in the mid-1950s to create a central depository system. In a long campaign, which lasted more than a decade, NYSE helped to change the statutes and to make necessary amendments that paved the way for the installation of such a system. In the late 1960s, a central depository became operative under the auspices of the Exchange's Clearing Corporation.

This affiliate, known as the Depository Trust Company, retains stock certificates in a cold storage. The selling broker advises DTC to debit his account and credit the buying broker's account without the necessity of moving the certificate. It is a simple book-entry operation that has received tremendous popularity during recent years because of its remedial effect on the operational problems of the industry.

Today, there are four securities depositories in the country — the Depository Trust Company in New York, the Midwest Securities Trust Company in Chicago, the Pacific Securities Depository Trust Company in San Francisco, and the Philadelphia Depository in Philadelphia.

The Depository Trust Company is capable of handling a variety of depository services. Although it accepts only securities eligible to its system, it expands its list continuously to include securities traded on the NYSE, AMEX, and on the over-the-counter market.

Certificates are registered in the name of Cede & Co. — nominee name for the Depository Trust Company — and are beneficially owned by the participants. The participant, whether broker, bank, or an institution, merely instructs DTC through the use of various forms to debit his account and credit the buyer's account. A broker may also utilize the securities held on deposit as collateral for a loan. DTC attaches a lien on these securities until the loan is paid off.

The participant also may instruct DTC to have shares held on deposit to be transferred in the name of his customer. The procedures, although technical in nature, are clerically routine. Forms representing a particular instruction travel back and forth and ignore the certificate altogether. Dividends are received from the disbursing agents and credited to the respective participant's account.

SERVICES PROVIDED BY DTC

Deposit of Securities

A participating organization may deposit the securities eligible with DTC. All deposited securities are credited to the participant's account.

Institutional Delivery System (ID)

This service will assist brokers and institutions to complete their security transactions. An institutional account may be able to receive credit of shares that it has purchased via the book-entry system.

ID users have the option to have acknowledged trades entered into the Continuous Net Settlement System of the National Securities Clearing Corporation. This is permissible if the security is CNS eligible and the broker, the institution, and the agent–bank subscribe to the ID/CNS interface.

Pre-Authorized Delivery System (PDQ)

The Pre-Authorized Delivery System (PDQ) is a method of delivering securities without the use of delivery instructions, envelopes, or credit lists.

Withdrawal of Nominee Certificates

A participating organization may withdraw a physical stock or bond certificate from DTC. To satisfy this need, DTC permits participants to withdraw securities in round lots, registered in the name of and endorsed by Cede & Co. (DTC's nominee name).

Withdrawal of Certificate Under the Fast Program

DTC provides a program called FAST that entitles the participants to withdraw certain securities in round lots, odd-lots, or mixed lots, registered in a name specified previously by the participant.

Dividends and Interest Payments

Cash and/or stock dividends and bond interest payments received by DTC are credited to the participants' account.

Dividend Reinvestment Service

The Dividend Reinvestment Service permits DTC to utilize programs of automatic reinvestment of dividends of certain securities. DTC, acting on behalf of the participant, will arrange for the reinvestment of dividends of these securities.

Collateral Loan

A participant may pledge securities credited to his own free account as collateral for a loan with any pledgee bank participating in DTC's Collateral Loan Program.

Overnight Loan

The DTC overnight collateral loan service gives participants the opportunity to pledge securities for an overnight bank loan while anticipating their automatic release the next morning for a book-entry delivery to other participants.

Conversions

The DTC conversion program enables participants to exercise conversion of securities from one class to another class within the book-entry environment. Participants wishing to offer the conversion of a security authorize DTC to surrender the qualifying convertible securities on deposit to the conversion agent.

Reorganizations

DTC provides services for mergers, acquisitions, and tender offers of securities on deposit.

Roll Over on U.S. Treasury Bills

A participant may roll-over maturing U.S. Treasury Bills for new ones issued every Thursday and available to the public the preceding Monday.

U.S. Government Securities

U.S. Treasury Bonds, Notes, and Federal Agency securities are eligible for DTC through a system developed with the Federal Reserve Bank of New York. The system uses the Fed's and DTC's book-entry systems so that all participants may deliver and store U.S. government securities. Actual certificates of U.S. government securities are thus eliminated, minimizing the risk of their loss, theft, or destruction. Regular DTC services for collecting and distributing interest payments and redemption proceeds apply to U.S. government securities.

DTC does not handle or hold in its vault certificates of U.S. government securities. These are kept at the Federal Reserve Bank of New York for the account of DTC. A participant wishing to deposit a U.S. government security at DTC will forward the certificate to the Federal Reserve Bank of New York, which will accept the security on behalf of DTC; DTC will add the security to the participant's DTC account after being notified by the Federal Reserve that the deposit has been made.

The deposit of U.S. government securities also may be made at any Federal Reserve District Bank. The Federal District Bank will notify the New York Fed and appropriate credits will be allocated to the DTC's account.

Once the eligible securities have been credited to a participant's DTC account, they become available for delivery to other participants.

A participant may withdraw registered U.S. government securities from its DTC account by giving appropriate instructions to DTC. The securities are made available for pickup by participants at the Federal Reserve Bank of New York.

Proxies

DTC does not directly exercise any voting rights for shares registered in the name of Cede & Co. Instead, DTC facilitates the voting of Cede & Co. shares by extending the voting rights to the appropriate DTC participant.

THE MIDWEST SECURITIES TRUST COMPANY

A smaller, but nevertheless, representative depository for stock certificates is the Midwest Securities Trust Company, the depository arm of the Midwest Stock Exchange in Chicago. Operating in conjunction with the Midwest Clearing Corporation, the two subsidiaries provide a wide range of services for their participants. MSTC also provides a location for stock certificates while enabling participants full use of the deposited shares to transact their business. Through the use of book-entry movements share quantities may be moved from participant to participant or from participant to a non-member firm with an account at another depository without actual physical movement of the certificates. In addition, shares may be used to collateralize short option positions with the Options Clearing Corporation or to facilitate loans with participating institutions.

Operation of the MSTC Depository

The Midwest Securities Trust Company holds stock certificates on behalf of participants. These certificates are held in fungible form (in the name of Kray & Co.) by security issue and represent each participant's total Depository Free position.

The Depository Free position itself is a segregated position. Stocks in this position cannot be used for the completion of trades; they have to be moved via book-entry into another free position on instructions of the participant. Since the certificates held in the Depository are immobilized, movements of securities between participants or within a participant's own account are completed by a book-entry system.

Services

1. *Participant Delivery Program.* Because of the increasing number of trades made by institutions on behalf of their trust customers, MSTC has developed the Participant Delivery Program (PDP) to simplify and streamline broker/institutional trades within the MST System. PDP creates a trade recording and comparison cycle between the broker and the bank. Both the bank and the broker receive special reports that indicate the status of each trade from day to day, within the five-day settlement cycle. The bank must acknowledge each of its trades via special acknowledgement cards before the trade enters the MST System for settlement. Actual settlement of the trade involves book-entry movement of securities from one participant to another.

2. *Pledge Loan Program.* The Pledge Loan Program is a computerized book-entry method for effecting long-term collateral loans between a broker–dealer and a bank by pledging as collateral securities held within the Depository. After the terms of the loan have been arranged between the two parties, securities to be used as collateral are entered into a pledged position until the completion of the loan. Securities never leave the Depository; all movements are made by book-entry. If, during the life of the loan, there is a need to substitute other securities, the substitution can be arranged — provided that the pledgee bank accepts the substitution of other securities as collateral.

CHAPTER TWENTY TWO

INSURANCE COVERAGE IN THE SECURITIES BUSINESS

SECURITIES INVESTORS PROTECTION CORPORATION

In the early 1970s, Congress established the Securities Investors Protection Corporation to insure customers of stricken brokerage firms, similar to the insurance program provided by the FDIC for commercial banks and FSLIC for savings and loan associations.

The Securities Investors Protection Corporation, known as SIPC, is a private corporation sponsored by the U.S. government. It is funded by assessments of member brokerage firms. The assessment is based on the gross revenues, with a minimum fee of $25 a year. Membership is mandatory for all broker–dealers registered under the Securities Exchange Act of 1934, except those engaged in mutual funds, variable annuities, insurance, or advisory activities.

When a brokerage firm is in the process of liquidation, SIPC will petition the federal court to appoint a trustee to assume the control of the firm. The trustee will have the responsibility to liquidate the firm's assets and satisfy customers' insured accounts.

The trustee's first responsibility will be to notify customers and creditors of the firm's insolvency. All claims must be submitted to the trustee for processing within a certain date. Claims presented six months after the filing date are not honored.

The trustee will distribute cash and securities to customers whose accounts show the money and security positions properly identified. This will be securities actually registered in customers' names and held in safekeeping with the broker–dealer. These securities will not be part of the insurance coverage provided by SIPC.

The trustee will request the amount of the margin debit from margin customers. After receipt of the funds, securities will be transferred in the customers' names and shipped to them.

SIPC insures up to $500,000 in each customer account, of which no more than $100,000 can be in cash. Each individual is insured up to $500,000, no matter how many accounts he may have carried with the broker–dealer. For SIPC purposes, the customer's cash, margin, short sales, options, and other accounts are combined into one. Commodity accounts are not insured by SIPC.

The trustee will establish the value of the customers' securities held in Street name as of the date of the SIPC's application to the court for the appointment of the trustee.

The uninsured portion of the customer accounts and claims from general creditors will be satisfied only after the insured customers' claims have been satisfied. This will be to the extent of the remaining assets of the firm on a pro rata basis.

NASD RULES ON INSURANCE COVERAGE

Brokerage firms must have adequate insurance coverage for every aspect of their operation. The NASD requires the brokerage firm to carry a blanket fidelity bond to cover officers and employees of the firm against losses in securities, losses due to forgery and alteration of securities and checks, and losses due to fraudulant trading.

There are different types of insurance coverage: mail loss insurance, miscellaneous insurance, umbrella coverage, wrongful retention coverage, legal liability coverage for directors and officers, key man insurance, computer insurance, foreign insurance, and employee benefit insurance.

The securities firm must maintain a minimum insurance coverage of 120 percent of its net capital if its net capital is less than $500,000.

The firm is required to review the adequacy of its insurance coverage at least once a year. Any termination, cancellation, or substantial modification of the insurance policy must be reported to the NASD within 10 business days.

SEC RULE OF LOST, MISSING, STOLEN SECURITIES

The SEC Rule 17f–1 requires all brokers, dealers, registered transfer agents, clearing corporations, securities exchanges, and banks to report and make inquiries with respect to missing, lost, counterfeit, or stolen securities.

Reporting of lost securities must be done to the Securities Information Corporation (SIC) of Cambridge, Massachusetts.

Reporting Requirements

- *Missing or lost securities.* Every institution must report missing or lost securities to the SIC and the transfer agents. Such reporting must be done within two business days of the discovery of the loss.

- *Securities lost in transit.* These securities must be reported by the delivering institution no later than two business days after the notice of non-receipt.

- *Securities considered lost as a result of securities count.* These securities must be reported no later than 10 business days after the completion of such securities count or as soon as the certificate numbers can be ascertained.

- *Delivery through a clearing entity.* If a security is not received, the delivering institution must supply the receiving institution with the certificate numbers of the security within two business days from the date of the request. Where the delivery is made by mail or via drafts and payment is not received within 10 business days, the delivering institution must confirm the failure to receive the delivery and must report within two business days of such confirmation.

- *Counterfeit securities.* These securities must be reported within one business day of their discovery. The appropriate law enforcement agencies must also be notified.

- *Information to be reported.* The reports must have the following information:
  1. Name of issuer
  2. Type of security
  3. Date of issue
  4. Maturity date

5. Denomination
6. Interest rate
7. Certificate numbers
8. Name of registered holder
9. Date of discovery
10. CUSIP and FINS numbers

Reporting must be made on Form X-17f-1A.

Recovery

When a security previously reported missing, lost, or stolen is recovered, the SIC and the transfer agent must be promptly notified within one business day of the recovery.

Requirements for Inquiry

Every reporting institution, except a registered transfer agent, must inquire from SIC before processing a security to ascertain whether the security has been reported as missing, lost, stolen, or counterfeit. No inquiry is necessary:

1. If the security is received from the issuer or its agent.
2. If the security is received from another reporting institution or the Federal Reserve Bank.
3. If the security is received from the customer of the reporting institution and is registered in the name of the customer.
4. If the value of the security is $10,000 or less.
5. If the security is received directly from a depository facility.

The following securities are exempted from the reporting and inquiry requirements of Rule 17f-1:

1. U.S. government and federal agency securities
2. Securities not assigned CUSIP numbers
3. Bond coupons

Record-Keeping

The reporting institutions must retain copies of Form 17F-1A filed pursuant to the rule, in an easily accessible place for a minimum of three years.

PROCEDURE FOR REPLACING LOST CERTIFICATES

Corporations have special procedures to have lost or destroyed certificates replaced. The transfer agent acting on behalf of the corporation has the responsibility to replace a lost certificate under the Uniform Commercial Code.

When the certificate is reported lost, the securities firm will contact its insurance carrier to execute a surety bond for the replacement of the certificate. The bond will hold the corporation, the transfer agent, and the registrar free and harmless from any liability in duplicating the security.

A partially mutilated or destroyed certificate may be replaced without the need of an indemnity bond if certain distinguishing marks on the certificate have remained visible and identifiable.

For lost bearer or coupon bonds, "stop" payments are placed with the paying agent. No "stop" payment may be placed, however, for U.S. Treasury obligations and certain municipal securities.

CHAPTER TWENTY THREE

TAXATION IN SECURITIES
TRANSACTIONS

In discussing taxation in securities transactions, one must consider the following factors:

- *An account or a security may be taxable.* The taxpayer must pay income tax based on his tax bracket.
- *An account or a security may be tax-exempt.* The taxpayer pays no income tax.
- *An account may be tax-deductible.* The taxpayer may reduce the amount from his taxable income.
- *An account may be tax-deferred.* The taxpayer may defer the payment of income tax to a future year. This applies to tax-deferred accounts such as IRAs and recognized but not realized gains in the sale of properties. The taxpayer will sell a property for a gain and use the proceeds to buy another property. The gain in the transaction is recognized but not realized, since it has been used immediately to purchase another property. The tax on the recognized gain may be deferred until the second property is sold for a gain.

BASIS

For tax purposes, *basis* is the cost or the book value of the asset at the time of acquisition. The basis is the total cost of the acquisition, which may include commissions, charges, interest, the replacement costs, and the capital improvements of the property. The depreciation of the property will reduce the basis. The costs and commissions for the sale of the property will increase the basis.

ORDINARY INCOME AND CAPITAL GAINS

The Tax Code classifies income as *ordinary* and *personal service*. The ordinary income is the passive income, such as dividends, interests, rents, and royalties. It is taxed on a progressive scale. Personal service income is earned income. This consists of salaries, wages, and income in providing personal service. This is also taxed on a progressive scale.

Under the Tax Code, stocks, bonds, options, warrants, U.S. Treasury notes, U.S. Treasury bonds, and other similar securities are considered as capital assets, but not the U.S. Treasury bills. One may never have a capital gain or loss in transactions of U.S. Treasury bills.

The purchase and sale of a capital asset establishes a tax basis.

EXAMPLE

	Debit	Credit
a. Purchase 100 Bee Corp. at $35	$3,500	
b. Commissions	$ 45	
Tax basis	$3,545	

	Debit	Credit
a. Sell short 100 Bee Corp. at $35		$3,500
b. Commissions	$ 45	
c. SEC fee	$ 1	
Tax basis		$3,454

THE HOLDING PERIOD

The holding period is the length of time the investor owns the property. The period starts with the acquisition of the capital asset, from the day after the trade date of the purchase until the trade date of the sale. The holding period determines the tax rate and the tax deductibility for capital gains and losses. For short sales, the holding period does not start at the time when the short sale is executed; it starts when the short sale is covered.

EXAMPLE

The investor buys 100 Bee Corporation on trade date March 17, 1986, and sells it on trade date March 18, 1987. The holding period is one year.

The investor sells short 100 Bee Corporation on trade date March 17, 1986, and buys it back on March 18, 1987, to cover the short. The holding period is zero, since it starts with the purchase on March 18, 1987.

If the holding period is six months or less, the gain or loss is considered short term. If the holding period is six months and one day or longer, the gain or loss is considered as long term.

EXAMPLE

Date Purchased	Date Sold	Short Term	Long Term
a. 100 Bee Corp. March 16, 1986	100 Bee Corp. March 16, 1987		Long term
b. 100 Bee Corp. March 16, 1987	100 Bee Corp. March 17, 1987	Short term	
c. Buy to cover short sale 100 Bee Corp. April 16, 1987	Sell short 100 Bee Corp. March 15, 1986	Short term	

TAXABLE GAINS AND LOSSES

To compute short-term capital gains for the year, the investor will add all his short-term gains and subtract from the total all his short-term losses. The result will be the *net* short-term gain for the year. 100 percent of this amount will be taxable as ordinary income for the year.

Short-term gain − Short-term loss = Net short-term gain

To compute long-term gains for the year, the investor will add all his long-term gains for the year and subtract from the total all his long-term losses. The result will be net long-term gain for the year. Only 40 percent of this amount will be taxable as ordinary income.

$$\text{Long-term gain} - \text{Long-term loss} = \text{Net long-term gain}$$

EXAMPLE

a.	Long-term gain on 100 Bee Corp.	$5,000
b.	Long-term distribution on Bee Mutual Fund	$1,000
	Total long-term gains	$6,000
c.	Long-term loss on 100 Bee Corp.	−$1,000
	Net long-term gain	$5,000

Only 40 percent of this $5,000 will be added to the taxable income.

Capital Losses

If the investor has a net short-term loss or a net long-term loss, he must do the computation in the following manner:

1. He must offset the net long-term gain by net short-term loss.
2. He must offset the net short-term gain by net long-term loss.

$$\text{Long-term gain} - \text{Short term loss} = \text{Long-term gain}$$
$$\text{Short-term gain} - \text{Long term loss} = \text{Short-term gain}$$

EXAMPLE 1

Net long-term gain:	$10,000
Net short-term loss:	−$ 6,000
Net long-term gain:	$ 4,000

EXAMPLE 2

Net short-term gain:	$10,000
Net long-term loss:	−$ 6,000
Net short-term gain:	$ 4,000

The arithmetic can be the other way around if the investor reports a net loss minus long or short term.

EXAMPLE 3

Net long-term gain:	$10,000
Net short-term loss:	−$12,000
Net short-term loss:	($ 2,000)

The entire $2,000 may be deducted from the investor's ordinary income.

EXAMPLE 4

Net short-term gain:	$10,000
Net long-term loss:	−$12,000
Net long-term loss:	($ 2,000)

Only 50 percent of $2,000 may be deducted from the investor's ordinary income.

Through this netting process, the investor may never have a net short-term loss and a net long-term gain during the same taxable year.

Net short-term losses are deductible dollar for dollar, against ordinary income up to $3,000 a year. Long-term losses reduce the ordinary income only 50 cents on the dollar up to $3,000 a year. Capital losses in excess of the $3,000 a year may be carried forward to future years. This carry-forward provision does not include worthless securities. The investor must consider that he had sold the worthless security for zero during the year that the corporation had gone bankrupt. The $3,000 limit applies to individuals filing single tax returns and people filing joint returns.

Advisory fees, rental fees for safe-deposit boxes, fees for statistical services, stock transfer tax, interest on margin accounts, if paid, are considered deductible items for tax calculation purposes. Interest on funds borrowed to purchase tax-exempt securities may not be deductible.

THE TIMING OF SECURITIES TRANSACTIONS

To include a gain in his taxable income for the year, the investor must make sure that the *settlement date* of the securities transaction is not later than the last business day of the year.

To include a loss in the taxable income for the year, the investor must make sure that the *trade date* of the securities transaction is not later than the last business day of the year.

The investor will plan the year and securities transactions in the following way:

For short-term gain: He will cover the short-term gain by first taking long-term losses, then short-term losses. He will take the additional losses to offset ordinary income.

For long-term gain: He will cover long-term gain by first taking long-term losses then short-term losses. He will take the additional losses to offset ordinary income.

For long-term loss: He will consider taking short-term loss to offset ordinary income and carry over full long-term loss to offset future short-term gain.

Points to Consider at Year-End

1. Long-term losses are used most advantageously against short-term gains, but they must first be used against long-term gains, if any.

2. If long-term gains are contemplated, the investor will postpone the long-term gain by selling short against the box. After the end of the tax year, he will close out the short by delivering the shares in his long position.

3. The investor may consider it advantageous to take the unrealized losses in his security positions for the current year. This loss carry-over will provide the investor with a means of offsetting gains realized on a future sale. The investor may use $3,000

of short-term loss, or $6,000 of long-term loss to offset up to
$3,000 of ordinary income each year.

4. The investor may consider a municipal bond swap at
year-end. He will sell the municipal bond that he is carrying at
a loss and remit the proceeds in higher yielding municipals. This
will allow the investor to shelter realized gains with realized
losses, and reinvest in higher yielding securities that could produce
additional tax-free income for the future.

Trades Made on the Last Day of the Month

For tax calculation purposes, every month has 30 days. If the
investor buys a security on the last day of a month, the holding
period will be calculated to the last day of the following months
regardless of the number of days in the month.

WASH SALE RULE

According to the Internal Revenue Code, a security position that
is established within 30 days before or 30 days after a completed
transaction and results in a loss will be disqualified as a tax-
deductible item. This is called the Wash Sale Rule. For example,
if the investor sells 100 Bee Corp. at a loss of $1,000 and purchases
100 Bee Corp. within 30 days of the trade day of the sale, he may
not deduct $1,000 as a loss from his ordinary income. The same
is true if the investor had purchased the security within 30 days
before the trade date of the sale transaction. The Wash Sale
period covers, therefore, 61 days. The investor may not offset a
loss against profit of the same security within the 61-day period.

EXAMPLE 1

	Debit	*Credit*
a. Investor buys 100 Bee Corp. at $50	$5,000	
b. Sells 100 Bee Corp. at $40		$4,000
c. Buys 100 Bee Corp. at $30 within 30 days of the sale trade	$3,000	

The investor may not use the original loss of $1,000 (5,000 − 4,000) to offset gains in other transactions or lower his taxable income. He must also carry the position of 100 Bee Corporation that he purchased at $30 on the basis of $4,000.

EXAMPLE 2

	Debit	Credit
a. Investor buys 100 Bee Corp. at $50	$5,000	
b. A year later he buys another 100 Bee Corp. at $40	$4,000	
c. He sells 100 Bee Corp. at $30 within 30 days of the trade date of the last purchase		$3,000

The loss of $1,000 (4,000 − 3,000) will be disallowed.

TAX ON ZERO BONDS

Zero bonds pay zero interest during the life of the bond but are sold at a discounted price from the face value. At maturity, the bondholder will receive the total face value. The difference between the purchase cost and the face value of the bond is called the Original Issue Discount (OID).

The Tax Code considers the Original Issue Discount as interest income for corporate zero bonds. Therefore, they accrue interest during the life of the bond.

For bonds issued before July 2, 1982, the Original Issue Discount is accrued into income on a ratable monthly basis over the life of the bond. This is known as Level Annual Accrual. For bonds issued after July 1, 1982, the Original Issue Discount is accrued into income using a progressive method. The accrual is small in the early years, but increases substantially in later years.

For corporate zero bonds, the bondholder is required to pay tax on interest income even though no interest is received. Taxable zero bonds are ideal investment vehicles for tax-deferred accounts, such as Keogh Plans and IRAs. No tax is levied on interest from zero municipal bonds, but if the bond is sold prior to maturity, the investor will be subject to pay tax on capital gain.

SHORT AGAINST THE BOX

In a short sale against the box, the investor holds a long security position in his brokerage account and sells the security short.

EXAMPLE

	Debit	Credit
a. Investor buys 100 Bee Corp. at $60	$6,000	
b. Sells 100 Bee Corp. short against the box at $80		$8,000
Net Credit		$2,000

The short against the box is done to defer the payment of income tax. It is not done to extend the holding period. Since the security position is not being closed, the customer is still considered as the owner of 100 Bee Corporation. But the $2,000 net credit will not be taxable in the year the short sale is executed. The customer will lock up profits for the year but postpone the tax liability on the profit until the following year. In the following year, the customer will instruct his broker to journal his long position to cover the short sale. His position will then be zero. Any resulting profit will be taxable for that year — the year the journal entry was made. The holding period is an important consideration. If the investor has a short-term long position and sells the security short against the box, the holding period of the long position becomes zero. The holding period starts when the customer covers the short position. The holding period remains unaffected if the customer has a long-term security position and sells it short against the box.

EXAMPLE

	Debit	Credit
a. Customer buys 100 Bee Corp. at $50 on March 2, 1984	$5,000	
b. Sells short 100 Bee Corp. at $60 against the box on August 30, 1984		$6,000
c. Covers the short on March 3, 1985 at $55	$5,500	
d. Sells 100 Bee Corp. at $65 on April 7, 1985		$6,500

The short sale against the box on August 30, 1984, will break the holding period of his long position that he had established on March 2, 1985, the day the customer covered the short. The subsequent sale of 100 Bee Corporation at $65 a month later will be considered as a short-term transaction. The result will be a short-term gain of $15 a share (original cost of $50 a share on March 2, 1984, and the final sale at $65 on April 2, 1985). The short sale would result in a short-term gain of $5 a share (sells short at $60 and covers it at $55).

Any gain resulted when purchasing the security to cover a short sale is considered as short term regardless of when the customer has covered the short. Even if the customer covers the short two years later, the gain will still be considered as short term. Any loss between the two transactions also would be considered as short term unless the customer holds a convertible security, a warrant, or a call option of the same security for more than six months at the time of the short sale. In that case, the resulting loss will be considered as long term. One-hundred percent of the short-term loss will be deductible against ordinary income, but only 50 percent of the long-term loss may be deductible. In both cases, the investor is allowed to deduct up to $3,000 a year.

FIRST-IN-FIRST-OUT (FIFO)

If the customer has established different positions of the same security at different times and prices, the sale transactions of these positions are applied on a first-in-first-out basis; unless the customer specifically instructs the broker to apply a particular position against the sale. The identification of a particular position is made by the date of the trade or by the certificate number of the security.

CASH DIVIDENDS AND INTERESTS

Interests on bonds and dividends on equity securities are taxed as ordinary income. The Tax Code allows an exclusion of $100 a person for dividend income. For joint return, the dividend exclusion is $200.

Cash dividends received by corporate accounts are subject

to an 85 percent exclusion from taxable income. The corporate account will only declare 15 percent of the cash dividends received as taxable income; the remaining 85 percent will be excluded from corporate tax liability. The corporation must own the security, however, for more than 15 days to qualify for the exclusion.

The Tax Code reduces the allowable dividend-received deduction for dividends on debt-financed stocks. This means, the dividend-received deduction (85 percent) is reduced by an amount equal to the interest paid on the loan when the corporation has borrowed money to purchase the dividend paying stock.

If a preferred security of a utility corporation organized before October 1, 1942, pays dividends to a corporation, the corporation will only be allowed to deduct 60 percent of the dividends from taxable income. If the utility corporation is organized after October 1, 1942, a corporation receiving cash dividends from the utility company is allowed to deduct 85 percent of the dividends from taxable income.

This exclusion does not apply to dividends received from foreign corporations.

STOCK DIVIDENDS

Stock dividends are not taxable unless the customer elects to receive cash instead of stock dividends. This is called Constructive Receipt. The investor must adjust the price per share of the original position after receiving the stock dividend. The additional stock dividend share will carry the same date as the purchase date of the original stock.

EXAMPLE

Customer buys 100 Bee Corp. at $50. The corporation distributes a 10 percent stock dividend. The customer receives 10 shares as stock dividend. His total holding will be 110 shares at a cost of $5,000 (100 × 5). The price per share will be adjusted to $45.45 (5,000 ÷ 110). For tax purposes, the holding period of the stock dividend will start from the date of the original purchase of 100 shares. The stock dividend will be taxable only when sold.

STOCK SPLITS

Stock splits are not taxable either. But the stockholder will adjust the price per share of his holdings. As in stock dividends, the additional shares received in stock splits will carry the same date as the purchase date of the original stock.

EXERCISE OF WARRANTS AND RIGHTS

When the customer exercises his warrants or subscription rights and receives shares through the exercise, the holding period starts on the purchase date of the original security.

INVESTMENT TAX CREDIT

For certain tangible and depreciable personal properties, taxpayers are allowed to take a 10 percent investment tax credit provided that the property has a minimum useful life of three years and it is located in the United States.

CORPORATE RETIREMENT PLANS

There are several different types of corporate plans through which the corporation offers retirement benefits to its employees. These plans may either be *qualified* or *non-qualified*. The non-qualified plans include:

1. *Payroll Deductions.* In this plan the funds are removed from the employee's salary after the federal, state, and FICA taxes are withheld. The funds will be invested by the management for the benefit of the employee.

2. *Employee Thrift Plan.* This may be qualified or non-qualified. In this plan, both the employer and the employee will contribute to the plan. The employee will contribute through payroll deduction. The employee's portion will be fully vested and may be withdrawn at any time.

3. *Deferred Compensation.* This plan is based on an agreement between the employee and the firm. The employee agrees to defer the receipt of a portion of his salary until retirement,

death, or disability. These plans do not require IRS approval but are subject to reporting and disclosure requirement of ERISA. The objective is to defer the payment of income tax on the deferred portion until retirement. Complications arise, however, when the corporation goes bankrupt.

The qualified plans include:

1. *Profit Sharing Plan.* The firm makes the contribution to the profit sharing plan based on its profit. The contribution may be fixed or discretionary. It is a defined contribution plan.

2. *Pension Plan.* The firm makes the contribution into a pension plan for the benefit of the employees. The plan may either have a *defined contribution* or a *defined benefit*. In a defined contribution plan, the firm makes a set contribution every year. In a defined benefit plan, the benefits are established and the firm will make contributions to meet the desired benefits.

The qualified plan requires the approval from IRS, and the firm must offer it to all full-time employees without any discrimination in favor of directors and stockholders. For defined benefit plans, the maximum benefit is $90,000 a year.

The following employees may be excluded from the plan:

- Seasonal employees
- Employees with less than 1,000 hours a year
- Employees under 25
- Employees with less than three years of employment at the firm.

These plans are subject to the following provisions of ERISA:

- The plan will be 100 percent vested after 10 years of employment.
- The plan will be 50 percent vested if the employee's age combined with the number of years of employment equals to 45. This applies only to employees with more than five years of employment.
- The funds must be placed in a trust with a trustee or trustees acting as fiduciaries.

A "top heavy" pension plan is one where the key employees receive more than 60 percent of the plan benefits of all the employees.

KEOGH PLANS

Under a Keogh Plan, a self-employed person may establish a personal retirement program under the custodianship of a bank, savings and loan association, mutual fund, and other qualified financial institutions. The assets in the program may consist of stocks, bonds, mutual funds, life insurance annuities, real estate mortgages, etc. The investment may be made by the person, but all the assets must be kept in the plan during the life of the program.

By establishing a Keogh plan, the self-employed individual will reduce his current tax liability while building assets for the future. The income earned in the plan is not taxable until the program is terminated and the assets are distributed to the planholders. This usually occurs after the planholder reaches the age of 60 — at which time, the individual may be in a lower tax bracket and the tax liability will be less.

In depositing funds in his Keogh plan, the investor must consider the allowable percentage on income generated from personal services. Passive income, such as dividends, interest, rent, limited partnership return, capital gains, may not be included.

In establishing a Keogh plan for himself, the owner of the company also must include all full-time employees with three or more consecutive years of service. Part-time and seasonal employees may not be included. A part-time employee is one who works not more than 1,000 hours a year. A seasonal employee is one who works less than five months a year. Contributions to the Keogh plan must be made at the same percentage rate for all employees in the plan, including the owner.

Generally no withdrawals from the plan are allowed until the plan participant is at least 59½ years old, or when he dies or becomes permanently disabled. The law requires that the distributions begin before the plan participant is 70½ years old, and the distribution must be completed within five years after the death of the planholder or the spouse, whichever occurs later.

Current law allows the person to deposit the lesser of $30,000 or 25 percent of net self-employed income in the Keogh plan. The contribution to the Keogh plan becomes a tax-deductible item. The calculation of 25 percent of net income is done in the following way:

Gross income	$75,000
Contribution to Keogh Plan	$15,000
Net income	$60,000

Twenty-five percent of $60,000 will be allowed to be deposited in a Keogh Plan.

The distribution of funds from a Keogh plan is taxed in the following way:

A. If the investor receives periodic payments of retirement benefits, these payments will be taxed as ordinary income when received.

B. If the investor receives lump-sum payments of retirement benefits, he will consider the payment as capital gains for the portion contributed before 1984. For deposits made after 1974, he may take the average of the deposits made during a four-year period or a special 10-year averaging for the entire amount.

There are penalties for contributions or withdrawals made in violation of the law. The investor may withdraw all excess contributions without any penalty, but the withdrawal must be done before the date of that year's tax return. If excess contribution is not removed, that portion will not be considered as deferred income and earnings on that amount will be taxable.

At death the distribution is considered as ordinary income to the beneficiary, but it is excluded from the decedent's estate.

INDIVIDUAL RETIREMENT ACCOUNT (IRA)

Individuals may establish an individual retirement program known as IRA. The contribution to the plan will reduce the individual's tax liability while building assets for the future. Income in the plan is not taxable to the individual until the plan is terminated.

IRA funds may be invested in certificates of deposit, savings accounts, endowments, mutual funds, stocks, and fixed income securities. The funds may not be invested in collectibles — such as coins, stamps, or art — and life insurance policies. Voluntary contributions may be withdrawn at any time without penalty. The funds may be rolled over and penalties for premature withdrawal are similar to the ones for Keogh. The rollover must be done within 60 days of receipt of funds. There is no penalty, therefore, if the person takes possession of the IRA funds for 60 days. At death the distribution is considered as ordinary income to the beneficiary, but it is excluded from the decedent's estate.

TAX DEFERRED OR TAX SHELTER ANNUITIES

Public school teachers and employees of nonprofit organizations are qualified to deposit funds in Tax Deferred or Tax Shelter Annuities based on a percentage of their salaries and years of service. Premature withdrawals are allowed without penalty. All withdrawals are considered as ordinary income and no income averaging is allowed. At death the distribution is considered as ordinary income to the beneficiary, but it is excluded from the decedent's estate.

To establish the programs, the employee signs a "Wage Reduction Agreement" allowing the employer to deduct a specified amount from his paycheck and deposit the amount in a Tax Sheltered Annuity Plan (TSA).

TAX SHELTERS AND DIRECT PARTICIPATION PROGRAMS

Limited partnerships offer direct participation programs to shelter the individual partner's income and at the same time allow the partner to share in the growth and the equity of the project. The sheltering is accomplished through depreciation, depletion, and intangible drilling costs of oil and gas projects. The individual partner is allowed to convert ordinary income into long-term capital gains. As a limited partner, his liabilities are limited to the amount of his investment with no management responsibility. The management of the project is conducted by a general partner.

Tax shelter programs usually do not have a secondary market. There is generally no liquidity. The individual partner may not sell his portion at any time he wishes. He must consider his proportionate revenue as taxable income less interest expenses, operating expenses, and depreciation.

The investor may purchase a privately offered Direct Participation Program on margin, but no margin purchases are allowed for publicly offered programs.

All tax shelter programs must be registered with the Securities and Exchange Commission before they are offered to the public. This applies to programs organized after August 31, 1984.

DONATIONS AND GIFT TAX

The Internal Revenue Code imposes a gift tax on transfer of properties as gifts. This will not include gifts to charitable entities and certain nonprofit organizations.

In making a donation to a charitable organization, the fair market value of the gift is deductible from ordinary taxable income. If the gift is a property, it will be advantageous for the donor to consider the holding period of the property. If the property is held long term and if at the time of the donation the value of the property has declined, the donor may consider selling the property first, taking a tax deduction on the loss, and then giving the cash as a gift to charity.

Gifts of properties are based on fair market value, and, as a general rule, property acquired by gift keeps the same holding period as it had in the possession of the donor.

Donations to Minors

Donations of monies, securities, or properties may be made to minors through a convenient law adopted by most states, called the Uniform Gifts to Minor's Act. The following are important considerations for this type of donation:

1. The gift once made may not be taken away from the minor. The minor becomes the beneficial owner, and the gift becomes irrevocable.

2. The donor will appoint a person of legal age to act as custodian for the minor. He may appoint himself, a trust bank, or another person as custodian.

3. There can only be one custodian for a minor.

4. The custodian must always act in the best interest of the minor.

5. Most states prohibit compensation to the custodian for services rendered.

6. The custodian may not use the security for personal needs. The security may not be pledged, loaned, or hypothecated.

7. The custodian may not open a margin account nor engage in speculative trading.

8. Interests and dividends on the securities in a custodian account are taxable to the minor. Therefore, the minor's Social Security number must be used in opening the account.

9. Under the Tax Code, the annual gift tax exclusion is $10,000 per donee per year. A husband and wife may give up to $20,000 a year to each child without incurring a gift tax.

10. When the minor attains majority age, he will request to have the security transferred into his individual name. A proof of age is required for this transfer.

Trusts for Minors

Instead of making donations to minors, a person may decide to establish a trust for the benefit of the minor. The following are some of the trust accounts used for minors:

Clifford Trust. A Clifford Trust is a revocable trust. In establishing this trust, the donor gives assets or money to a minor for a minimum period of 10 years and one day. At the termination of the trust, the gift reverts to the donor. In the absence of any specific provision, any capital gains on the gift are generally taxable to the donor.

Income Trust. An Income Trust is a living trust in which income generated from the trust is payable to the minor.

Crummey Trust. A Crummey Trust is similar to Income Trust, but, in this case, the minor has the right to withdraw the money from the trust account.

Crown Trust. Crown Trusts are demand loans made by a parent to a child. The child receives interests, dividends, or any appreciation on investments made with the funds. The child returns the principal on demand.

The purpose in establishing a Crown Trust is to transfer funds from the parent's high tax bracket to the child's low tax bracket. The Tax Code, however, assumes that the child is paying interest on the loan to his parent. This is called *imputing interest.* The imputed interest is treated as a gift from the lender to the borrower and the same amount is treated as interest payment from the borrower to the lender. This is, therefore, a round trip situation. On the out-bound, a gift tax is attached, and on the in-bound, income tax is attached. The gift tax is payable by the lender (parent) and income tax on interest received by the lender is also payable by the lender. The borrower (the child) is entitled to a tax deduction on interest given to the parent, but this may be negligible if the child is in a low tax bracket.

Income generated from a Crown Trust is excluded from the parent's estate.

Spousal Remainder Trust. A Spousal Remainder Trust is established by one of the parents for any fixed period of time for a child or a beneficiary. The beneficiary will receive income generated from the trust. When the trust is terminated, the remainder will go to the other parent. In establishing this trust, the funds must come from the individual account of the father or mother and not from their joint account.

ESTATE TAX

Estate tax is an excise tax on the value of the property transferred to beneficiaries at the time of death. The legal representative of the estate must value the decedent's gross estate and subtract the allowable deductions. The result will be the taxable portion of the estate. The property included in the gross estate must be valued at either the date of death or at an alternate valuation date, usually six months after death.

MARITAL DEDUCTIONS

The Economic Recovery Act of 1981 has removed the limits on the marital deductions for decedents dying and gifts made after 1981. All qualifying transfers between spouses pass free of both gift and estate taxes.

JOINT TENANCY

Effective after 1981, the estate of the first decedent will include one-half the value of the jointly held property, regardless of which spouse paid for the property.

STRADDLES AND OPTIONS TRANSACTIONS

Tax straddles are balanced positions in stock and other property with little chance of economic gain or loss. They are usually done to transform ordinary income and short-term capital gains into long-term capital gains and shift income from one year to the next. Under the Tax Code, straddles are required to be treated as a unified investment. Loss in one position could only be deducted to the extent it exceeded the unrealized gain in the other position. As such, straddles in Regulated Futures Contracts (RFCs), stock options, stock index options, stock index futures, and commodity options are subject to tax at year-end as if they were sold at the prevailing market price, even though the contracts may still be held by the taxpayer. The gain is taxed at 60 percent long term and 40 percent short term. All offsetting positions must be marked to the market at year-end. A loss realized in the closing of one position is deferred to the extent of any unrealized gain in the other position.

As in securities, option transactions may result in capital gain or loss, long term or short term. For options, the following trades are treated for short-term capital gain or loss:

- Closing purchases
- Closing sale if the option is held for six months or less
- Expiration of option

The following trades are treated for long-term capital gain or loss:

- Exercise of option when the underlying security is held for more than six months
- A long option held for more than 6 months

An option writer may not obtain a long-term capital gain or loss even if the position is held for over six months. Any loss realized from a covered in-the-money call will be a long-term capital loss, if the gain from the sale of the underlying security at the time such loss in the covered call is realized is long term.

WASH SALE RULE FOR OPTIONS

As in securities, the Wash Sale Rule also applies to option transactions. The loss from option trades will be disallowed if the underlying stock is sold in a subsequent tax year within 30 days of the closeout of the option in a covered call. The same rule applies when the customer writes an in-the-money put within the applicable period with respect to the stock sold at a loss.

EXAMPLE

   a. The investor sells 100 Bee Corp. at $50 a share on December 3, 1986, at a loss of $1,000.
   b. The following day, on December 4, 1986, the investor writes 1 put Bee Corp. exercise price 60. This option expires prior to February 1, 1987, and it is an in-the-money put.
   c. Due to the fact that the put is an in-the-money option, there is a strong likelihood that the put will be exercised and the writer would buy 100 Bee Corp. at 60. Therefore, according to the Wash Sale Rules, the put written by the investor was, in substance, a contract to acquire 100 Bee Corp.

SUMMARY OF TAXATION IN OPTION TRANSACTIONS

Type of Transaction	Short	Long
1. Buy options and sell 6 months and 1 day later.		Long
2. Buy call, exercise 3 months later.		Holding period starts at the time of exercise. Cost of the call will be part of the cost basis for the exercised stock.
3. Buy call, exercise 6 months and 1 day later.		Same as above
4. Buy put, exercise 3 months later.	Short	
5. Buy put, exercise 6 months and 1 day later.	Short	
6. Buy call. Call expires 3 months later.	Short	
7. Buy put. Put expires 3 months later.	Short	
8. Buy call. Call expires 6 months and 1 day later.		Long
9. Buy put. Put expires 6 months and 1 day later.		Long
10. Buy stock. 3 months later write call. 6 months later sell stock.		Long
11. Write call. Close it 3 months later.	Short	
12. Write call, uncovered. Close it 6 months and 1 day later.	Short	

SUMMARY OF TAXATION IN OPTION TRANSACTIONS (Continued)

Type of Transaction	Short	Long
13. Write put. Close it 3 months later.	Short	
14. Write put. Close it 6 months and 1 day later.	Short	
15. Write call. Get exercised 6 months and 1 day later.	Short	
16. Write call. Get exercised 3 months later.	Short	
17. Write put. Get exercised 3 months later.	Short	
18. Write put. Get exercised 6 months and 1 day later.	Short	
19. Buy stock. 3 months later buy put. Sell stock 6 months and 1 day later.	Short. The holding period is broken.	
20. Sell stock short. 2 months later write put. Buy stock back 6 months and 1 day later to cover the short.	Short for both stock and put.	
21. Write call. 6 months and 1 day later expires unexercised.	Short	
22. Write put. 3 months later expires unexercised.	Short	
23. Write put. 6 months and 1 day later expires unexercised.	Short	
24. Sell stock short. 2 months later write put. Close out the put 6 months and 1 day after writing put.	Short	
25. Sell stocks short. 2 months later write put. Close out put 3 months later.	Short	
26. Sell stock short. 6 months and 1 day later buy it back.	Short	
27. Sell stock short against the box. 3 months later cover it.	Short. Holding period for long stock is broken when selling stock short.	
28. Sell stock short against the box. 6 months and 1 day later cover it.	Short. Same as above.	

CHAPTER TWENTY FOUR

SECURITY ANALYSIS

Professional and individual investors use various statistics, averages, and indexes to chart the movement of securities prices. There are different schools of thought that attempt to determine the relative value of a security and its potential for growth. It has always been important for investors to forecast the price movement of securities to meet their investment objectives. There are basically three different methods of analyzing a security's price and forecasting its future direction: one is *fundamental*, the other *technical*, and the third *random walk*.

FUNDAMENTAL ANAYSIS

Fundamental analysis is based on the financial data of the corporation. The analyst considers the financial condition of the corporation, earnings, dividends, sales, marketing, new products, etc. and forecasts the price movement of the security. According to the fundamental analyst, if the corporation has good management and its profit picture is healthy, the stock of that corporation will have the tendency to go up.

TECHNICAL ANALYSIS

The technical analyst considers the historical trend of the security's price. He is usually not concerned with dividends, earnings, or sales. He will chart the price of the security at different periods and make his predictions as to the future movement of the security.

There are several methods used in Technical Analysis to chart movements of securities. One is *Point and Figure Charting*. Here the analyst charts the price movement on graph paper by putting an "X" when the price rises and an "O" when the price delines.

```
70 |  ×           ×
   |        o
60 |  ×           ×
50 |  ×     o     ×
40 |_____o_____
```

Another is *Vertical Line Charting*. Here the analyst uses a series of vertical lines to indicate the rise and fall of the security. Different patterns of these vertical lines give different indications as to the future direction of the stock market. The different patterns of vertical line charting are:

A. *Head and Shoulders Top.*

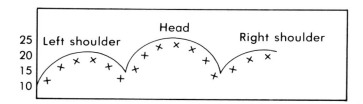

B. *Head and Shoulders Bottom.*

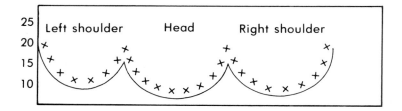

C. *Support and Resistance Level.* This chart will indicate the support and resistance level for a stock. The low point is considered a support; the high point is considered a resistance level.

D. *Double Tops and Bottoms.* This chart measures the forces of supply and demand. The chart generally forms an M or W because the plots will form the shape of these letters.

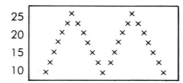 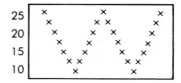

RANDOM WALK

The random walk analyst relates the price movement of a security to the walking pattern of a drunk. The step of a drunk does not give any indication as to the direction of his next step. The random walk analyst examines the security's price in the same way. According to him, the track record of the price of a security should not be taken as a basis for the future direction of the security.

Based on these three different schools of thought, there are various averages and indexes to measure the performance of the stock and bond market at a given period. Some averages are popular and some are not. Some use only a small group of securities and others use all the securities traded on the stock exchanges. The words *average* and *index* are used intermittently.

STOCK MARKET INDICATORS

The Dow Jones Averages

The most popular stock market indicators are the Dow Jones averages based on the writings of Charles Dow, an editor of *The Wall Street Journal* in 1884. Dow Jones has several different averages measuring the price movements of groups of securities in different industries. One is the Dow Jones Industrial Average, the other the Dow Jones Transportation Average, the third is the Dow Jones Utility Average, and the last one is the Dow Jones Composite Average. The most popular is the Dow Jones Industrial Average (DJIA). This is the average used by the press to report the performance of the stock market.

1. *Dow Jones Industrial Average.* The Dow Jones Industrial Average consists of 30 selected securities on the New York Stock Exchange. These are large industrial corporations. This average takes the market prices of each share of 30 stocks and divides the total sum by a divisor. This divisor is a figure that is adjusted periodically to reflect stock splits or stock dividends of a security in the group.

2. *The Dow Jones Transportation Average.* This average consists of 20 railroads, airline, and trucking companies listed on the New York Stock Exchange.

3. *The Dow Jones Utility Average.* This average consists of 15 utility stocks on the New York Stock Exchange.

4. *The Dow Jones Composite Average.* This average consists of 65 stocks that are included in the Industrial, Transportation, and Utility averages.

Historical Notes on the Dow Jones Industrial Average

Charles Dow's original model in 1884 consisted of only 12 corporate securities, primarily railroad stocks. In 1896, 12 other industrial corporations were added to the list; and in 1928, the list was expanded to 30 industrial securities, which is the current number. The market value of these 30 securities today account for almost 25 percent of the value of all securities traded on the New York Stock Exchange.

The following are the historical dates of the highs and lows of the Dow Jones Industrial Average:

1896:	First appeared in *The Wall Street Journal*
Jan. 12, 1906:	100.25
Oct. 28, 1929:	260.64
July 8, 1932:	41.22
Nov. 14, 1972:	1003.16
Jan. 11, 1973:	1051.70
Dec. 6, 1974:	577.60
Nov. 3, 1982:	1065.49

Feb. 24, 1983:   1121.81
April 26, 1983:   1209.46
May 20, 1985:   1304.88
Nov. 22, 1985:   1462.27
Jan. 16, 1986:   1541.63
April 17, 1986:   1855.03

Standard & Poor's Index

The Standard & Poor's Index of 500 stocks is more representative than the Dow Jones Industrial Average. It consists of 400 industrial corporations, 20 transportation stocks, 40 financial corporations, and 40 public utility companies.

Value Line Index

This is similar to the Standard & Poor's Index but has a broader base. The value line considers the price movement of approximately 1,685 common stocks.

New York Stock Exchange Index

This index computed by the New York Stock Exchange consists of all common stocks traded on a given day at the New York Stock Exchange. This is a composite index of four different groups of securities:

- Industrial
- Transportation
- Utilities
- Finance

The Index is published by the Exchange every half hour during the trading session. The Exchange computes the Index by multiplying the price of each stock by the number of shares listed on the Exchange. Unlike the DJIA and Standard & Poor's Index, this Index is expressed in dollars and cents. The New York Stock Exchange considers a base market value of a share at $50. This was the average price per share in 1965 when the Exchange initiated the Index. The Exchange adjusts this base value per share to reflect stock splits and stock dividends of corporations in the

Index just like the Dow Jones adjusts its divisor in the DJIA. The Exchange then computes the Index by the following formula:

$$\text{NYSE composite index} = \frac{\text{Current market value of all common stocks on NYSE}}{\text{Base market value}} \times 50$$

EXAMPLE

If the current market value of all NYSE common stocks is $500 billion and the base market value is $700 billion, the current NYSE composite index will be:

$$\frac{500}{700} \times 50 = 35.71$$

The Exchange determines the net money change in the average price by:

$$\text{Change in the average price per share} = \frac{\text{Average price per share listed on NYSE}}{\text{Composite Index}} \times \text{Change in Composite Index}$$

EXAMPLE

Let us assume that the Composite Index of 35.71 computed in the previous example goes up to 35.77. This is a rise of .06. If the average price per share listed on the NYSE is $45, the Exchange will compute the rise in the stock market by:

$$\frac{45.00}{35.71} \times .06 = .0756$$

This means the market is up 7.56 cents.

The NASDAQ–OTC Price Index

This index is computed by the NASD to measure the market activity of the over-the-counter securities traded on NASDAQ.

NASDAQ is a computerized system of OTC stocks initiated by the NASD in 1971. The NASDAQ Composite Index consists of all issues traded on NASDAQ. The Index is updated every five minutes and is computed by multiplying the total number of shares outstanding of all issues on NASDAQ by an average closing-bid price of that day. The total value for all stocks in the Index is then equated to a base figure.

The American Stock Exchange Price Change Index

This is, perhaps, the most simplistic of all averages. This index measures the activity on the American Stock Exchange. The Exchange considers all common stocks and warrants listed on Amex and computes the price change of the issues by the following formula:

$$\frac{\text{Total price change for all issues on Amex}}{\text{Number of issues on Amex}} = \frac{\text{Average change}}{\text{of price}}$$

EXAMPLE

Let us assume that there were 1,200 different stocks traded on a given day and each stock goes up ¾ point. The total price change will be:

$$\$800 \ (1,200 \times .75 \text{ cents})$$

The Amex will then divide $800 by the total number of issues traded:

$$\frac{800}{1,200} = .75$$

The index will show +.75. The Exchange computes this every hour during the trading session. New issues are added and deleted issues are removed.

Wilshire 5000 Equity Index

This is the broadest of all indexes. The Wilshire Index represents 5000 securities on the New York, American, and the Over-the-

Counter market. The index is value-weighted and it is prepared by Wilshire Associates of Santa Monica, California.

Barron's Group Stock Averages

These are arithmetic averages of stocks in 30 industrial groupings.

MARKET THEORIES USED FOR SECURITY ANALYSIS

There are many theories used by professionals and investors to chart their investment strategies. The theories most frequently used are the Dow Theory, the Odd-Lot Theory, the Advance–Decline Theory, the Short Interest Theory, the Confidence Theory, and there is even one called the Hemline Theory based on the length of ladies skirts. The theorists believe that the market will rise when the length of the ladies skirt goes up and the market will decline when the length of the skirts goes down. At times, this has produced extraordinary accuracy.

There is another interesting theory based on the moon. The analyst warns the investors to be wary of a full moon. He suggests that the market tends to lose points at the time of a full moon and gains during the new moon. In theory, therefore, one should sell the stock short the day before a full moon and cover the short three days later. This is the moon-market correlation!

The Dow Theory

The Dow Theory was developed by Charles Dow, the originator of the Dow Jones Averages. Based on the Dow Jones Averages, the theory makes predictions as to the future movement of securities. The Dow Theory suggests that the stock market acts in advance of business activity. The stock market will act now, for instance, if there will be a business downturn six months or a year in the future. One may predict the future market activity on this basis and make forecasts as to the movement of securities prices. The Dow Theory considers only the historical movement of stock prices and generally ignores sales, dividends, and earnings of the corporation.

It considers three movements in the market — The Primary Movement, the Secondary Movement, and Daily Fluctuations.

Primary Movement. This is a long-term (1 to 5 years) movement of the stock market. It will give the overall condition of the
market whether bullish or bearish.

Secondary Movement. This is a short-term (1 to 3 months)
movement of the market. There will be many Secondary Movements before the Primary Movement reverses itself. The Secondary Movement is used for short-term investment decisions.

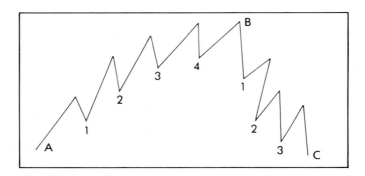

This graph shows the Primary and Secondary Movements. The
Primary Movement is the market's activity between A and B and
B and C. The Primary Movement shows a bullish market between
A and B and a bearish market between B and C. The Secondary
Movements are the short-term decline in the bullish market be-
tween A and B as indicated by 1, 2, 3, 4, and the short-term rise
in the bear market between B and C as indicated by 1, 2, 3.

Daily Fluctuations. The Dow Theory generally ignores the
daily movement of securities. It proposes that the daily fluctuations are the result of emotional attitudes of investors and do not
represent the Primary and Secondary movements of the market.

The Odd-Lot Theory

Shares between 1 and 99 are odd lots, and 100 shares and
multiples of 100 shares are round lots. The round-lot of certain
preferred stocks on the Exchange is 10 share units and odd-lot for
these securities are shares between 1 and 9. The odd-lot theory
measures the behavior of the small investor. The theory proposes

that the odd-lot customer generally buys stocks when the market nears its top and reduces the buying activity when the market declines. On the New York Stock Exchange, the odd-lot shares are usually purchased directly from a Specialist, not from another customer. There are more odd-lot buyers than sellers. This is due to the fact that the odd-lot investor accumulates shares by buying odd-lot but sells them as round-lot when the odd-lots become round-lots. The Odd-Lot Theory proposes that the professional round-lot investor should act in the reverse direction of the odd-lot customer. The odd-lot trading activities are reported daily and weekly. If the report indicates that there are more odd-lot sellers than buyers, this will give an indication to the round-lot customer to buy, and vice versa.

The Advance–Decline Theory

The Advance–Decline Theory is a simple calculation of the number of issues advanced and the number of issues declined in a given day. The analyst will make his predictions as to the future direction of the stock market based on the number of issues advanced and declined. He will record the percentage changes on a daily basis. The formula used to compute the index is a simple one:

$$\frac{\left(\begin{array}{c}\text{Number of}\\\text{issues advanced}\end{array}\right) - \left(\begin{array}{c}\text{Number of}\\\text{issues declined}\end{array}\right)}{\text{Total issues traded}} = \%\text{ change}$$

EXAMPLE

The day's activity is the following:

$$\begin{array}{rl}890 & \text{issues advanced} \\ 360 & \text{issues declined} \\ \underline{270} & \text{issues unchanged} \\ 1{,}520 & \text{total number of issues traded.}\end{array}$$

$$\frac{890 - 360}{1{,}520} = +3.4\%$$

If the number of issues declined exceed the number of issues advanced, the percentage will be a minus.

The Advance–Decline theorist proposes that if the number of issues advanced is higher than the number of issues declined in a period of days or weeks, the general movement of the market will be bullish and vice versa. The Advance–Decline Average is usually followed by the Dow Jones. If the Advance–Decline Average declines, the investor expects the Dow Jones to go up the following day.

The Short Interest Theory

The investor sells a stock short in anticipation that the market price will decline and he will buy the stock to cover his short. The difference in money will be his profit. He sells the stock short at $60 a share and buys it back at $50 a share. His profit will be $10 a share. In selling short, the investor borrows the security. This short trading activity is reported by the stock exchanges based on the short interest figures of the 15th of each month. The advocate of the Short Interest Theory studies this report and makes his investment decisions accordingly. The theory proposes that an *increase* in short sales indicates that the stock market will rise. This is due to the fact that the short seller will eventually buy the stock to limit his losses and this buying activity will push the market upward.

The Confidence Theory

The Confidence Theory is based on the behavior of the investing public about a particular issue or about the stock market in general. Are investors more anxious to buy stocks or to sell? This is generally determined by the yields on bonds. The Confidence Index measures the yields of high quality and low quality bonds. If the yields on high quality bonds advance, that means the investors are leaving the stock market and buying high grade bonds. Conversely, if the yields on low quality bonds decline, that means the investor is buying stocks.

ECONOMIC INDICATORS

Security analysis is based on economics, price expectations, and government activities.

Economists tell us that there are various business cycles—expansion, peak, recession, and trough. The leading economic indicators are: the stock market, machine tool orders, housing starts, Consumer Price Index, and Wholesale Price Index. The last two determine the rate of inflation on a monthly basis. The coincident indicators are: the Gross National Product, production per hour, and industrial production. The lagging indicator is the rate of unemployment, which is generally dependent on the other indicators.

Price changes affect the economy. There are several different types of price changes: *Demand–pull* inflation, *cost–push* inflation, and *stagflation*. Demand–pull inflation is the result of too much money, but very few goods. Cost–push inflation is the result of increase in cost of production, resources, and labor. Price freeze is a governmental control on prices. Stagflation (stagnation and inflation) means production is stagnant but the economy is inflationary.

Government activities particularly those of the Federal Reserve Board affect the economy and the stock market. These activities include the government's ability to control the budget deficit and the balance of payments. The Federal Reserve Board establishes monetary policies and controls credit.

The country is said to be in *Recession* when there is economic decline during six consecutive months. It is said to be in *Depression* when there is economic decline during six consecutive quarters.

METHODS OF INVESTING

Professionals have devised different methods to make investments in the securities market. Some methods use a combination of stocks and bonds on a formula basis and others use dollar-cost averaging to buy securities.

Constant-Ratio Plan

Through this plan, the investor maintains a constant balance between stocks and bonds. If he intends to maintain, let us say, a 60-40 percentage ratio, 60 percent bond and 40 percent stock, he will make his investments on that basis and will maintain this 60-40 ratio all the time. If the market of the stock portion of his investment rises, he will sell a portion of the stock and with the proceeds of the sale buy more bonds to maintain the 60-40 ratio.

Constant-Dollar Plan

Here the percentage relates to the amount of money invested and not the number of shares or bonds. The investor will invest, let us say, $50,000 in stocks and $50,000 in bonds, and he will maintain this ratio all the time. This is generally used in dollar-cost averaging for mutual funds and other investment companies. In dollar-cost averaging, the investor invests a sum of money and the mutual fund buys a number of shares.

$$\frac{\text{Amount of money invested}}{\text{Price per share}} = \text{Number of shares acquired.}$$

The investment company will send a monthly statement to the customer, reporting the accumulated shares in his account. The dollar-cost averaging is generally done for long-term investment purposes.

ANALYSIS OF RISKS

In conducting a security analysis one must consider various risks associated with securities.

- *Financial Risk*: The financial condition of the corporation.

- *Market Risk*: The public's attitude toward the security.

- *Interest Rate Risk*: Fluctuations of interest rates affect the security prices.

- *Inflation Risk*: Rise in inflation may shrink the value of the security.

- *Liquidity Risk*: Due to inadequate depth in the securities market, the investor may not be able to liquidate his security or will be forced to liquidate it at an unfavorable price.

- *Economic Risk*: This refers to the general economic condition in the country, risk of economic recessions or depressions.

Based on these various risks, the investor will develop his own perception on the relationship between risk and reward. An investment with high risk may bring large rewards, but may also bring disappointment and failure.

GLOSSARY

ABC Agreement An agreement between a brokerage firm and its employee that states the firm is prepared to finance the cost of purchasing a seat at the Exchange.

Above Par A security valued in excess of its face value.

Accounts Receivable Money due to a business organization.

ACRS Accelerated Cost Recovery System. This method will allow assets to be undervalued in the early years. Also known as 3-5-10 Rule.

Accretion A method of adjusting the price of a bond purchased at discount from the face value.

Accrued Interest Interest representing the period during which the seller of the bond owned the security.

Accumulation Unit In purchasing a variable annuity contract, the customer purchases accumulation units similar to mutual fund shares.

Actuarial Tables Tables giving the life expectancy of individuals.

Actuary A mathematician that calculates risk based on mortality tables for insurance companies.

Ad Valorem A method of assessing taxes on properties.

Adjusted Debit Balance The amount of money representing the net balance that the customer borrows and that the customer owes the broker; the difference between the total debits and the total credits.

Adjusted Strike Price The strike price of an option is changed to reflect dividends or the stock split of the underlying security.

Advance–Decline Theory A market theory that calculates the number of issues advanced and declined in a given day.

After Market The secondary market. The market following immediately after the initial offering of a security to the public.

Aggregate Exercise Price This is the strike price of an option multiplied by the number of shares of the underlying security. 50 × 200 shares = 10,000.

AIR Assumed Interest Rate.

Air Pocket Stock A security whose price declines suddenly and dramatically.

All or Nothing A type of underwriting. The underwriter is required to sell all the shares to the public or none at all.

Allied Member An employee of a brokerage firm, either a general partner or a voting stockholder, who is not a member of the stock exchange, therefore not allowed to trade on the exchange floor.

Allottee A person or a brokerage house to whom securities are allotted in an underwriting.

Allotment Amount of shares or bonds assigned to each member of the syndicate team in an underwriting of a security.

American Bankers Association Trade organization for banks in the United States.

American Depositary Receipts — ADR A security issued by a U.S. bank representing shares of a foreign corporation.

American Stock Exchange Price Change Index An index computed by the American Stock Exchange consisting of all common stocks and warrants listed on Amex.

Amortization Gradual elimination of debt.

Annual Depreciation A method of annualizing the depreciation of a property. If the cost of the property is $10,000 and its usable life is 5 years, by using the Annual Depreciation method, the corporation will spread out the cost of $10,000 for a period of 5 years.

Annuitize To start the pay-out period in an annuity program.

Annuity A contract under which funds are paid at regular intervals.

Annuity Contracts A contractual obligation to pay a sum of money at regular intervals or periodically to subscribers.

Annuity Unit Annuity unit represents the customer's proportionate ownership in a variable annuity contract after the insurance company commences its distribution to the subscriber.

Appreciation Increase in value of the property or security.

Arbitrage The mechanics of buying securities in one market and selling them in a different market.

Arbitrage House A securities firm which specializes in arbitrage transactions.

Asked Price The price that the seller is offering to sell.

Assented Securities Securities of a corporation in the process of reorganization.

Assessed Valuation   The value of a property for the purposes of assessing taxes.

Asset Coverage   An amount in the corporation's net assets that covers the securities issued by the corporation.

Assets   The properties or the resources of a company. Appears on the left side of the Balance Sheet.

Asset-Liability Management   Managing the amount of debt against assets.

At Risk   Exposure of risk or loss in a property or a security.

Auction   A type of market where there is one seller but many buyers.

Authorized Shares   Shares of a corporation approved by the Secretary of State after a certificate of incorporation has been filed.

Average Unit Cost   Total cost of purchasing products divided by the number of units purchased during a given period.

Away from the Market   A phrase used when the limit price is too far away from the current market price of the security.

Back Office   The operations department of a securities firm.

Backdating   A phrase used for mutual fund transactions. The customer backdates his agreement to purchase the mutual fund to take advantage of reduced sales charge particularly for large transactions.

Backspread   This is a neutral spread consisting of two option series with the same expiration month. The holder has more long options than short options.

Backwardation   A method of pricing commodities. Near-term commodities will have higher value than those delivered in the future.

Bad Delivery   A security not acceptable to consummate a securities transaction.

Balance Sheet   A summary of all the assets, the liabilities, and the net worth of an organization.

Balanced Company   An investment company that invests its cash in different types of securities, common stocks, bonds, preferred stocks, and so on.

Banking Act of 1933   The Glass-Steagall Act of 1933.

Barometer Stock   Stock which indicates the general trend of the marketplace.

Basis   Purchase price of an asset.

BD Form   Broker–Dealer form filed with the SEC by broker–dealers. The form indicates the firm's financial condition and the names of the officers.

Bear Option Spread   A spread combination using calls and puts. It becomes profitable when the underlying security declines in value.

Bear Raid   The activity in the stock market where large blocks of securities are sold short for purposes of manipulating the price of the security.

Bellwhether   A blue chip security such as IBM that indicates the general condition of the stock market.

Best Efforts   A type of underwriting. The underwriter acts as an agent between the issuer and investors in selling securities to the public.

Bid Price   The price that the buyer is bidding to buy the security.

Big Eight   Eight large accounting firms in the United States.

Blanket Fidelity Bond   Insurance coverage for brokerage houses to protect the firm against losses due to employee dishonesty, fraud, lost certificates, and forgery.

Block   A security in excess of 10,000 shares for stocks and $200,000 for bonds.

Block Positioner   A broker–dealer engaged in block transactions.

Blowout   A condition where the securities in a public offering are sold immediately. A Hot Issue.

Blue Chip Company   A company with a reputation of earnings, stability, and marketability.

Blue List   A listing reporting bids and offers of municipal bonds.

Blue Sky   Securities laws of a state.

Board of Arbitration   A group of people selected by a regulatory agency to resolve disputes in securities transactions.

Board Broker   A member of an option exchange using the market maker concept. The board broker keeps the books of public orders.

Boiler Room   An office where salespeople use pressure tactics to sell securities to customers.

Boilerplate   A standard phrase used in legal documents.

Bond and Preferred Stock Company   An investment company that invests its assets in bonds and preferred stocks.

Bond Ratio   A ratio determined by dividing the face value of the bond by the total capitalization of the company.

Book-Entry Certificates   Securities with no physical certificates representing ownership.

Book Value of Common Shares   Total assets minus liabilities and preferred stock, and divided by the number of outstanding shares.

Bottom Dropped Out   Sharp decline in securities prices.

Bottom Fisher   A person who is generally interested to purchase securities of near-bankrupt corporations.

Box   Physical location of certificates in a securities firm.

Box Spread   This is a combination of a call and a put spread. It may be vertical, horizontal, diagonal, or butterfly. The investor will establish a spread using calls and a spread using puts. The result may be a debit or a credit. Also known as *jelly rolls*.

Bracket Creep   Approaching a higher tax bracket.

Break   Sharp decline in securities prices.

Breakeven Point   The point at which the sales proceeds will be equal to the cost of purchasing the security.

Breaking the Syndicate   Breaking the syndicate team which was organized to underwrite a security.

Breakout   The rise or fall of a security price above or below a certain level.

Breakpoint   The management company will offer a reduced sales charge when the amount of money invested by the customer reaches a particular level — or "breakpoint."

Break-Up Point   Liquidating value.

Bridge Loan   A short term loan.

Bring Out   To make a public distribution of a security.

Broad Market   A term that describes that a large number of listed securities are being traded.

Broad Tape   The stock market tape projected on a wide screen in a brokerage office.

Broker–Dealer Credit Account   A special account used by the brokerage house to effect or finance transactions of any of its owners, partners, or voting stockholders.

Broker Loan Rate   A special interest rate charged by banks to broker–dealers. It is usually lower than the prime rate that the bank charges to its preferential customers.

Broker's Blanket Bond   An insurance policy that covers losses resulting from fraudulent practices in brokerage houses.

Brokers Originated Window Ticket   A ticket prepared by brokerage personnel in submitting items to transfer agents.

Bucket Shop   A brokerage house that does not execute customer orders immediately as instructed. It executes only when it is advantageous for the broker to do so.

Bucketeer   A broker who operates a bucket shop.

Bulge   A term that describes a small but sudden rise in securities prices.

Bulk Segregation   A procedure in the cashiers department to segregate customers' fully paid for and margin excess securities in bulk form. A certificate with a large denomination will be segregated for several customers.

Bull Spread   A spread using calls or puts. It becomes profitable when the underlying security rises.

Bunching   Combining the odd lot orders and executing them as round lots to save the odd lot differential.

Business Cycle   Different periods in economic activity.

Butterfly Spread or Sandwich Spread   A spread combination using calls or puts. The spread has 3 different strike prices. Example: The customer writes 2 calls on-the-money and buys 1 call in-the-money and 1 call out-of-the-money.

Buyers' Market   A condition in the marketplace that is advantageous for the investor to buy.

Buy-In   A trading procedure. A firm has the right to buy-in the security if the selling broker has not delivered the security within a prescribed period of time.

Buyer's Option   Type of settlement of securities transaction. The delivery of the security is made on the day the option expires on the buy side.

Buying Climax   The level at which the price of a security has risen.

Buying Power   The amount of securities that the customer may purchase using the credit balance or the excess equity in the account. The formula used to determine the buying power:

$$\text{Buying power} = \frac{\text{Excess equity}}{\text{Margin requirement}}$$

Buyout   Purchasing the controlling interest of a corporation.

Cabinet Crowd   The brokers on the floor of the New York Stock Exchange engaged in trading inactive bonds.

Cabinet Security   An inactive security in the stock market.

Cage   The cashiers department of a brokerage house.

Calendar Spread   Also called horizontal spread or time spread. A combination of a long and short of the same class of option with the same strike price, but different expiration months.

Call   An option giving the holder the privilege to buy the underlying security at a specific price within a specified period of time.

Call Money   Loans made by bank to broker–dealers.

Callable Security A security that may be called by the issuer at any time before maturity.

Called Away A security redeemed before maturity or an option exercised against the writer.

Capital The net worth of the business, the owner's equity.

Capital Excess See Capital Surplus.

Capital Gain Gain on capital asset.

Capital Gains Distribution Distribution of profits generated from the sale of securities in a mutual fund portfolio.

Capital Gains Tax Tax on property held longer than the required holding period.

Capital Goods Machinery, equipment, and buildings belonging to a corporation.

Capital Loss Loss on capital asset.

Capital Market The stock, bond, and the money market.

Capital Stock Generally the same as common stock. Usually used when the corporation does not have a preferred stock issued.

Capital Surplus An amount of money that the company receives from the sale of the common stock to the public in excess of the par value of the stock. Also known as Paid-In Capital or Capital Excess.

Capital Turnover A ratio determined by dividing the annual sales by stockholders' equity.

Capitalization Leverage The ratio of total debt vs. tangible net worth.

Carrying Broker Broker–dealer who carries customer accounts.

Cash Account A brokerage account. The customer must make full payment to the broker when purchasing securities in a cash account.

Cash Asset Ratio The ratio between the cash asset and current liability. It is determined by dividing cash assets with current liabilities.

Cash Commodity A transaction in a commodity consummated upon the delivery of the actual commodity.

Cash Cow A type of organization that continuously generates cash.

Cash Market A transaction in a commodity that is consummated upon the delivery of the commodity.

Cash Ratio A ratio of cash to current liabilities of a corporation.

Cash Surrender Value The amount of money that the insurance company will give to the customer upon the surrender of the insurance policy.

Cash Trade A securities transaction in a cash trade settles on the day of the trade.

Cashier's Department   The department in a brokerage house responsible for securities processing, transfer, receive, deliver, and control of cash.

Cats and Dogs   Speculative securities.

CBOE   Chicago Board Options Exchange. Organized in 1973, it is the first organized options exchange in the U.S.

Cede & Co.   A nominee name for DTC.

Certificate of Incorporation   When incorporating a business, a certificate must be filed with that state's Secretary of State.

Chartist   A person who charts the prices of securities.

Cheap Money   Loan with low interest rates.

Churning   Excessive trading activities to generate commissions.

Circle   A method of determining potential investors interested to purchase a security before the effective date of the Registration Statement in a public offering.

Clifford Trust   A short-term revocable trust with a minimum life of 10 years and 1 day.

Close Money   Loan with high interest rates.

Closed-End Management Company   A company with fixed capitalization. It sells a fixed amount of shares to the public.

Closely Held Corporation   A company with a few voting stockholders.

Closing Purchase Transaction   An option trade in which the customer reduces or eliminates an existing short position by buying the identical option series back.

Closing Sale Transaction   An option trade where the customer reduces or eliminates a long position by selling the identical option.

COD or DVP   Cash on delivery or deliver vs. payment. The customer will instruct the broker to deliver the security to a designated bank against payment.

Coincident Indicators   Economic indicators that analyze the condition of the economy, such as the Gross National Product and industrial production.

Cold Comfort Letter   An auditor's letter certifying that information in the prospectus or the Registration Statement is correct.

Collateral   Securities or other properties pledged by a borrower to secure a loan.

Comingling   Combining customer securities with those owned by broker–dealers.

Commodity Dividends   Dividends paid in commodities.

Commodity Futures Trading Commission (CFTC) This is the federal agency created in 1974 responsible for regulating the futures trading at commodity exchanges.

Commodity Option An option for a specific commodity futures contract to purchase or sell within a specified period of time.

Common Stock A type of capital stock. A corporation is required to issue a common stock.

Common Stock Ratio A ratio determined by dividing common stock, capital surplus, and retained earnings by the total capitalization of a company.

Comparison A ticket issued by a broker–dealer and presented to the contra-broker for comparison.

Compensating Balance An amount of money required by a bank to establish a line of credit for a customer.

Competitive Underwriting A type of underwriting. Dealers are required to send their bids to the issuer. The issuer will sell the security to the dealer who has submitted the most favorable bid.

Compound Interest Interest compounded during a period of time.

Concession The amount of compensation given to a selling group member in an underwriting.

Conduit or Pipeline Theory Internal Revenue Code. A regulated investment company is not subject to pay income tax if 90 percent of its income is distributed to shareholders.

Confidence Theory A market theory that measures the behavior of the investing public about a particular issue or the stock market in general.

Confirmation A ticket issued by the broker–dealer confirming the trade of a customer.

Conglomerate A corporation engaged in diverse industries.

Consent of Service Process Form A form to be filed by a corporation to register securities within a state under the Blue Sky requirements.

Consolidated Tape A stock market tape reporting the transactions of New York, American and regional stock exchanges.

Consols British government bonds.

Constant Dollar Plan A method of investment. The percentage of investment relates to the amount of money invested.

Constant Ratio Plan A method of investment. The investor maintains a constant balance between stocks and bonds.

Constructive Receipt Stock dividend issued by a corporation but the stockholder elects to receive cash instead.

Consumer Price Index   An economic indicator that measures the prices of goods and services that consumers buy or use.

Continuous Net Settlement (CNS)   A clearing procedure. The securities transactions are cleared on a continuous basis. Security positions are updated continuously by the clearing corporation.

Contrarian   A person who acts contrary to what other investors are doing in the stock market.

Control Person   A major stockholder or a decision making person of a corporation. Also known as Affiliated Person.

Control Stock   A security owned by control persons.

Controlled Commodity   A commodity regulated by the Commodity Exchange Act.

Contractual Payment Plan   Under this plan, the customer agrees to make deposits in fixed amounts at specified intervals when buying shares in mutual funds.

Conventional Option   An option traded in the over-the-counter market not on an options exchange.

Conversion Agent   The agent responsible for converting a security from one type to another type.

Conversion Parity   The level at which the convertible security is converted into a number of shares of common.

Conversion Premium   The level by which the price of a convertible security exceeds the price of the security to which it can be converted.

Conversion Price   The price at which a share of common stock will be valued if the preferred stock or bond is converted into common stock.

Convertible Preferred   A type of preferred stock. The stockholder has the privilege to convert the security into common shares.

Cooling-Off Period   The period between the filing and the effective date of the Registration Statement.

Cornering the Market   The activity of purchasing large volume of securities for the purposes of controlling the price in the marketplace.

Corporate Bond Fund   An investment company that invests its assets in corporate bonds.

Correspondent Broker–Dealer   A broker–dealer acting as agent for another broker–dealer located in another city.

Cost Basis   For tax purposes, basis is the cost or the book value of asset at the time of acquisition.

Cost–Push Inflation   Inflation due to the cost of producing the product.

Covered Option A short position in which the writer has deposited the underlying security on a call or the aggregate exercise price on a put option.

Credit Agreement An agreement disclosing the terms of the credit when the broker lends money to a margin customer. This is in compliance with SEC Rule 10b-16.

Credit Department The margin department; the department in a brokerage firm that oversees the customer's cash and margin activities.

Credit Union A non-profit organization formed by employees of a company or a labor union to provide financial services.

Crowd Brokers around a trading post on the floor of the stock exchange.

Crown Trust A living trust established for the benefit of a minor. The minor pays the principal on demand.

Crummey Trust A living trust established for the benefit of a minor. The minor has the right to withdraw money from the account.

Cum-Rights With rights. The purchaser of the security will be entitled to receive subscription rights.

Cumulative Preferred A type of preferred stock. The stockholder will never lose the right to receive dividends.

Cumulative Voting A procedure for voting. The stockholder has one vote for each share he owns, but unlike the statutory method he will multiply the votes by the number of proposals placed on the agenda at a corporate meeting.

Curb The American Stock Exchange.

Curb Broker A broker who transacts business on the American Stock Exchange.

Current Assets Assets that can be converted into cash within a one-year period such as marketable securities, accounts receivable, etc.

Current Liabilities Short-term obligations of the firm to be paid within a period of one year.

Current Ratio Ratio of current assets to current liabilities, computed by dividing the amount of assets by current liabilities.

Current Yield on Common Stock This is determined by dividing the stock's annual dividends by its current market price.

CUSIP A number that identifies a security.

Custodian Bank A commercial bank appointed by the investment company to act as custodian and bookkeeper for monies and securities of the investment company.

Customer Agreement *Also* hypothecation or margin agreement. The agreement that sets forth the conditions under which the broker finances the customer's margin transactions.

Customer's Man The registered representative, account executive.

Cyclical Stock A security whose price fluctuations are based on economic upturns or downturns.

Daisy Chain A manipulative device. A series of transactions in a security to attract investors to purchase the security.

Day Loan Lending money to a broker–dealer with the understanding that it wiH be repaid before the end of the day.

Day Trade The purchase and sale of the same security in a margin account on the same day, or selling a security short and purchasing the same security on the same day.

Daylight Trading Bona fide arbitrage transaction.

Debenture Stock A security that promises to make fixed payments at different intervals.

Debt Equity Ratio Ratio of total debt to total equity.

Debt Service Amount of money required to make payments of interest and principal during a given period.

Default Risk The risk that payment of interest or principal of a bond will not be paid.

Defensive Stock A stock that continues to earn income during periods of economic downturn.

Deferred Charges Charges incurred in the organization of a new division or the manufacturing of a new product.

Deferred Compensation An agreement between the employee and the firm. The employee agrees to defer receipt of a portion of his salary until retirement.

Deficiency Letter Notice from the SEC to the issuer advising the issuer that the Registration Statement needs to be revised or amended.

Defined Benefit Plan In this pension plan, the firm will establish certain benefits and make the contribution to meet the desired benefits.

Defined Contribution Plan In this pension plan, the firm makes a set contribution every year.

Deflation The reverse of inflation. The period in which prices of goods and services decline.

Delayed Delivery The delivery of a security passed the settlement date.

Delisting Removal of a security from exchange listing.

Demand Deposit An amount of money that may be withdrawn without prior notice to the bank holding it.

Demand Loan Loan that can be called by the lender at any time.

Demand–Pull Inflation Inflation due to the buying activity of consumers.

Demonetization The withdrawal of a specific currency from circulation.

Depreciation A decrease in value of the property as the property gets older. Tax deductible amount representing the cost of fixed assets over their useful life.

Deregulation Removal of government regulation to stimulate the efficiency in the marketplace.

Designated Order Turnaround (DOT) A procedure to transmit orders directly to the trading post for execution.

Devaluation Decline in the value of a country's currency against the currencies of other countries.

Diagonal Spread A combination of a long and a short option with different strike prices and different expiration dates.

Dilution The condition where convertible securities are converted into common stock and warrants and options are exercised.

Dip A drop in the stock price.

Direct Participation Program Limited partnership in oil and gas and real estate where the investor may have direct participation in the profit and tax benefits of the program.

Discount Broker A broker that charges reduced commission rates to customers.

Discretionary Account A securities account. The customer will authorize the broker to transact trades in his account at the broker's discretion.

Disinflation The rate by which the rise of prices of goods and services is reduced.

Disintermediation Removal of funds from bank accounts to higher yielding securities in the marketplace.

Disposable Income Income at the disposal of the consumer after taxes have been paid.

Distribution Stock Stock sold in a primary or a secondary distribution.

Distributing Syndicate A group of brokers formed to distribute a large block of securities.

Diversified Management Company A diversified management company invests 75 percent of its assets in cash, government securities, other securities, and other investment companies, and 25 percent is invested at the discretion of the management.

Divestiture   Disposition of assets or securities.

Dividend Payout Ratio   Percentage of earnings paid to shareholders as dividends.

Dividend Reinvestment Plan   Reinvestment of cash dividend to purchase additional shares in the company.

Dollar Cost Averaging   A program through which a specific sum of money is invested in a number of shares of mutual funds on a regularly specified basis.

Don't Fight the Tape   Don't buy when the stocks are falling and don't sell short when the stocks are rising.

"Don't Know" Trade   A notice issued by the financial institution advising the contra broker–dealer that it does not know the trade.

Double Declining Balance Depreciation   A method of determining the depreciation of a property. This method does not consider the salvage value of the property in determining the amount of annual depreciation.

Double Option   Generally used in commodity options trading. Exercise of the call makes the put expire, and the exercise of the put makes the call expire.

Dow Theory   A market theory developed by Charles Dow. The theory makes predictions as to the future movement of securities. The theory considers three movements: primary, secondary, and daily fluctuations.

Dow Jones Averages   A popular stock market indicator based on the writings of Charles Dow, the editor of *The Wall Street Journal* in 1884.

Downstream   Flow of funds from a corporate parent to its subsidiary.

Downtick   Transaction of a security at a price below the preceding transaction.

Downturn   Shift in the direction of the stock market from bullish to bearish.

DSO   Number of days sales are outstanding.

DTC   The Depository Trust Company that offers depository services.

Dual Listing   Listing of a security in more than one stock exchange.

Dual Purpose Company   An investment company that invests its assets, based on two objectives — income and capital. Income is based on the income that the management company receives in dividends and interest on the securities in the portfolio. Capital represents the capital gain based on the appreciation of the securities in the portfolio.

Due Bill Check A promissory note. The deliverer promises to pay dividends and interests to the receiver after the payable date.

Due Diligence Meeting Meeting among the underwriters of a security held prior to the effective date. Underwriters discuss all pertinent details about the offering.

Dutch Auction A system in which the price of a security is gradually lowered until it approaches an acceptable bid.

Earnings Per Common Share The net income minus dividends on preferred stock divided by the number of outstanding shares.

Eastern Account An underwriting account. Underwriters are required to sell their allocated shares and the shares of co-underwriters.

EBIT Earnings before interest and taxes.

Econometrics Mathematical interpretation to describe relationships between economic factors.

Edge The difference between the market price and the theoretical value of the option or the futures contract.

Effective Date The date when the securities are allowed to be sold to the public.

Employee Thrift Plan An employee plan. The employee will make contribution to the plan through a payroll deduction matched by the employer.

Equity Net worth, assets minus liabilities.

Equity Financing Raising money through sale of equity securities.

Equity REIT A type of real estate investment trust that invests its assets in office buildings, shopping centers, and warehouses.

ERISA Employee Retirement Income Security Act.

ERTA Economic Recovery Tax Act of 1981.

Escheat The return of abandoned properties or securities to the state.

Escrow Monies or securities held by a bank or a financial institution under a contractual arrangement.

Escrow Receipts A receipt issued by an OCC-approved bank against a deposit of underlying security to cover a short option position.

Estate An individual's total worth exclusive of any liabilities.

European Option This option is exercised only on the expiration date, not before.

Ex-All Securities transaction without dividends, rights, or warrants.

Exact Interest Interest calculated on the basis of 365 days a year.

Exchange Privilege The stockholder's privilege to switch from one type of mutual fund into another.

Ex-Dividend Date   The date established by the stock exchange or the NASD. Trades on ex-dividend date will pay no dividend to the purchaser.

Exempt Securities   Exempt from registration requirement of the Securities Act of 1933; U.S. government securities, municipal securities, securities issued by banks, short-term money market instruments, securities issued by savings and loan associations and farmers' cooperative groups, receivers' certificates, securities issued by religious and nonprofit organizations, and insurance policies.

Exempt Transactions   Transactions that are exempt from registration requirements of the Securities Act of 1933.

Exercise Price   The specified price per share for which the underlying security may be purchased or sold by the option holder — also called strike price, or predetermined price.

Ex-Pit Trade   A transaction executed off the floor of the commodity exchange.

Ex-Rights   Without rights. The purchaser of the security will not be entitled to receive subscription rights.

Extraordinary Income/Expense   Unrelated income and expense. These items are not related to producing operating revenue. Examples: interest income, interest cost, sale of assets.

Eyeball Analysis   A fast evaluation of key items on the Balance Sheet of a company.

Face Amount Certificate Company   The face amount certificate company will issue bond certificate based on the funds invested by the customer. The face amount of the certificate will be in excess of funds received from the customer. The difference in money will be compounded as interest.

Factoring   A type of financing. The corporation sells its accounts receivable to a factoring company.

Fail to Deliver   A securities house account. The securities firm is failing to deliver securities.

Fail to Receive   A securities house account. The securities firm is failing to receive securities.

FAST   A system of DTC that enables participants to withdraw securities registered in a name specified by the participant.

Federal Call   A Regulation T call.

FIFO (First-In-First-Out)   An inventory accounting method based on the assumption that goods were sold in the order by which they were acquired. Goods unsold at the close of an accounting period were those most recently purchased.

Financial Future   A futures contract on a financial instrument.

Financial Statement   A report listing the assets, liabilities, operating expenses, anticipated revenues, and net earnings of a business organization.

FINS   A number that identifies a financial institution.

Firm Commitment Underwriting   A type of underwriting securities. The underwriter is committed to sell the securities purchased from the issuer.

Firm Quote   As opposed to nominal or subject quote. The firm bid or asked price of a market maker.

First Preferred Stock   A preferred stock that has priority over any other preferred security of the same corporation. Also known as Prior Preferred.

Fiscal Year   A period covering 12 consecutive months.

Fitch Sheets   Sheets published by Fitch Investor Services reporting prices of securities listed on stock exchanges.

Fixed Annuity Contract   Under this contract the life insurance company pays a fixed amount of money to the subscribers.

Fixed Assets   Tangible assets with a useful life of one year or longer, such as real estate and equipment.

Fixed Expenses   Uncontrollable expenses of a firm, such as depreciation of equipment, rent, insurance premiums, taxes, licenses, cost of interest on loan, etc.

Fixed Liabilities   The company's long-term obligations, such as bonds maturing in five years or more, mortgages, long-term bank loans, etc.

Fixed Trust   A type of unit investment trust. The portfolio is composed of tax-exempt government securities. The size of the fund will diminish as the securities in the portfolio approach their maturity date. At maturity, the board of trustees will liquidate the fund and distribute the assets to the shareholders.

Flash   Indication on the ticker tape advising that the volume is heavy and the tape is behind.

Flat Market   Low activity in the stock market where securities prices are moved horizontally.

Fleece   A naive investor who buys a security blindly.

Float   Number of corporate shares traded in the marketplace.

Floatation Cost   The cost of issuing a new security.

Floor Brokers   Members on the floor of NYSE representing their firms.

Floor Official   An employee of the stock exchange assigned to resolve disputes on the floor of the exchange.

FOCUS   A report issued monthly and quarterly by broker–dealers and submitted to the self-regulatory organizations and the SEC reporting the financial and the operational condition of the brokerage house. It stands for Financial and Operational Combined Uniform Single Report.

Form 8-K   A form required by the SEC from a publicly held corporation. The corporation must report any material change in its financial condition or corporate charter.

Form 10-K   An annual report required by the SEC from a publicly held corporation. The corporation is required to report total sales, revenues, operating income and other pertinent details to the Commission.

Form 10-Q   A quarterly form required by the SEC from a publicly held corporation.

Fortune 500   500 largest industrial corporations in the United States ranked by sales, selected annually by Fortune magazine.

45-Day Letter   This is known as the "free look." The customer has the right to withdraw from the mutual fund plan within 45 days after the custodian bank has sent him the notice of particulars.

401 (K) Plan   An Internal Revenue Code that allows an employee to contribute to a plan through a salary reduction method.

Fourth Market   The market for trading stock exchange listed securities among institutional accounts without any broker.

Free Box   Location of securities in a securities firm.

Freed Up   The members of the syndicate are free to sell the security at any price in distributing the security to the public.

Free Riding   A practice in underwriting securities. The underwriter withholds a number of shares of a new issue and sells them at a higher price later on. This practice is prohibited by the SEC.

Free Riding and Withholding Rule   NASD rule. Under this rule broker–dealers are not allowed to sell "hot" issues to certain affiliated or non-affiliated investors.

Front-End Mutual Fund   A type of mutual fund where most of the first year's deposits will be applied to sales charge.

Front Running   Trading securities with advance knowledge that a buy or sell recommendation will be made by an analyst.

Frozen Account   A customer account is said to be frozen for a period of 90 calendar days if the customer sells the security that he has purchased before having paid for it in full.

Full Service Broker   A broker providing a variety of financial services to his customers.

Full Trading Authorization   A document empowering a third party to withdraw funds and/or securities from the account of another person.

Fundamental Analysis   A method of analyzing and forecasting the price movement of a security. The analyst considers the financial condition of the corporation, its earnings, dividends, sales, marketing, and so on.

Fungible   Interchangeable.

GAAP   Generally Accepted Accounting Principles used in preparing financial statements.

Gather in the Stops   Trading activity to push the price of a security down to the level of stop orders.

General and Administrative Expenses (GAE)   The administrative expenses of the firm, such as compensation to non-producing employees, telephone, legal, insurance, accounting, printing, postage and office supplies. These do not include the cost of warehousing the products.

Gilt-Edged Security   A corporation that has acquired the reputation of always paying dividends on stocks and interest on bonds in a dependable manner.

Give-Up   A procedure in securities transactions on the floor of the stock exchange. Example: Floor broker A buys a security for broker B, *gives up* the name of Broker B to Broker C, who has sold the security. Broker A charges commission to Broker B.

Glamour Stock   Usually a Blue Chip stock. The security of a corporation with dependable reputation for growth and earnings.

Glass-Steagall Act   A federal legislation enacted in 1933 prohibiting banks to engage in the securities business and underwriting corporate issues.

GNP   The Gross National Product. The value of goods and services produced in the United States over a one year period.

Go-Go Fund   A term used for investment companies that invest aggressively in speculative issues.

Going Ahead   A manipulative device. The broker executes the order first for his own account and then executes the customer's order.

Going-Concern Value   A term used to describe the intangible asset (goodwill) of a corporation.

Going Long   Purchasing a security.

Going Private   Converting a publicly held corporation into a private enterprise.

Going Public   A term used when a private company distributes its shares to the public.

Going Short   Selling a security without owning it.

Gold Mutual Fund   An investment company that invests in gold stocks.

Gold Standard   A system under which currency is converted into gold.

Goldbug   An investor who considers gold as a good investment.

Golden Handcuffs   A term that describes the contractual agreement of a broker with the brokerage house.

Golden Parachute   A term that describes the agreement of a corporation to make a lucrative compensation to an executive. This is usually done in the event the executive loses his job due to an acquisition or a takeover.

Good Faith Margin   The amount of margin a broker would require for a specified security position.

Good-Till Cancelled Order (GTC)   A limit order that remains in effect until cancelled by the customer or executed by the broker.

Good-This-Month Order   A limit order with a life of only one month. If not executed, the order will be cancelled.

Government Securities   Securities issued by agencies of the U.S. government.

Graduated Security   A security that has graduated from a regional stock exchange or the over-the-counter market to a national stock exchange.

Graveyard Market   A depressed bear market.

Green Shoe   A term that describes the procedure whereby a corporation will issue more shares to meet the demand of the investing public when the security in an underwriting has been oversold.

Greenmail   A term that describes payment by a corporation to an individual who is attempting to acquire the company. The person receiving the payment agrees not to pursue his bid to take over the company.

Gross Margin   Net sales minus cost of goods.

Gross Profit   Gross margin. Net sales minus the cost of goods sold.

Gross Sales   Total sales.

Gross Spread   The difference in money between the underwriter's cost of purchasing the security from the issuer and the public offering price.

Group Sales   Block orders sold to institutional customers.

Growth Company   A company that is growing faster than other companies in the same industry.

Gun Jumping   Selling a security before the Registration Statement has been filed with the Securities and Exchange Commission.

Haircut   The amount of deduction that a broker is required to take from the value of securities used to compute broker–dealer's net capital.

Half-Stock   An old term referring to a security with a par value of $50 a share instead of $100.

Hard Dollars   Payment made for services.

Hammering the Market   Speculators constantly selling a stock short.

Heavy Market   A bear market with more sell orders than buy orders.

Hedge   A strategy to eliminate or reduce risks by making offsetting transactions.

Hedge Clause   A disclaimer notice on a document or on a securities recommendation list advising the reader that the writer of the document will not guarantee the accuracy of information obtained to prepare the document.

Hedge Fund   Investment companies that use hedging strategies.

Hedged Tender   Selling a security short in a tender offer.

Hemline Theory   A security analysis based on the hemline of women's skirts. Analyst thinks that when the hemline goes up, so will the stock market and vice-versa.

High Flyer   Highly speculative security.

High-Tech Stock   High technology security.

Historical Yield   Yield covering a certain period of time.

Hit the Bid   A term that describes the trading practice when the broker accepts the highest price offered for a security.

Holder of Record   The stockholder or the bondholder of a security.

Holding Company   A corporation that owns other companies.

Holding Period   The length of time the investor owns the security.

Holding the Market   Buying securities to stabilize the price of the security.

Horizontal Spread   See Calendar Spread.

Hot Issue   A security that will trade at a premium immediately after the effective date of the underwriting.

Hot Stock   Stolen security.

House Account   An account used to maintain trading or security positions of a brokerage firm.

House Call   Maintenance margin call.

Hybrid Annuity   These are part-guaranteed dollar contracts and variable contracts.

Hypothecation   Pledging of securities as collateral for a loan.

Illiquid   An account or a security is illiquid if it cannot be converted into cash readily.

In-and-Out Trader   A trader who constantly buys and sells the same security.

In-the-Money   A call option is in-the-money when the strike price is below the current market price of the underlying security. A put option is in-the-money when the strike price is above the current market price of the underlying security.

In the Tank   A term advising that prices of securities are declining.

Inactive Post   The trading post for preferred securities on the floor of the New York Stock Exchange.

Income Company   An investment company that invests its assets in dividend and interest paying securities.

Income Shares   One of the types of shares of a dual purpose mutual fund.

Income Statement   The statement of the firm's earnings over a period of time — a month, a quarter, or the fiscal year.

Income Stocks   Stocks with a high pay-out ratio.

Income Trust   A living trust in which income generated from the trust is payable to the minor.

Indenture   An agreement, trust, or contract.

Independent Broker   A member of the stock exchange who executes orders for other members.

Index Fund   A mutual fund that compares its performance with stock market indexes.

Inflation   Rise in the value of goods and services.

Ingot of Gold   A bar of gold.

Inside Market   Quotes of securities between market makers.

Insider   A person who has inside information about a corporation or a security.

Instinet   A computerized trading facility allowing institutional accounts to trade stock exchange listed securities.

Institutional Delivery System   A system of DTC that provides facility for brokers and institutions to complete their securities transactions.

Insured Account A customer account insured by Federal Deposit Insurance Corporation, Federal Savings and Loan Insurance Corporation or by Securities Investors Protection Corporation.

Intangible Assets The intangible assets of a company are the patents, good will, and franchises.

Interest Amount of money paid for the use of funds.

Interest Coverage This determines the company's ability to pay interest to the bondholders of the outstanding bonds.

Intermediation Making investments through a financial institution.

International Mutual Fund An investment company that invests in foreign securities.

Interpositioning A type of trade where the broker purchases the security from a non-market maker who, in turn, purchases the security from the market maker.

Intrinsic Value Cash value of the option. It is the amount that is in-the-money.

Inventory Turnover The ratio of net sales vs. inventory. It is determined by dividing the net sales by the year-end inventory.

Inventory Value Total inventory multiplied by average unit cost.

Investment Advisers Act Federal legislation enacted in 1940 regulating the activities of investment advisers.

Investment Adviser A company or a person that advises the type of security to be purchased or sold by the investment company.

Investment Company A company organized to invest customer funds in securities or properties. It will manage the portfolio for the interest of shareholders.

Investment Company Act Federal legislation enacted in 1940 regulating the operation and management of investment companies.

Investment Company Yield A yield determined by dividing the annual dividend of the fund share by the current offering price.

Investment Letter A letter written by the purchaser of a security in a private placement certifying that he has purchased the security for investment purposes with no immediate plans to sell.

Investment Tax Credit The taxpayer may take an investment tax credit on certain tangible and depreciable personal properties.

IRA Individual Retirement Account. A retirement account established by individuals.

Irrevocable Trust A trust that cannot be terminated before the term of the trust.

Issue Security.

Issued and Outstanding Shares Number of shares sold to stockholders.

Issuer The entity that issued securities.

Joint and Survivor Annuity An annuity program. Periodic payments are made during the lifetime of two people. Payments will continue until both die.

Joint Venture A form of partnership where one partner has the authority to run the business and the others act as limited partners.

Jumbo Certificate A certificate with a large denomination.

Kaffirs Gold mining securities in South Africa.

Keogh A retirement program for self-employed individuals.

Key Indicators Used to evaluate the financial condition and the profitability of the firm.

Killer Bees A term describing the brokerage house that uses techniques to protect a corporation against a takeover attempt.

Kiting Stocks Manipulative device used to create artificial prices for securities.

Kray & Co. A nominee name for MSTC.

Lagging Indicator Economic indicator that determines the rate of unemployment in the country.

LaSalle Street Chicago's financial district.

Leading Economic Indicators Economic indicators that analyze the condition of the economy, such as the stock market, machine tool orders, housing starts, the Consumer Price Index.

Leg One side of a spread option combination.

Legal Transfers Securities transfers that require documents to transfer.

Letter of Credit A letter issued by a bank indicating the bank's commitment to lend a specified amount of funds for a limited term.

Letter of Intent The customer may sign a letter of intent indicating his intention to invest funds in the future. This is done to qualify the transaction for a reduced sales charge.

Letter Stock, Letter Bond Restricted securities, sold in a private placement not registered with the SEC.

Leverage The use of borrowed money to purchase securities.

Leverage Buyout Acquiring a company by using borrowed money.

Leveraged Company A company with more debt than equity in its capital base.

Leveraged Investment Company An investment company allowed to borrow funds for its capital.

Liabilities   The obligation that the company owes to creditors.

LIFO (Last-In-First-Out)   An inventory accounting method based on the assumption that goods sold were the most recently purchased. Goods unsold at the close of an accounting period were those acquired at earlier dates.

Lift   Rise in the price of a security against the rise of stock market averages.

Lifting-Leg   Closing one side of a hedge combination, leaving the other side intact.

Limited Partner   The limited partner has no active role in the firm. His liabilities are limited to the amount of money he has contributed to the firm.

Limited Trading Authorization   A document empowering a third party to enter an order on behalf of another person.

Lipper Mutual Fund Average   Average indicating the performance of mutual funds.

Liquid Market   A market where investors buy or sell securities with no difficulty.

Liquidating Dividends   Distributions made to stockholders at the time of dissolution of the corporation.

Liquidity   The feature of a security that will allow it to be converted into cash readily.

Liquidity Ratio   See Quick Asset Ratio.

Listed Option   An option listed at an options exchange for trading.

Listed Security   A security listed on an exchange.

Load   Sales charge of a mutual fund.

Load Fund   Mutual fund with a sales charge.

Loan Consent Agreement   An agreement that allows the broker to lend the customer's securities to finance the margin transaction.

Loan Value   The amount of credit the broker is allowed to lend to the customer; the complement of the margin requirement. Example: If the margin requirement is 65%, the loan value is 35%; if the margin is 70%, the loan value is 30%. With Regulation T currently at 50%, the loan value for marginable securities is 50%. With the loan value at 30%, the loan value of $10,000 worth of security is $3,000 (30% of $10,000).

Locals   Floor traders who trade for their own account.

Lock Box   A method of collecting checks due from customers of a company. Customers send checks to a Post Office Box to be collected by a bank for the account of the company.

Lombard Street   Financial district in London.

Long-Term Assets   Tangible assets with a life greater than one year.

Long-Term Debt   Long-term obligations of the firm to be paid in one year or longer.

Long-Term Gain   Gain on capital asset held longer than six months.

Long-Term Loss   Loss on capital asset held longer than six months.

Macroeconomics   Analysis of the nation's general economic condition.

Maintenance Excess or House Excess   The amount of equity in the margin account over and above the margin maintenance requirement.

Maintenance Margin Call   A demand for additional funds from the customer to maintain the required equity in the account.

Maintenance Margin Requirement   The requirement to maintain a minimum amount of equity in a margin account as set forth by the stock exchanges, NASD, and the securities firm.

Making a Market   A broker's activity that establishes and maintains the price on a security.

Maloney Act   Federal legislation enacted in 1938 creating the National Association of Securities Dealers to oversee transactions on the over-the-counter market.

Managing Underwriter   The principal underwriter.

Management Company   A type of investment company. It invests investor's funds in securities and manages the portfolio.

Management Group   The investment advisers.

Margin   Cash or securities that a customer is required to submit to the broker as collateral.

Margin Account   A brokerage account. The customer will make the partial payment to the broker in purchasing securities on margin.

Margin Call   A request to the customer to put up additional cash or securities to meet the margin requirements.

Margin Credit   The credit balance in a margin account as a result of sale of securities, deposit of cash, dividends and interest received for securities long in the account.

Margin Debit   The amount of money that the customer owes the broker.

Margin Department   The credit department of a brokerage firm.

Margin Deficiency   The amount by which the required margin exceeds the equity in the margin account.

Margin of Profit Ratio   This is determined by dividing the operating income by net sales.

Marginable Security   Equity securities and convertible bonds listed at a national stock exchange and over-the-counter securities approved by the Federal Reserve Board are considered as marginable securities for purposes of margin transactions.

Marital Deduction   Federal legislation that will allow assets of a deceased spouse to pass to the surviving spouse free from estate taxes.

Mark to the Market   The procedure for determining the market value of a security position against the current market price.

Market Letter   A newsletter issued or prepared by an investment analyst or adviser.

Market Maker   A broker–dealer engaged in maintaining a market of a security or a group of securities in a stock exchange or in the over-the-counter market.

Market Out Clause   A provision in the underwriting agreement that will allow a member of the syndicate to withdraw from the underwriting team without any liability or penalty.

Marketable Security   A security that can be traded in the marketplace.

Match Maker   The option buyer and the writer are entering the market at the same time.

Matched Orders   Buying and selling the same security to create a fictitious volume of transactions.

Matched Trades   Information submitted to the clearing corporation by both selling and buying brokers is matched.

MCC   Midwest Clearing Corporation. A clearing entity that clears transactions on the Midwest Stock Exchange.

Melon   Extraordinary distribution of corporate profits to stockholders.

Member Firm   A securities firm, member of a stock exchange.

Member Firm Surveillance Department   A department at the NYSE responsible for overseeing the business conduct of members and member organizations.

Merchant Bank   A bank, usually located in Europe, engaged in investment banking.

Mezzanine Bracket   A term describing the member of a syndicate team whose allocated portion of the underwritten security is second to the member who has the largest allocation.

Mill   1/10 of a cent.

Minority Interest   Interest of stockholders with less than half of total corporate shares.

Minus Tick   Downtick.

Microeconomics   Analysis of economic units.

Mini-Maxi A type of underwriting. The underwriter sells a minimum number of shares to the public, then proceeds to sell the remaining shares until the maximum level is reached.

Missing the Market Failing to execute a trade contrary to the customer's instructions.

Mixed Spread A neutral spread that is a vertical spread or a backspread. Usually includes more than two series of options.

Monetarist A person who believes that the money supply is extremely vital for economic growth.

Money Market The market for short term money market instruments.

Money Market Mutual Fund An investment company that invests its assets in money market instruments, such as commercial papers, certificates of deposit, and so on.

Mortgage REIT A type of real estate investment trust that finances the construction of commercial and residential properties.

MST System A wide range of integrated services offered by the Midwest Clearing Corporation.

MSTC Midwest Securities Trust Company that offers depository services to member financial institutions.

Municipal Bond Fund An investment company that invests its assets in municipal bonds.

Mutual Fund An open-end investment company.

Mutual Fund Custodian A commercial bank acting as custodian and bookkeeper for a mutual fund.

Naked Options See uncovered options.

Narrow Market Low volume transactions of a security in the marketplace.

NASD The National Association of Securities Dealers. A self-regulatory organization that regulates the over-the-counter market.

NASDAQ The National Association of Securities Dealers Automated Quotation System. An electronic data terminal system providing computerized facility to trade securities.

NASDAQ-OTC Price Index An index computed by the NASD. It measures the market activity of over-the-counter securities traded on NASDAQ.

National Market System The market for certain securities on the over-the-counter market under the supervision of the National Association of Securities Dealers.

Negative Cash Flow Occurs when a business spends more than it takes in.

Negative Working Capital   Occurs when current liabilities exceed current assets.

Negotiable   A security that can be used for delivery or transfer.

Negotiated Underwriting   A type of underwriting in which the terms are negotiated between the issuer and the underwriters.

Net Asset Value (NAV)   The bid price of the investment company shares. It is determined by:

$$\frac{\left(\begin{array}{c}\text{Market value of securities}\\ \text{in the portfolio}\end{array}\right) + (\text{Other assets}) - (\text{Total liabilities})}{\text{Number of shares outstanding}}$$

Net-by-Net Settlement   A clearing procedure. Securities transactions are cleared on a daily basis by the clearing corporation.

Net Capital Requirement   An SEC requirement for broker–dealers to maintain a certain amount of capital to operate the business.

Net Cost of the Property   The actual cost minus the salvage value of the property.

Net Income Before Taxes   Net operating income minus net operating expenses.

Net Income to Net Worth Ratio   A ratio determined by dividing net worth into net income.

Net Investment Income (NII)   Total amount of dividends and interest that the investment company receives from securities in its portfolio.

Net Operating Income   Income after cost of goods sold.

Net Quick Assets   Assets obtained by adding cash, securities, and accounts receivable and subtracting current liabilities.

Net Worth   The capital of the company. Assets minus liabilities.

Neutral Hedge   This is a combination of long and short positions in related securities. It becomes equally profitable if the stock moves a little in either direction.

Neutral Spread   A combination of long and short option contracts in which the theoretical value changes very little against the changes in the price of the underlying index.

Neutral Strategy   A strategy that is neither bullish nor bearish.

New York Stock Exchange Composite Index   An index computed by the New York Stock Exchange consisting of all common stocks traded on a given day.

Nifty Fifty   Fifty securities on the floor of the New York Stock Exchange that are generally favored by investors.

No-Action Letter   Notification from the SEC that it will take no action with respect to a specific transaction.

No-Load Fund   A mutual fund that charges no sales commission.

Nominal Quotation   In making a nominal quotation, the market maker is revealing the quotation for information purposes only. He has no firm commitment to accept the bid or the offer.

Nominee Name   Street name. A term used to describe securities held in the name of the bank or brokerage house for the account of customers.

Non Clearing Member   A member of the stock exchange with no affiliations.

Non-Cumulative Preferred   A type of preferred stock. The stockholder will lose the right to receive dividends if the corporation decides not to distribute them.

Non-Diversified Management Company   Similar to a venture capital company. It has no limitation as to its investment activity or the selection of the portfolio.

Nonmarginable Security   A security that may not be purchased on margin.

Non Member Firm   Broker–dealer with no membership at the stock exchange.

Non Public Information   Information not available to the public.

Non Purpose Loan   Money borrowed for purposes other than purchasing securities.

Nonrecurring Charge   Extraordinary charge. A corporate charge that does not occur frequently.

Not Held Order   A market order giving the broker discretion to execute the trade at the best available price. The broker assumes no responsibility.

Not Rated   The securities that are not rated by a rating agency such as Moody's or S & P.

NQB   National Quotation Bureau. Publishes and distributes daily lists of securities and bids and offers of the market makers in the over-the-counter market.

NSCC   National Securities Clearing Corporation. A clearing entity that clears transactions on the New York and American Stock Exchanges and the NASDAQ over-the-counter market.

NYSE Call   Margin call for additional margin to maintain the minimum required by Rule 431 of the New York Stock Exchange.

Odd Lot Shares between 1 and 99 for common stocks and 1 to 9 for preferred securities.

Odd-Lot Dealer A dealer engaged in odd-lot transactions.

Odd-Lot Theory A market theory that analyzes the trading activity of small investors, particularly those purchasing and selling odd lots.

OCC The Options Clearing Corporation.

Off-Board A trade made off the floor of the stock exchange.

Offer Wanted (OW) A term generally used in the over-the-counter market where a potential buyer of a security is looking for an offer from a seller.

Offering Circular Prospectus.

Offering Date Date on which the securities will be available for distribution to the public.

Offering Price The offering price of an investment company share is the net asset value (NAV) plus the sales charge.

Offset Closing a securities transaction.

Omnibus Proxy A proxy used by depositories or custodian banks.

On-the-Money Also called at-the-money. The strike price is equal to the current market price of the underlying security.

Open-End Management Company The company does not have a fixed capitalization. Shares are issued continuously to meet the demand of the shareholders.

Open Interest The number of outstanding option contracts.

Open on the Point A term used by a block positioner that a block trade has been completed and printed on the tape.

Open Order Limit order that has not been cancelled or executed.

Open Outcry A term describing the shouting practice by brokers on the floor of commodity, options, or stock exchanges when executing buy and sell orders.

Opening Purchase Transaction An option trade in which the customer creates a long position in an option series.

Opening Writing Transaction An option trade in which the customer creates a short position in an option series.

Operating Income Net sales minus the operating expense.

Operating Ratio Also known as Expense Ratio. Determined by dividing the operating cost by net sales.

Option Certificate A certificate issued by OCC indicating the ownership of an option contract. This practice is now discontinued.

Option Contract A put or call.

Option Hedge   See Ratio writing.

Option Mutual Fund   Investment company that buys and sells options on securities in its portfolio.

Optional Dividend   Dividend that can be distributed either in cash or in shares.

Optional Stock   Underlying stock.

Or Better (OB)   Limit order to execute the trade at a price better than the price specified on the order.

Ordinary Income   Passive income, such as dividends, interests, rent, and royalties.

Ordinary Interest   Interest computed on a 360-day a year basis.

Originator   Principal underwriter of a new security.

OTC Margin Security   Securities on the over-the-counter market approved by the Federal Reserve Board for margin trading.

OTC Option   An option not listed at an options exchange, traded on the over-the-counter market.

Out of Line Stock   A stock whose price is too high or too low compared with similar stocks.

Out-of-the-Money   A call option is out-of-the-money when the strike price is above the current market price of the underlying security. A put option is out-of-the-money when the strike price is below the current market price.

Out the Window   A term describing a successful way of distributing new securities to the public.

Outstanding Option   An option contract that has neither been closed, exercised, nor reached its expiration date.

Overheated Economy   Rapidly expanding economy.

Overnight Loan   A fully secured short-term loan to a broker–dealer.

Over-the-Window   Direct delivery of a security made to the receiving window of a securities firm.

Overbooked   Oversold.

Overhang   A term used when a large block of securities sold on the trading floor will depress the market price of the security.

Overhead   Cost of running a business minus the cost of manufacturing or buying the product that is being sold.

Overissue   Shares issued in excess of the amount authorized by the Secretary of State of the state of incorporation.

Overstayed   A term used to describe an investor who has an unrealized profit but waits for a larger profit.

Oversubscribed Oversold. A term used in an underwriting of a new security.

Owner's Investment Turnover The ratio of net sales vs. tangible net worth.

Pac-Man Strategy Strategy used by corporation A to buy shares of corporation B when corporation B is threatening to acquire corporation A. The action may force corporation B to discontinue its takeover fight.

Pacific & Co. A nominee name for PSDTC.

Paid-in-Capital See Capital Surplus.

Painting the Tape Manipulative device. Speculators buy and sell a certain security to create the impression of heavy trading activity in the security.

Paper Profit Unrealized profit.

Par Face value of the security.

Par Value An arbitrary determination of the value of a corporate share. The par value has no relationship to the market value of the stock.

Parent Company Holding company.

Parking Investing in safe securities.

Partial Call The issuer is making a partial redemption of outstanding securities.

Partial Delivery A delivery of security with less than the amount indicated on the contract.

Participant Delivery Program (PDP) A system at MSTC that provides facility for brokers and institutions to complete their securities transactions.

Participating Preferred A type of preferred stock. The stockholder may receive extra dividend if declared by the corporation.

Participating Trust A type of unit investment trust. It makes investments in other investment companies.

Payable Date A date established by the corporation. The corporation is required to distribute dividends or interests by the payable date.

Pay-In Period This is the accumulation period in which the customer is depositing funds in the annuity plan.

Pay-Out Period The annuity period. The customer starts receiving the annuity payments.

Pay-Out Ratio This is determined by dividing the total dividends paid on common stock by the total net earnings.

PCC Pacific Clearing Corporation. A clearing entity that clears transactions on the Pacific Stock Exchange.

Pegging A term that describes the activity of the principal underwriter in stabilizing the price of a new issue in the marketplace.

Penny Stock Securities that sell for less than $1 a share.

Percentage Order A day limit or a day market order. The broker will execute an order after a certain number of shares have been traded.

Performance Fund Mutual fund that invests in growth stocks.

Performance Stock Growth stock.

Period of Digestion Period in which the market price of a new issue is determined in the marketplace.

Periodic Purchase Deferred Contract Annuity contract with fixed payments made after a period of time specified by the customer.

Perpetual Warrant A warrant with no expiration date.

Personal Service Income Earned income, such as wages and salaries.

Phantom Stock Plan Incentive program for corporate executives. The executive will receive a bonus based on the rise of the corporation's security in the marketplace.

Piggyback Registration The public distribution of existing shares of a corporation together with new shares issued by the same corporation.

Pink Sheet A listing published by the National Quotation Bureau. It reports bids and offers of market makers for equity securities.

Pipeline Proposed public distribution of a security.

Plan Completion Insurance An insurance policy that will complete the customer's continuous investment program in a mutual fund in the event the customer dies before the plan is completed.

Pledge Hypothecation of securities.

Plow Back A term used when a company reinvests earnings instead of distributing them as dividends.

Plus Tick A term used when the security is traded at a price higher than the previous transaction.

Point $1 for stocks, $10 for bonds. A point in the Dow Jones Average refers to the units in the average and not to the change in the dollar amount.

Poison Pill A technique used by a company to make its stock less attractive to avoid a takeover attempt.

Pool Manipulative device for securities. A group of investors will pool their resources to manipulate the price of a security in the marketplace.

Portfolio Securities holdings.

Position Trader Commodities or options trader.

Pot Shares returned to the principal underwriter by a participating underwriter to effect sales to institutional investors.

Pot Is Clean All the shares in the pot are sold to institutional investors.

Pre-Authorized Delivery System (PDQ) A system at DTC that provides a method of delivering securities without the use of delivery instructions, envelopes, or credit lists.

Preemptive Right Right given to stockholders to purchase shares of a new issue.

Preferred Dividend Coverage This measures the company's ability to pay dividends on preferred stock.

Preferred Stock A type of capital stock. A preferred stockholder generally has no voting rights.

Preferred Stock Ratio A ratio determined by dividing the preferred stock by the total capitalization of the company.

Premium The trading price of an option.

Prepaid Expenses Payments for materials in advance of their receipt, such as rent payments and insurance premiums.

Prepayment Giving the proceeds of the sale to the customer before the settlement date of the trade.

Price Earning Ratio The market price of a share divided by the earning per share.

Price Spread See Vertical Spread.

Pricey Unrealistic securities price.

Prime Rate Interest rate charged by banks to preferential customers.

Primary Distribution Sale of a new issue to the public.

Primary Market The market for securities listed at a primary stock exchange.

Principal Amount Face amount of the security.

Prior Preferred A type of preferred stock. The prior preferred has seniority over any other preferred in the event of liquidation.

Private Placement Sale of securities to a limited number of investors.

Probate Process whereby the last will and testament is presented to court and the appointment of the legal representative of the estate is completed.

Progressive Tax A system of income tax. More taxes are levied as income rises.

Pro Rata Proportionate allocation.

Prospective Purchaser–Investor Suitability Statement A form executed by the customer in a private placement. In examining the form, the broker will determine whether the customer is suitable for a particular investment.

Prospectus A document prepared by a corporation in offering securities to the public.

Proxy A voting authorization signed by the stockholder authorizing another person to vote his company shares on his behalf.

Proxy Fight Strategy used by a person to gain control of a company.

PSDTC Pacific Securities Depository Trust Company that offers depository services to member financial institutions.

Public Offering Price The price at which the new issue is sold to the public.

Public Securities Association Trade organization of dealers engaged in underwriting municipal bonds, U.S. government, and federal agency securities.

Public Utility Holding Company Act Federal legislation enacted in 1935 regulating utility corporations.

Pure Play A term that describes a company in a particular business, for instance, IBM is a pure play for computers.

Purpose Loan Money borrowed to buy securities.

Put An option contract giving the holder the privilege to sell the underlying security at a specific price within a specified period of time.

Qualifying Annuity Annuity program approved by the IRS.

Quasi-Public Corporation Private corporation whose stock is sometimes traded publicly.

Quick Assets Assets that can be converted into cash readily within a 30-day period, such as marketable securities and accounts receivable. Quick assets may not include the value of the inventory, since inventory cannot be converted readily into cash.

$$\text{Quick Assets} = \text{Current Assets} - \text{Inventory}.$$

Quick Asset Ratio The ratio between the Quick Assets and Current Liabilities. It is determined by dividing the Quick Assets by Current Liabilities.

Quiet Period A period immediately following the effective date. Broker–dealers must be quiet about the security being offered to the public. They are only allowed to send a copy of the prospectus to interested customers during this period.

Radar Alert Procedure to forecast a corporate takeover attempt.

Raider A person who attempts to takeover a company.

Rally Rise in the price of a security.

Random Walk Analysis A method of analyzing and forecasting the price movement of a security. The analyst does not consider the track record of the security to forecast the direction of the price.

Ratio of Current Debt to Tangible Net Worth This ratio indicates the relationship between short-term credit and the owners' investment in the business. It is determined by dividing current debt by tangible net worth.

Rate of Return The rate of return on an investment, takes into account dividend and capital appreciation.

Ratio Ratios measure the relationship between two or more items in the financial statement.

Ratio of Total Debt to Tangible Net Worth This ratio indicates the relationship between total debt and the owners' investment in the business. It is determined by dividing total debt by tangible net worth.

Ratio Writing Writing more than one option against each long position — also called variable hedging, or option hedge.

Reading the Tape Monitoring the performance of stocks.

Real Interest Rate Current interest rate minus the rate of inflation.

Real Estate Investment Trust (REIT) An investment company that invests its assets in real estate properties.

Real Return Rate of return adjusted by rate of inflation. If the rate of return is 10 percent and the inflation rate is 6 percent, the real return is 4 percent.

Recapitalization Changing the capitalization of a corporation.

Receive and Deliver Section A section of the cashiers department responsible to receive and deliver securities.

Recession The economy is said to be in recession when it declines during six consecutive months.

Reclamation Rejection of a security delivery.

Record Date A date established by the corporation. Only stockholders of record will be entitled to receive dividends or interests from the issuing entity.

Red Herring A preliminary prospectus.

Refinancing Issuing stocks and using the proceeds of the sale to redeem an existing bond.

Regional Stock Exchange A stock exchange not located in New York.

Registered Company A corporation registered with the Securities and Exchange Commission.

Registered Representative Account executive, customer's man, the securities salesperson.

Registered Security Security registered with the SEC or a security registered in the name of the holder of record.

Registrar An agency assigned by the corporation to authenticate the issuance of new certificates.

Registration Statement A document submitted to the SEC for a public distribution of a security. It makes full disclosure of all essential facts about the issuer of the security.

Regular Way Trade A type of settlement of securities transactions. For equity trades, the transaction settles on the fifth business day after the trade day; for U.S. Treasury obligations, the transaction settles on the business day following the trade day.

Regulated Commodity Commodity regulated by the Commodity Futures Trading Commission.

Regulation A SEC regulation allowing corporations to sell securities valued up to $1.5 million within a 12-month period.

Regulation G A regulation of the Federal Reserve System that regulates credit by persons other than banks and brokers.

Regulation T A regulation of the Federal Reserve System that governs the extension of credit by broker–dealers.

Regulation T Excess Excess margin. The equity in the customer's account exceeding the margin required under Regulation T.

Regulation U A regulation of the Federal Reserve System that regulates loans extended by banks for securities trading.

Regulation X A regulation of the Federal Reserve Board that governs the activities of borrowers who obtain credit for securities transactions.

Regulation Z *Also* Truth in Lending Law. A regulation of the Federal Reserve Board that requires the creditor to make full disclosure as to the terms of the credit arrangement.

Remargining Depositing more cash or securities to meet the broker's margin requirements.

Restricted Account An account with an equity below the existing margin requirement.

Retail House Brokerage house serving public customers.

Retained Earnings Profits that are not distributed as dividends.

Return on Equity This is determined by dividing the net income by stockholders' equity.

Return on Invested Capital This is determined by dividing the net income and interest on debt by the total capitalization.

Reverse Split A corporate restructuring of a security's price. A corporation will increase the price per share in the marketplace by correspondingly reducing the number of shares outstanding.

Rigged Market Manipulated market.

Right of Accumulation The management company will offer a right to the investor to accumulate shares in his plan.

Ring Trading location on the floor of the stock exchange. Pit for commodity exchange.

Riskless Transaction Also known as Simultaneous Transaction. A non-market maker will buy the security from a market maker after receiving instructions from the customer to purchase the security.

Rolling Stock Rolling equipment such as railroad cars and aircrafts.

Rollover Moving money from one investment to another.

ROR The actual rate of return.

Round Lot Trading unit. For common stocks, the round lot is 100 shares and multiples of 100 shares. For preferred stocks, the round lot is 10 shares and multiples of 10 shares.

Round Trip Purchase and sale of the same security within a period of time.

Rule 15c3-3 A SEC rule, also known as Customer Protection Rule.

Rule 17a-5 SEC rule. Under this rule, broker–dealers are required to file a FOCUS report with the SEC and the stock exchange on a monthly and quarterly basis.

Rule 17a-13 A SEC rule. Under this rule, broker–dealers carrying customer accounts are required to count their security positions and resolve the differences.

Rule 144 SEC rule allowing investors to sell restricted, unregistered securities.

Rule 147 SEC rule, also known as Intrastate or Safe Harbor rule. Allows corporations to sell securities within a state.

Rule 237 SEC rule allowing non-affiliated persons to sell restricted securities.

Rule 405 A New York Stock Exchange rule. The rule requires broker-dealers to know the essential facts about their customers.

Rule 415 SEC rule allowing corporations to file only one Registration Statement with the SEC covering current and future public distributions of securities.

Rule 505 of Regulation D SEC rule allowing the corporation to sell securities valued up to $5 million to 35 investors during a 12-month period.

Rule 506 of Regulation D SEC rule allowing the corporation to sell unregistered securities in a private placement.

Running Ahead A term that describes the broker's activity of executing his own trades first before executing customer orders.

Runoff The final reporting of security prices on the ticker tape after the conclusion of the trading session.

RVP Receive versus payment. Receipt of securities against payment.

Same-Day Substitution The sale of a security in a restricted account and the purchase of another security on the same day.

Scale Order An order to purchase or sell the security at different intervals.

Scalper Usually refers to the speculator who manipulates the price of a security.

SCCP Stock Clearing Corporation of Philadelphia. A clearing entity that clears transactions on the Philadelphia Stock Exchange.

Schedule E SEC procedure allowing a broker–dealer to sell his own securities to the public. Also known as the self-underwriting rule.

Schedule 13D A form required by the SEC from investors who acquire more than 5% of a corporation. The form must be filed with the SEC within 10 business days after the acquisition of shares has taken place.

Schedule 14b A form required by the SEC filed by a dissident group in a proxy contest.

Scorched-Earth Strategy Strategy used by a company to make its securities unattractive to protect itself from a takeover attempt.

Scrip Dividend Dividends paid in the form of certificates or promissory instruments.

Scripophily A practice of collecting certificates of bonds and stocks as collector's items.

Seat Membership at the stock exchange.

Seasoned Security A widely traded security of an established company.

Secondary Market The market for securities listed at a primary exchange but traded at a different stock exchange.

Secondary Offering The public distribution of a security which has previously been issued.

Securities Act of 1933 Federal legislation that requires securities to be registered with the SEC before their distribution to the public.

Securities Act Amendments of 1975 Federal legislation that amended some of the provisions of the Securities Exchange Act of 1934.

Securities Exchange Act of 1934 Federal legislation that regulates the securities exchanges, brokerage house activities, and corporate securities in America.

Securities Industry Association (SIA) Trade organization of broker–dealers.

Securities Industry Automation Corporation (SIAC) Facilities management company that provides computer services for New York and American Stock Exchanges and clearing corporations.

Securities Investors Protection Corporation (SIPC) Corporation established by Congress in 1970 that insures customer accounts at brokerage organizations.

Security As defined under the Securities Act of 1933: note, stock, bond, interest in profit-sharing agreement, investment contract, voting trust certificates, oil and gas participation unit, warrants.

Segregated Securities Fully paid-for and excess margin securities.

Segregation A procedure in the cashiers department to segregate customers' fully paid for and margin excess securities.

Selected Dealer Agreement Agreement that specifies the terms for selling group members in an underwriting.

Self-Regulatory Organization (SRO) A non-governmental organization that has statutory responsibility to regulate its own members and establish ethical and business standards. Examples: The New York Stock Exchange, the NASD, the Chicago Board Options Exchange.

Seed Money Funds invested in new ventures.

Seller's Option A type of settlement of securities transaction. The delivery of the security is made on the day the option expires on the sale side.

Selling Expenses Cost of selling or marketing the products or services of the company, such as advertising and compensation to salespeople.

Selling Group Member A broker–dealer who is not a member of an underwriting syndicate invited to sell securities in a public offering.

Selling Short Selling a security without owning it.

Sensitive Market Market that is easily influenced by political or economic news.

Separate Accounts An account maintained for the variable annuity contracts. The management company invests funds in securities and places the securities in the "separate account."

Settlement Date Date on which the securities trade is settled.

Shadow Calendar Registration statements for new securities still pending at the SEC.

Shark Repellent Strategy used by a corporation to fight against a takeover attempt.

Shelf Registration SEC Rule 415.

Short Against the Box A trading procedure. The investor holds a long position and sells the security short.

Short Cover Purchase of security to cover the short sale.

Short Interest Theory A market theory that measures the trading activity of short sellers.

Short Sale Selling the security without owning it.

Short-Term Gain Gain on capital asset held shorter than six months.

Short-Term Loss Loss on capital asset held shorter than six months.

Sideways Market Horizontal price movement of securities in the marketplace.

Simple Interest Interest paid on the principal not compounded.

Sleeper Stock Inactive stock.

Sleeping Beauty A company considered a good target for takeover.

Small Investor Individual investor.

Soft Market Market where the supply is greater than the demand to purchase securities.

Solicited Trades Transactions solicited by the broker–dealer.

Special Bid Procedure of purchasing large blocks of securities on the stock exchange.

Special Memorandum Account (SMA) A special account used by the brokerage house to record excess funds in customer margin accounts.

Special Offering Procedure to sell large blocks of securities on the stock exchange.

Special Omnibus Account A brokerage account generally used by investment advisers.

Specialist The market maker on the floor of the Exchange responsible for maintaining a fair and equitable market for a group of securities assigned to him.

Specialist's Book The book maintained by the Specialist.

Specialist Joint Account   An account that provides for the mingling of the security position of the participants and the sharing of profits and losses from the account on a predetermined ratio.

Specialized Company   An investment company that invests its assets in specialized industries, such as bank stocks, high-tech stocks, and so on.

Spin-Off   Corporation breaking up into smaller units. The units will act as independent entities.

Split Commission   Commission divided between a broker and an investment adviser.

Split Down   Reverse split.

Split Order   A large order broken down into smaller orders to facilitate the execution.

Sponsor   The distributor, the underwriter, the wholesaler.

Spot Price   Cash price of the commodity.

Spousal Remainder Trust   A living trust established by one parent for the benefit of a minor. At termination of the trust, the minor returns the principal to the other parent.

Spread   A long and a short option of the same type but different series.

Squeeze   A condition in the stock market where short sellers are forced to buy the securities to cover their shorts.

Stabilization   Procedure of maintaining the public offering price of a new security in the after market.

Stabilization Period   The period in which the managing underwriters stabilize the price of a security in the secondary market.

Stag   Agile investor who trades securities for fast profit.

Stagflation   Stagnation and inflation in the economy. Production is stagnant but the economy is inflationary.

Stamped Bonds   Corporations during the period of reorganization will stamp their bonds to reflect the adoption of a new plan.

Standard & Poor's Index   A stock market indicator based on the price movement of 500 securities.

Standby Underwriter   An underwriter engaged in selling or exercising unexercised subscription rights.

State Street   Financial district in Boston.

Statutory Voting   A procedure for voting. The stockholder will have one vote for each share he holds. He will cast his votes for each of the proposals placed on the agenda at a corporate meeting.

Statutory Underwriter   A market maker purchasing unregistered securities from the customer.

Sticky Deal   A new issue which is difficult to distribute to the public.

Stock Ahead   The order that will be executed first due to its chronological entry into the trading floor.

Stock Dividend   Dividends issued in shares.

Stock Loan   A securities house account. The securities firm has loaned the securities to another firm.

Stock Split   A corporate restructuring of a security's price. The corporation will reduce the price per share in the marketplace by correspondingly increasing the number of shares outstanding.

Stock Transfer Section   A section of the cashiers department responsible for preparing securities for transfer.

Stockholders' Equity   The amount of money that the stockholders have in a corporation. Assets − liabilities = stockholders' equity.

Stop Order   A stop issued by the SEC or the state securities administrator halting the registration process of a security.

Straddle   A combination of a put and a call on the same underlying security with the same strike price and expiration month.

Straddle the Market   A situation when a speculator is short on one stock and long on another.

Straight Line Depreciation Method   A method of determining the depreciation of the property. Through this method the annual depreciation is determined by dividing the net cost of the property by the number of years of usable life.

Street   The New York financial district. It refers to Wall Street.

Street Name   Nominee name.

Subchapter M   Internal Revenue Code that deals with investment companies. Also known as Conduit or Pipeline Theory.

Subchapter S Corporation   A form of corporation that is taxed as a partnership.

"Subject Market"   In revealing his quotation, the market maker is not ready to trade the security at that price.

Subscription Right   A short-term instrument allowing the stockholder to buy more shares through subscription.

Subscription Warrant   Warrant issued in conjunction with a stock or a bond entitling the holder to purchase additional shares.

Substitution   The purchase and sale of securities in a restricted account on the same day.

Sums-of-Years Digits Depreciation   A method to determine annual depreciation of a property. Through this method, the number of years of the property's usable life is added together.

Sundry Assets Miscellaneous assets of a company, such as unimproved land and prepaid expenses.

Support Trend The price at which the security will stop its downward trend.

Surrender Right The surrender right of the mutual fund is the amount of money that will be returned to the customer after the customer rescinds the transaction.

Surveillance Coordination Department A department at the NYSE responsible for ensuring that member organizations submit audit reports and financial statements to the Exchange.

Suspense Accounts A temporary house account to solve unresolved items.

Syndicate A team of underwriters.

Systematic Risk Risk that is common to all securities in the same industry.

T-Call A demand for funds to cover initial margin requirement.

Tailgating Manipulative device. The broker executes the order in his own account immediately after receiving customer orders for the same security.

Take a Flier Act of speculation in low grade securities.

Tangible Net Worth The net worth of the firm minus the intangible assets, such as copyright and goodwill.

Tax Credit A reduction of a tax liability.

Tax Equity and Fiscal Responsibility Act (TEFRA) Federal legislation enacted in 1982 to raise tax revenues for the federal government.

Tax Deductible The loss in a transaction may be deducted from ordinary income.

Tax Deferred The payment of tax is deferred to a future year.

Tax Deferred Annuity Tax shelter annuity (TSA). A plan for employees of nonprofit organizations. A percentage of their salaries is deducted and placed in a retirement program.

Tax Exempt The account, the security, or the earning is not subject to tax.

Tax Umbrella Tax loss carry forward.

Taxable The account, the security, or the earning is subject to tax.

Technical Analysis A method of analyzing and forecasting the price movement of a security. The analyst considers the price movement of the security at different time periods.

Technical Rally Short rise in stock prices.

Tender Offer   An offer by a person interested in purchasing a security from the stockholder of a corporation.

Third Market   The market for trading stock exchange listed securities in the over-the-counter market.

Tick   Minimum fluctuation in the price of a security.

Ticker Tape   A medium that reports securities transactions on the floor of the exchange.

Tight Market   Market where the spread between the bid and asked prices is very narrow.

Time Deposit   Amount deposited at a bank for a specified period of time.

Time Spread   See calendar or horizontal spread.

Time Value Premium   An amount by which option's premium exceeds the amount that is in in-the-money.

Toehold Purchase   Purchasing the security of a corporation in amounts less than 5% of the total outstanding shares.

Tombstone   An advertisement placed by the managing underwriter announcing a public offering.

Topping Out   The highest point that the security's price is expected to reach.

Touting   Aggressive method to sell a particular security.

Trade Credit   The ratio of current debt vs. tangible net worth.

Trade Date   The execution date of the trade.

Traders   Independent members of the exchange who trade only for their own accounts.

"Trading Market"   A firm market. In revealing his quotation, the market maker is making firm commitment that he will trade the security at that price.

Trading Rotation   A procedure allowing broker–dealers on the floor of the options exchange to make bids and offers in certain options, a series at a time.

Transfer Agent   An agency assigned by the corporation to maintain stockholder records and to transfer securities.

Transfer Agents Turnaround Rule   A SEC requirement. Under this rule, transfer agents are required to complete a transfer within three business days of receipt.

Treasury Stock   Stock sold by the company in a public offering, but repurchased by the company at a later date. These shares do not carry voting rights. No dividends are issued on these shares.

Trust Indenture Act   Federal legislation enacted in 1939 to regulate corporations issuing debt instruments.

12B-1 Mutual Fund   No load investment company that charges shareholders fees for its administrative expenses only.

Two-Dollar Brokers   Independent members of the Exchange. They execute orders on behalf of other member organizations.

Uncompared Trades   Information sent to the clearing corporation by the seller and buyer are not matched.

Uncovered Option   Or naked option. A short position where the writer of the call has not deposited the underlying security or the writer of the put has not deposited the aggregate exercise price of the put.

Underbanked   A new underwriting. The principal underwriter is having difficulty forming a syndicate.

Underbooked   A new underwriting. The underwriter has not received favorable response from prospective customers to purchase the security.

Underlying Security   The security that the option writer is obligated to sell (call) or purchase (put) upon exercise of the option.

Undermargined   An account in which the equity is below the required margin percentage.

Underwriter   A person or an entity acting as an intermediary between the issuer and the investing public in securities distributions.

Underwriting Spread   The difference between the cost of purchasing the security from the issuer and the public offering price.

Undigested Issues   New securities not yet distributed to the public.

Uniform Gifts to Minors Act   A state law allowing individuals to make donations to minors.

Uniform Practice Code   The NASD code that regulates the mechanics of effecting and completing securities transactions between member firms of the NASD.

Uniform Securities Agent State Law   Examination required by various states for prospective registered representatives.

Unit Investment Trust   A company organized under a trust agreement. It will issue redeemable Shares of Beneficial Interest (SBI). The shares will represent a participation in a unit of specified securities in the portfolio.

Units of Trading   The unit of trading for stocks is 100 shares and multiples of 100 shares; for bonds $1,000 face value up to $100,000 face value; for warrants 100 warrants.

Unlisted Securities   Securities that are not listed at a securities exchange.

Unloading   Selling securities in a declining market.

Unregistered Security   Security not registered with the SEC.

Unrestricted Account   A customer's margin account where the equity is equal to or greater than the Regulation T margin requirement for initial margin.

Unsegregated Securities   Securities that may be used to finance the customer's margin indebtedness.

Unsolicited Trades   Transactions executed on instructions from the customer without any solicitation by the broker–dealer.

Upstairs Market   Order executed in the broker's office and not in the stock market.

Uptick   Trade executed at a price higher than the preceding transaction.

Usury   The interest rate authorized by law.

Value Line Index   A broad base stock market indicator based on price and movement of approximately 1,700 securities.

Variable Annuity Contract   Under this contract, the amount of annuity payment will be based on the investment performance of the securities in the portfolio.

Variable Expenses   Controllable expenses of a firm, such as salaries, telephone, utilities, supplies, etc.

Variable Hedging   See Ratio writing.

Variable Ratio Write   An option strategy in which the customer writes more calls than shares of the underlying security. Example: The customer owns 200 shares of the underlying security and writes 4 calls.

Variable Spread   A spread combination of long and short options on the same option class and the same underlying security but at different strike price and expiration dates. The number of short contracts may be different from the number of long contracts.

Vertical Bear Spread   Spread combination using calls or puts where the long side has a higher strike price than the short side. Both sides will have the same expiration month.

Vertical Bull Spread   Spread combination using calls or puts where the long side has a lower strike price than the short side. Both sides will have the same expiration month.

Vertical Spread   Also called price spread, perpendicular spread, or money spread. A combination of a long option and a short option with the same expiration dates but with different strike prices.

Volatility   Expected fluctuation of security prices.

Voting Trust Certificates   A type of corporate security where voting privileges are assumed by a bank acting as trustee on behalf of stockholders.

Wage Reduction Agreement An agreement signed by the employee allowing the employer to deduct an amount of money from his paycheck.

Waiting Period Cooling off period in an underwriting.

Wallflower A security not favored by investors any more.

Warrant A corporate instrument that offers the holder the privilege to buy more shares through exercise.

Wash Sale Rule A rule in the Tax Code. The loss resulting from a security position established 30 days before and 30 days after a completed transaction is not considered as a tax-deductible item.

Watered Stock Stock of corporations where total worth is less than its capital.

Weak Market A market where there are more sellers than buyers.

Western Account An underwriting account. Underwriters are required to sell only their allocated portion.

When Distributed Transaction in a security not yet distributed.

When-Issued A term to describe a transaction of an unissued security. The security is authorized but at the time of the trade is not issued yet. The trade is made on a "when, and if issued" basis.

White Knight A person who is attempting to takeover a company in a friendly manner acceptable to the management.

Whipsawed A situation where the investor buys before the price of the security falls down and sells before it goes up.

Wholesale Price Index An economic indicator that measures the prices of goods and services that wholesalers buy or use.

Wide Opening Wide spread between bid and asked prices of a security.

Widow-and-Orphan Stock Safe and a high dividend paying security.

Wild Cat Security Speculative security.

Williams Act Federal legislation enacted in 1968 to regulate tender offers.

Wire House Brokerage house with a communications network. Also known as commission house.

Wire Room Order room of a brokerage house.

Working Capital The company's current operating fund. Current assets minus current liabilities.

"Work-Out Market" A market where the broker is not sure about his ability to trade the security. He will check the market first and then he will make a commitment to buy or sell.

Wraparound Annuity   Annuity contract that will give the holder the right to choose the type of investments for the insurance company issuing the annuity.

Write   Selling an option in an opening transaction.

Writer   A customer having a short position of an option contract. A person who is making a commitment to purchase or sell the underlying security upon exercise of the option.

Yellow Sheet   A listing published by the National Quotation Bureau. It reports bids and offers of market makers of corporate bonds.

Yield   The percentage return that one expects on investments.

Yo-Yo-Stock   Highly volatile stock.

Zero-Minus Tick   Price of a security traded at the same price than the previous transaction but higher than the last different price.

INDEX